IRONCLADS
AND
COLUMBIADS

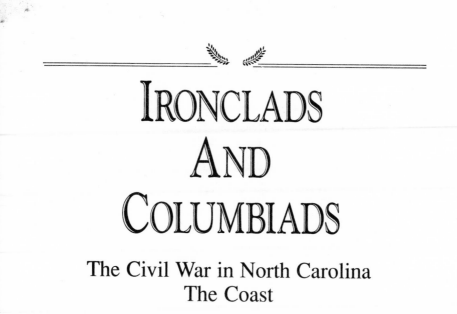

IRONCLADS AND COLUMBIADS

The Civil War in North Carolina
The Coast

William R. Trotter

John F. Blair, Publisher
Winston-Salem, North Carolina

This book is printed on acid-free paper.

Library of Congress Cataloging-in-Publication Data

Trotter, William R.
Ironclads and columbiads : the coast / William R. Trotter.
    p.   cm. — (The Civil War in North Carolina ; v. 3)
Includes bibliographical references and index.
ISBN 0-89587-088-6 (pbk.)
1. North Carolina—History—Civil War, 1861–1865—Naval operations.
2. United States—History—Civil War, 1861–1865—Naval operations.
I. Title. II. Series: Trotter, William R. Civil War in North Carolina ; v. 3.
E591.T76   1991
973.7'5—dc20
90-28711

TABLE OF CONTENTS

ACKNOW-
LEDGEMENTS

As the scope of this project has grown, so has the number of people who have materially aided in its completion and in the distribution of the books themselves. My deepest thanks therefore to the following people:

Bede Mitchell of the Jackson Library, University of North Carolina at Greensboro, who made it possible for me to enter "The Cage" at my convenience, there to commune peacefully with the *Official Records*, both land and naval;

Richard Mansfield and Tom Halfhill for their patient and sympathetic editing;

Debi Nash, whose dedication to marketing these volumes far surpassed the call of duty;

Donna Royals, Lee Noel, and Amy Pruette, for making the books look so good;

Tom Valentino, who gave up a sunny weekend to help launch this series;

Mrs. Elizabeth Herman of the Greensboro Public Library, for her persistent and invaluable aid in getting rare source material through the interlibrary loan pipeline.

INTRODUCTION

There was more fighting along the coastal strip of North Carolina than in all other sections of the state combined. The reason for this was simple: There were tempting strategic objectives to be won along the coast, and they were within easy striking distance of the main Federal naval base at Hampton Roads, at the mouth of the Chesapeake Bay.

The unusual configuration of North Carolina's coastline, and the relationship of its navigable waters to the state's interior communications, were the most important strategic factors influencing what took place there during the Civil War. Running through the sandhills section of the eastern Piedmont was the Wilmington & Weldon Railroad. If supplies delivered through the blockade or transported from the deeper South were to get through to the Virginia front — where they were most urgently needed — that railroad was vital. There were other rail lines running through the state, of course, including important routes through Charlotte and Raleigh, but the coastal railroad would become increasingly vital as fewer supplies came up from the Deep South and the Confederacy relied more and more on the blockade runners.

North-south movement of men and supplies was also possible by water, along North Carolina's extensive intracoastal waterway system. Pamlico and Albemarle sounds connected with the sea and with the coastal rivers; they also connected with Virginia, via the Great Dismal Swamp Canal and the Albemarle and Chesapeake canals. A series of great rivers connected the coast with the interior of the state: the Cape Fear, the Neuse, the Pasquotank, the Roanoke, the Tar, the Chowan. Together, these and other navigable rivers reached far enough inland to give access to fully one-third of the state.

Whoever controlled those rivers controlled the coastal railway. Whoever controlled the sounds, controlled the rivers. And whoever controlled the Outer Banks controlled access to everything else. If the entire coastal sector remained in Confederate hands, the South retained a valuable gateway to foreign sources of aid, the resources of North Carolina's richest agricultural counties, and a communications network ideally suited for delivering food and material to Confederate field armies.

The Outer Banks — that long, thin necklace of barrier islands that shelters the sounds and the riverine estuaries from the sea — acted as a shield, an outer wall, protecting the entire coastal region. The only way a Federal force could get at the rivers and their inland ports was by penetrating from the open sea into the sheltered waters of the sounds, and that was possible only through a small number of inlets. There were only seven such inlets, in fact, and not all of them were passable by large warships. These constituted, in modern military parlance, "choke points": narrow, treacherous channels which could easily be dominated by the heavy artillery of the day.

The Confederate officers and state officials responsible for protecting these gateways were quite aware of their importance. Any fool looking at a map, they assumed, ought to be able to see that at a glance. Unfortunately for North Carolina, and ultimately for the entire Southern cause, the Confederate government -- with that peculiarly obdurate refusal to set priorities which characterized so much of its strategic thinking -- neglected to act quickly or decisively to fortify these easily defensible positions. Instead, the Richmond government left the local commanders to do the best they could with inadequate supplies, no real naval support, wretchedly untrained levies of raw troops, and artillery that was either low on ammunition, insufficient in caliber, or in such dismal condition that it was almost as dangerous to the gunners as it was to the enemy. *(For an explanation of the types of artillery described in this volume, see Appendix A.)*

The campaigns that resulted from this strategic situation are highly interesting, partly because of their pioneering use of amphibious tactics, which foreshadowed the "island-hopping" campaigns of World War II. These campaigns were not, however, among the more inspiring examples of Southern military prowess. The story of the coastal war in North Carolina is one of frustrations, missed opportunities for both sides, lopsided victories, and needless defeats. Yet it is also, now and then, a tale illuminated by flashes of extraordinary gallantry and tactical brilliance. There is, for example, no more heroic saga in the annals of the Civil War than the epic defense of Fort Fisher, the Gibraltar of the Confederacy and the greatest earthwork fortress ever built on American soil. Yet Fort Fisher, too, eventually fell as a direct result of Richmond's negligence and incompetence. And when it fell, the Confederacy staggered from a mortal blow.

"The greatest mistake of the South was neglecting her Navy."

-- Commander John Maffitt, CSN

PART 1

THE COAST
ATTACKED

SEIZING THE FORTS

The first acts of open militancy in North Carolina occurred in the Cape Fear region, where passions against the Lincoln administration were high. On the last day of 1860, the secessionist citizens of Wilmington sent a telegram to Governor John Ellis, asking for permission to seize two Federal posts in their neighborhood.

The posts occupied very strategic locations. Fort Caswell, a stout masonry fortress, lay 30 miles south of Wilmington on the west bank of the Cape Fear River. And between Fort Caswell and Wilmington, at Smithville (now Southport), lay a Federal barracks called Fort Johnston. There were no Federal garrisons at either place — just a couple of ordnance sergeants who acted as caretakers. But there was concern in Wilmington that Lincoln was prepared to dispatch troops in sufficient numbers to turn these positions into genuine bastions, just as a similar concern was felt throughout the lower Piedmont about the Federal arsenal at Fayetteville.

When Governor Ellis turned down the telegraphed request, a delegation from Wilmington took the train to Raleigh and argued the case for seizure directly to the governor. Their main argument derived from strong rumors that a Federal warship, the revenue cutter *Harriet Lane*, had been loaded with troops and might, even at that moment, be on its way to the Cape Fear outposts. Ellis sympathized with the Wilmington firebrands, but he stood firm on the matter. For the moment, North Carolina was still a part of the Union, and the armed seizure of two Federal posts would be inflammatory as well as unlawful.

Champing at the bit, the secessionists of Wilmington prepared for war nonetheless. A militia unit was formed, its ranks filled with

7

hotbloods and would-be gallants, called "The Cape Fear Minute Men." Not long after the company began drilling and strutting, a report arrived on January 8, 1861. The report stated that a Federal cutter was indeed on its way, bearing 50 soldiers and eight guns, destined for Fort Caswell.

Now began the first campaign of the Cape Fear Minute Men. They engaged a small schooner, packed it with a week's supply of food and water, rounded up a motley assortment of arms — including ancient flintlocks, shotguns, and Bowie knives — and sailed down the river. They reached Fort Johnston in Smithville during the wee hours of January 9. At 4 a.m. they banged loudly on the door of the barracks. The "Fort Keeper," Ordnance Sergeant James Reilly, who comprised the entire garrison, groggily responded. Reilly had no choice but to surrender the post to his visitors, after demanding and obtaining a proper receipt. He probably wasn't too indignant about the incident, since his sympathies lay with the South. Indeed, James Reilly would soon enlist in the Confederate Army, attain the rank of major, and serve gallantly at Fort Fisher.

After detailing 15 men to stay behind and man Fort Johnston, the Cape Fear bravos -- now in high spirits indeed -- set sail on January 10 to "capture" Fort Caswell. In contrast to Fort Johnston, Caswell really was a fort. Construction had started in 1827 and was completed in 1838. Caswell was built in the classic pentagonal design so common in masonry forts of the early 19th century. It was surrounded by a moat and could be entered by passing through two protected sally ports as well as the main gate. Its peacetime garrison was ostensibly 50 men (to be reinforced in wartime to 450), but at the start of 1861 there was only a single man stationed there — the Fort Keeper, another ordnance sergeant with the intriguing name of Dardingkiller.

Dardingkiller's thoughts are not a matter of record, but the appearance of the Cape Fear Minute Men was probably the most interesting thing that had happened to him since he had left his last posting. The life of the Fort Keeper must have been solitary almost beyond endurance. The one extant piece of correspondence known to have been written by one of these men (Ordnance Sergeant Corlette, in a letter dated April 19, 1853) indicates that one of his primary duties -- and pastimes -- was to collect a fee from people who came out to fish on the fort's beaches.[1]

Dardingkiller surrendered at about 7 p.m. on January 10. The commander of the Cape Fear company, Major John Hedrick, now set about doing what he could to prepare the place to resist Federal attack. He must have been a frustrated man in this regard, for he found only two cannon on the ramparts of Fort Caswell, and neither of them could be fired because exposure to the salt air had rotted their mountings. So Hedrick's men patrolled the walls, scouted the beaches, and kept a keen lookout, making a bold show of things despite the fact that most of them were armed with shotguns and varmint rifles.

When Governor Ellis learned of these goings-on, he promptly wired Colonel John Cantwell, commander of a militia regiment in Wilmington and the only man in the area who outranked Hedrick. Ellis explained to Cantwell the possible political repercussions of Hedrick's actions, and ordered Cantwell to restore things to their proper status. Ellis had already wired President James Buchanan, both informing him of the situation and asking him, point-blank, what he planned to do with the forts. When Buchanan's secretary of war telegraphed back that nothing was planned for the moment, Ellis decided that his initial response was the correct one: North Carolina had nothing to lose by adhering to the letter of the law.

Colonel Cantwell made a difficult and thankless trek out to Fort Caswell. After his boat was becalmed in the river, he had to walk the last few miles into Smithville, where he located a steam launch to take him to the fort. Once there, he presented Major Hedrick with the governor's order. Hedrick and his men grumbled at this negation of their dashing achievement, but he replied to the governor's message: "We, as North Carolinians, will obey the command."[2] Reilly and Dardingkiller eventually reported to Washington that everything in their respective posts had been "returned in good order" (which wasn't saying much, considering how shabbily Washington had maintained the two places over the years).

One inhabitant of Smithville recalled discussing the condition of Fort Caswell with some of the Minute Men. After seizing the fort, they told him, they had been ordered to "be ready for action at the first alarm."

But no alarm followed and they settled themselves down to get as much ease as they could, which was mighty little. On inspection the fort was found to be dilapidated and almost unfit for human habitation. There were no guns mounted which could be fired, the moat was nearly filled with sand and muck, and there was not a room in the fort, finished or unfinished; mosquitos were the only energetical objects that made an appearance. To the troops who had performed this service for their country, there did not seem to be any of the pomp or circumstance of "glorious war"; but it was necessary to keep up some form of military display and the sentinels posted on the walls were ordered to give immediate notice of the approach of any hostile ships...None came however and after waiting a few days a...steamer was seen approaching which they found to be the bearer of dispatches to the effect that the troops occupying Fort Johnston and Fort Caswell should evacuate those places and return immediately to Wilmington where they were to disperse and return to their homes. It was explained that North Carolina had not yet seceded from the Union, and until she had done so, the United States were the rightful possessors of all such property...[When the Minute Men returned] the inhabitants of Smithville looked at each other and wondered. They had not thought that the war would end so soon, without the loss of a single man.[3]

Three months later, on April 15, 1861 — just after sending his feisty "you can get no troops from North Carolina" wire to Washington in response to Lincoln's call for soldiers to subdue the rebellious South — Governor Ellis sent new orders to Colonel Cantwell. This time, Ellis instructed the militia officer to seize Forts Johnston and Caswell "without delay."

Colonel Cantwell set sail with 120 men on the morning after he received the governor's telegram. The militia companies that comprised his command were given a spirited farewell by the populace. They boarded a steamer and set sail for Smithville, where, for the second time, Sergeant Reilly was relieved of his keys. A few hours later, the equally hapless Sergeant Dardingkiller experienced a similar episode of *deja vu*.

Ellis had also ordered the seizure of Fort Macon, across Bogue Sound, opposite the little port of Beaufort. Fort Macon was already in rebel hands, however, for Captain Josiah Pender and a detachment of volunteers from Beaufort had taken it on April 14 (from its one-man garrison, Ordnance Sergeant William Alexander).

Fort Caswell was still in its original forlorn condition, and Fort Macon was found to be just as bad. Captain Pender reported that its ironwork was pitted, the embankments and sides of the moat had collapsed, and of the fort's 17 cannon only 4 were mounted — and those on carriages which looked as if they would disintegrate with the recoil of the first shot. Cantwell, getting his first really detailed look at Fort Caswell, was so unimpressed that he wired Governor Ellis and proposed that the fort be placed under strict blackout so that no passing Federal ship could see that it had been garrisoned and perhaps be tempted to attack. In its present condition, Cantwell averred, the fort was indefensible.

By the end of May, however, the industrious garrison had mounted 22 guns, deepened the moat, and erected a supporting battery (Fort Campbell) about half a mile to the southwest, covering the beaches. Over the next two years, Caswell would gradually be improved until it was second only to Fort Fisher in terms of strength. Its gun emplacements would be protected by thick casemates of pine logs, sand, and overlays of railroad iron. Attempts to strengthen Fort Macon proved less successful, and it was far from ready when its baptism of fire took place.

Once the garrisons had done whatever was in their power to arm and repair the forts, their lives settled into a dreary, monotonous, and uncomfortable pattern. One letter written from Fort Caswell in the summer of 1862 recounts that the soldiers spent their days lying around in the shade, if they could find any, "and when night comes, instead of getting cooler it positively gets warmer and the mosquitoes come out in swarms...some of them as large as a hummingbird with bills half an inch long...there is no such thing as sleeping.[4]

Another letter home described the daily routine of the Caswell garrison:

> I will try and give you a routine of my daily labors. I have to be on parade ground [to answer to] my name, I then have my face to wash and hair to come which is quite a job here as it generally takes about half an hour to find a basin...at [7:30 a.m.] I have again to be on parade ground to answer to my name for breakfast. We are then marched into our mess room when we have a chief of mess appointed from our company to superintend the cooking. Those that cannot get plates at the first table (which is very hard to do) will have to take a seat on the

bricks, and wait their turn. We have rice[,] bacon bread...which we
relish very well as our work gives us a good appetite. At 8 after
breakfast we are drilled until night, resting at short times every hour
or so. If we are not drilled at the cannons we are drilled at the sea
beach with our muskets. We have to answer to our names for every
meal, and also at 9 o'clock before we go to bed, and such scrambling
to get to sleep you never saw.[5]

That was at Fort Caswell. Up the coast at Fort Macon — and at
the newly constructed Forts Hatteras, Clark, Oregon, and Ocracoke
— things were less regimented. Aside from the (so far) false
alarms concerning vast armadas of approaching Federal ships, life
for the garrisons was not too bad during those early weeks of the
war. The main enemy was boredom. A man who could play a good
tune on a fiddle was accorded a place of honor. An officer who
could arrange a brass band concert for his men (the cornet and
trumpet ensemble from Fayetteville was especially in demand),
was assured of their loyalty. Marathon card games were held on
the parapets. Men answered the morning roll calls with fishing
poles in their hands instead of muskets. The gentle art of surf-
casting was brought to perfection, with the crudest of equipment,
during the long off-duty hours of tedium.

Other than gambling, gabbing, and fishing, however, the main
pastime appears to have been the soldiers' traditional favorite:
drinking. Local purveyors of spirits did a thriving business dis-
pensing alcohols of various strengths and contents. Since the
officers drank too, as much if not more than the men, drunkenness
on duty was usually treated as a minor offense. Harsh disciplinary
punishments were reserved for troopers found guilty of grossly
indecent behavior toward the local female population, such as it
was on the Outer Banks in 1861.

Across the sounds, the inhabitants of North Carolina's coastal
towns made the transition from peace to war after their own
individual styles. Wilmington bustled with patriotism and bellicosity, while down river, the peaceful little town of Smithville held a
public meeting and formed a Home Guard company that was
probably the shortest-lived unit in the Confederate order of battle.
The incident was drolly recounted in the memoirs of Dr. Walter
Curtis, a Smithville native who served for 30 years as quarantine

surgeon for the Port of Wilmington:

> Mr. John Bell was elected Captain, his chief qualifications being that
> he was good natured and not likely to enforce any military discipline
> whatever. Much wisdom was apparent in the...conversation of these
> ancient gentlemen. They proposed to the Captain a great number of
> things heretofore unheard of in any military organization; the prin-
> ciple one being that as they were liable to become fatigued by the
> exertion of marching and inquiring of the citizens "if they were well"
> and listening to their replies that "they were not well, that they had
> a mighty hurting in their heads and a misery in their backs" which
> being duly reported to Captain Bell he would reply by saying that "he
> was sorry for their infirmities but that Mustang linament was a good
> thing to rub on the aching places and that a small quantity of
> Plantation Bitters taken internally would finish the cure."
>
> Captain Bell issued orders that they should all meet for drill the
> next morning and one member of the force proposed to the Captain
> that the soldiers of the "home guard" should be required to bring
> camp stools with them so that when they were tired they could sit
> down and rest. Captain Bell then gave the order of "attention" and put
> them through the various drills marching them around town and it
> was observed that when one of the company got opposite to his own
> home he left the ranks and was no more seen. The "home guard"
> being thus weakened so that they could not face any kind of enemy,
> it was moved and seconded ...that the "home guard" ought to be
> disbanded, to which motion Captain Bell remarked that "he thought
> so too...."[6]

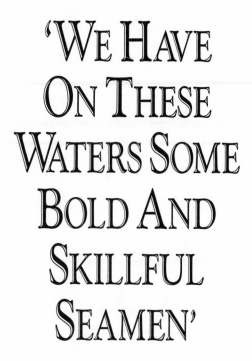

'WE HAVE ON THESE WATERS SOME BOLD AND SKILLFUL SEAMEN'

Governor John Ellis reported on the coastal situation in a letter to Confederate President Jefferson Davis dated April 27, 1861. The letter reveals that Ellis had a clear understanding of both the vulnerability and the strategic importance of the coastline:

> The State is to all intents and purposes practically out of the Old Union, and we are deciding on the speediest mode of giving legal sanction to this State of facts...All lights have been extinguished on the coast. Vessels have been sunk in the Ocrachoche [sic] Inlet and a fleet of armed vessels (small) is now being fitted out to protect our grain crops lying on the inland waters of the [northeastern] part of the State. A good Ship Canal connects those waters with the Chesapeake at Norfolk.
>
> Beaufort harbor, protected by Fort Macon is a most eligible point for privateering & c...we have on these waters some bold and Skilful Seamen who are ready to go out as privateers at once. The forms required in procuring letters of Marque present a great obstacle. Had you an authorized agent here who could deliver letters and receive the

bonds &c. the work would be greatly facilitated. The enemy's
commerce between N. York and all the West Indies and South
American ports could be cut off by privateers on the coast of No.
Carolina.[1]

Orders went out from Raleigh in the last days of April to erect
fortifications at Ocracoke and Hatteras, two of the most strategic
points on the Outer Banks. On the last day of the month, the
Confederate government authorized the transfer to North Carolina
of 20 13-pounder fieldpieces. These guns were intended to provide
landward protection for Forts Macon and Caswell, as well as to
guard the landing sites along the banks of the Neuse River. This
gesture seemed to indicate an awareness on Richmond's part of the
urgent need to protect the state's coastline. Unfortunately, this
token transfer of artillery was the last such gesture Richmond
would make until it was too late. And field artillery was not needed
as much as heavy coastal guns with enough range and punch to
discourage Federal naval operations. The Confederacy had enough
such guns to do the job, but the government was unable to sort out
its priorities. Few of those weapons were sent to the coast in time
to be useful, and those that did were supplied only with token
amounts of ammunition, much of it scandalously inferior.

Fate also took a hand, for in May the sagacious and politically
well-connected Governor Ellis died suddenly. He was replaced by
Henry T. Clark, speaker of the state senate. Clark was an active
governor, and not without energy or intelligence, but he was nearly
overwhelmed by the magnitude of the job and lacked the clout with
Richmond that Ellis had enjoyed. Most of his pleas for weapons,
men, and artillery specialists were dismissed by Richmond as mere
nagging — no matter how closely reasoned were the governor's
arguments, and no matter how imminent were the threats he sought
to address.

One of Clark's first steps was to create a Military and Naval
Board to coordinate all military activities in North Carolina. So
vast was the coastal region that it was thought best to divide it into
two "departments." The northern theater ran from Norfolk to
Onslow County, with the New River as its southern boundary. The
southern department embraced everything from there to South
Carolina. Brigadier General Walter Gwynn was appointed com-

mander of the northern department; his southern counterpart was Brigadier General Theophilus Holmes, a Mexican War hero with a reputation for professionalism.

By mid-summer of 1861, the state had enough troops to man the coastal defenses adequately. They were not mustered into organized units, however, because there were no arms. By August 1861, 22 infantry regiments had been raised in North Carolina, but 16 of the best-trained and best-equipped units had been sent to Virginia. That left a grand total of six regiments to guard a coastline almost 400 miles long, and every one of these regiments was green and poorly armed.

The strategic situation was eased, however, by the facts of geography. Only six channels -- Hatteras, Oregon, Ocracoke, Beaufort, and the two Cape Fear inlets -- were passable by ocean-going craft. As long as these key positions were held, North Carolina could not be invaded from the sea, nor could her internal communications and agricultural production be disturbed by seaborne incursions.

Closest to the enemy was General Gwynn's northern department. It was also the most vulnerable, because there were no existing fortifications on that part of the Outer Banks. Defensive works would have to be erected on barren windswept sand spits, and "everything but the sand" — even the drinking water — had to be hauled across Pamlico Sound, most of it from New Bern, 90 miles away. Heavy guns had to be dismounted and transported from the Norfolk Navy Yard to the Outer Banks, and once there, emplaced on whatever sorts of mounts and carriages could be hammered together by local workmen. After the 7,000-pound gun barrels had been hoisted from their railroad cars, the whole process of shipping, transporting, and remounting them was just as slow, tedious, and labor-intensive as it had been in George Washington's time. General Gwynn soon found it necessary to issue an appeal to the civilians on the mainland, urging them to send whatever slaves or free laborers they could spare to assist in the fortification projects. The work was, after all, being done for their protection. The response to this plea, however, was slow, grudging, and meager.

Hatteras Inlet was the single most strategic point in Gwynn's department. Here, two forts were erected: Fort Clark, at the seaward mouth of the inlet, with seven guns (five smoothbore 32-pounders and two smaller fieldpieces); and Fort Hatteras, sited to command the western exit of the inlet, with lanes of fire that overlapped those of Fort Clark.

Fort Hatteras was perhaps the weaker of the two forts. It was built of dirt and sand, its outer walls shaped and given added protection by thick wooden planks driven into the sand at a glancing angle, and then layered with mats of sod. The fort measured about 250 feet square and mounted a dozen 32-pounders. The 32-pounder had been a common coastal defensive weapon in the decades following the War of 1812, and against wooden sailing ships armed with smoothbore cannon it had proven more than adequate, for it fired solid shot that struck with tremendous smashing power. But since they were inaccurate smoothbore weapons, the 32-pounders could only be "pointed at" the enemy, not really "aimed." Their effective range was only about 2,000 yards.

Fort Clark was smaller, lower, and from any angle not a very impressive sight. In the words of one naval historian, both positions "resembled pigpens more than bastions." Nevertheless, Gwynn's men had done a reasonably good job of construction -- a Federal engineering officer who later inspected the positions, with an eye toward retaining them as Federal outposts, reported that he was "not able to suggest any improvements" in their construction or location.

What General Gwynn's engineers could not do was to provide these works with the kind of long-range rifled artillery needed to fend off the U.S. Navy. Nor, for all his good intentions, could Gwynn conjure up an extra regiment of well-armed infantry to repel any landing parties that might try to outflank the forts from the beaches to the north.

Work on the Hatteras forts, and on the lesser works at Oregon and Ocracoke Inlets, was given added urgency by the fact that Federal ships sometimes appeared offshore, just out of range, to observe the progress of construction. That progress was violently interrupted on July 10 when the Federal side-wheeler *Harriet Lane* steamed into range at high speed and fired three broadsides at the Hatteras earthworks. The shells did no damage but provoked a wild scramble among the workers.

Far worse than the slight danger of a Federal shelling were, in the troops' opinion, the mosquitos. When the sea breeze died down, the bugs were so bad that men had to be detached to stand alongside each workman and shoo the insects away with handfuls of sea oats. Modern-day visitors to the area will surely sympathize.

All things considered, it was a long, hot summer for the Outer Banks garrisons. Despite the acknowledged importance and vulnerability of the North Carolina coast, by mid-summer there were still less than 600 men available to guard the whole vast stretch. These consisted of 350 men of the 7th North Carolina Regiment stationed at the Hatteras works, and another 230-odd men divided between the outposts at Oregon and Ocracoke Inlets. Since most of the manual labor, predictably, was done by Negro slaves from the mainland, the soldiers passed the time as best they could. According to contemporary accounts, most of the time they sat in the shade, swatted insects, and drank. Or went fishing and drank. Or played cards and drank. The only place where any sort of rest and recreation could be had was at the tiny fishing village of Portsmouth, near Fort Ocracoke, an impoverished and squalid place whose inhabitants alternately profited and suffered from the boredom of the local Confederate garrisons.

What little action there was during the late spring and early summer of 1861 centered around the activities of the "North Carolina Navy," better known to those who served in it as the "Mosquito Fleet." There were five ships in all: small, shallow-draft steamers that had originally been canal tugboats or intracoastal trading vessels. The fastest and best-armed was the CSS *Winslow*, a former coastal trading ship armed with a 32-pounder forward and a smaller rifled cannon on her afterdeck. The other four ships (the *Oregon*, *Ellis*, *Beaufort*, and *Raleigh*) were each armed with a single small cannon apiece. General D.H. Hill, who became intimately acquainted with the Mosquito Fleet during his tenure as commander of the northern coastal district, did not consider the little ships much of an asset:

> In the absence of a regular supply of coal they frequently had to tie up on shore and cut green wood to keep steam in their boilers. Their crews were not gunners, but fishermen, soldiers, or farmers, hur-

riedly taught to fire a gun. Their fuses were uncertain and their guns liable to burst after a few rounds...If the stakes had not been life and the issues desperation, blood, [and] death, the laugh of the satirist would have driven the "mosquito fleet"...from the waters.[2]

Typical of the vessels in question was the 92-foot *Beaufort*. Formerly a tugboat on the Dismal Swamp Canal, the *Beaufort* was 17 feet wide and her ironwork a quarter-inch thick. She had been strengthened with timbers to accept a rifled 32-pounder and was crewed by 35 men. Her captain was Commander William H. Parker, an experienced career naval officer who had resigned his U.S. Navy commission to fight for the Confederacy. Parker was not impressed with this little ship's warlike potential when he first saw her tied up to a dock at New Bern. The first thing he noticed was that both the powder magazine and the boiler were situated above the waterline, where they were almost certain to be hit during a lengthy engagement.

Unprepossessing as she was, the *Beaufort* achieved the signal honor of engaging in the first ship-to-ship naval battle of the Civil War. On July 21, 1861, the little tugboat duelled with a much larger Federal ship in the vicinity of Oregon Inlet. Both ships kept the narrow barrier island between them as they fired, using the sand dunes for cover. No hits were scored by either vessel during the 45-minute exchange, but after observing a few close splashes, the Confederates were exhilarated by the sight of their more powerful adversary finally ducking behind a large dune and hiding from the *Beaufort*'s guns.

Although the Mosquito Fleet's vessels were limited as men-of-war, they were much more suited for a less conventional role, one which would prove far more damaging to the enemy. Given the geography of the South's coastline and the virtual nonexistence of her naval forces, the ancient and romantic practice of privateering quickly suggested itself as a natural course of action. To that end, Jefferson Davis, on April 17, 1861, authorized the Confederate Congress to issue "letters of marque" -- official sanctions for privately owned vessels to be armed and take to the seas in search of vulnerable enemy merchant ships. The value of any cargo taken from such ships would be divided between the crew who captured the ship and the Confederate government.

Throughout history, weaker naval powers had frequently been able to wound much stronger opponents with such a strategy. Privateers in the War of 1812 did much more damage to Great Britain than did the U.S. Navy. And in 1761, at a time when Louis XV's French navy had virtually been swept from the seas, his privateers nevertheless claimed more than 800 English merchant vessels. When Captain Albert Thayer Mahan wrote his brilliantly perceptive book *The Influence of Sea Power Upon History* -- the first in-depth discussion of the relationship between naval strategies and the economic health of combatant nations -- he penned a summary of the ideal conditions for waging a campaign with privateers. He could well have been writing with the coastline of North Carolina specifically in mind:

> The advantage of geographical nearness to an enemy, or to the object of attack, is nowhere more apparent than in that form of warfare which has lately received the name of commerce-destroying, which the French call *guerre de course*. This operation of war, being directed against peaceful merchant vessels which are usually defenceless, calls for ships of small military force. Such ships, having little power to defend themselves, need a refuge or point of support near at hand; which will be found in certain parts of the sea controlled by the fighting ships of their country, or in friendly harbors. The latter give the strongest support, because they are always in the same place, and the approaches of them are more familiar to the commerce destroyer than to his enemy.[3]

The Confederacy had a real opportunity to use its coastal waters as a base for a determined campaign of *guerre de course*, and the value of this strategy was proven by the brief but sensational career of a handful of dashing privateers that did operate from the protected waters of Hatteras Inlet during the war's early months. In the summer of 1861, the naval authorities in Washington regarded the coast of North Carolina as "the most dangerous stretch of shore in the whole Confederacy." It formed, in their eyes, an immense watery bastion, with the sounds as moats, the Outer Banks as ramparts, and Hatteras Inlet as its chief sally port. A relatively modest concentration of forces and resources there by Richmond would have enormously improved the South's overall strategic posture. With only a few good regiments, some easy-to-build shallow-draft gunboats, and a few dozen pieces of reliable heavy artillery, the Confederacy's long-range prospects would have been much healthier.

Nature seemed almost to have designed the North Carolina coast with an offensive defense in mind. Along the entire East Coast, Cape Hatteras is the easternmost jut of land into the Atlantic. In 1860, most of North America's coastal shipping skirted the treacherous Cape Hatteras shoals within sight of the Cape Hatteras lighthouse. So, too, did a significant portion of the lucrative commerce with the West Indies. As the German U-boats were to find in World War II, there was no shortage of targets off the North Carolina coast.

The first vessels to try their hand at buccaneering were three ships from the Mosquito Fleet: the side-wheeler *Winslow* and two of the converted canal boats, the *Raleigh* and the *Beaufort*. The *Winslow*, skippered by Lieutenant Commander Thomas M. Crossan, was the fastest ship and enjoyed the most success.

Crossan's first prize was the brig *Lydia Francis*, of Bridgeport, carrying a cargo of Cuban sugar. Equally valuable was the next capture, the bark *Linwood*, whose cargo of Cuban coffee fetched a handsome price. All together, in May and June, the *Winslow* captured five vessels. The richest was the schooner *Herbert Manton*, loaded with $30,000 worth of Cuban molasses. On June 25, while steaming in the Gulf Stream about 25 miles off Cape Hatteras, the *Winslow* took the brig *Hannah White* — a Confederate blockade runner which itself had been captured only five days earlier by a Federal ship off Savannah, Georgia. The *Hannah White*'s valuable cargo of molasses thus reached a Confederate port after all.

At the end of July, at about the same time the North Carolina Navy was absorbed into the Confederate States Navy, civilian privateers began operating out of Hatteras Inlet. Most of them were ships from other Confederate states, drawn to North Carolina by Hatteras Inlet's reputation as the handiest and most secure place on the eastern seaboard from which to go a-raiding.

A trim little ex-pilot boat from Norfolk, the *York*, enjoyed amazing success on July 13 — at first, that is. After taking the brig *P.T. Martin*, out of Philadelphia, the Confederates discovered in her hold a complete sugar mill, originally destined for Havana, Cuba. When another Federal ship suddenly appeared, the crew of the *York* got nervous and ran the captured *P.T. Martin* aground, then fled into the trees just beyond the beach. The Federal ship, the USS *Union*, anchored offshore and shelled the forest for awhile, then landed an armed party which set fire to the brig and its cargo. The *York* itself was forced to run aground on August 9, not long after taking her final prize, the schooner *George T. Baker*. The *George T. Baker* was recaptured by the Federals, too, and her Confederate crew thrown into irons for their voyage to New York.

July 25 proved to be a busy day off the Outer Banks. First, the three-gun screw-steamer *Mariner*, out of Wilmington, captured a Yankee schooner. Next, the fast side-wheeler *Gordon*, a three-gun ship that had been drawn north from Charleston by reports of good hunting in the Hatteras waters, overhauled and captured a brig out of Bangor, Maine -- the *William McGilvery*. The *William McGilvery* proved to be loaded with Cuban molasses. Its skipper, Master Hiram Carlisle, at first refused to heave to, compelling the *Gordon* to open fire. When a shell went whistling between his main stays and foresail, accompanied by a signal from the *Gordon* threatening to sink him, Carlisle had second thoughts.

Not long after the capture of the *William McGilvery*, the *Gordon* took a schooner making for Philadelphia with a precious load of Cuban fruit. The busy little privateer was spotted by a Federal warship on July 30, but she nimbly ducked between two sand bars and reached safety in Beaufort harbor. Three days later she was back off Hatteras, scanning the sea for more targets. Soon she found them. During the first week of August, the *Gordon* took two more prizes, both schooners, laden with cargoes of fresh fruit and mahogany.

On August 9, six of the largest maritime insurance companies in the United States addressed a joint petition to the Honorable Gideon Welles, U.S. Secretary of the Navy, bewailing their "very heavy" losses and demanding that the "nest of pirates" at Hatteras be cleaned out. A situation report on the privateering reached Welles's desk one day later from an officer aboard the blockade sloop USS *Cumberland*:

It seems that the coast of Carolina is infested with a nest of privateers that have thus far escaped capture, and, in the ingenious method of their cruising, are probably likely to avoid the clutches of our cruisers.

Hatteras Inlet, a little south of Cape Hatteras Light, seems their principle rendezvous. Here they have a fortification that protects them from assault. A look-out in the lighthouse proclaims the coast clear, and a merchantman in sight; they dash out and are back again in a day with their prize. So long as these remain it will be impossible to entirely prevent their depredations, for they do not venture out when men-of-war are in sight; and, in the bad weather of the coming season, cruisers cannot always keep their stations off these inlets without great risk of going ashore.[4]

Even as this frustrated officer was writing his report, Federal plans were being developed for an expedition under General Benjamin Butler that would wrest control of the Outer Banks from the Confederacy. The last prize of the Hatteras privateers -- captured by the doughty *Winslow* -- was a coastal steamer taken on August 20, 1861. Exactly one week later, the Federal invasion fleet was spotted by the lookouts in Cape Hatteras Light.

THE
ANACONDA STIRS

On the Union side, the strategy and conduct of the war's first six months might be described as a continuation of the Mexican War experience. The commander-in-chief of the U.S. Army, General Winfield Scott, had also commanded all of the land forces in the war with Mexico. Several ranking U.S. Navy officers, men such as Samuel DuPont, had also held positions of high responsibility in that conflict. In their minds, there were many similarities between Mexico and the Confederacy. Both nations were geographically immense, with vast stretches of sparsely inhabited territory; both had extensive coastlines, but only a handful of significant ports; both had navigable river systems that penetrated deeply into the interior; both depended largely on imports for manufactured goods; and neither nation had a real navy, nor the industry and resources to build one.

If a combination of blockade and amphibious attack — coupled eventually with a massive thrust against the capital city — had beaten the Mexicans, it ought to work as well against the South. This was the reasoning behind the strategic plans formulated in May 1861, and the Lincoln administration, thankful to have some kind of coherent scheme (and too inexperienced to look for a better plan), accepted Scott's concept. Scott liked to call it the "Anaconda Plan," after the large tropical snake that slowly squeezes the life out of its prey with gradual contractions of its muscles. To coordinate the various elements of this strategy, a central planning committee, the Blockade Strategy Board, was formed in late May. During the next two months, its members met several times a week, working out the details.

Curiously enough, one of the board's first recommendations was to leave the coast of North Carolina pretty much alone, except for the offshore blockade. To bottle up the privateers, a proposal was advanced to sink a number of stone-filled old hulks in the channels between the sounds and the ocean. Other than that, the "sterile and half-drowned shores of North Carolina" were of little interest. This attitude changed rather quickly when the Confederate privateers began their sorties into the trade routes and the marine insurance rates in New York, Boston, and Philadelphia began soaring.

One Federal general who began thinking about North Carolina was Benjamin F. Butler, commander of the Union garrison at Fort Monroe. Early in June, despite his own blustering amateurishness and the raw condition of his undisciplined men, Butler had successfully expelled a much smaller Confederate force from Newport News. Eager to win more laurels, Butler pursued the retreating Colonel John Magruder and attacked the Confederates in a fortified position at Big Bethel on June 10. Butler was trounced. Desperately seeking to redeem his reputation, Butler almost immediately began submitting proposals to lead a combined operation against the privateers' base at Hatteras Inlet. As it happened, Butler's memos began arriving only a week or so before the first really serious Union defeat of the war — the Battle of Manassas (Bull Run). This defeat created intense public clamor for the Lincoln administration to take some kind of vigorous, and successful, action against the enemy. Since the U.S. Army was in no condition to resume offensive operations in Virginia, the strategists in Washington began looking around for some spot where the Confederacy was not too strong, and where the Union's monopoly on naval power, combined with a modest investment in ground troops, might produce a quick, cheap, headline-grabbing victory.

As the summer dragged on and the Northern newspaper editorials grew more vociferous in their demands for action, North Carolina came more and more into focus as a probable target. Intelligence reports of an unusually fresh and reliable nature confirmed Federal suspicions that the Outer Banks were not yet protected by formidable defenses. These reports came from two Yankee sea captains, Daniel Campbell of Maine and Henry Penny of New York, whose vessels had been seized by Confederate privateers. Campbell and Penny had spent their time as prisoners --

loosely guarded prisoners, it would seem -- snooping around and memorizing details of the Confederate forts and the condition of their garrisons. When the two seamen were freed in a prisoner exchange, they immediately told all they knew to Commodore Silas Stringham, Union commander of the Atlantic Blockading Squadron.

The works guarding Hatteras Inlet, Stringham learned, were weakly held by about three companies of men. Morale was low, ammunition was limited, and the powder was known to be damp from exposure to the coastal elements. The beaches north of the forts were not regularly patrolled, and Federal troops could probably come ashore undisturbed anywhere along the length of Hatteras Island. The two skippers also provided some useful details about tides, winds, currents, and surf conditions.

These first-hand accounts dovetailed with a number of strategic assessments that landed on the desk of Navy Secretary Welles during late June and July 1861, documenting the growing menace of the Confederate privateers and their method of operation. All of these factors — from General Butler's importuning memos to the repatriated skippers' intelligence summaries — converged to create a strong impression that there was nowhere else along the entire Southern coast where the Union might apply its naval power so easily, and to such great gain, as the coast of North Carolina.

For the U.S. Navy, an expedition against Hatteras would be something of a test case. The Navy Department, in the spring of 1861, was not ready for the tasks it would be called upon to perform. Long years of peace and bureaucratic inertia had fostered a system choked at the top by superannuated gold braid. Before the Civil War, promotions in the Navy had been awarded solely on the basis of seniority, which by 1861 was very senior indeed. Vigorous, imaginative young officers remained frozen in subordinate ranks for years, sometimes decades, until their best and keenest qualities had faded away. Any officer who simply lived long enough, unless he was an outright criminal or some kind of scandalous degenerate, could be sure of eventually reaching the top rungs of the promotional ladder. Ability and initiative counted for nothing. In the absence of any real incentive to lead, think, or perform with distinction, conformity and mediocrity became virtues. At the time the war broke out, the high command of the U.S. Navy was fossilized — staffed entirely, as one contemporary observer acidly remarked, by "worn out men without brains."

One reason for this sad state of affairs was that for the past two centuries, until the 1840s, ship design and the science of naval ordnance had not changed in any fundamental way. The men-of-war that carried the flag in 1840 looked, except for the odd detail of rigging and architecture, very much like the vessels of the Revolutionary War era. They were massive wooden sailing ships of two or three decks, armed with broadsides of smoothbore cannon that fired solid shot at relatively close range.

But the dawning Industrial Age produced several byproducts, including steam power and rapidly evolving ordnance technology — although by 1861, the process of modernization, in the U.S. Navy at least, was still spotty. When war came, the Navy had 90 ships, but 50 of them were sailing vessels, and a significant number had been docked for so long that they proved too worm-eaten to be seaworthy. There were 38 steam-powered vessels, but a quick survey ordered by Navy Secretary Welles revealed that five of them had engines that wouldn't even start. Of the others, one was patrolling the Great Lakes, and three others were judged structurally unfit for service. The total of modern vessels actually in commission and at sea was a mere 24. And almost all of them were showing the flag in overseas regions, some as far away as Africa and Japan.

The total of serviceable modern warships on hand with the "Home Squadron" when war broke out — the total number of warships immediately available to patrol an enemy coastline almost 4,000 miles long — was exactly three, mounting a total of 24 guns. No wonder the Confederates scoffed when Lincoln declared a blockade.

Still, the potential for great expansion was there, and at its core were five modern steam frigates, constructed during the last decade, which were among the most powerful warships, ton for ton, on Earth. Long and sleek, with rounded sterns and gracefully raked bows, these ships were strong, seaworthy, and powerfully armed. Typical was the USS *Minnesota*, a vessel that would see much wartime service off the coast of North Carolina. The *Minne-*

sota's main battery consisted of 42 nine-inch rifled guns, augmented by four 100-pounder rifles, one 11-inch rifle, and one enormous 150-pounder gun. At the start of the conflict, all five of these vessels were laid up for repairs, but work on them was accelerated, and soon the Confederacy would feel the weight of their broadsides.

Until the exigencies of war dictated new standardized designs, the U.S. Navy had to make do with civilian craft hastily converted for military roles -- a process that was underway at a feverish pace when the Hatteras privateers began their attacks. In the war's first months, anything that could float, move, and carry a cannon without capsizing was bought and pressed into service: yachts, Staten Island ferry boats, tugs, fishing craft, whalers, even garbage scows. A surprising number of these converted craft, once armed, proved quite useful to the military, although the sheer variety of vessels made logistics a nightmare, and control of any large formation was all but impossible.

Officers were recruited in a similarly helter-skelter manner: from ferry boats, the merchant service, and fishing craft. The training course at the U.S. Naval Academy at Annapolis was streamlined for rapid turnaround, the theory being that any man who had earned his living at sea would already know the basics of navigation and seamanship. Enlisted men were attracted by bonus offers, sometimes as high as $1,000.

The strategic prospects for employing this newly expanded naval force were striking. Fortunately for the Confederacy, they were but dimly and erratically perceived at the highest levels of the Federal command. And just as the vast extent of the rebel coastline posed great problems for the blockaders, it also posed an almost insoluble dilemma for the Confederate government. The two things most desperately needed by Richmond on the battlefields of Virginia were trained manpower and artillery -- the very things needed to protect the coastline. If men and guns were withdrawn from the area around Richmond, the reasoning went, the capital would become vulnerable to the Federal armies massing on the other side of the Potomac. Yet if the coastline were not strengthened by the Confederate government, the various state governors — already angry over the amount of manpower and resources being committed to Virginia — might decide to hold back their regiments, their cannon, and their gunpowder for regional protection.

For a nation as strapped for military resources as the Confederacy, this basic strategic conundrum was crippling. Early efforts to cope with it did divert attention and resources from the Virginia front, but always in the form of halting, parsimonious half-measures that did little to strengthen the coast. Always, the cannon were too few or too late, their powder and shot too limited, experienced gunners too rare, and good engineers too overworked or underequipped to create any kind of coherent defensive front. Nowhere was this waffling policy of too-little-too-late more dramatic in its failures and more tantalizing in its might-have-beens than on the North Carolina coast in 1861.

Fortunately for the Confederacy, even though the U.S. government had an instrument of tremendous power in its hands -- a navy capable of launching large-scale amphibious attacks virtually at will, anywhere along the rebel shore -- the Union failed to appreciate what a tremendous shock a successful landing always delivers to the enemy's morale. The lesson was right there, in front of their eyes, in the panic that would be generated by the loss of the Hatteras forts. And the remarkable later success of the Burnside expedition, which would establish Union control over all of coastal North Carolina at a ridiculously low cost in blood, reprised the lesson in spectacular fashion. Yet even then, President Lincoln and his generals remained fixated on a Napoleonic concept of great land armies locked in a death struggle. Amphibious operations remained, until the last winter of the war, strictly one-shot affairs, localized in their objectives and in their effect on the enemy.

The Civil War would therefore be decided by huge, grinding, land campaigns. The North's vast naval power was fully employed only in the realm of blockading operations, where its success was erratic and for the first two years very disappointing. Had Lincoln correctly interpreted the lessons of Butler's and Burnside's successes, and committed a massive infusion of men and firepower to the North Carolina coast, the Army of Northern Virginia would have been cut off from most of its supplies, the Confederate railroad system would have been savaged, North Carolina would have been knocked out of the war, and tens of thousands of lives would have been saved. Once the Federals had taken the Outer Banks, Roanoke Island, and the river estuaries, there was little but distance standing in their way. Even a single strategic thrust toward the rail junction at Goldsboro, executed while the invaders still had momentum on their side, would have dealt the Rebellion a staggering blow.

If the Northern generals missed a golden opportunity, however, so too did the leadership of the South. For if the coast of North Carolina had been afforded the priority it deserved, in terms of fortifications and firepower, the North's blockade would have been rendered vastly more difficult, costly, and ineffective. And the cost, to Richmond, would have been cheap indeed.

HATTERAS LOST

On the morning of August 27, 1861, a Confederate telegraphist in Norfolk flashed some electrifying news to Raleigh: "Enemy's fleet...left last evening; passed out of the capes and steered south...."

The fleet in question was the largest yet assembled by the North for a single operation: the steam frigates *Minnesota* and *Wabash*, the sloop *Cumberland*, three gunboats (the *Pawnee*, *Monticello*, and the former revenue cutter *Harriet Lane*), and a side-wheel steamer, the *Susquehanna* -- mounting a total of 149 guns. Tagging along were two chartered civilian vessels being used as transports for the 900-odd infantry of the 9th and 20th New York Regiments, along with a gaggle of surf boats and a couple of auxiliary tugs. General Benjamin Butler was in command of the landing force. His naval counterpart, Commodore Silas Stringham, looked like a character from a Nathaniel Hawthorne story: a bony, hollow-eyed Yankee gentleman who habitually wore a puritanical black knee-length coat and a stiff white collar. He was decidedly a product of the hallowed seniority system of the U.S. Navy and had a reputation, not entirely deserved as it turned out, for being slow, cautious, and dull-witted.

Federal lookouts aboard Stringham's ships spotted the Cape Hatteras lighthouse at 9:30 a.m. on the morning of August 27. On the other side of the surf, the Confederate commander of the forts, Colonel William F. Martin, realized that his worst fears were about to materialize. Despite repeated soothing assurances, not so much as a round of ammunition had come through from Richmond in weeks. Martin would have to deal with the assault with the pathetically inadequate forces he already had -- about 350 men of the 7th

North Carolina. As he counted the enemy masts gradually coming over the horizon, Martin correctly concluded that he did not stand a chance. (He might have been comforted somewhat if he had known that his adversaries, crammed tightly in the holds of their converted troop carriers, had spent the night vomiting all over one another as they endured the typically rough Hatteras seas.)

Martin also figured that the odds would be more even if the Confederate garrison at Portsmouth, near Fort Ocracoke -- some 230 men -- could reach Hatteras before the enemy did. There being no telegraph line, Martin searched the sound for a Confederate steamer to take the word quickly to the neighboring island. Usually, there were two or three Mosquito Fleet vessels within hailing distance. But it was typical of the bad luck that was to dog Confederate efforts during the whole battle that on this particular morning there was not a vessel in sight. Martin had no choice but to send his dispatch with a man in a small open launch. It didn't reach Colonel G.W. Johnston, commander of the forces at Portsmouth, until 24 hours later.

In contrast, Stringham's amphibious landing -- the first such operation undertaken by the U.S. Navy since the Mexican War -- got cracking rather smartly. The towed landing craft were drawn up alongside the transports, and by 10:00 a.m. Stringham's warships were ready to open fire on Fort Clark.

Stringham may have been an old mossback, but he deserves credit for a sound tactical innovation. Instead of firing from anchor, the traditional "Old Navy" manner of dueling with coastal guns, he steamed his ships in a large circle, firing their guns in rotation as they came to bear on the enemy. This was the first recorded use of such a tactic by the U.S. Navy, and later it would be refined and used to great effect in the attack on Port Royal, South Carolina.

Puffs of smoke soon appeared over the gun positions of the fort as the defenders returned fire. Stringham's crews held their breath with apprehension — they could actually see the ponderous solid-shot rounds arcing through the air toward their ships. Fear changed to hoots of derisive laughter, however, when the Confederates' shot plopped harmlessly into the sea a good half-mile short of the nearest Federal ship. Undisturbed, Stringham's ships fired as though on a training exercise, each one closing with the fort, unleashing a broadside, and then pulling away to let the next ship have a turn. After an hour of this steady firing, the smoke between ships and shoreline grew so dense that the fort was no longer visible. Nevertheless, the ship's gunners kept heaving shells into the murk, confident that they had long ago zeroed in on the range.

At mid-day, protected by three gunboats, the Federal infantry started coming ashore. In typical Hatteras fashion, however, a sudden strong southerly wind whipped the surf into turbulence. Surprisingly, nobody was drowned, but so many of the landing boats were wrecked that the landing had to be called off after only 318 men of the 20th New York and two small howitzers had been landed. The troops on shore were German- speaking New Yorkers, led by Colonel Max Weber, and their situation was suddenly very grave. They were soaked to the skin, most of their ammunition was wet, they had no food, and their only drinking water -- under an August sun on the Outer Banks -- was what they carried in their canteens. The morning had begun as an adventurous lark, but it was now something entirely different.

To those watching on the offshore ships, it looked for a time as if the little landing force was about to get in even more trouble. A detachment of what appeared, at first glance, to be rebel cavalry was spotted bearing down on them from the direction of the forts. The gunboats promptly opened fire on this "cavalry," which responded in a manner too hysterical to seem credible. Closer and cooler examination proved this formation to be nothing more than a terrified herd of wild Hatteras ponies who were fleeing, first, from the bombardment of Fort Clark, and then from the fire directed at them personally.

The Union troops on the beachhead were not actually in as much trouble as their discomfort suggested. Fort Clark had run out of ammunition shortly after noon, and by 12:30 the garrison had spiked the guns and was withdrawing across a narrow marsh-straddling causeway toward Fort Hatteras. The withdrawal came under heavy fire from the offshore guns and, as viewed from the ships, looked like a rebel rout. Men were stumbling and falling, running and diving for cover in the marsh grass. This impression of total collapse was reinforced when General Butler observed boats filled with men apparently pulling away from the island on the sound side. Since no Confederate flag was visible at either bastion, Butler assumed that the Fort Hatteras garrison, too, had begun to evacuate.

While Colonel Weber led his bedraggled landing force inside the scarred walls of the now-abandoned Fort Clark, and there hoisted the first Union flag ever to be raised above a captured rebel fortress, Commodore Stringham ordered the shallow-draft steam gunboat *Monticello* to pass through the treacherous inlet and take possession of the seemingly abandoned Fort Hatteras. But the men Butler had seen in the retreating boats were stragglers from Fort Clark. The Fort Hatteras garrison was still there, and when the *Monticello* slowed down to run the inlet, the Confederates had their first chance to fire at a target within range.

They made the most of it. The *Monticello* began to retire as soon as the first shells started splashing around her. The *Monticello*'s captain realized his ship was a sitting duck, but the channel was too narrow for any fancy maneuvering at high speed. Before the gunboat managed to extricate itself, the rebel gunners scored at least five solid hits, blowing away the *Monticello*'s boat davits, riddling her galley, pantry, and armory with shell fragments, and tearing a great gash across her main deck.

Sunset came, and Commodore Stringham's assessment of the situation was not hopeful. The sea was getting rough, forcing his ships farther out from shore and making it impossible for him to dispatch any further aid to the stranded New Yorkers at Fort Clark. Colonel Weber's little force was demoralized. Alone, unsupported by friendly guns, three-fourths of its ammunition ruined by seawater, bone-tired from the day's exertions, the 20th New York was exceedingly vulnerable to a rebel counterattack. The men were also tormented by thirst, for no fresh water had been found in the abandoned fort. Despite their officers' warnings, they had emptied their canteens by mid-afternoon, and by nightfall their thirst was so great that they were digging holes in the sand and attempting to drink the brackish sludge that seeped in from the bottom. Hunger proved less of a problem, however. Several sheep and a goose were found roaming on the island, and they were promptly spitted on bayonets and roasted over open fires.

A few hundred yards to the west of Fort Clark, Confederate

reinforcements had finally arrived from Portsmouth. Arriving with them was Commodore Samuel Barron, commander-in-chief of the coastal defenses for the district of upper North Carolina and lower Virginia. Colonel Martin, completely worn out from the day's tension and combat, offered command to Barron, who accepted. Barron seemed confident; additional troops would arrive from New Bern before midnight, he told Martin, and with them he proposed to retake Fort Clark by bayonet.

Given the virtually defenseless condition of Weber's dog-tired men, and the fact that the combined rebel forces on Hatteras now outnumbered the Yankees, Fort Clark probably could have been retaken that night by men armed with nothing but rocks and clubs. Commodore Barron, unfortunately, didn't seem to appreciate the urgency of dislodging the Federal invaders. When the expected troops from New Bern failed to show, he abandoned plans for a counterattack and concentrated his men's energies on strengthening Fort Hatteras. It apparently never occurred to him that without Fort Clark to guard the mouth of the inlet, Fort Hatteras was too isolated. It could be brought under fire from too great a distance, and from too extensive an arc, for its own weak armament to effectively reply.

Committed now to a passive, defensive role, there wasn't much the garrison of Fort Hatteras could do for the rest of the night except eat their first decent meal in 24 hours and catch whatever sleep the mosquitos would permit. At first light the next day, it was clear that the weather had moderated and the Federal fleet was preparing to close in. At about 7:30 a.m., after two hours of maneuvering, the bombardment began.

"It was like a hailstorm," recorded one survivor, and indeed it must have been. More than 3,000 shells and balls were fired by the ships, with up to 28 shells per minute exploding inside the fort or against its sandy parapets. "[The] firing of shells became...literally tremendous," wrote another witness, "as we had falling into and immediately around the work not less on average of ten each minute, and the sea being smooth, the firing was remarkably accurate."[1]

Broadsides from the ships tore into the mud walls like some sort of brutal tilling machine, uprooting great fountains of muck and turf whose particles hung in the humid air like liquid smears before raining back down over the sweating, and frustrated, Confederate gun crews. A few rounds from the fort came near some of Stringham's ships, cutting some rigging and chipping some woodwork, but otherwise no damage was done by the fort. At approximately 11 o'clock, a gunboat shell fell into the fort's ventilator shaft, not far from the main ammunition magazine, filling the vicinity with smoke and creating the appearance of a much more serious hit than it really was. But by then, the garrison had taken all they could. The white flag was run up at 11:07.

When he spotted the surrender colors, General Butler sent an aide ashore to talk terms. Commodore Barron sought honorable terms -- officers to keep their sidearms, and so forth -- but Butler was in a stern and vindicated mood, and he refused all terms other than full capitulation. Barron had no choice but to accept. Following the formal signing of surrender documents aboard the *Minnesota*, General Butler went ashore, took a place beside Colonel Weber, and led the Federal infantry into the still-smoldering Fort Hatteras for a flag-raising ceremony. Butler had certainly gained an impressive victory, even though the precise instrument of victory was not his generalship but rather the weight and accuracy of Stringham's broadsides. Moreover, the victory was gained at a bargain price: one man seriously wounded, three or four with mere scratches, and not a single man killed. Confederate losses were variously reported as four to seven killed and 20 to 45 wounded.

More than 600 Confederate soldiers surrendered. All of the prisoners were suffering from thirst and exhaustion. "Their thirst appeared unquenchable," wrote one of the victors, "[and they] said they had had no water fit to drink since they had been in the fort."[2]

It really wasn't much of a battle. Barron could have won the cheap victory for himself if he had shown a little more spunk and ordered an assault on Fort Clark during the night. Stringham would never have shelled his own men, and without naval gunfire support, Butler would have been forced to head for home and face certain disgrace.

In the North, of course, news of the fall of Hatteras Island was greeted with great rejoicing, and Commodore Stringham was feted as though he were Horatio Nelson returning from Trafalgar. The

North badly needed a victory after the humiliation of First Manassas/Bull Run, and the newspapers played this one up for every headline it was worth and then some. Strategically, the fall of Forts Hatteras and Clark meant that the Union could force the inland waterways whenever it wanted to, interrupt the flow of supplies to Virginia, and seal off the upper Outer Banks as a refuge for blockade runners and privateers. Pamlico Sound now lay open, and indeed, the entire coast of North Carolina had been unlocked between Wilmington and Roanoke Island. Butler and Stringham, for all their dour mediocrity, had managed to accomplish all this without losing a single man, in the space of 48 hours.

Confederate Secretary of the Navy Stephen R. Mallory got sick to his stomach when he heard the news. Why it should have surprised him is a mystery, as a Federal attack on Hatteras Island had been rumored for weeks and the urgent pleas from Governor Clark, begging for adequate protection, had crossed his desk many times. He might well have asked himself why, with all that advance warning, the forts had not been supplied at least with decent gunpowder -- surely a few boatloads of that wouldn't have strained the Confederacy's resources or left Richmond open to casual plunder. Nor would have the loan of a few good engineers and ordnance men to make sure the powder was put to good use.

One Petersburg editorial writer tried to make levity from the disaster, writing that by staying on the island "Old Butler will have to take his brandy and whiskey undiluted, and such as we have been informed he generaly [sic] uses, will speedily consume his vitals."[3] Not many other people were laughing, however. An official inquiry into the debacle came up with plenty of blame to spread around. The Ordnance Department was censured for failing to arm the forts properly, and the commanders on the spot, Commodore Barron in particular, were berated for their lack of aggressive tactics. It was even rumored that most of the Confederate garrison was drunk on the day of the enemy landings. "Most" might be an exaggeration, but surely "some" is not. To the other North Carolina firsts in the war now belonged the chagrin of being the site of the first Confederate defeat.

Astonishingly, General Butler's orders now called for him to evacuate the coast after tearing down the forts and sinking block-ships in the Hatteras channel. These instructions seemed, at the very least, an illogical follow-up to the victory just obtained. Butler had enough basic military sense to see that it was important to hold Hatteras and, if possible, to expand the Federal presence on the Outer Banks. He even journeyed back to Washington to get his orders changed, only to find that the Secretary of War had already altered them to meet the new realities.

Even more astonishingly, the Confederates abandoned without a fight the stout little forts at Ocracoke and Oregon Inlets, thus opening two more gateways into the southern waters of Pamlico Sound. To be sure, the value of those positions had been somewhat compromised by the fall of the Hatteras forts, but they retained some value, both tactical and psychological, and it is difficult to see any sound military judgment in the decision to abandon them. Instead, the decision seems to have been motivated by sheer panic. Some regional officers argued strongly against the withdrawal, pointing out that in many ways these forts were better able to protect themselves than either Hatteras or Clark had been. Nevertheless, the forts were abandoned, and nine precious cannon were either spiked or were accidentally dropped into the sea during attempts to load them onto ships. When news of the forts' abandonment broke, the state rang with cries of revulsion and accusations of cowardice. "The entire state joined in surprise and consternation over the evacuation of these two costly and skillfully constructed forts before even a ramrod was waved in their direction."[4]

After thus handing the enemy the equivalent of two more victories, the Confederates began to shift their attention, and most of their remaining forces, to Roanoke Island. From this strategic location they could at least dominate Albemarle Sound and the vital waterway connection to Virginia, the so-called "back door to Norfolk."

Thus did the North obtain its first foothold on Southern soil, at the cost of a handful of wounded men. Rarely in all military history has such strategic advantage been gained so cheaply. About the only consolation for the South was that Butler didn't have enough ships or men to push on and take the port towns on the mainland. There was really nothing to stop him except his own lack of resources.

After the Confederates were dislodged from Hatteras and Ocracoke, a "domino effect" followed with a vengeance. The way was now clear to attack poorly defended Roanoke Island, and once Roanoke Island fell, the whole coast all the way up to Norfolk was rendered vulnerable. The importance of the Hatteras victory was clearly recognized at the time by intelligent men on both sides. Only one side, however, followed up with appropriate measures. The Confederate side, lacking decisive leadership from Richmond, could only scramble to catch up with events.

Admiral David D. Porter had this to say about the Hatteras battle: "This was our first naval victory, indeed our first victory of any kind, and should not be forgotten. The Union cause was then in a depressed condition, owing to the reverses it had experienced. The moral effect of this affair was very great, as it gave us...possession of the sounds of North Carolina if we chose to occupy them. It was a deathblow to blockade running in that vicinity and ultimately proved one of the most important events of the war."[5]

A DAY AT THE RACES

General Butler had left the Hatteras Island garrison under the command of a brave, able, but somewhat vainglorious young officer, Colonel Rush C. Hawkins of the 9th New York. Enough reinforcements arrived in August and September 1861 to give Hawkins sufficient manpower not only to strengthen Fort Hatteras, but also to make some reconnaissance probes on the other islands. On September 16, Hawkins dispatched a force to Fort Ocracoke with orders to disable any guns the rebels might have left behind, and to blow up the place when they were done. While this was being carried out, a patrol was sent by launch to Portsmouth, which was found to have been abandoned by nearly all of its former inhabitants.

Hawkins's main concern was the concentration of rebel forces on Roanoke Island. Fortifications were being built there and the Confederates appeared to have a sizable number of men at their disposal. Hawkins expected them, sooner or later, to cross over to Hatteras Island, land somewhere to the north of the forts, and then try to attack from the landward side. To forestall such a move, Hawkins ordered the 20th Indiana Regiment, 600 men under Colonel W.L. Brown, to take up a defensive position at the beach hamlet of Chicamacomico.

On October 1, 1861, the armed tugboat *Fanny* was loaded to the gunwales with supplies for the new Chicamacomico outpost. She steamed north over the placid sound waters on what was intended to be a routine supply mission. Instead, the *Fanny* triggered one of the most confused and indecisive engagements of the war — one which would go down in history under the derisive name "The

Chicamacomico Races."

Waiting for the *Fanny* were three units of the Mosquito Fleet, now expanded to its maximum strength, thanks to reinforcements that had come down from Norfolk via the Dismal Swamp Canal. Since Commodore Barron had been sacked after the Hatteras catastrophe, the valiant little flotilla now had a new commander: Commodore William F. Lynch, a Virginian who had resigned his captain's rank in the U.S. Navy following the secession of his native state. Among the new vessels under his command were the *Curlew* and the *Seabird*, two side-wheeler riverboats. The *Curlew*'s forward gun was a 32-pounder taken from one of the abandoned forts, and its aft gun was an ancient 12-pounder fieldpiece, still on its wheeled carriage. The *Seabird* had a rifled 32-pounder mounted forward and a 30-pounder Parrott gun mounted aft. These vessels, along with the *Raleigh*, were now the best-armed ships in the Mosquito Fleet.

At the other end of the scale was the little ex-canal tug *Junaluska*, which had only enough space and stamina to carry a six-pounder popgun, a type of fieldpiece known in earlier days as a "grasshopper." The gun crews were not sailors at all, but infantrymen from the 3rd Georgia Regiment. Their only gunnery training -- and their only experience on the water, for that matter -- was acquired during the two-day trip down the Dismal Swamp Canal from Norfolk.

When the *Fanny* sailed, laden with supplies, it was of course spotted by Confederate lookouts, and word was sent to Colonel A.R. Wright, at that time the senior officer on Roanoke Island. Wright had worked out a scheme with Lynch whereby a Federal steamer was to be bushwhacked and captured, and her crew grilled for information about Union intentions.

The *Raleigh*, the *Curlew*, and the *Junaluska* ganged up on the *Fanny*. According to a contemporary account, the *Fanny*'s guns were "well worked and aimed with precision," but it was the Mosquito Fleet that struck the first (and only) recorded hit of the battle. After a half-hour chase and the exchange of about two dozen shots, a shell — probably from the *Curlew* — exploded on the *Fanny*'s deck. Although it caused no known casualties, the damage was sufficient to induce the *Fanny*'s skipper to strike his colors. It was the Mosquito Fleet's moment of glory -- they had won a naval engagement, and they had captured the first Union vessel ever taken by rebel arms.

Better still, from a practical point of view, they had won a boatload of much-needed supplies, including two rifled cannon and a cargo of military stores valued at $100,000. Among the stores were 1,000 overcoats, which were promptly distributed to the 3rd Georgia -- whose amateur gunners, after all, had won them. The rebels also obtained some interesting news from interrogating the crew: the 20th Indiana had bivouacked at Chicamacomico.

Colonel Brown of the 20th Indiana didn't need anyone to tell him what had happened to his supply ship -- he had watched the engagement from the shore and seen his rations, overcoats, and ammunition sailing away under the enemy's flag. He had only himself to blame. The *Fanny* had been lying at anchor for two and a half hours waiting for Brown to organize a detail to unload her. That was how Lynch and the Mosquitos managed to get the drop on her so decisively.

When he learned about the Federal outpost at Chicamacomico, Colonel Wright mobilized the entire Mosquito Fleet to transport every available Confederate soldier to the island. The idea was to land one force, the 3rd Georgia, to the north of the Federal position, and then land the 8th North Carolina Regiment, under Colonel H.M. Shaw, to their south, thus catching the hapless Hoosiers between two fires. Phase 2 of the plan called for the united, and presumably victorious, Confederate units to sweep down the island and attack Hawkins and his men at the captured forts. It was such a bold and ambitious scheme that something almost had to go wrong with it.

It took three days to prepare for the operation. The mood of the troops was optimistic, their officers were excited, the weather in the sound was cool and calm, and the water was as smooth as glass. Conditions would never be better.

Just after midnight on October 5, the expedition sailed. In all, there were six armed steamers, including the *Fanny* (now flying a Confederate flag), towing numerous barges and launches filled with soldiers. Just after sunrise, the little fleet appeared offshore from the 20th Indiana's camp. Colonel Brown realized that his unit was about to be cut off. He gave the order to abandon the camp and fall back on Fort Hatteras. His men obeyed with undignified alacrity, leaving everything behind but their rifles. They poured south along the sand dunes even as Colonel Wright's Georgia troops landed behind them and took up pursuit.

Thus began the Chicamacomico Races. In the lead were the terrified and helpless civilian inhabitants of the little village, followed by the routed members of the 20th Indiana. Both soldiers and civilians alike began to suffer mightily from the hot white glare of the sun and sand as they lurched and staggered through the dunes. Many of the Hoosier troops were barefooted, and after a mile or so the sand began to rub the skin from their feet. Thirst was another torment. The influx of 600 extra mouths had exhausted the little village's water reserves, and the water rations sent up by Hawkins had been captured on the *Fanny*, so most of the Federal infantry were running with dry canteens. Behind the fleeing mob came the excited Georgians, scourging their prey with volleys of musketry. Now and then a Minie ball would tag a fleeing man, toppling him headlong into the sand.

While the chase moved south, the Confederate fleet tried to get into position to cut off the retreating Union troops. But the bad luck which had so far plagued every Confederate effort in this sector once more intervened. The pursuing vessels went aground on an uncharted sandbar some two miles from their objective. Many of the North Carolina troops, eager to avenge the fall of Forts Hatteras and Clark, wanted to attempt a landing anyway, in small boats. Had they done so, even a hundred of them could have made quick work of the desperate and exhausted Indiana men. But Colonel Wright seems to have suffered a failure of nerve at this point, and by withholding permission for the men to use his small boats, he guaranteed the failure of his plan.

Staggering with exhaustion, the Indiana soldiers finally reached the Cape Hatteras lighthouse at about midnight, where at last they found a supply of potable water. They turned the old landmark into a fortress and waited all night for an attack that never came. They woke the next morning, in the words of one survivor, "feeling like sandcrabs, and ready, like them, to go into our holes, could we find them."

The pursuing Georgians were winded, too. Still unaware that Shaw's North Carolinians had not landed, they encamped for the night somewhere between the Cape Hatteras lighthouse and Kinnakeet. When they learned the next morning about how the plan had miscarried, great was their disgust. Sullenly, they broke camp and prepared to march back to Chicamacomico, taking some consolation from their rout of the 20th Indiana. They had killed eight Hoosiers and captured about 40 others.

But the Chicamacomico Races were not over yet — there was one final act still to come, a kind of hysterical grand finale. While the Georgians were about-facing, the 9th New York, which had been marching north from Hatteras since daybreak, came within sight and began chasing *them*.

Then, just after mid-day, the gunboat *Monticello* anchored off the coast and put the retreating Georgians under fire from every gun that could be brought to bear. "Of course we could offer no resistance...we had to march down the beach and take it," wrote one survivor. The retreat took place mostly on the sound side, where there was at least an illusion of cover. Ducking shells, the Confederates trudged southward, often through tidal pools two or three feet deep, for a distance of 18 miles. The men behaved well, all things considered. And although the noise, tension, and fear were terrific, the Yankee cannonade proved remarkably benign. A half-dozen Confederates were wounded, but there were no re-corded fatalities. The Confederate fleet tried to get within range to provide support, but couldn't find enough deep water to do so. Considering the untrained gun crews of the Mosquito Fleet, it was probably just as well that they couldn't get close enough to attempt to return the Union fire over the heads of the Georgia column.

The Confederate expeditionary force was safely withdrawn and sailed forlornly back to Roanoke Island. The Federals abandoned their outpost at Chicamacomico and concentrated again at Hatteras. Although the whole episode did absolutely nothing to change the balance of military power in the region, both sides managed to convince themselves that they had thwarted a major enemy offen-sive.

As an immediate consequence of the little battle, Colonel Hawkins was removed from overall command of the Union garrison on Hatteras Island, although he was retained at the head of his regiment. Hawkins was replaced by Brigadier General J.F.K. Mansfield.

In his own defense, Hawkins cited the need to protect the civilian population of Chicamacomico, whose Unionist sympathies he considered quite strong. Indeed, Unionist sympathies in this part of the coastal region did appear strong, for logical reasons. In the first place, most able-bodied Confederate sympathizers were already in the field. For the unprotected population which remained, the only rational attitudes were indifference or a predisposition to be nice to the Federal invaders, when and if they appeared. After all, thus far the Confederacy had proven quite unable to stop the invaders from landing and moving anywhere they liked, and from occupying any place they felt like occupying.

Hawkins continued to importune Washington with reports which spoke of ardent Unionism throughout the Pamlico Sound region. President Lincoln became convinced that it was vital to raise a regiment of Unionist Outer Bankers, and he proposed that New York Governor William H. Seward's nephew, Clarence, go to Hatteras and "play colonel," even if the number of recruits amounted to only a company. In fact, so few men came forward to enlist under the Union flag that "it was not found necessary to convert young Seward into a colonel."[1] Eventually, a total of only 56 Hatteras men swore allegiance to the Union. They were duly (and optimistically) designated the "1st Company" of the 1st North Carolina Union Regiment, and were relegated to garrison duty in the two island forts.

During his tenure as commander of the Federal garrison, Hawkins also issued an "Address to the People of North Carolina," assuring everyone who read the flyer that Federal troops had come to restore constitutional law and peace, not to plunder and abuse. His message might have been more convincing had his own regiment not been busily plundering the wretchedly poor islanders. Even Hawkins himself, in one candid report, was forced to refer to his men as "vandals." Word of the looting got around, and the trickle of Unionist recruits dried up, along with much of the passive sympathy Hawkins had noted earlier.

Another attempt by Washington to capitalize on the supposed

Unionist sympathies along the coast involved the appearance of two opportunistic scoundrels named Marble Nash Taylor and Charles Henry Foster. These crafty gentlemen organized something called the Hatteras Convention, held on November 18, 1861, which passed a set of surreal resolutions declaring all state offices vacant, the Federal constitution in full force again, and appointing Taylor as the new "provisional governor." The deliberations of this august-sounding body were somewhat compromised by the fact that only eight men attended the meeting. Foster set up a farcical "election" -- one which attracted only 400 of the 9,000 registered voters in the district -- and then attempted to take his seat in Congress. When word of these shenanigans appeared in the Northern press, Congress balked at the transparency of the fraud and refused to confirm Taylor or let Foster take his seat on Capitol Hill. The whole shabby business thereupon collapsed and the two adventurers, unable after all to conjure glory from the sands, faded back into the obscurity from which they had briefly emerged -- carpetbaggers ahead of their time.

PART 2

BURNSIDE'S EXPEDITION –THE COAST CONQUERED

CHANGES IN COMMAND

One of the more momentous casualties of the Union defeat at Manassas/Bull Run was General Winfield Scott's mental equilibrium. All thoughts of grand strategy were pushed from the old general's mind by that debacle, and he became obsessed with one thing only: protecting Washington. While that objective was no doubt desirable, something more ambitious would be required in order to defeat the Confederacy and save the Union. The stout-hearted but superannuated Scott had to go, and his replacement was General George C. McClellan.

McClellan was never a success on the battlefield. His arrogance and vanity, particularly as reflected in his testy relationship with Abraham Lincoln, have become part of Civil War legend. Yet at the time he assumed command of all Federal forces on November 1, 1861, he was one of the ablest and most progressive minds in the American military establishment. His strategic plans set in motion the operations that would result in the conquest of the North Carolina coast, and had his battlefield ineptness in Virginia not undone him, those plans probably would have resulted in the fall of Raleigh, the cutting of one of the South's most vital rail lines, and a much earlier conclusion to the entire war.

In the interim between the Union defeat at Manassas and the arrival of McClellan as commander-in-chief, the war was locked in a stalemate. There were two exceptions: the Hatteras expedition, and Admiral DuPont's attack on Port Royal, South Carolina, between Charleston and Savannah. Although the latter operation did not take place until early November 1861, it was set into motion long before McClellan took over, and Scott deserves credit for approving it.

Admiral DuPont's startling success in overwhelming what had been regarded as one of the South's most impressive bastions had profound, though indirect, consequences for future operations off the North Carolina coast. DuPont's victory confirmed what Stringham's tactics against Forts Hatteras and Clark had suggested — it blew to smithereens the conventional rule that one gun mounted in a land fort was worth five guns on a ship. Rifled artillery and steam-propelled firing platforms had rendered that hoary formula as obsolete as a Spanish galleon. No longer would Federal naval officers balk at the prospect of fighting ship-versus-fort engagements. Indeed, after the Port Royal victory, they became rather keen on it.

DuPont's victory also gave the North a centrally located supply base right in the middle of the Atlantic coastline. Rapid construction soon expanded Port Royal into a major depot. Chartered merchant ships sailed there regularly from Northern ports, bringing powder, beef, vegetables, coal, clothing, rope, nails, tobacco, and spare parts -- everything needed to run the Atlantic blockade squadrons. From late November 1861, blockaders off the North Carolina coast wouldn't have to sail all the way back to Hampton Roads for resupply. After a quick run down the coast, with a day or two's layover for loading and a bit of shore leave for the men, the vessel would be back on station.

The capture of Port Royal fit in nicely with McClellan's plans. Those plans, in turn, were based on the military realities of the mid-19th century, not those of Winfield Scott's heyday. In 1855, McClellan had gone to the Crimea as part of an American commission whose job was to report back on all the latest tactics, equipment, and organization of the armies that had been involved in that critically transitional conflict.

McClellan took home several very important and up-to-date impressions. First and foremost was the way in which new industrial technologies, particularly the mass production of rifled cannon and small arms, had tilted the tactical advantage toward the defender. Against slow-loading smoothbore muskets that had a maximum effective range of 100 to 150 yards, the bayonet charge was a useful tactic. But against rifles that could accurately hit a target at five times that distance, mass charges were murderous and usually futile. McClellan reasoned that if an attacking army could seize sensitive points and fortify them quickly, it would compel the enemy to attack, at a radical disadvantage, and permit the defender to shoot his attacker to pieces from behind earthworks.

Equally important were the technological advances of the telegraph and the railroad. For an army operating on internal lines of communication -- i.e., the Confederate army -- those two inventions offered tremendous advantages. The telegraph permitted instant communications of enemy moves, and the railroads permitted the rapid concentration of men and supplies to counter his moves with localized superiority. The telegraph and the railroad, McClellan realized, were what had given the South its victory at Manassas, not some mythical concept of invincibility on the battlefield.

McClellan therefore studied his maps of the South not just to see where the enemy's field armies were deployed, but to find the most sensitive and vulnerable centers of communications. If these rail junctions, bridges, and telegraph stations could be neutralized, the Confederate armies would be left blind, immobilized, and without supplies. It was not necessary, McClellan realized, to crush the South's armies in vast Napoleonic land battles. The South's war effort was absolutely dependent upon two rail networks — the lines going east through the Mississippi Valley, and those running north-south along the Atlantic seaboard. To paralyze the Confederacy, all the North had to do was seize the points where the main rail lines joined with connecting lines: Jackson, Corinth, Nashville, Knoxville, Decatur, Selma, Montgomery, Charleston...and Goldsboro, North Carolina. If those junctions were in Federal hands, the Confederate army would be fragmented. To regain control of the junctions, the Confederates would be forced to attack fortified Union positions. The resulting casualties, coupled with the paralysis of internal communications, would be enough to make the rebel leaders see that their struggle was futile.

McClellan could also see from his maps that all of those strategic junctions, except Knoxville, could be reached by water. Another impression McClellan had brought home from the Crimea was an understanding of the importance of sea power as a means of putting armies ashore suddenly and unexpectedly at vulnerable points inside the enemy's borders.

Even before he rose to commander-in-chief, McClellan was hard at work forging the tools to implement this grand strategy. During August 1861, he met frequently with the Blockade Strategy Board. He found sympathetic officers on the board who shared his enthusiasm for combined operations, and won permission to form an "amphibious division." It would be led by his old friend, Major General Ambrose Burnside, and would be comprised of hardy New Englanders, organized for the purpose of capturing the North Carolina towns of Beaufort and New Bern. Possession of Beaufort and New Bern would give Burnside secure bases for a threatening advance against the Wilmington & Weldon Railroad, not only at Goldsboro, but also against the important bridges north of that junction.

When McClellan assumed command of the Federal armies on November 1, he fitted the Burnside expedition into his grand strategy. Combined land-sea attacks on rebel strongholds in South Carolina, Florida, and New Orleans — along with the Burnside thrust into North Carolina — would strike at those communications centers McClellan had selected. Success at those points would distract the rebels, pin down their reserves, force them to disperse in order to meet these peripheral threats, disrupt the flow of supplies to Virginia, and permit McClellan's main blow against Richmond to proceed with every advantage.

Meanwhile, the Confederates were doing some strategic rethinking of their own. Petitions from the coastal towns flooded into Raleigh, demanding more military assistance. But Governor Clark could respond only by reminding the coastal inhabitants that he and his predecessor had already sent to Richmond all of North Carolina's organized regiments, plus all of the modern firearms, powder, and cannon to be found within the state. There was nothing left for coastal defense except regiments that were totally unarmed, or that were so raw and undisciplined that the Confederacy had not yet agreed to accept them.

Two weeks after General Butler seized the Confederate forts on Hatteras Island, Governor Clark sent delegates to Richmond to beg Jefferson Davis to return some of the veteran North Carolina regiments so they could be deployed to protect New Bern,

Wilmington, and Roanoke Island. Davis replied that the enemy was making these coastal demonstrations precisely to lure the Confederacy into dissipating its strength in Virginia, and he was not going to be fooled by the ruse.

Governor Clark and his military advisers were especially worried about Roanoke Island. Its strategic importance was immense. It dominated Croatan Sound, which linked Albemarle and Pamlico Sounds, and it was the choke point for the entire system of waterways that connected the sea with the state's river network. By means of canals, these waterways afforded a direct water link with Norfolk and, thence, Richmond itself. Anyone could see this by looking at a map, just as any fool could see that Roanoke Island was within easy striking distance of the Federal base on Hatteras Island. Yet all of Governor Clark's pleas for arms, trained men, and supplies met first with indifference and eventually with pique. Finally, the governor himself was castigated by Richmond for his "damned meddling."

To the professional soldiers of North Carolina, no less than to the governor, it seemed inexplicable that Richmond should wantonly neglect the defense of such an obviously vital point. This attitude fed the growing suspicion that there was an anti-North Carolina cabal within the Davis administration, comprised of men who disliked and distrusted the state for its Unionist history and its reluctance to secede (North Carolina was the last state to join the Confederacy). There was some truth in those suspicions, but the neglect of the coastal defenses can probably be attributed more to sheer confusion, and a chronic inability to sort out strategic priorities, than it can to sinister political motives. Davis and his aides were already basing too many of their decisions, as they were to do throughout the war, on short-sighted political considerations. The threat to Richmond in the early autumn of 1861 was much less real than they perceived it to be, but Richmond continued to be a blinding priority. Every other front, regardless of its real value to the South, was relegated to the same subordinate category. When Governor Clark wrote to Secretary of War Judah P. Benjamin on September 27, he stated North Carolina's grievances plainly:

Besides the arms sent to Virginia in the hands of our volunteers, we

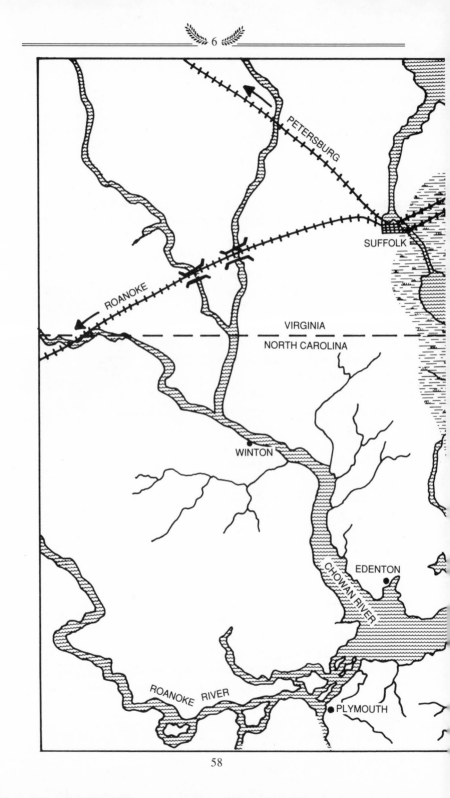

PETERSBURG

SUFFOLK

ROANOKE

VIRGINIA

NORTH CAROLINA

WINTON

EDENTON

CHOWAN RIVER

ROANOKE RIVER

PLYMOUTH

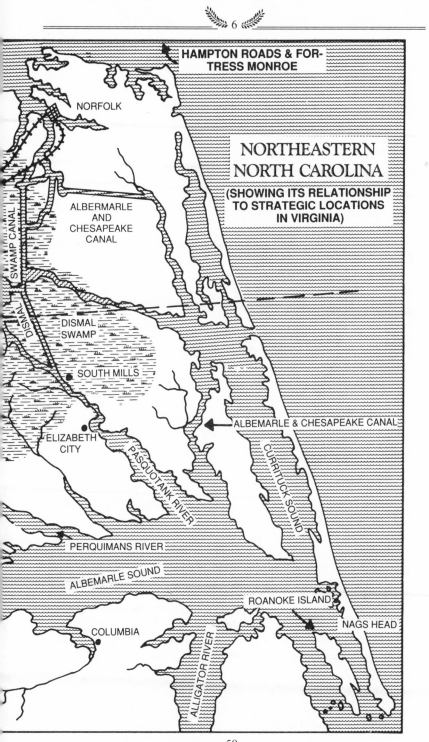

HAMPTON ROADS & FOR-
TRESS MONROE

NORFOLK

NORTHEASTERN
NORTH CAROLINA
(SHOWING ITS RELATIONSHIP
TO STRATEGIC LOCATIONS
IN VIRGINIA)

ALBERMARLE
AND
CHESAPEAKE
CANAL

SWAMP CANAL

DISMAL

DISMAL
SWAMP

SOUTH MILLS

ELIZABETH
CITY

PASQUOTANK RIVER

ALBEMARLE & CHESAPEAKE CANAL

CURRITUCK SOUND

PERQUIMANS RIVER

ALBEMARLE SOUND

ROANOKE ISLAND

COLUMBIA

NAGS HEAD

ALLIGATOR RIVER

have sent to Virginia 13,500 stands of arms, and now we are out of arms, and our soil is invaded, and you refuse our request to send us back some of our own armed regiments to defend us...we have disarmed ourselves to arm you...the recent invasion compels us again to buy a Navy for our protection, not receiving it from the Confederate States. We are denied powder, on the ground that we have received more than any other state, without advertising the fact that the powder has been made into cartridges and sent back to Virginia with every regiment....[1]

Benjamin's reply was a masterpiece of bureaucratic unction and evasion. He admitted, on the one hand, that circumstances had conspired to dilute the efforts made on behalf of the North Carolina coast, but he excused this neglect because "the war has recently assumed such formidable dimensions as to make it impossible that human beings can satisfy all the exigencies or all the people at every point that may be exposed or threatened with attack...." In closing, Benjamin hollowly asked for the governor's "hearty cooperation" in defending his "own coast" -- nowhere acknowledging the importance of that coast for the Confederacy as a whole. In a summary, he equated North Carolina's calls for protection with similar clamorous demands inundating Richmond from such faraway and strategically secondary theaters as Missouri and southern Texas.

Unfortunately, the things needed to defend the coast of North Carolina were among the military items in shortest supply. Governor Clark's little jab about the absence of a Confederate States Navy, for example, went beyond the bounds of realism -- no government can conjure a navy out of thin air in six months' time. The heavy ordnance and the trained specialists required for a navy were among the rarest commodities in the Confederate inventory. Matters were made even more complex by the division between Richmond and Raleigh of financial responsibility for military expenditures. Lines of authority and responsibility were blurred, tangled, and obscure even to the men on the spot. When the North Carolina General Assembly asked Governor Clark to supply certain basic information about what sort of guns, ammunition, and artillery specialists might be available for redeployment to the coast, he was unable to provide accurate figures because his authority to obtain them conflicted with the Davis government's authority to keep them secret. Had the enemy cooperated by not attacking the North Carolina coast until the summer of 1862, there might have been time to straighten out most of these matters. But the enemy had a more immediate timetable. The state's coastal defenses, instead of getting better during the six-month interval between the fall of Hatteras Island and the attack on Roanoke Island, deteriorated even further.

About the only thing Richmond did to counter the threat -- aside from authorizing the transfer, in late summer, of two worn-out cannon and a few barrels of powder -- was to send down some new officers. Brigadier General Richard C. Gatlin was assigned to command the Department of North Carolina; under him, Brigadier General Joseph Anderson was assigned to command the Wilmington-area defenses; and the vigorous General D.H. Hill was given command of the defenses of Albemarle and Pamlico Sounds. Gatlin established his headquarters at Goldsboro, the central point of the coastal region and, as it happened, one of the enemy's prime objectives. Richmond also authorized, on September 29, the purchase or construction of shallow-draft gunboats to contest the inland waters. Unfortunately, there weren't any significant boat-building facilities in the state, nor adequate materials for the limited facilities that did exist. The armed ships on hand when the Yankees struck were, in D.H. Hill's phrase, "farcically unfit for wartime service."[2]

Even without any significant naval resources, Gatlin drew up a sound and thoroughly professional strategy for defending the coast. His plan was to strongly defend the "exposed" points, such as New Bern and Roanoke Island, giving each place sufficient local reserves and artillery to pin down any Federal landings. Meanwhile, in Goldsboro, he would establish a strong theater reserve of four to six regiments which would not be committed until after the Yankees had tipped their hand.[3]

But without the cooperation of the Confederate government, without trained reserves anywhere, and with orders that made it difficult for him to do anything else, Gatlin was forced to adopt a weak and vulnerable strategic posture. This posture was tied to the remaining fortified points in rebel hands, scattered and in some cases badly sited. He also had to do all he could to defend the vulnerable towns along the rivers and sounds. This meant he was forced to try to hold many widely separated locations with small numbers of troops and guns, rather than to concentrate all of his resources at a few important points.

General Anderson's command, ostensibly protecting the whole Cape Fear region, numbered only 4,669 men at this time. And he soon lost one-fourth of his manpower when Richmond ordered him to send two of his regiments to Charleston. The Union missed a golden opportunity by not taking advantage of this, for the important blockade-running port of Wilmington could have been captured easily at this stage of the war.

D.H. Hill, for his part, was appalled at the condition of the defenses in his sector. His first act upon arriving to take command was to begin a tour of inspection. He was amazed to find that it took him 15 days just to inspect every spot that was listed on his maps as a defensive position. And positions that had taken him more than two weeks to reach by horseback and railroad could be reached by the enemy, by water, in a day or two. Shortly after returning from this tour, on October 18, 1861, Hill submitted a report on conditions in his sector:

> Fort Macon has but four guns of long range, and these are badly supplied with ammunition, and are on very inferior carriages.
>
> New Bern has a tolerable battery, two 8-inch Columbiads and two 32-pounders. It is, however, badly supplied with powder. This is also the condition of Washington [N.C.]. Hyde, the richest county in the state, had ten landings and only one gun -- an English 9-pounder of great age and venerable aspect.
>
> Roanoke Island is the key to one-third of North Carolina, and whose occupancy by the enemy would enable him to reach the great railroad from Richmond to New Orleans. Four additional regiments are absolutely indispensable to the protection of this island. The batteries also need four rifled cannon of heavy caliber. I would most earnestly call the attention of the Secretary of War to this island...the towns of Elizabeth City, Edenton, Plymouth, and Williamston will all be taken should Roanoke be captured or passed. The inhabitants of those towns have been most criminally indifferent about efforts to fortify them.[4]

Unable to obtain sufficient cannon and powder to make either Roanoke Island or Fort Macon the formidable bastions they needed to be, Hill did what he could with passive defenses. "The spade had been set a-going wherever I have been," he wrote to General Gatlin. One of his pet projects was a line of truly formidable earthworks across the center of Roanoke Island, crossing the isle from one beach to the other. But Hill was not destined to supervise the completion of these valuable works. Before he had been in command long enough to do much more than take a look around and draw up an outline of what needed to be done, he was recalled for duty in Virginia. This kind of bad timing would be repeated: In 1864, just as he was about to wrest New Bern from the Federals, General Robert Hoke, too, would be ordered back to Virginia.

Hill was replaced by General L. O'B. Branch, whom Governor Clark's military adviser, General Henry King Burgwyn, Sr., regarded as "the youngest and least experienced brigadier in the service." General Burgwyn now began an unsuccessful attempt to gain command of the upper coastal sector himself, not because he wanted the glory but because he had good ideas about how to defend it. His son, the brave young Harry King Burgwyn — then serving a dreary tour of garrison duty with Zebulon Vance's 26th North Carolina regiment out on Bogue Bank — agreed with his father. "Roanoke Island, from what I hear will be taken without difficulty if the enemy attack it," he wrote in December. "I sincerely hope you may succeed [in gaining command] for Branch is not competent."[5]

At this point, General Gatlin suggested to Richmond that, because of its sheer size and irregular shape, the coast should be divided into three commands rather than the existing two. He had made that suggestion before, but Richmond hadn't paid much attention. This time, the reorganization was authorized. The Cape Fear district remained under General Anderson; the Pamlico Sound/New Bern area was still under Branch; and the newly redrawn sector, comprising Albemarle Sound and Roanoke Island, was entrusted to General Henry A. Wise. Unfortunately, Richmond didn't stop there. The Confederate government saw fit in its wisdom to separate that sector administratively from the rest of North Carolina and place it in the Department of Norfolk, then commanded by one of the worst Confederate generals of the war, the bumbling and indolent Benjamin Huger (described by one colleague as "a barnacle on the Confederacy").

Sour-faced and lazy, Huger was not without ability as an engineer, but was completely out of his depth as commander of a vital and vulnerable Confederate stronghold. He was almost maniacally single-minded in his obsession with Norfolk, and he was unshakably convinced that every Federal warship and transport seen loading across the water at Hampton Roads was part of a gigantic assault about to descend on his own headquarters. He had little interest in what was going on in North Carolina, and he had no intention of weakening his resources by so much as a single company. At the time Roanoke Island was most direly threatened -- a time, as well, when the Federals had no intention of attacking Norfolk, and in fact were not even demonstrating against it -- Huger kept control of 15,000 idle troops. One-fifth of that number probably would have been sufficient to hold Roanoke Island.

Huger never seemed to take seriously the possibility that the enemy might come up through North Carolina and attack him from the south. This obsessive concern with threats from the north is surely the only rational explanation for the odd defenses on Roanoke Island. The defenses were on the northern half of the island, with the guns facing Albemarle Sound -- which was still, of course, in Confederate hands. Toward the south, where the enemy already had a foothold, defenses were largely ignored. Not that the Roanoke defenses were that formidable, anyway. They were, in fact, rather pathetic: "[the] forts had no gunners, no rifled cannon, no supplies, no anything except undrilled and unpaid country bumpkins posing as troops."[6]

When General Wise took his first tour of the island, he too was aghast. He found a steamy, swampy, pesthole of a place, manned by troops who were poorly armed, untrained, raggedly clad, and almost hopelessly demoralized. Indeed, the only thing warlike about them were the names they had chosen for their companies: The Hatteras Avengers, the Yankee Killers, and so forth. Henry Wise was a politically appointed general, not a professional military man, but he was not stupid. He ordered more earthworks dug, and pilings driven into the river to impede the Yankee gunboats. But there was nothing he could do about the shortage of guns and trained troops, and it was much too late to do anything about the idiotic way in which the island's forts had been emplaced.

Wise started bombarding Huger with frantic pleas for engineers, gunners, powder, shot, entrenching tools, and trained infantry -- all things which Huger had in relative abundance. Huger responded with patronizing bromides. In reply to one of Wise's more vexatious telegrams, he wired back: "You want...hard work and coolness among the troops you do have, instead of more men." Indeed, Huger actually withdrew Wise's best unit -- the veteran 3rd Georgia -- and sent nothing to replace it. Governor Clark stepped in and dispatched the 31st North Carolina Regiment, but it was a very poor trade.

Near the end of the year, hoping perhaps to get better results from the imperturbable Huger by arguing with him in person, Wise journeyed to Norfolk. Huger listened with obvious impatience while Wise recited his litany of need. Huger waved it all away, expressing his doubts that the defense of the island was really as urgent a matter as Wise claimed it was, and once more assuring Wise that he could make do with what he already had if he but showed a "cool head" and a commanding presence.

Having wasted his breath in Norfolk, Wise decided to go over Huger's head by traveling west and entering the snakepit of Richmond's bureaucracy. He camped out in Secretary of War Benjamin's offices until Benjamin agreed to hear him out. Always cool and phlegmatic himself, Benjamin was instantly offended by this obnoxious young man, who leaned on his desk and passionately harangued him about imminent perils in North Carolina. Benjamin wanted only to get rid of the pest. He finally agreed to "seek consultation" and then get back to Wise with his recommendations.

Benjamin then consulted, of all people, General Huger, who assured him that the Roanoke Island situation was not all that urgent and agreed with Benjamin that Wise was a brash young upstart. All Wise got for his trouble was a snippy little order telling him, in effect, to stop bothering the government and to go back and do the best he could with what he had. The only concession

Richmond finally made was to permit Wise's own unit, "Wise's Legion," to join him on the island. Even then, movement of the unit was so badly botched that none of its cavalry or cannon arrived in time for the Federal attack. All that got through the pipeline were 450 infantry, exactly 10 percent of the number Wise had requested as the minimum needed to defend the island.

Therefore, to defend the most strategically vital island on the entire Atlantic coast of the Confederacy, Wise had a grand total of 1,493 soldiers: the Virginians of his own legion; the 31st North Carolina, commanded by Colonel J.V. Jordan; and the 8th North Carolina, led by Colonel H.M. Shaw. Both North Carolina regiments were greener than spring grass, armed with an attic-sale collection of fowling pieces, shotguns, and small-game rifles. What little artillery was on hand did not inspire confidence, either, for its gun crews were "infantrymen who a week before did not know a ramrod from a lanyard."[7]

These men went into battle -- unless they were completely dull-witted or insensitive to rumor -- with the full knowledge that they were hopelessly outnumbered, and that they were facing well-trained and -equipped soldiers who were supported by the powerful mobile artillery of an armada of naval vessels, and who were led by West Point officers decorated for bravery in the Mexican War. There would be no miraculous victories for these men. But given the odds against them, it was something of a marvel that they fought at all, and vastly to their credit that they would give the Yankees more than a few rough moments.

STORMY WEATHER

Generals Ambrose Burnside and George McClellan were close personal friends. In 1852 Burnside had staked much of his personal wealth on a breech-loading carbine he had invented, manufactured in token quantities, and hoped to sell to the government. When the government decided not to buy the carbine, leaving Burnside in serious financial trouble, it was McClellan, then an officer with the Illinois Central Railroad, who stepped in and offered his old friend a good job with the firm. Burnside did well in the railroad business -- better, indeed, than he would in most of his military assignments -- and rose to become treasurer of the corporation.

In addition to being a well-connected businessman, Burnside was also a West Point graduate (Class of 1847). When the Civil War broke out, he was a natural choice for command. Appointed leader of the 1st Rhode Island Regiment, Burnside got his initial taste of combat at the First Battle of Manassas/Bull Run. He did rather poorly in that battle, but since so many other Federal officers had done as badly or worse, no one paid much attention. He was promoted to brigadier general in August 1861.

One month later, McClellan summoned him to Washington and placed him in charge of raising a 15,000-man "coastal division" for use in one of the planned amphibious operations. Burnside was 37 years old, and a fearsome figure of a man. He had a lofty, bald cranium whose wispy fringe of hair was turned into a bristling statement of virility by the bushy muttonchop whiskers that hung from his cheeks, arched over his clean-shaven chin, and met at the philtrum of his nose -- the famous "burnsides" from which the modern term "sideburns" is derived. His eyes were penetrating and stern, his brows beetling, and in most of his photos he scowled

67

ferociously.

He found it harder than he had anticipated to raise the needed troops, due to the competition. General Ben Butler was gathering men for his expedition, as was General Thomas Sherman, whom McClellan had put in charge of the attack on Fort Pulaski. After setting up his headquarters in New York, Burnside made the rounds of state capitols in New England, asking the various governors for regiments of men comprised of veteran seafarers. He had to settle, mostly, for men who were farmers, merchants, and mechanics, but they performed well when the time came.

Burnside could call upon the Navy for fire support -- ships of the North Atlantic Blockading Squadron, led by the gruff, pipe-smoking, cane-waving Rear Admiral Louis M. Goldsborough -- but he himself would have to arrange the fleet of transports, supply vessels, and in-shore gunboats. During his long and exhaustive inspection of vessels for sale in the New York area, Burnside was taken by more than one waterfront sharpie who sold him a leaky, worn-out civilian craft. He ended up purchasing old ferry boats, passenger steamers, tugs, former slave ships, and even a couple of garbage scows. Admiral Goldsborough's shipfitters did what they could to strengthen these vessels and plug their holes, but on most of the transports the quarters assigned to the infantry were some-what inferior to those enjoyed by the average convict. Crowded into cramped, airless holds, the men slept, or tried to sleep, on lumpy mattresses stuffed with evil-smelling wads of seaweed.

Goldsborough's naval force was comprised of 20 ships, mounting 62 guns. A total of 15 of those guns were the new nine-inch rifles, respected for their range, accuracy, and the bursting power of their shells. Burnside assembled his own flotilla of steam gunboats as well, nine of them ranging in size from 200 to 400 tons and mounting, on the average, three cannon apiece. He also had five rundown canal boats converted into floating batteries. These, of course, had to be towed to North Carolina — and into battle, too, for that matter. They were "armored" with sandbags and bales of hay, and armed with Dahlgren boat howitzers. In all, Burnside's waterborne firepower amounted to a formidable total of 108 pieces.

Annapolis, Maryland, was selected as the rendezvous point for the expedition, ships and men alike. Beginning on October 21,

1861, the assigned regiments trickled in over a period of two months. Here, the mostly raw recruits were drilled in the rudiments of soldiering. The rudiments were all that Burnside had time to hammer into them; there was neither the time nor the equipment to conduct any special amphibious training. Goldsborough's officers worked out a seat-of-the-pants technique for getting the landing boats to the beach, and let it go at that.

Three of Burnside's friends were selected to lead the three brigades that comprised the Coast Division. All three were Regular Army officers and, like Burnside himself, were trained as engineers and ordnance experts. The regiments were organized in the division as follows:

First Brigade (Brigadier General John G. Foster)

10th Connecticut
23rd Massachusetts
24th Massachusetts
25th Massachusetts
27th Massachusetts

Second Brigade (Brigadier General Jesse Reno)

21st Massachusetts
51st Pennsylvania
9th New Jersey
51st New York
6th New Hampshire

Third Brigade (Brigadier General John G. Parke)

53rd New York
89th New York
8th Connecticut
11th Connecticut
4th Rhode Island
5th Rhode Island Battalion

Artillery (Captain James Belger)

Battery F, 1st Rhode Island Light Artillery
1st New York Marine Artillery (attached under Colonel William
A. Howard)

One of these units did not last long in North Carolina. Plagued by acrimonious disputes among its officers, and wracked by one mutiny that ended with several of those officers clapped in irons, the 53rd New York was sent back to Annapolis soon after it reached the coast. Burnside had decided it was more trouble than it was worth. The Army Department agreed and disbanded the regiment completely in March 1862.

Burnside's Coast Division was ready to sail by the start of the new year: 12,000 men and 80 ships. Embarkation orders went out on January 6, 1862. The ships rendezvoused at Fort Monroe, then sailed to Annapolis, where three days were spent loading the troops, guns, horses, and supplies. Burnside himself arrived on January 9 with a touch of Victorian melodrama — he passed through the fleet standing in the pilothouse of a little picket boat, waving at his men and bowing in response to their lusty cheers.

Great care had been taken to insure secrecy, and the ships' captains were sailing under sealed orders. Many of them had guessed, of course, in a general sort of way, what their destination would be. McClellan's specific orders outlining Burnside's objectives were detailed, ambitious, and rather sensitive politically:

— Capture Roanoke Island.
— Seize or block the canal system connecting North Carolina waters with Norfolk.
— Capture New Bern and Beaufort.
— Capture or neutralize Fort Macon.
— Destroy as much of the Wilmington & Weldon Railroad as possible, including the vital bridge near Goldsboro.
— A demonstration against Raleigh was permissible, as was a move against Wilmington, but only if the risks were not too great.

The orders concluded with an admonition that any proclamations issued by Burnside should say "as little as possible about politics or the Negro; merely state that the true issue for which we are fighting is the preservation of the Union."

It was hard to keep this sprawling polyglot fleet together even on the first night of the voyage, the clear, calm, moonlit evening of January 11. There were just too many types of vessels, some steam powered, some still hauling under canvas, and all of them with different sea-keeping characteristics.

For many of those who participated, the voyage to Pamlico Sound was more harrowing than most of the fighting. The skipper of the vessel transporting the 21st Massachusetts was found to be so drunk as to be entirely incapable of handling his ship; General Reno ordered him thrown into the brig and scrounged up a substitute skipper on the spot. The troops' accommodations and provisions were abominable. One member of the 45th Massachusetts described his transport as being "dirty as a stable" and was even less complimentary about what the men were given to drink: "I should think the water casks were a cemetery for dead rats, by the way [it] tastes," he wrote in his diary.[1] On some ships, a cup of rainwater would fetch a dollar, and those who had the foresight or the means to collect what fell from the sky earned a tidy sum.

"Worst of all," remembered another Massachusetts veteran, "was the poor food furnished the men, which was fast becoming almost disgusting: the meat ration consisted entirely of pork, which had been boiled and put in barrels before leaving Annapolis and had now become sour and moldy."[2] Indeed, when Burnside later promulgated orders forbidding the troops to molest the civilians or plunder their livestock, one of the Massachusetts officers recorded this prophetic response: "There is a feeling among the men, which will be apt to show itself when the time comes, that, if they happen on anything really good to eat, they ought to have it, after the vile food furnished them on [the transports]."[3]

There was precious little eating done on the last stage of the voyage. Almost as soon as the armada rounded Cape Henry, Virginia, it ran into the teeth of a Hatteras nor'easter. The storm escalated into a full gale that raked the ships on January 13-15. The towering seas and furious winds made it impossible for the ships to attempt crossing the bar from the open sea into Pamlico Sound. Instead, they were forced to ride out the storm at anchor. Virtually every ship in the fleet suffered some collision damage as it slammed broadside into its neighbors. To the romantically inclined, the storm was "a scene of wildest terror and grandeur." To most of the soldiers, it was an ordeal. The rails were lined, day and night, with whey-faced infantrymen "paying the customary tribute to Neptune." Burnside actually suffered heavier naval losses during the storm than he did during the campaign. Five ships were grounded or simply battered to pieces by the Hatteras seas, including one of the floating batteries and a transport carrying 100 horses.

Admiral Goldsborough's naval contingent joined the Burnside fleet at Hatteras, just in time to sample some of the second gale that battered the expedition on January 22-24. While the ships rode it out, Burnside made heroic efforts to keep up the morale of his men. He made sure he was highly visible, dashing hither and thither aboard his little steamer, herding his ships back into formation, waving jauntily to his seasick and thirst-tortured soldiers, and demonstrating his willingness to endure the situation alongside them. They liked him for it. Despite their misery, the men never failed to cheer Burnside when he appeared. After all, the storms were not his fault.

The weather finally moderated in late January, and the next week or so was spent in the Herculean task of getting the ships over the "swash," as the treacherous channel was called by Outer Bankers. This process proved almost as nightmarish as enduring the gales. Some of the ships Burnside had bought in New York — from salesmen who had assured him that the vessels drew only six feet of water when loaded — turned out to have drafts of eight, nine, and ten feet. The channel was impassable for any ship drawing more than seven and a half feet. Some of the bigger ships simply could not squeeze through, so their cargos and soldiers were unloaded at Hatteras, and the ships were sent back to Annapolis.

Swearing and heaving, drenched by intermittent squalls of icy rain, the troops lightened their ships by jettisoning ballast and unloading supplies and animals onto the beach. Once lightened, the ships were towed by doughty little tugs that strained to pull or push the transports and gunboats into the sound. While the Army did all the straining and swearing, Admiral Goldsborough did little to help. He remained snugly on his flagship, stolidly puffing his pipe and playing endless games of backgammon. He did, however, take note of the trouble that was resulting from the Army and Navy each having command over part of the same combined operation, and he drew the obvious conclusion that in the future the Navy ought to have sole command over everything that floated, and the Army over everything that walked. It was not until late in the war, however, that such a common-sense arrangement became doctrine rather than exception.

While the ships were being manhandled into Pamlico Sound, some of the New England soldiers got a chance to stretch their legs on Hatteras Island. They were not impressed. "Of all the lonely, God-forsaken looking places I ever saw, this Hatteras Island takes the premium," wrote one in his diary.[4] The inhabitants of the Outer Banks were a source of great curiosity to the New Englanders. One soldier in the 24th Massachusetts wrote home: "Queer folks in this region! Several hundred are scattered along the bar, who get their living by fishing, gathering oysters, wrecking and piloting. Most of them were born here, never saw any other locality, and all are happy. There are women here who never wore shoes...."[5]

For the moment, the New Englanders' worst enemy seemed to be sand. It was everywhere and got into everything. "Everyman expects to eat his peck of dirt before he dies," lamented one Massachusetts trooper, "but no one thinks to get it all in one short [week]...."[6] When the company cooks made coffee, they would invariably find from two to three inches of sand at the bottom of the pots. And because of the grit adhering to the baked beans, they could not be chewed, but had to be swallowed whole.

About the only local attractions of any interest, other than the natives themselves, were the two captured rebel forts, but they proved disappointing, too. "Small, water-flooded, and insignificant looking," was how one soldier described them.

By the night of February 4, the entire expedition -- less the five ships that had joined the legion of wrecks along the Outer Banks, and the deep-draft vessels that had been sent home -- was over the swash and safely at anchor in the sound. Preparations immediately began for the attack on Roanoke Island. The New England infantry showed the same naive zest that the early North Carolina regiments had displayed, and the same fragile concept of war as a great adventure. One of the more thoughtful soldiers wrote in his diary:

> One would have supposed, to have heard the boys talk last night, that we were all Napoleons. They talked of booming guns, the rattle of infantry, of splendid bayonet charges, daring and heroism...on the principle, I suppose, that those who know nothing fear nothing.[7]

Later that day, the same soldier recorded his feelings just after his regiment, the 45th Massachusetts, was issued live ammunition for the first time since their training exercises back at Annapolis:

> This loading with ball and cartridge was a new order to me; it implied that our holiday soldiering was over. A peculiar feeling such as I had never before experienced came over me; I felt it to the very taps of my brogans, and thought that I would rather be excused...."[8]

THE BATTLE
OF ROANOKE
ISLAND

Had the Richmond administration been tending to its priorities, the delays and discomforts afflicting the Burnside expedition would have furnished a valuable opportunity to rush reinforcements to Roanoke Island. Nowhere in Virginia at that time was there as grave a threat looming to the Confederate cause than that posed by Burnside's force in Albemarle Sound; few vital points in the South were so vulnerable. The place should have been turned into a Confederate Gibraltar. Instead, newspapers in Richmond blithely exaggerated the damage inflicted on the Burnside expedition by the Hatteras storms, and assured their readers that Burnside was as good as defeated by the hand of a protective God. Except for the too-long-delayed, and incomplete, transfer of Wise's Legion, not a single man or cannon was dispatched to General Wise's front. As had been the case at Forts Hatteras and Clark, the local troops were on their own.

The troops did what they could. On the northwest side of Roanoke Island, three forts had been erected, their sand ramparts faced with turf, mounting a combined total of 25 cannon. From north to south, they were Fort Huger, Fort Blanchard, and Fort Bartow. Only Fort Bartow would be involved in the coming battle - - the others, for reasons so irrational as to border on the whimsical, were sited too far north for their guns to reach any Federal targets.

Wise had reinforced Fort Bartow so that it now mounted nine guns: seven smoothbore 32-pounders and a pair of rifled cannon of similar caliber, all commanded by a Confederate Navy lieutenant with the reassuring name of Benjamin P. Loyall. On the eastern side of Roanoke Island, at the mouth of Shallowbag Bay, a pair of guns had been mounted at Ballast Point to command the channel between the island and the small Outer Banks village of Nags Head. To the west, on the mainland, was Fort Forrest, which supported the works on the island directly opposite Fort Blanchard. Fort Forrest, however, was a "fort" only by courtesy of description. It consisted of two ancient canal barges that had been rammed into the bank, lashed together, and reinforced with walls of sandbags and cotton bales. There was room on the decks for seven more 32-pounders. The channel between the mainland and the western shore of the island had been blocked -- not very effectively, as it turned out -- by a double row of sunken ships, 16 in all, augmented by pilings which were still being driven into the bottom on the day Burnside attacked.

Roanoke Island itself was 12 miles long and about 3 miles wide. It was low, swampy, densely covered with brush, and much frequented by pestilential fogs and clouds of mosquitos. There was but a single road running the length of the island, and whoever commanded that artery controlled the whole place. Therefore, Wise's men had thrown up an earthen rampart about 80 feet long at right angles to the road. Its flanks were secured by earth and timber breastworks, and by large patches of swampy terrain which were thought to be impassable by infantry. In the center of the earth-work, commanding the road, was a redoubt mounting three can-non: an 18-pounder that was a trophy from the Mexican War, a 24-pounder howitzer, and a dinky little 6-pounder that had formerly been used in Edenton to fire salutes on the Fourth of July. Ammu-nition for these weapons, and for the guns in the forts, was severely limited, and virtually all of it was roundshot (for the 32-pounders) or grapeshot (for the infantry-support weapons). Wise had only a few dozen explosive shells in his entire inventory.

Nevertheless, Wise was reasonably confident in his earthworks. Because the terrain was so restricted in front of the three-gun redoubt, Burnside's numerical advantage was largely canceled out. As for the swamps on the flanks, "the engineers who laid off the line, the scouts who tried to penetrate their jungles, and the native islanders who were questioned all united in pronouncing the vine-tangled cypress swamps...as absolutely impenetrable." Indeed, when asked about these bogs, one of the natives merely shrugged and replied, "When one of our cows gets in there, we leave her there, for we know we can't get her out."[1]

To man all of these works, Wise could deploy about 1,400 men. He had three North Carolina regiments — the 2nd, 31st, and 8th — along with two Virginia regiments from Wise's Legion, the 45th and 59th. Their condition was not encouraging, for at least one-fourth of the men were on the sick list on any given day, thanks mainly to the damp malarial climate and monotonous diet. The Virginia units were adequately clothed and armed, but the condition of the North Carolina regiments was pathetic. They were clad in rags, armed with shotguns and small-game rifles, and not a few of them went into battle with nothing more than their personal homemade Bowie knives.

Henry Wise had good intentions and was determined to rouse his sickly force by personal example. Unfortunately — in yet one more instance of the chronic bad luck that plagued every well-intentioned Confederate commander on the coast — Wise was in bed with pneumonia, in a hotel at Nags Head, on the day Burnside made his move. In his absence, command of Roanoke Island rested on the somewhat unsteady shoulders of Colonel H.M. Shaw, nominally commander of the 8th North Carolina. Already suspect for being a transplanted New Englander, Shaw did nothing to endear himself to his men. He largely ignored their discomforts and spent most of his time playing chess in his tent rather than taking an active part in the defensive preparations. In the opinion of one of his subordinate officers, Shaw was "not worth the powder and ball it would take to kill him."[2]

Thus, when Burnside drew near Roanoke Island on the morning of February 5, 1862, he possessed every possible advantage. His armada of 67 vessels, its transports carrying 13,000 well-drilled infantry, made a brave sight as it came up the sound. The ships anchored south of the island at sunset and stayed there all during February 6, when the onset of a soupy winter fog made any military action out of the question.

On the other side of the Confederate forts and block-ships, the Mosquito Fleet made ready to offer what resistance it could. At 4 p.m., the little *Appomattox* sailed down through the cold and gloomy weather to observe what she could of Admiral Goldsborough's fleet. Goldsborough was apprised of the Confederate ship's approach, but he ordered that not a shot be fired at her. Indeed, he wanted the rebels to know what they were up against.

Since the Federals seemed settled in for the night, the Mosquito Fleet's captains did the same. They anchored on their side of the river obstacles, put out picket boats to prevent any nocturnal surprises, and then cooked supper. Commodore Lynch spent the night in as civilized a manner as possible — clad in a dressing gown, he retired to his cabin and read *Ivanhoe*. An hour or so after he finished dining, he received a visitor, his friend Captain William H. Parker.

Both men agreed that their prospects for the morrow were not good. Their little fleet mounted a total of 9 guns, while Goldsborough's 19 warships mounted more than 50, including 100-pounders and 9-inch rifles. Neither officer believed the South would win the coming engagement, nor did any other officer in the squadron entertain such a delusion. After conferring on these unpleasant subjects, both men somehow drifted into a discussion of literature. It turned out they shared a passion for the romances of Sir Walter Scott, and they took turns recalling their favorite incidents from novel after novel. The spell was broken when the ship's bell tolled midnight. Lynch escorted Parker to the deck, saw him tucked into his rowboat, and bid him a fond goodnight by exclaiming, "Ah, if we could only hope for success...but come again when you can!" As Parker rowed back to his own ship, he reflected on "what strangely constituted beings...we are after all. Here were two men looking forward to death in less than 24 hours -- death, too, in defeat, not in victory -- and yet able to lose themselves in works of fiction."[3]

The fog was gone, but otherwise the weather over the sound was vile on the morning of February 7. Cold rain squalls pimpled the water and gusty winds roughened it. But aboard the Federal ships everything proceeded in a businesslike manner. Sawdust was poured on the decks to absorb any slippery blood-puddles that might form, and the infantry companies were mustered on the decks of their transports. Those with the stomach for it fueled themselves with hot coffee and hardtack. (Some officers added a grog ration to this spartan fare.) They mulled over the appropriate but cliched signal hanging wetly from the flag-lines on Goldsborough's ship: "Today the country expects every man to do his duty."

At about 9:30 a.m. the Federal gunboats began threading their way into the channel between the island and the mainland. An hour later, the first shot of the day was fired by the Confederates at Fort Bartow. By mid-day, Goldsborough had deployed his Union ships. Some of his vessels were close to the sunken block-ships, engaging the Mosquito Fleet on the other side; the rest were grouped near Fort Bartow. Only three of the fort's cannon could depress far enough to engage Goldsborough's ships -- the rest had been positioned to deal with that imaginary threat from the north. All of the other rebel forts were too far away to fire effectively, although they periodically lobbed experimental shots, just in case. On two occasions the Mosquito Fleet sallied into the pilings and block-ships, trying to bait Goldsborough into chasing them into range of the batteries at Forts Blanchard, Forrest, and Huger. But Goldsborough didn't need to chase the pesky Mosquitos. They weren't bothering him that much, and he was scoring sufficient hits on them at long range.

The CSS *Forrest*'s engine was struck fairly early in the fight, and her young captain's scalp was laid open by a shell fragment. At about 4 p.m., the CSS *Curlew* was badly hit by a shell from the USS *Southfield*. The shell plunged through the *Curlew*'s main deck and tore out through her bottom, "as though they had been made of paper," said a witness. Her skipper, nicknamed "Tornado" Hunter because of his excitability, was already wild with excitement from the battle. The shock of realizing that his ship was sinking snapped him out of the berserk trance he had been in for the past three hours, and also made him realize that he wasn't wearing any pants. He later confessed to Captain Parker that he had absolutely no idea how this state of affairs came about, "as he had certainly put on a pair in the morning."[4] Within minutes, the *Curlew* began settling in the water, and Hunter steered her west, intending to ground her so that she might be salvaged later. Unfortunately, he put her ashore right under the muzzles of Fort Forrest's guns, effectively taking that position out of the battle.

Lynch's raw gun crews did about as well as could be expected, maybe better. Parker thought their shooting "entirely too rapid and not particularly accurate." Still, they manfully endured a hailstorm of fire from Goldsborough's powerful fleet, trading shot for shot with the superior Federal force until they ran out of ammunition and were compelled to withdraw to the north. At the height of the battle, Parker ordered his engineer to send every spare man topside to work the 32-pounder. Every time a Federal shell burst overhead, the green crew would flop to the deck and had to be ordered up again. All of the new men responded, except for one coal-passer who was obviously gripped by fear. Parker, standing exposed on the upper deck, thought that the man resembled a turtle, turning his head from side to side as though looking for an escape route. Parker drew his Navy Colt, cocked it, aimed at the man's head, and calmly said, "Get up or I will kill you." The man leaped back to the 32-pounder and served bravely for the remainder of the engagement. Later, he shamefacedly apologized to Parker, saying of his first combat experience: "...it's all in gettin' used to it, Cap."[5]

Most of the Federal fleet concentrated its fire on Fort Bartow, which took a seven-hour pounding from approximately 2,600 projectiles. As the 100-pounder and 9-inch rounds slammed into the sod ramparts, columns of sand and marsh grass spouted 40 feet into the air. For virtually all of the Federal soldiers on the transports, this was their first experience of a massed bombardment. The sound of it was just as awesome as the sight: "...the balls from the great smoothbores puffed like locomotives, while the projectiles from the rifled guns whirred like partridges, and occasionally a Whitworth bolt gave a dismal shriek."[6]

Although Fort Bartow looked like it was disintegrating, it really wasn't seriously damaged. Its garrison suffered only one man killed and four wounded, and its gunners managed to keep up a slow but steady return fire throughout the afternoon, earning the grudging admiration of Admiral Goldsborough. Lieutenant Loyall had trained his "country bumpkins" well. Between the fire from Fort Bartow, and the odd lucky shot from the Mosquito Fleet, Goldsborough's ships sustained 27 hits. The USS *Commodore Perry*, commanded by the gallant Lieutenant Charles Flusser, took eight hits, three of them below the waterline. She certainly would have sunk had one or two of those hits been explosive shells, but since all were roundshot, the damage was contained. The *Hunch-back*, too, sustained eight hits, and the *Hetzel* was put out of action when a cannonball holed her below the waterline. Otherwise, the damage to the Federal fleet was superficial and Goldsborough's casualties very light. He lost 6 men killed and 17 wounded — or 3 killed and 11 wounded, depending on which reports you read — and 6 of those were injured when their own gun blew up (something that Civil War cannon were prone to do with alarming frequency). Aboard the Mosquito Fleet, Lynch's casualties amounted to a mere 6 wounded.

While the artillery duel was raging, the Federal transports were laboriously completing their passage through the narrow channel, aiming at a landing beach called Ashby's Harbor about three miles below Fort Bartow. Burnside had sent a reconnaissance patrol toward the beach at noon, consisting of an officer, a half-dozen soldiers, and a Negro boy named Tom Robinson who had lived on the island for years. The detachment sailed right into the muzzles of 200 Confederate rifles and two cannon -- under the lethargic command of Colonel J.V. Jordan -- concealed behind a screen of heavy underbrush. Yet for some inexplicable reason, the Confederates didn't fire a single shot at them.

The actual landings went smoothly. Shallow-draft steamers towed long lines of rowboats and barges, crammed with men and equipment, straight toward the beach. At a predetermined distance, the tow lines were cut and the towing craft veered sharply away; the landing craft coasted forward into the shallow water. It all went off with drill-field precision and was characterized by excellent seamanship.

Astonishingly, although the landing boats were sitting ducks for the 200 Confederate riflemen hidden in the bushes, Burnside lost not a single man to their fire. Colonel Jordan seems to have been quite unnerved by the spectacle of the little bay filling up with thousands of bluecoats. His concealed men were eventually spotted -- according to one account, by the sunlight glinting from their bayonets -- and fired upon by at least two Union gunboats. As the first salvos of grapeshot came crashing into the trees, Jordan pulled out his entire force, without having fired so much as one token

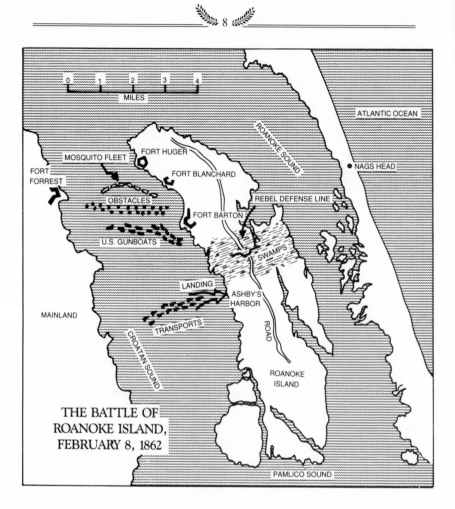

THE BATTLE OF
ROANOKE ISLAND,
FEBRUARY 8, 1862

volley. Had a braver man been in charge, the Yankees would have suffered severe casualties during the landing, and might even have been forced to retire. As it was, Burnside landed 4,000 men and six pieces of artillery as though it were all a training exercise. Most of his infantry didn't even get wet above the knees.

Undisturbed from any direction, Burnside calmly put the rest of his force ashore by midnight. At first light the next day, February 8, he advanced on the Confederate earthworks. Colonel Shaw, meanwhile, was quite properly alarmed at the size and power of the force coming against him. He sent a series of increasingly frantic telegrams to General Huger in Norfolk, imploring for reinforcements. Huger replied with maddening equanimity, "Keep cool...stand by the guns," but he sent no more troops or cannon.

Burnside's plan of attack was simple. It had to be, given the nature of the terrain and the existence of only a single road. General Foster's brigade would move in first, spearheaded by the 25th Massachusetts; General Reno's brigade would follow; and General Parke's brigade would be kept in reserve.

It was slow going. Intermittent rains during the night had turned the dirt road into mud, and Shaw's Confederates had felled trees in front of the roadway redoubt to a distance of 700 yards. Because of the restricted maneuvering room available to his attackers, and the supposedly impassable swamps on his flanks, Shaw evidently thought his inferior force could hold its own. But the restrictive terrain hampered the defenders, too. Shaw could find room to deploy only 400 men at the point of contact and was forced to keep the other 1,050 -- three-fourths of his command -- in reserve, some 250 yards behind the earthworks. As it turned out, they were too far away to be of much use when needed.

The Confederates opened fire on the 25th Massachusetts as soon as its lead companies became visible at the edge of the cleared strip. Burnside's artillery, a naval battery that would serve with great determination throughout the battle, pulled up at the edge of the trees and began firing. On either side of the road, Yankee infantrymen struggled and cursed and flopped about in the bogs, some men sinking to their waists in gummy muck. Because of the ooze and dense tangles of briars that ripped at uniforms and clutched at belts and rifle slings, it was impossible for the Union officers to form coherent battle formations. Within minutes, to make matters even more confused, the entire center of the island was shrouded by dense clouds of powder smoke hanging like curtains in the air. Aimed fire became impossible. One Massachusetts veteran recalled that "we could see nothing to shoot at, but taking our range by the smoke of the enemy's guns we blazed away. We fired high, low and obliquely, thinking if we covered a wide range of ground we might possibly lame somebody...."[7]

One officer from the 25th Massachusetts was observed calmly emptying his revolver into the air at an approximate elevation of 80 degrees. Someone asked him what he was doing. "Why, you see my shots attain their summit directly over the enemy, and if one of those shots in falling should hit a man on top of his head, his goose is cooked just as effectually as though he had been hit with a cannon ball."[8] If the Confederates suffered any losses from this experiment in ballistics, it was not recorded.

The muddy road now assumed the status of a kind of causeway, since it was the only practical way to move through the surrounding swamps. Despite their inferior numbers, Shaw's men kept up a blistering fire on the bluecoats, augmented by grapeshot from the motley trio of cannon. This storm of lead swept the roadway like a broom; to advance upright was to be hit for certain. The 25th Massachusetts was forced to advance at a crawl. They loaded their rifles in a prone position, rose up to fire, and then hit the ground again. It was slow work, and it gave no promise of carrying the rebel line. After two hours of this grinding punishment, the 10th Connecticut was brought up to relieve the Massachusetts regiment.

Sizing up the situation as a stalemate, General Foster ordered the 23rd and 27th Massachusetts to leave the high ground alongside the road and try to force their way through the thickets on the Confederate left. At about the same time as the bedraggled 25th Massachusetts was being withdrawn to the rear, General Reno came to a similar conclusion and ordered his brigade -- the 9th New Jersey, 21st Massachusetts, and 51st New York -- to try the swampy ground on the rebel right. Both flanking movements went forward bravely, through waist-deep muck and tangles of briars that cut like barbed wire. One old veteran of the Seminole Wars later described the terrain as being "worse than the Ever Glades of

Florida."[9]

The attackers were fired up. Some yelled "No Bull Run here!" as they advanced. When a staff officer of the 21st Massachusetts was grazed in the forehead by a Minie ball, he coolly wrapped a bandanna around the wound, grinned at the man nearest him, and called out above the din: "A man never gets hit twice in the same fight, does he, Captain?" Two seconds later he was knocked flat, struck in the neck by another rifle ball.

Advancing with the 51st New York was George Washington Whitman, the brother of poet Walt Whitman. In a letter to his mother, dated February 9, he described the flanking movement this way:

> [We] worked around on their right flank through a thicket that you would think it was impossible for a man to pass through[.] it was mighty trying to a fellows nerves as the balls was flying around pretty thick cutting the twigs off overhead and knocking the bark off trees all around us, but our regiment behaved finely and pressed on as fast as possible[.] we were under fire for about an hour and a half before our regiment dare fire a shot for fear of hitting our friends as we could not see 10 yards on either side. As soon as our regt [regiment] got sight of the Batrey [battery] Gen. Renno [sic] gave the order to charge and away we went[,] water flying over our heads as we splashed through it....[10]

Amazingly, Reno's men succeeded in traversing the "impassable" swamps on the rebel right. They stormed out of the wilderness with bayonets leveled, cleaned out the nearest Confederate breastworks, and then opened a brisk fire on the main line of earthworks from an oblique angle behind the Confederates. A few minutes later, over on the defenders' left flank, the 23rd Massachusetts — scratched and muddy but otherwise unharmed by its passage through the "impenetrable swamps" — opened fire from a position of similar advantage. The Confederate line began to crack.

The grand finale came in the form of a melodramatic charge by the 9th New York, whose glory-hungry commander, Rush Hawkins, was chafing in his position astride the roadway behind the 10th Connecticut. There was even, according to some sources, a marvelously Victorian bit of dialogue between Hawkins and General Foster. Detecting a sudden weakening of fire from the redoubt across the road -- a direct result of the sudden appearance of the two Massachusetts regiments on the Confederate flanks -- Hawkins implored Foster for permission to attack. Foster is supposed to have replied, "You are the very man, and this is the very minute! Zouaves, storm the battery!"

Hawkins' Zouaves needed no encouragement. They poured down the road, literally leaping over the heads of the astonished 10th Connecticut, howling their war-cry: "*Zou-zou-zou!*" Although Hawkins would soon loudly claim that it was this impetuous act which broke the rebel line, in truth his men encountered resistance only from a few stragglers. Most of the Confederate troops were already pulling back, stunned by the sudden and almost simultaneous appearance of hostile regiments on both of their supposedly invulnerable flanks. As a matter of historical fact, the only genuine bayonet charge against organized resistance on Roanoke Island was the brief, jerky assault launched by the 21st Massachusetts when it emerged from the swamp-thickets on the rebel right. When Rush Hawkins later claimed the hero's laurels bestowed on him by the New York press, which lionized him as the hero of the Roanoke Island battle, the Massachusetts veterans took umbrage. Well into the 20th century, bitter arguments raged between the two regiments in the pages of memoirs, regimental histories, and veterans' magazines.

About 30 minutes after the roadway redoubt was outflanked, the wretched Colonel Shaw hoisted a white flag over his tent. Incredibly, the gun crews at the other Confederate forts on Roanoke Island -- three-fourths of whom had yet to fire a single shot at a Federal target -- resentfully began spiking their guns and throwing their gunpowder into the sound. A handful of Shaw's men managed to escape, either by slipping away in small boats or by hiding in the dense underbrush, but that was the only bright spot in an otherwise catastrophic day for the Southern cause. Shaw had fallen victim to his own rather bizarre passivity and to one of the oldest traps a commander can fall into: assuming that your flanks are secured by terrain features that someone else tells you are "impenetrable." In only two days, Burnside had taken the most important military objective between Wilmington and Norfolk, and he had done it at a cost of only 37 men killed and 214 wounded. Shaw's men suffered

23 killed and 58 wounded, along with a staggering 2,500 men taken prisoner.

Understandably, the victors were curious to get their first close look at the enemy. One member of the 25th Massachusetts recorded in his diary:

> February 10: The prisoners are a motley looking set, all clothed (I can hardly say uniformed) in a dirty looking homespun gray cloth. I should think every man's suit was cut from a design of his own. Some wore what was probably meant for a frock coat, others wore jackets or roundabouts; some of the coats were long skirted, some short; some tight fitting, others loose; and no two men were dressed alike. Their head covering was in unison with the rest of their rig...from stovepipe hats to coonskin caps; with everything for blankets, from old bedquilts, cotton bagging, strips of carpet to Buffalo robes."[11]

Once the fighting was over, there was little animosity between the two sides. A certain measure of gloating on the part of Burnside's men, and a very understandable sullenness on the part of Shaw's, was about as deep as the ill-feeling seemed to go. Casual friendships were commonly struck: <quote>

> I came across one young man from Richmond; he was smart appearing and loquacious...he said: "This has turned out not as I wished, but not different from what I expected when we saw the force you had...I accept the situation and am glad it is no worse. I am Secesh [Secessionist] clear through, and after I am exchanged, shall be at you again. [But] when this little dispute is settled, if any of you fellows ever come to Richmond, hunt me up. If alive, you will be welcome for as long as you choose to stay, and when you leave, if you don't say you've had as right smart a time as you ever had, call me a liar and I will call you a gentleman."[12]

The victorious Yankees were surprised by the number of fearsome Bowie knives they found littering the battlefield. They later questioned some of the local ex-slaves about the rebels' preference for carrying that kind of weapon:

> The rebels, as the negroes told us, had cut many a fine caper with their knives before groups of awe-struck darkies, but a single fight had showed them the wisdom of the rule, that a soldier should be made to put his whole reliance upon the regular weapon of his arm of the

service...for while almost every rebel at Roanoke Island carried a bowie knife, we almost never saw them generally carried in any subsequent battle.[13]

The Battle Of Elizabeth City

Before moving against his other objectives on land, General Burnside wanted to mop up by terminating the career of the pesky Mosquito Fleet. Not that Commodore Lynch's little fleet had enough ships and guns to do Burnside any real harm, but there was always the possibility of nautical guerrilla raids, such as the ambush of the *Fanny*.

After shooting off all his ammunition during the battle of February 8, Lynch retired to Elizabeth City, hoping to find supplies there. He found only a small quantity of powder and shot, so he ordered one of his ships, the *Raleigh*, to proceed to Norfolk, via the Dismal Swamp Canal, to fetch more. Lynch then took the two vessels he had been able to resupply -- *Appomattox* and *Seabird* -- and gamely headed back toward Roanoke Island. Not far from the mouth of the Pasquotank River, Lynch learned that the island had fallen. He surmised that Elizabeth City would be one of the Yankees' next objectives, and he returned there to make whatever defensive preparations he could.

There was a fort, of sorts, erected at Cobb's Point near Elizabeth City. Lynch moored one of his gunboats, the *Black Warrior*, across the river from Cobb's Point. Upstream a short distance, he positioned the rest of the Mosquito Fleet in a line: the *Seabird*, *Ellis*, *Appomattox*, *Beaufort*, and the *Fanny*. Urgently, he approached the local militia commander and asked him to call out his troops. Only a few dozen men showed up, badly armed and shaking with fear. It was only on the morning of February 10, after two frantically busy days, that Lynch actually had time to go ashore and inspect the fort at Cobb's Point. What he found there was not encouraging. There were four guns, but they were crewed by only eight frightened militiamen, some of them mere boys.

While Lynch was ashore, Commander Stephen C. Rowan, Goldsborough's tactical commander, was bearing down on the Confederate battle line. His ships came into view at about 8:30 a.m., and firing commenced shortly after 9:00. When Rowan's vessels were just a mile from Lynch's, the Union commander hoisted the signal: "Dash at the enemy!" His ships opened their throttles wide and surged forward, cleaving angry white wakes from their bows.

As if on cue, the militia at Cobb's Point disappeared. Since Lynch regarded the little fort as the key to his defensive scheme, he quickly sent a messenger to Parker aboard the *Beaufort*, requesting him to send gun crews and ammunition. Parker read the message incredulously, then asked the young man who had carried it, "Where the devil are the men who were in that fort?" The lad shrugged and said, "All run away."

Parker left a skeleton crew on his ship and rowed for shore with the requested gunners. He only had enough men to work two of the guns, and only enough time to load them once before the Federal fleet was abreast of his position, gunports belching flame. At that moment, Parker discovered that none of the weapons had been emplaced so they could swivel in an upstream direction. Thus, as soon as the enemy passed by the fort, the guns became useless.

Disgusted, Parker spiked the guns, lowered the flag, and help-lessly watched while the Federal ships tore into the tiny Confeder-ate squadron. The *Black Warrior* was the first casualty, battered so badly that her crew set fire to her and jumped into the river. The *Commodore Perry* rammed the *Seabird*, splitting open the little Confederate ship and sending her to the bottom. The USS *Ceres* closed with the *Ellis* and grappled for boarding. The skipper of the Confederate ship, Captain J.W. Cooke, ordered his crew over the side. Some went, but some stayed with Cooke, and together they met the boarding party bravely, cutlasses in hand. There was a furious hand-to-hand melee that ended only when Cooke was gravely wounded. The *Fanny* took several shell hits; she caught fire, was run aground, and abandoned. The *Beaufort* somehow broke free and escaped to Norfolk. She was followed by the only other Confederate survivor, the *Appomattox*, whose captain soon discovered that the vessel was two inches too wide to pass through the canal. The *Appomattox*, too, ended up being scuttled and burned.

Federal losses in the Battle of Elizabeth City were two men killed and seven wounded. Lynch's Mosquito Fleet lost four men killed, six wounded, and 34 captured.

From that day on, the waters of North Carolina would belong to the Yankees. Their rule would be challenged only once, and that briefly, by the great ironclad ram *Albemarle*. Admiral David Porter gave Commander Rowan high marks for his slashing attack, describing the battle as "just such a scene as naval officers delight in...one of the best conceived and best executed battles of the war."

Having thus disposed of the Mosquito Fleet, Commander Rowan's flotilla proceeded upriver to Elizabeth City, where panicky citizens had set fire to two square blocks of the town. There was no Confederate defense -- what troops there had been in the vicinity had joined the civilians in a desperate exodus.

Two days later, four ships from Rowan's squadron went to Edenton. This town was found undefended and was, in effect, surrendered to them by a Mr. James Norcum, who introduced himself as the town's leading Unionist. Rowan's final action was also unopposed -- the sinking of a big dredge to block the Chesapeake and Albemarle Canal. This concluded a very busy and productive week for the Burnside expedition. In seven days, the amphibious force had captured Roanoke Island, taken two important coastal towns, knocked out all Confederate sea power in North Carolina, and blockaded an important canal -- all at a cost of a relative handful of casualties and some superficial damage to a few ships.

Now, finally, weeks too late, General Huger took some action. He rushed 1,000 men to Suffolk, Virginia, and five companies more to South Mills, to protect the canal. A North Carolina regiment was also taken from the front at Petersburg and entrained for its home state. In North Carolina itself, news of the fall of Roanoke Island triggered a panic which led to a wave of enlistments — seven new companies were mustered in two days. In Raleigh, the panic was reflected in newspaper editorials and letters to the editors. "The Southern Confederacy," wailed one citizen, "is a `gone coon'!" Another reader demanded that the Confederate officials responsible for the neglect of Roanoke Island's defenses "ought to be shot...cashiered...and horse-whipped."[14]

An official inquiry into the disaster exonerated General Wise (whose own son died from wounds received in the battle), and noted that both Secretary of War Benjamin and General Huger had received timely, accurate warnings about the Yankee threat and the dire condition of the island's defenses. Benjamin continued to serve in the government, although his days as Secretary of War were numbered, but Huger was never again entrusted with a significant command.

Perhaps the most telling and prophetic remarks about the debacle were those which appeared in a letter to the *Richmond Examiner*, written in response to a series of fanciful battle accounts that praised the valor and deeds of the two Virginia regiments on the island:

> The Roanoke affair is perfectly incomprehensible. The [Southern] newspapers are filled with extravagant laudations of our valor; the annals of Greece and Rome offer no parallel. Whole regiments were defeated by companies, and we yielded only to death...and what is the loss? Richmond Blues, two killed and five wounded; McCulloch Rangers, one killed and two wounded; the other [Virginia] companies lost in all two killed and eleven wounded. Comment is needless. The whole army had better surrender at once, for it will eventually come to it.
>
> I am sir, etc., "An Officer"[15]

ZOUAVES AMOK -- THE BURNING OF WINTON

Rush C. Hawkins was a self-made man with a thirst for military glory. A native of Pomfret, Vermont, Hawkins had run away from home at age 15, lied about his age, and enlisted in the U.S. Army to fight in Mexico. When the Civil War broke out, he was a successful New York lawyer and had no trouble getting himself elected colonel of a regiment, the 9th New York — more commonly known as "Hawkins's Zouaves" because of the baggy pantaloons, colorful blouses, jaunty garrison caps, and rakish pointed beards affected by its men and their commander.

In February 1862, Hawkins was 30 years old. Although the impetuous charge of his unit at Roanoke Island had been delivered against already-crumbling resistance, Hawkins managed to convince himself that it was a moment of Napoleonic glory. He was still in the throes of self-infatuation when he received orders for his next assignment: an expedition up the Chowan River to the little port town of Winton.

Winton was of interest to General Burnside for two reasons. First, there were two vital Confederate railroad bridges within easy striking distance of any troops landing there. Second, reports had reached Burnside that Winton was packed with 500 Union sympathizers who had taken over the town, raised Old Glory atop the

Hertford County Courthouse, and were waiting with open arms to welcome the Federal army. If Winton really were his for the asking, Burnside would acquire a valuable base deep inside rebel territory. From there, he could do serious harm to the Confederate rail network at little risk to his own troops.

The expedition sailed on February 18, under the leadership of Commander Rowan. There were eight gunboats, carrying approximately 1,000 men of the 9th New York, along with several companies of the 4th Rhode Island.

Winton at this time had a population of about 300. There was little of importance in the town, save for the Hertford County Courthouse, and contemporary accounts ascribe to the place an overall look of genteel dilapidation. The Confederate authorities, however, were as aware as Burnside of the strategic value of the town, and they had rushed troops to Winton as part of their knee-jerk reaction to the fall of Roanoke Island. On the morning Hawkins and Rowan began their expedition, Winton was guarded by 400 Confederate infantry — the 1st Battalion of North Carolina Volunteers, under Lieutenant Colonel William T. Williams — and a four-gun battery of the Virginia Mounted Artillery, under Captain J.N. Nichols.

Williams had no sooner set up his headquarters and fed his men than reports reached him that the Federal squadron had been spotted steaming upriver. He deployed his battalion for a giant ambush, taking skillful advantage of the terrain. The town of Winton was situated behind a waterfront bluff covered with oak trees and dense underbrush. At the foot of the bluff was the town wharf. Williams's plan was to lure the Union boats to the wharf, from where they would be unable to elevate their deck guns high enough to shoot at the bluff. Then the Confederates would pour fire onto them from concealed positions on the summit.

To bait the trap, he hired the services of a mulatto woman named Martha Keen, the wife of a local brick mason. Mrs. Keen agreed to stand on the wharf as the Union ships hove into sight, and signal them that it was safe to land.

While Williams was setting up his clever ambush, Rowan's little fleet was enjoying a leisurely cruise up the Chowan. The men didn't expect any fighting, having taken seriously the reports that

Winton had been overrun by Unionists. The weather was clear and brisk, and the scenery pastoral. A New York correspondent on board Rowan's flagship, the USS *Delaware*, described the trip this way:

> The greater portion of the day was spent in admiring the picturesque scenery which is to be found on the banks of the Chowan. Here and there were deserted houses, and small boats drawn up on the shore by their timid owners, who had left them upon our approach. Solitary contrabands (slaves) at intervals might be seen waving their hats with perfect delight, with the belief, apparently, that 'Massa Bobolition' had come to free them. Not a single white man, however, was to be seen until within twenty miles of Winton, when a party of fifteen horsemen, apparently reconnoitering, was discovered on a hill some distance inland.[1]

At 4 p.m., with mist rising over the river, Rowan's lookouts spotted the dock at Winton. One of the first men to see the objective was Rush Hawkins himself. Hawkins was skeptical about the reported Unionist takeover in Winton, and he had stationed himself up in the crosstrees of the *Delaware*'s mast as a lookout. When Hawkins spotted a dark-skinned woman on the wharf, vigorously waving a piece of cloth and seeming to imply that it was safe for the ships to land, his suspicions grew that they were sailing into a trap.

Nevertheless, not a shot was fired as the *Delaware* approached the dock. The little town up on the bluff seemed peaceful and deserted. Then, when the *Delaware* was only 50 yards from shore, Hawkins' keen eyes spotted sunlight glinting on rifle barrels. Lifting his gaze, he saw the muzzles of two cannon.

"Ring on, sheer off!" he cried to the ship's pilot. "Rebels on shore! Sheer off!" Hawkins repeated his warning at least six times before the stunned pilot comprehended what was happening; the *Delaware* veered away only ten feet from the wharf.

Williams' North Carolinians unleashed a tremendous fusillade from their hiding places. Minie balls whanged and zinged and beat like hailstones on the little gunboat as its paddlewheels desperately churned water. Fortunately for Hawkins, the rebel cannon atop the bluff were unable to depress their barrels low enough to hit the *Delaware* -- their shots splashed into the river several yards beyond their target. Later, more than 125 holes were counted in the *Delaware*'s deck and superstructure. Amazingly, however, the only casualty was Rush Hawkins' dignity. Shots cut through the lines he was holding as he tried to climb down from the mast. "My descent," he later wrote, "...was rapid and not graceful."

Rowan conned his ship into midstream, sailed upriver until he was out of musket range, and then turned the boat so his own Dahlgren and Parrott guns could shell the bluff. The naval guns threw much heavier metal than the little rebel battery could match. Branches, leaves, and chunks of reddish mud erupted from the bluff. Williams's men endured the shelling just long enough to suffer two wounded, and then they scattered.

Clearly, it was time for Rowan to fall back and regroup. After tossing a few more rounds at the bluff, he rejoined the rest of the flotilla and led them downstream for a distance of about seven miles. It was on this retreat that the day's only fatality occurred. As one Rhode Island soldier recalled, "On our way down the river, as we passed an opening in the woods, we espied a rebel picket, standing, leaning on his horse, and watching us very closely. He was somewhat out of range of our rifles, but our mate trained his gun on him...and let fly. The great shell seemed to burst in his face, and when the smoke cleared away, nothing of him or the horse could be seen."[2]

Rowan's ships huddled together in mid-river that night in a kind of "wagon train" formation, expecting anything from sniper attacks to boarding parties. Instead, the night was quiet and passed without incident.

The next morning, Hawkins and his men made ready to take little Winton by storm. Expecting desperate resistance now, Rowan's sailors grimly lashed mattresses and flour bags around the pilot houses of their ships; piles of revolvers and cutlasses were laid on deck where they could be snatched up quickly. Hawkins also made sure every man in his unit was armed with some oakum and kindling wood. Infuriated by the ambush, he was determined that the rebellious citizens of Winton would never forget their visit by the Zouaves.

The reappearance of the Union flotilla caused great alarm in the village. Colonel Williams and his men had spent a very enjoyable night being feted as heroes, and the citizens had settled down for the first peaceful night's sleep they had known since the fall of Roanoke Island. Everyone was eating breakfast when Rowan's supposedly defeated ships reappeared. Williams couldn't try his ambush trick again, and any one of Rowan's eight ships packed more firepower than his little battery of field guns. To stand and fight within range of the Union vessels would be suicidal. He therefore hurriedly withdrew his men to some prepared breastworks near Mt. Tabor Church, on Potecasi Creek.

Even while the civilians were fleeing, the first Union shells began plowing up the waterfront. Rowan aggressively shelled the bluff and the riverside part of town until he was satisfied there would be no return fire. Hawkins himself led the landing party: six companies of the 9th New York, supported by three little boat howitzers.

Charging up the hill and onto the main street, the Zouaves found Winton deserted except for some Negroes and a handful of old people. One of the Negroes turned out to be Martha Keen, the woman who had baited the ambush the day before. Mrs. Keen managed to escape a hanging only by claiming that she was the slave of one of the rebel officers, and that he had threatened to kill her if she didn't perform the ruse. Hawkins believed her and let her go.

The town itself was not so lucky. Barrels of tar and turpentine were rolled into the buildings — including the courthouse, with all of its historical records — and then ignited. Before and during the burning, the Zouaves ran wild. Since the civilians had left so precipitously, there was plenty of loot. In a frenzy of pillage, the Zouaves dragged feather beds into the street and ripped them open with bayonets, shot and stabbed all the pigs and chickens they could find, tore down velvet drapes and dragged them through the mud, and loaded themselves down with whatever took their fancy, from rare books to chamber pots. Pianos were smashed to kindling. Mountains of clothing were carried onto the ships, including stacks of children's clothes. Two hapless felons, still locked inside the courthouse when the flames took hold, were chopped free by some sailors with axes, and immediately fled into the woods.

From scattered surviving letters and diaries, it is clear that not all of the New York soldiers approved of or participated in the vandalism, but most of them shared Hawkins's unbending attitude toward the South. The Confederates started the war, they reasoned, and should be made to pay a harsh penalty for doing so.

When the ships were low in the water with loot, the landing party reboarded, their faces black with soot and their eyes still wild with the excitement of plundering. Behind them, the little village of Winton, and all of Hertford County's historical records, lay in ashes. Even though Colonel Williams's force was equal to the Zouaves, and even though he could have ambushed them handily while the rampage was at its height, he remained in his earthworks at Mt. Tabor Church and did nothing. When the Federals sailed away, he marched his men back toward Virginia. "Courage," wrote one local historian, "was not Williams's strongest quality." Confederate authorities agreed, and found his passivity inexcusable. He resigned from the Confederate Army in disgrace in 1863.

There were other repercussions from these incidents. In New York, a newspaper editor had been collecting contributions in order to have medals struck to commemorate the Zouaves' so-called bayonet charge at Roanoke Island. A few days later, *The New York Times* dashed cold water on the fund-raising campaign by accusing the regiment of "promiscuous plunder and violence." Southern newspapers, of course, trumpeted the sack of Winton as though it had been the work of blood-crazed Visigoths.

Perhaps the worst casualty of the affair was General Burnside's policy of conciliation toward the coastal inhabitants. Just two days before the Zouaves hit Winton, Burnside had issued a general proclamation assuring the local citizens that his men would behave in a "Christian manner" and would commit no violence against them unless fired upon. The actions of the Zouaves, however mitigated by their aggravation, made a mockery of the general's words. After such an act of vandalism, the Southern newspapers protested, how could anyone trust the Yankees' promises again? "Let us listen to no such pretenses," trumpeted the *Raleigh Standard*. "Let every man buckle on his armor and fight to the death."

Burnside glossed over the burning of Winton in his official report. The buildings set afire, he claimed, had demonstrably been used by the Confederates for military purposes, and the other buildings had unfortunately caught fire due to a sudden shift in the wind -- an excuse contradicted by the gunboats' logs, which agreed that the wind that morning was blowing at only two miles per hour. Washington preferred to accept Burnside's version, and there was no official inquiry into the matter.

Hawkins' subsequent military career was colorful. He was undoubtedly brave, but he could at times be recklessly insubordinate. Before the war was over he would be thrown in jail twice for picking fights, verbal and otherwise, with superior officers, including General George McClellan. After the war, he returned to the practice of law, served in the New York legislature, and became a rich man. He died in 1920, at the age of 89, when he was run over by an automobile. He left his entire fortune, nearly $1 million, to the Society for the Prevention of Cruelty to Animals.

Winton was not rebuilt during the war. The part of North Carolina between the Chowan and Roanoke Rivers became a no-man's land. Protected by neither army but periodically scourged by both, it would become the center of activity for the bushwhackers known as "Buffaloes," and by the war's end it was a desolate place.

With Roanoke Island strongly garrisoned, his supply lines to Fort Monroe secure, Albemarle Sound swept clean of the valiant but hopelessly outgunned Mosquito Fleet, and a strip of coastal territory from the Virginia state line down to Hyde County under Federal control, General Burnside felt ready to make his next big move of the campaign: the attack on New Bern.

'YOU MAY RELY ON A HARD FIGHT' - - DISASTER AT NEW BERN

Mobilized in July and August 1861 at Camp Crab Tree near Raleigh, the 26th North Carolina Regiment was preparing, in late April 1862, to go into battle for the first time. In command of the regiment since late August was Colonel Zebulon Baird Vance, destined to become the famous wartime governor of North Carolina. In charge of the regiment's training, however, was his second-in-command, the brilliantly able 20-year-old Lieutenant Colonel Harry King Burgwyn. And Harry Burgwyn had his doubts.

A plantation aristocrat by birth, Harry Burgwyn was an honors graduate of the University of North Carolina and of the Virginia Military Institute. He had also taken some courses at West Point, where one of his instructors was John G. Foster, the man who would succeed Ambrose Burnside as commander of Union forces in North Carolina. Burgwyn's records at these military schools was distinguished. At V.M.I. he had even attracted compliments from a taciturn professor of artillery who would later become known as Stonewall Jackson. Harry's father, Henry Burgwyn, Sr., was serving as one of Governor Clark's military advisers at the time

Harry was elected second-in-command of the 26th North Carolina. Father and son corresponded frequently on matters political and military.

In early September 1861, the regiment had found itself encamped on Bogue Bank, protecting Fort Macon. There, young Harry had his "first brush with the enemy" -- mosquitos. "Oh, how they did trouble me," he wrote in his diary.[1] Insects were not the only problem. An attitude of lethargy seeped into the men stationed on that windswept sandspit. They felt abandoned, and for all practical purposes they were. Ragged, sunburned, subsisting on a monotonous and unhealthy diet, tormented at night by the mosquitos, they did the minimum required of them and as little else as they could get by with. Harry Burgwyn busied himself by drawing up detailed, and quite insightful, plans for defending Bogue Bank, including a system of bombproofs, supply roads, and earthworks that would have enabled the troops to guard 3.5 miles of coast instead of the 2,000 yards or so their lines actually encompassed.

Zebulon Vance was worried about the condition of his troops. In an appeal to Governor Clark dated September 18, he sketched their state of mind:

> I am sorry to say that a portion of my regiment are almost in a state of mutiny on account of the non-reception of their pay -- most of them are suffering for the most ordinary articles of everyday use which they are unable to purchase, whilst many others left behind them destitute and dependent families who are daily appealing to them for aid...this state of things cannot be endured much longer by men who have nearly four months pay due them. If not relieved soon, I fear I shall not be able to maintain discipline.[2]

With the coming of cool weather, the regiment was shifted from the Outer Banks to the mainland, and a winter camp was established between Morehead City and Carolina City. Here, as autumn yielded to winter, the regiment drilled and drilled and drilled. Discipline and training were left in the hands of Harry Burgwyn, who rapidly earned a reputation as a martinet. Vance, knowing himself to be strictly a military amateur, wisely left such professional matters in the hands of his vigorous young lieutenant colonel. The troops, who had originally responded enthusiastically to Harry Burgwyn's appointment, came to hate him for his strict-

ness and severity. It was not until after the Battle of New Bern —
when Burgwyn's insistence on discipline enabled the 26th to acquit
itself well on the field, and to survive intact while other units
disgracefully fell apart — that the men learned to appreciate the
young officer for the professional he was. They were devoted to
him thereafter, until the day they buried him in a gun case under a
walnut tree on the field at Gettysburg.

Relations between Burgwyn and Vance were sometimes uneasy,
and Harry's letters leave little doubt that he was frequently vexed
beyond endurance by Vance's easy-going style as a commander.
When the regiment finally got its marching orders, on January 26,
1862, Vance took six companies and went ahead to New Bern to
locate a campsite. When Burgwyn arrived a few days later, he was
appalled to discover that Vance had chosen a location with very
poor natural drainage. When Burgwyn suggested they relocate to a
healthier spot, Vance dismissed the notion by saying the men
wouldn't want to move because they "have built chimneys to their
tents." Vance himself promptly became sick from the dampness
and general foetor of the location, but stubbornly refused to move
so much as one tent.

About this and many similar differences of opinion, young
Harry fretted constantly in letters to his father, such as the following, dated January 19:

> None of our regiments [at New Bern] are so efficient as they should
> be. My own is the best & if it had a good Colonel would be a most
> capital reg. Col. Vance is however a man without any system or
> regularity whatever and has so little of an engineering mind as to say
> that the Croatan entrenchments are worthless unless the enemy land
> and attack us there. His abilities appear to me to be more overrated
> than those of any other person I know of. As an instance of his
> procrastinating habits: We have been in the service as an organized
> reg. since the 27 of August & until today we have not had a color
> bearer...appointed. Today he appointed him. If I have mentioned the
> matter to him once I have done so 20 times....[3]

A week or so after Burgwyn lodged his first protests to Vance
about the camp, a fierce winter deluge tore up the tents and turned
the place into a mud wallow. Burgwyn was furious: "I have
remonstrated with Vance time & time again & yesterday Col.

Sinclair (whose regiment together with ours is to form the vanguard) told him that if he remained here all his men would be sick...."[4]

Vance's correspondence, by contrast, reveals that he held his punctilious young assistant in high regard and trusted his military expertise totally. Vance was surely playing his favorite role -- the easy-going mountaineer -- as a means of gaining the emotional loyalty of his men while Burgwyn whipped them into shape as soldiers. If Vance felt a real affection for Burgwyn, which seems almost totally absent from Harry's letters, Burgwyn for his part was not entirely immune to Vance's personal charm. Considering the poor raw material both colonels had to work with, their respective virtues probably complemented one another more often than not. As Harry Burgwyn's chief modern biographer expressed it: "Harry's penchant for perfection probably encouraged Vance to play a more relaxed role for the sake of balance. Both were born leaders, and each respected the virtues of the other in their respective fields. They made a good team in spite of their personality differences."[5]

Besides the unsteady condition of the troops, both Burgwyn and Vance instinctively smelled another Richmond-sired fiasco shaping up at New Bern. The town was certain to be General Burnside's next objective, and its loss would be nearly as devastating as the loss of Roanoke Island. Common sense dictated that the defense of New Bern be entrusted to someone with a professional military background, preferably someone who knew a lot about fortifications and artillery. Harry Burgwyn's father, who had made several personal reconnaissances of the coastal defenses, would have been an ideal choice. Instead, Jefferson Davis made another of his political appointments, another Virginian, in fact — General L. O'B. Branch.

Branch was an ardent secessionist from an old and politically powerful Virginia family. His uncle, John Branch, had served as governor. Before being appointed to command the New Bern district, Branch's service to the Confederacy had been limited to a term of service as paymaster general, and a brief, non-combat, stint as colonel of the 33rd North Carolina Regiment. Like Henry Wise, however, Branch was neither a fool nor a sluggard. He did the best he could with what Richmond provided him.

That wasn't much. In several letters from early 1862, Harry Burgwyn pointed out what he and other officers saw as the self-evident idiocy of Richmond's dispositions. Since it was obvious, by mid-February at the latest, that New Bern was Burnside's next target, why wasn't every available man and gun being rushed to the vicinity, instead of remaining strung out in weak pockets all along the coastline? As was the case before the Roanoke Island disaster, a kind of stupor seemed to have settled over the authorities in Richmond.

In his usual precise manner, Harry Burgwyn went out one day and actually measured the entrenchments from the Neuse River, at Fort Thompson, to Bryce's Creek, which marked and protected the Confederate right flank. He stated flatly that the entrenchments could not be adequately defended by less than 6,130 men (drawn up in two ranks, each man one yard apart, and with 1,500 men in tactical reserve). General Branch had about 4,000 men, a fair percentage of whom were poorly armed and/or sick on any given day. New Bern, Burgwyn concluded, was "absolutely defenceless."

Nevertheless, Burgwyn and his comrades were determined that it would be defended. In his final letter before the battle, Harry wrote his mother:

> Intelligence deemed to be very reliable & in fact undoubtedly so has been received to the effect that the enemy are close at hand and preparing to attack us...The news was received by our own men with no cheering[,] no undue exultation[,] no efforts to keep their courage up by noisy demonstrations[,] but every eye brightened[,] every arm grew nervous & the most deadly determination is on all. You may rely on a hard fight....[6]

Extensive fortifications had been sketched out to cover New Bern from the seaward side. The best defensive ground lay about ten miles below the city. Here, a strong series of earthworks, dubbed the "Croatan Works," had been erected. Work had started back when D.H. Hill had toured the region, and had proceeded intermittently ever since. Unfortunately, the lines were too long for Branch to man with the 4,000 troops he had. He therefore elected to concentrate along a shorter, secondary line of defenses about four miles above the Croatan Works.

Branch's left flank was solidly anchored on the Neuse River and on Fort Thompson, a stout little earthwork mounting 13 guns -- though only three of them, alas, were able to bear on the landward approaches. Upriver from Fort Thompson were a half-dozen other protected batteries and forts. Not a single one, however, was designed to protect the city's landward approaches along the main road from Morehead City and the rail line that ran parallel to it. They were poorly located to meet any Federal move more subtle than a head-on frontal attack from the water. One Confederate officer, after touring the defenses, pronounced them "a disgrace to any engineer."

General Branch did all he could to correct the situation. He sent out desperate appeals for laborers; the lukewarm local population sent him a few dozen free Negroes, men desperate for work of any kind, and a grand total of one slave. This meant that Branch had to use hundreds of his own men as labor troops. Nor were the civilians more generous in supplying construction equipment -- Branch's men had to scrape out their entrenchments bare-handed, or with broken and worn-out implements scavenged from local plantations. Every day that passed saw Branch begging Richmond for enough reinforcements to man the Croatan Works, but Richmond sent not a single company. Nor were any additional North Carolina troops freed from their not-very-pressing duties elsewhere and allowed to bolster the New Bern defenses.

Nevertheless, Branch maintained an optimistic front before his subordinates, and they, in turn, were lulled by the still-prevalent notion that one Southerner could lick five Yankees without half trying. The astonishing complacency of Branch's officers was vividly recounted in the memoirs of Colonel Estvan, a European soldier of fortune who had served with distinction in the defense of Sevastopol during the Crimean War, and who had enlisted in the Confederate Army for the adventure of it.

Estvan had ridden down from Raleigh, where he was serving as an adviser, for a firsthand look. He was unimpressed with both the fortifications and the troops who manned them. The officer in charge of Fort Ellis, the next work north of Fort Thompson, had imparted no sense of urgency to his men. As a consequence, the entrenchments were still far from finished only days before Burnside struck. Colonel Estvan wrote:

> The works were carried on here just as if no danger was apprehended. The commander of the place was an easy-going sort of man, smoking his pipe by the fireside and apparently caring as little about [General Branch] as he did about Burnside and his fleet. The man's coolness and unconcern were quite astounding. "If my comrades," said he, "should really attempt to defend the place, I will stand by them; should they run away, I am not far from the bridge. So I may as well smoke my pipe quietly, and not bother myself by anticipating the course of events."[7]

At Fort Thompson, the gunners were having a practice shoot when Estvan arrived. "My astonishment, I must admit, was aroused at the precision the artillerymen displayed in *not* hitting their mark; and I came to the conclusion that if General Burnside had only the slightest notion of how matters stood, he would at once make sail for Newbern, and take the place without risking the loss of a man."[8]

Before returning to Raleigh, Colonel Estvan attended a formal dinner in New Bern that was presided over by General Branch and attended by all the local Confederate commanders. The attitude he observed, in contrast to the military realities he had witnessed that day, was remarkable:

> As long as dinner lasted, which, by the way, was a very good one, all went smoothly. But as soon as the champagne went round every man present was eager to make a speech. Americans, I have observed, are all fond of displaying their oratorical powers on festive occasions. After a speech of some half-hour's duration, General Branch proposed a toast in honor of the Confederacy, which was responded to in a speech scarcely inferior in length, by the Colonel of the 2nd regiment of cavalry, in the course of which he dilated in glowing terms on the matchless gallantry of his troops, their prowess being such as to throw the deed of the Greeks and Romans into the shade; according to him the whole corps was ready to die, if needful, to the last man. I need not add that this speech was received with tumultuous applause. "Gentlemen," concluded the gallant colonel, "let us make Newbern a second Sevastopol, before the walls of which the enemy must perish!" Cheers resounded on all sides. "Yes, Newbern shall be a second Sevastopol!"

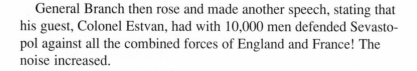

General Branch then rose and made another speech, stating that his guest, Colonel Estvan, had with 10,000 men defended Sevastopol against all the combined forces of England and France! The noise increased.

> Colonel Spreil [Spruill, Branch's cavalry commander] was again on his legs and said that with ten thousand of his own brave fellows, he would have taken Sevastopol in ten days, and not left one stone upon another. I was now called upon to make a speech in reply. "My friends," said I, "how would you go to work if General Branch, with ten thousand of his best men, undertook the defense of Sevastopol, and Colonel Spreil, with ten thousand of his cavalry, attacked it? What would be the result?" They stared in astonishment at these words, and I sat down curious to see how they would solve their own problem. Another subject was then broached, but I soon perceived that I had lost their favor.[9]

The Attack On New Bern

Burnside embarked his invasion force -- approximately 11,000 men -- from Roanoke Island on March 11, 1862. He sailed without Rear Admiral Goldsborough, who had just received orders to return to Hampton Roads and take charge of the crisis that had erupted there when the Confederate ironclad *Virginia* (formerly USS *Merrimac*) steamed out and challenged Federal naval power as it had never been challenged before. The aggressive Commodore Rowan was left in charge of Burnside's flotilla. His job was made easier by the fact that, for once, the weather all around Cape Hatteras was perfectly calm. The fleet steamed majestically across Pamlico Sound beneath a cloudless blue sky.

When Burnside's ships anchored at Slocum Creek just after dark on March 12, his force was 17 miles (overland) from New Bern. The Union fleet had been under observation for hours, of course, and its arrival had been signaled to New Bern via a chain of bonfires. Burnside's final orders before the landing admonished his troops to march light: blankets, haversacks, canteens, and 60 rounds per man were the only impedimenta to be carried ashore.

The New Englanders who landed represented a cross-section of northeastern America in the mid-19th century. Some of their regimental histories list the men according to occupation as well as age and place of birth. In the ranks of the 45th Massachusetts, for example, there were 166 farmers, 124 clerks, 77 seamen, 50 carpenters, and 34 teamsters; the rest, in batches of a dozen or less, were blacksmiths, coopers, glass blowers, masons, rope makers, grocers, plumbers, wheelwrights, watchmakers, sextons, milkmen, and one individual who listed his occupation simply as "gentleman." Their average age was 25.5 years, but in this regiment alone were 50-odd soldiers who were over age 40, and several — drummer boys mostly — who were as young as 15.[10]

Probably the oldest, and surely one of the most interesting, Yankees who fought at New Bern was a gentleman named John Fide who belonged to one of the Massachusetts regiments. A Frenchman by birth, he was a naturalized American citizen, more than 70 years old, who had dyed his hair, eyebrows, and whiskers in order to sneak past the 45-year-old age limit when he enlisted at his home in Plymouth, Massachusetts. Fide had served in the army of Napoleon and had been wounded at Waterloo in 1815. He carried his full share in the New Bern engagement, which he later said had been every bit as hard-fought as any battle in which he had participated a half-century earlier.

March 13 was devoted to landing the men and their artillery (a single battery of boat howitzers; the ship carrying the regular field artillery had run aground). No sooner had this been completed, at about 1 p.m., than the rains began to fall. "It always rains when the 24th marches," was the saying among the men of the 24th Massachusetts, and this day was no exception. The march toward the rebel lines which now began was, in Burnside's own words, "one of the most difficult and disagreeable I witnessed during the entire war."[11]

The roads, wrote one Massachusetts soldier decades later, were so bad that "even after forty-four years [the memory of them] can give me about as good a rhetorical start in the way of profanity as any inspiration at my command."[12] Even the mud seemed different -- more glutinous, more impassable -- than New England mud. "North Carolina soil...in connection with a good vigorous rain, is a combination hard to beat in opposition to the march of large bodies of troops; at its best it seemed as though when one got his foot well stuck in the mud and attempted to get it out it was a question whether the mud or the ankle would give way."[13]

Meanwhile, beginning at daybreak, Commodore Rowan's gunboats provided constant fire support. They started with a blistering bombardment of the landing zone at Slocum's Creek, then advanced with the struggling, cursing troops, keeping slightly ahead of Burnside's columns, blasting any terrain feature that looked as if it might be concealing Confederate troops or guns; none did. After a six-mile hump through soaking rains and deepening muck, Burnside's men reached the strongly fortified Croatan Works, which they were astonished to find deserted. Pressing ahead, Burnside went into bivouac just beyond range of the defenses along the Fort Thompson line. His men spent a miserable night trying to stay warm under a more or less constant pelting by chilly torrential rains.

One camp wit was so moved by the weather that he penned the following quatrain, which enjoyed wide circulation among Burnside's regiments in the weeks to come:

> Now I lay me down to sleep
> In mud that's many fathoms deep;
> If I should die before I wake,
> Just hunt me up with an oyster rake.[14]

They awoke the following morning, March 14, to a soggy fog, the moss in the trees looking "weird and mournful." The New Englanders then discovered that the weather had given them some practical problems. First of all, not surprisingly, the gunpowder in everyone's rifle was damp. Aside from that, there was a more serious, and less easily corrected, problem with the British-made Enfield rifles with which several regiments were equipped. It was found that the stocks of these weapons had swollen in the dampness to such an extent that their ramrods couldn't be withdrawn for reloading. Hundreds of men went into battle that day armed only with their bayonets, unable to fire a single round until they were able to pick up a functioning weapon from a fallen enemy.

Facing the Yankee soldiers, counting eastward from Fort Thompson to the tracks of the Atlantic & North Carolina Railroad, General Branch had the following regiments: the 27th North Carolina, 37th North Carolina, 7th North Carolina, and 35th North

Carolina. On the right flank of the 35th North Carolina was Wood's Brickyard, dominated by an old brick kiln which had been loopholed for rifles. To fully protect the landward approach to New Bern, however, Branch had to cover the additional mile of distance from the railroad tracks out to the Weathersby Road. The land between the tracks and the road was rough and broken, and cut in two by a strip of swampy ground spawned and watered by a tributary of Bullen's Creek. The uneven ground forced Branch to pull back the righthand portion of his line for a distance of 150 yards.

In the center, right where the Confederate battle line intersected the railroad, was the brick kiln. This was more than just a weak spot -- it was a rupture in the continuity of Branch's entire line, a major sin in the book of Napoleonic tactics. Branch should have covered this piece of ground with at least half of his 12 cannon and one of his best regiments. Instead, he assigned it to his poorest unit: a militia battalion under Colonel H.J.B. Clark, green recruits with only two weeks' service, armed mostly with shotguns and hunting rifles. At the last minute, Branch seems to have recognized the danger, for he hurriedly ordered up a two-gun battery of 24-pounders and told them to entrench near the brick kiln. Unfortunately, the guns were just being unlimbered when the enemy struck that very point in the Confederate line.

From the brick kiln to the Weathersby Road stretched Vance's 26th North Carolina Regiment, occupying a line of earthwork rifle pits fronted by an abatis of slashed and sharpened timber. The Weathersby Road itself was the anchor of Branch's right flank, and there, at least, he had the sense to throw up a small earthen redoubt and mount two cannon, supported by a few companies of the poorly armed 2nd North Carolina Cavalry. Because Vance's front was so rough and irregular, he prudently placed one of his officers, Major Carmichael, in command of the companies near the railroad line. Harry Burgwyn was given command of the companies on the right, over to and including the gun battery on the Weathersby Road.

In reserve, about 1,000 yards behind the brick kiln, was the 33rd North Carolina, led by Colonel C.M. Avery. Branch stationed himself between the reserves and the militia company at the

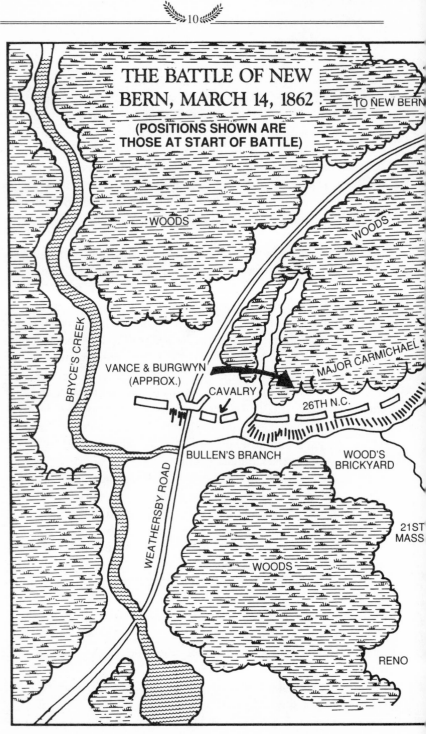

THE BATTLE OF NEW BERN, MARCH 14, 1862

(POSITIONS SHOWN ARE THOSE AT START OF BATTLE)

TO NEW BERN

WOODS

WOODS

BRYCE'S CREEK

VANCE & BURGWYN (APPROX.)

CAVALRY

MAJOR CARMICHAEL

26TH N.C.

BULLEN'S BRANCH

WOOD'S BRICKYARD

WEATHERSBY ROAD

WOODS

21ST MASS

RENO

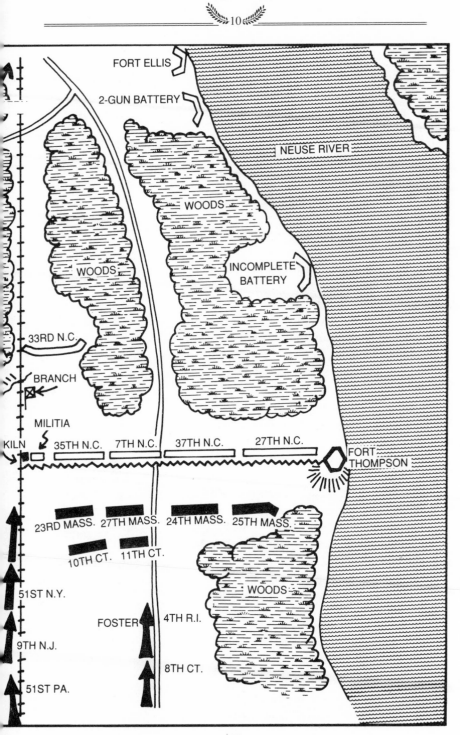

FORT ELLIS

2-GUN BATTERY

NEUSE RIVER

WOODS

INCOMPLETE BATTERY

WOODS

33RD N.C.

BRANCH

MILITIA

KILN   35TH N.C.   7TH N.C.   37TH N.C.   27TH N.C.   FORT THOMPSON

23RD MASS.   27TH MASS.   24TH MASS.   25TH MASS.

10TH CT.   11TH CT.

WOODS

51ST N.Y.

FOSTER   4TH R.I.

9TH N.J.

8TH CT.

51ST PA.

brickyard angle, a position which put him about equidistant from both flanks. His left wing was supported by no less than ten pieces of artillery, not counting the three landward-firing guns at Fort Thompson.

Burnside chose to attack with a reprise of the plan that had proven so successful at Roanoke Island. General Foster's brigade would attack on the right, aiming to hit Branch's line just west of Fort Thompson, using the Beaufort-Morehead City Road as its axis of advance. General Reno's brigade would attack using the railroad as their line of approach. General Parke's men would again be held in reserve, between the other two attacking columns, and would be ordered forward to reinforce whichever brigade seemed to be making the most progress.

Burnside himself was a target of the battle's first shot. He rode forward with some aides, halted at a treeline about 350 yards from the 37th North Carolina's part of the battle line, and strained to see through the mist. They were spotted by Confederate gunners. A Parrott gun roared, and its shell exploded in the trees not far from the general's party, scattering them quite effectively. Firing erupted all along the line within minutes.

Foster's brigade attacked first and ran into galling fire. The three guns mounted at Fort Thompson proved especially deadly, bowling over bluecoats with virtually every discharge. Adding to the carnage were overshots from Commodore Rowan's Union gun-boats firing from the Neuse River. Rowan's gunners were lustily shelling the whole area, without regard to the precise locations of friends or foes. Like Lord Cornwallis at the Battle of Guilford Courthouse in the Revolutionary War, Rowan was willing to sacrifice some friendly casualties in return for the moral effect of his cannonade on the enemy. One of the soldiers pinned down under this crossfire remembered it this way:

> To add to the pandemonium of legitimate battle our gun boats in the river behind us a half mile or more away, but cut off from view by the timber, their commanders thinking to help us, opened fire in our rear with their big guns, the shots from which came tearing through our ranks with a roar such as an ordinary freight train might have made if running at a hundred miles an hour, and their shots were quite as well aimed to reach us and as destructive as those of the enemy...to

my left almost within reach, one of the smaller of their shots carried
away the arm of one of our boys, and within ten feet of me smashed
the intestines of another to jelly, almost severing his body in two.[15]

New Bern may not have been a big engagement as Civil War
battles go, but it was hard-fought. "I myself had a variety of
experiences in battle...but I was never engaged in anything quite so
peppery as the battle of New Berne," recalled one survivor.[16]
Foster's leading regiment, the 27th Massachusetts, suffering heavy
casualties, burned up all its ammunition without getting near the
rebel entrenchments and had to be replaced by the 11th Connecticut. Another of Foster's spearhead units, the 23rd Massachusetts,
eventually cracked under the heavy fire, and many of its men fled
from the field.

Boldly replacing the 23rd was the 10th Connecticut, which dug
in about 200 yards from the Confederate breastworks and fought an
intense rifle duel with the 27th and 37th North Carolina Regiments.
The New Englanders worked their new Enfields -- those that
weren't out of commission from the rain -- like demons, pouring
out about three shots per minute. Some men jammed their ramrods
into the dirt beside their positions to permit faster reloading. It was
a valiant performance, one that earned the admiration of friend and
foe alike, but it was not enough to get Foster's attack rolling again.
The entire Federal right had been pummeled to a standstill.

It was a very different story on General Reno's front. Quite
possibly guided by treachery — in the form of some very detailed
reports on General Branch's dispositions — Reno from the start
focused his attentions on the hapless militia unit covering the brick
kiln. From Reno's vantage point, it must have looked as if the
Confederate right flank just ended in mid-air. This was partly due
to the smoke and confusion on the battlefield, and to the fact that
the breastworks of the 26th North Carolina were 150 yards behind
the rest of the Confederate line.

Just as the Confederates began unlimbering the two 24-pounders
Branch had dispatched to the brickyard, they were spotted by
Reno. Reno accosted Lieutenant Colonel William Clark of the 21st
Massachusetts and ordered him to take the guns. Rallying about
200 of his men within shouting distance, Clark attacked. His men

killed three gunners and two horses; the rest fled.

Clark now found himself in the middle of the brickyard, under fire from two directions, with no friendly troops anywhere near. He had two choices: retreat, or continue attacking. He decided to attack. The next target was the militia battalion. Disregarding the mostly wild fire coming from the 26th North Carolina's line, Reno formed up his men at right angles to the militia's line and smote the raw country boys with a thunderous assault. The two-week soldiers broke and fled the field in terror after Reno's men poured two volleys into them.

This sudden rupture in the Confederate center exposed the flank of the next regiment in line, the 35th North Carolina. Colonel James Sinclair tried desperately to rally his men and keep them in formation, but changing fronts under fire was something only a veteran regiment could do, and the 35th began to drift toward the rear in spite of Sinclair's efforts. Some companies of the 7th North Carolina, sensing that their own right flank was now in the air, did manage to face about and shore up the sagging rebel line.

Reno now hurried up the remaining units of his brigade to reinforce Clark's breakthrough. All of this movement attracted intense, if wildly inaccurate, fire from the breastworks of the 26th North Carolina, forcing Reno to call off his massive attack on the brickyard and redeploy to engage Vance's men.

Meanwhile, General Branch, now fully aware of the mortal danger to his center, hurried forward his reserves, the 33rd North Carolina. Four or five companies of that regiment, under Major Gaston Lewis, made their stand on the hottest part of the field -- between the left flank of the 26th North Carolina and the brick kiln. For a time they succeeded in checking the Yankees' progress. They threw back several determined Federal attacks and twice counterattacked with bayonets to regain lost ground. An eyewitness to Lewis's stand, Lieutenant Colonel (later General) Robert F. Hoke, said later that Lewis "had to fight to his front, right, and left, but still maintained his position...no one could have behaved with more coolness, bravery, and determination."[17]

The Battle of New Bern hung in the balance. Reno's original spearhead -- the four Massachusetts companies under Lieutenant Colonel Clark -- had continued to fight very much alone, and by now were almost totally surrounded by Confederates. Clark finally pulled them out and began searching for reinforcements, certain that the rebel center was ready to fold. The first Union commander he encountered was Colonel Isaac Rodman of the 4th Rhode Island Regiment, the vanguard of Parke's reserve column. Rodman's men were chafing to get into the fight, having done nothing so far except squat under cover behind the lefthand units of Foster's stalled attack.

Sending a runner to inform General Parke what he was doing, but not waiting for a reply, Rodman ordered his men to charge. They advanced in formation until they were 100 yards from the Confederate breastworks, then broke into a wild jog, cheering as they ran. Parke was galvanized by the news of Rodman's stroke, and instantly dispatched two more nearby units to reinforce the attack.

This time the Federal assault had sufficient weight to break the whole rebel line. Hardest hit was the 7th North Carolina, in the midst of reforming after its hard work in clearing Clark's men out of the brickyard. Parke's assault smashed that regiment hard on its right flank and drove it from its entrenchments. Observing this sudden turn of events at the enemy center, General Foster, on the Federal right wing, ordered a renewed general assault that swept irresistibly over every rebel position between the railroad tracks and the Neuse.

To avoid a complete rout, General Branch issued orders for a general Confederate retreat. But the order never got through to Colonel Vance over on the right flank of the 26th North Carolina, near Harry Burgwyn. Nor did it get through to Major Carmichael, the man Vance had left in charge of the regiment's left, near the railroad tracks. Just as the 4th Rhode Island was preparing to charge, Major Carmichael had been struck in the open mouth by a Minie ball that passed through his palate and tore through his neck, killing him instantly. Several men who were near Carmichael later surmised that he had attracted the attention of a Federal sniper because of a small rebel flag he was wearing on his cap. The insignia was a token from his girlfriend in New Bern, and Carmichael had promised to wear it in his first battle.

Now the only part of the rebel line still intact was manned by

Vance's regiment and five companies of the 33rd North Carolina, which had dug in between Carmichael's left flank and the edge of the brickyard. For a time, these men resisted stubbornly, maintaining heavy fire. But the combined weight of Reno's and Clarke's brigades put them under so much pressure that they, too, were forced to withdraw. All things considered, both of the North Carolina regiments performed well; the battle actually had been lost by about 8:45 that morning, but they hung on to their part of the line until noon.

By that time, orders or no orders, it was clear to Vance, Burgwyn, and every other Confederate officer on the spot that the rest of Branch's troops had evaporated. The Federal breakthrough prevented them from retreating along the Beaufort Road or the railway embankment, so the 26th and the attached companies of the 33rd had no choice but to retreat across Bryce's Creek.

By all accounts, there was "great confusion" at the crossing point, as well as some danger. Due to spring rains, Bryce's Creek was deep and swift enough to qualify as a river. The Yankees were fast approaching from the rear, and the extent of the Confederate defeat was gradually sinking in; there was a real chance of panic. Three men drowned in the first rush to get across. Colonel Vance almost became the fourth. With more bravado than good sense, he tried to inspire his men by riding into the stream. His horse had other ideas. The future governor was bucked into the water, and the weight of his accoutrements pulled him under. Fortunately, several men managed to pull him out.

Every survivor agreed it was Harry Burgwyn who rose best to the occasion. Drawing his sword, he moved tirelessly among the milling troops, urging discipline and calm, and making it clear that he wouldn't hesitate to skewer any man who lost his head and endangered the majority. Scouts were sent along the shore, and they succeeded in locating enough boats to take the men over in small groups. It required several hours to complete the crossing, and Harry Burgwyn was the last man over.

The other retreating Confederate regiments did not maintain such discipline. One officer who tried to stop some fleeing soldiers urged them to think of their reputations. The newspapers, he cried, would blaze with tales of their cowardice, disgracing them in the eyes of their families and of posterity. One terrified refugee slowed his pace long enough to retort, "I'd rather fill 20 newspapers than one grave!"[8]

In all, 64 Confederate graves were filled as a result of the day's fighting. Federal fatalities numbered 88. The intensity of the combat is reflected more accurately in the numbers of wounded: 89 Confederate and 370 Federal.

The bullet-pocked brick kiln was turned into a field hospital by the victors, under the supervision of the regimental surgeon of the 21st Massachusetts — a gentleman aptly named "Dr. Cutter". Wrote one Massachusetts soldier, "The saddest sight I saw [at the aid post] was some Rebel officer's splendid gray charger, both of whose forelegs had been carried away at the knee by a cannon ball, standing immobile and silent upon the stumps -- a sickening monument to man's barbarity."[9]

Most of Branch's demoralized force fled across the Trent River bridge into New Bern. After the last of them seemed to be over, the bridge was set afire, effectively halting any Federal pursuit. Commodore Rowan's gunboats, however, were not unduly troubled by the pilings and obstructions that had been laboriously placed across the Neuse River. Most of the Confederate emplacements along the shore were abandoned before the gunboats came within range, but there was some exchange of cannon fire, and three of Rowan's vessels sustained light damage during their passage upriver.

Several Union ships arrived off New Bern in time to lob a few shells at the last of Branch's men as they fled the town. Rowan conned his flagship, the USS *Delaware*, up to the town's main wharf. He ordered his guns secured, since there seemed to be no possibility of further resistance, and climbed out to get a closer view of the town. At the foot of the dock, he was greeted by a single New Bernian, whom he later described as "an old darky lady." Rowan inquired if there were any rebel soldiers still in town.

"Massa," replied the woman, "if you believe me, they is runnin' as hard as they kin!"[20]

AFTERMATH – THE SKIRMISH AT SOUTH MILLS

Burnside's army occupied New Bern late on the afternoon of March 14, 1862. Parts of the city were on fire, possibly from the shells of Commodore Rowan's gunboats, but more likely from the panicky actions of the fleeing Confederates. Except for newly liberated Negroes and some "poor whites," the town was deserted. For two days New Bern was pillaged by the unrestrained Negroes and their liberators, soldiers and sailors alike. Burnside finally had to bring in a strong garrison and post guards to restore order. Some of the looted property was returned, but much of what was brought back consisted of items stolen by the ex-slaves. Burnside's men kept most of what they took for themselves.

A volume of history looted from a home in New Bern by a member of the 24th Massachusetts contained an inscription left by one of the departing civilians: "If this book should into a Yankee's hands fall, remember you did force to flee from home and friends, a peaceful family, and may the memory forever haunt thee." The regiment's official chronicler dryly remarked, "The present possessor of the volume says that no ghosts of the `peaceful family' have troubled him for his part in the dispossession."[1]

Meanwhile, General Branch established new headquarters in Kinston, the next town of any significance upriver, and sent out patrols to help round up the scattered remnants of his defeated army. For the next five days, bands of Confederate stragglers wandered into Kinston, muddy, disheveled, and ravenously hungry. About the only units that kept together and reported for duty in good spirits were Zebulon Vance's 26th North Carolina and its attached companies from the 33rd — and that was mainly because the enterprising future governor had managed to locate a keg of brandy for his boys somewhere along the march. As Vance led his men into town, they were greeted by the regimental band, the "Johnny Rebs" (Moravian brass players from Salem, mostly), who greeted them with a rousing rendition of "Dixie."

When the shock of New Bern's loss began to sink in, the people of North Carolina demanded an accounting. After all, North Carolina's troops had now been in three battles on the state's own soil, and they had lost every one of them without inflicting so much as a day's delay on the enemy. Responsibility devolved upon General Richard Gatlin, whom Richmond had appointed commander-in-chief of the Department of North Carolina. Basically a decent and capable man, Gatlin's chief fault seems to have been a lack of galvanizing energy. He remained, most of the time, at his headquarters in Goldsboro, trying to conduct the war by correspondence instead of setting a personal example to the scattered and shaky defensive garrisons under his command. He had also managed to make some enemies. On the day the battle was fought at New Bern, Gatlin was sick in bed, but that didn't stop his enemies from spreading the rumor that he had been too drunk to stand up. Gatlin, for his part, claimed that the campaign had been lost because Richmond had ignored his pleas for guns, men, and supplies. There was plenty of truth in that accusation, but Gatlin's own lack of energy was surely a contributing factor as well. In the end, he was sacked in response to the statewide clamor that followed the Battle of New Bern.

Less blame was attached to General Branch. A "political general" of the type then commonly found in both armies, Branch had made only one real mistake during the battle: putting a raw militia company, unsupported by artillery, in the most fragile section of his line. But even if he had stationed his best battalion and half of his artillery at the brickyard, the outcome of the battle would almost certainly have been the same. Branch simply had too few men to do the job. Burnside came against him with a three-to-one advantage in bayonets, supported by a powerful naval squadron which sooner or later would have blown Fort Thompson into the river. If Branch had properly fortified the "brickyard angle," he might have held Burnside at bay for ten hours instead of four, making the Yankees pay a higher price in blood, but Burnside still would have taken New Bern.

Immediately following the defeat, the state's newspapers, seeking some aspect of the New Bern debacle that was not wholly disgraceful, began pumping up the reputation of the 26th North Carolina and its commander, Colonel Vance. Reports appeared in print of heroic (and nonexistent) charges launched upon the enemy, and of stubborn defensive actions waged long after the rest of Branch's army was swept away like chaff. This was all nonsense, and it angered the men who had actually been there and knew the truth. Only those companies of the 26th which had been under command of Major Carmichael were hotly engaged. Over on the regiment's right flank, where Vance and Harry Burgwyn were standing, it was a different story. Nothing in the historical record indicates that Vance's behavior at New Bern was other than steadfast and honorable, and mostly cool-headed, except for that reckless plunge into Bryce's Creek. On the other hand, Vance was never actually under fire, except for the odd stray round passing overhead, and it is quite possible that he never saw a Yankee soldier all day -- not one close enough to shoot at, anyway.

The stiffest resistance put up by any North Carolina unit that day was offered by the 33rd, which lost more men than all of Branch's other units combined. The 33rd had plugged the gap at the brickyard and held it against several aggressive attacks, which bought the Confederates time for a less-than-catastrophic retreat. And when increasing Federal pressure finally forced the 33rd to retire, the regiment withdrew in a steady and disciplined manner. Officers and men of the 33rd naturally resented the inflated accounts of heroic deeds supposedly performed by Vance's men, or by Vance himself, for that matter.

When Vance's editorial supporters beat the drums for him during the 1862 gubernatorial election, they revived all of the old

New Bern legends, and this time there was rebuttal in the form of articles and letters in the press. The assistant surgeon of the 33rd North Carolina, Dr. J.F. Shaffner, wrote to a correspondent in Salem: "It is pitiable to see the endeavors of some partisan presses to bolster up the name of Vance, on what was to us a humiliating defeat. If Col. Vance is foolish enough to allow [Editor William] Holden and Co. to run him for Governor for deeds of heroism performed at New Bern, I will freely confess I have been deceived in the man. -- Col. Vance himself was not in the fight...."[2]

On Vance's behalf, however, it needs to be said that there is no evidence from his correspondence that he connived to inflate his reputation at the expense of his comrades. As for Vance's personal courage, that would soon be demonstrated plainly enough at the Battle of Malvern Hill, where he experienced combat in all its horror and gained high marks from his men for leadership.

As the strategic situation came into focus again after the fall of New Bern, things began to look grim indeed. The entire tidewater region of North Carolina, except for Wilmington and its immediate vicinity, was now either in Yankee hands, or open to easy occupation. There seemed to be no good reason why Burnside would not rapidly obtain reinforcements and boldly thrust inland, severing the important Wilmington & Weldon Railroad. He might even drive on to Raleigh, and possibly even knife lengthwise through the Piedmont region of the state. That would allow him to link up with the Unionists in eastern Tennessee, effectively cutting Virginia off from the rest of the Confederacy. For a period of time after New Bern, there was virtually nothing to stop him. Branch's demoralized troops, scarcely 3,000 men in all, were a flimsy shield.

On March 15, the day after the defeat, General Gatlin felt compelled to issue a general order for all naval stores, cotton, and tobacco to be moved west along the railroad lines, far enough inland from any navigable river to protect them from enemy raids.

Fortunately for the Confederates, Burnside was more concerned about consolidating his victories, fortifying his coastal enclaves, bringing in reinforcements, and eliminating Fort Macon -- the one remaining rebel bastion on the Outer Banks -- than he was about striking inland. If Burnside had won his victories cheaply in terms of human blood, he had suffered considerable losses of draft animals and wagons, for a good many of both had not survived the stormy crossing from the sea to Pamlico Sound. He would need large numbers of animals, wagons, and substantial railroad equipment before he could even contemplate an attack on Kinston or Goldsboro, much less Raleigh or Norfolk.

On the Confederate side, there were a few positive effects from the New Bern fiasco. No one was talking anymore about a short and glorious war against a craven and incompetent foe. From now on, North Carolinians had to take the conflict seriously, and from now on Richmond would pay more attention to the defensive needs of the state. Indeed, the Jefferson Davis government reacted to the loss of New Bern with a spurt of energy that was no less welcome for being several months too late. General Gatlin was relieved of command on the same day he ordered the coastal supplies sent inland, and he was replaced by General Theophilus Holmes. General Anderson, at Wilmington, was replaced by the crusty and highly professional Brigadier General Samuel G. French. The crucial job of consolidating the defenses around Goldsboro was assigned to the very able Brigadier General Robert Ransom.

More important than the shuffle of high command was the fact that Richmond poured reinforcements into North Carolina at an unprecedented rate during the first two weeks after the fall of New Bern. By the end of March, more than 20,000 men had arrived, augmenting the 3,000 to 4,000 already on hand. If even half that number had been available four weeks earlier -- and there wasn't a single compelling reason why they couldn't have been -- Burnside would have been outnumbered. He almost certainly would have been crushed at New Bern, if he had dared attack at all.

General Holmes reorganized the state's manpower into four brigades, and started drilling them hard in camps centered around Kinston and Goldsboro. In May, a blockade runner brought in a shipment of new Enfield rifles from Great Britain, enabling Holmes to modernize the armament of several regiments. Sickness, apathy, and growing disillusionment continued to hamper Holmes's activities, however.

Burnside continued to move in his typical methodical way. He did plan to attack Goldsboro, but not until Fort Macon was subdued. To prepare for that he sent a detachment under General Parke to occupy Morehead City and Beaufort, across the channel from Fort Macon. From those points, Parke was able to establish reliable communications with Federal naval units stationed off that part of the coast.

An offensive against Fort Macon would have to wait awhile longer, however, because just as he was about to start closing in on the fortress, Burnside received electrifying intelligence reports that the rebels were planning to sneak some ironclad vessels into Albemarle Sound by way of Currituck Sound and the Dismal Swamp Canal. Burnside knew his wooden-hulled ships were no match for even a small ironclad, so he immediately detailed the reliable General Reno to move up to South Mills, at the Albemarle Sound end of the Dismal Swamp Canal, and blow up the Culpepper Locks there.

Reno's command numbered 3,000 men and included the 51st Pennsylvania, 21st Massachusetts, 6th New Hampshire, 89th New York, and Hawkins's Zouaves (the 9th New York). A four-gun battery provided artillery support. The expedition reached the Pasquotank River after nightfall on April 18, 1862. About four miles below Elizabeth City, at Chantilly, the troops waded ashore through shallow water and established a beachhead by midnight. Two of Reno's regiments were delayed, however, when their transport ran aground. Reno was anxious to get on with his mission, because Burnside had ordered him to blow up the locks quickly and get home before the enemy could concentrate against him. Yet, he was also anxious not to lose track of his missing units, so he decided to wait awhile at the landing site. At about 3 a.m., Reno ordered Hawkins to march ahead to South Mills and to hold the locks until the remaining troops could catch up. Hawkins set off, accompanied by the artillery and two wagons crammed with explosives.

Hawkins' guide was a mulatto man who seemed to know the area well. Well enough, that is, to purposely lead Hawkins down the wrong road. This cost the Federals several hours of time and, more seriously, all hope of surprise. The Zouaves' advance guard soon ran into a rebel cavalry picket, who galloped off through a hail of Minie balls and gave warning of the Yankees' approach. The so-called "guide," meanwhile, scooted into the trees and tried

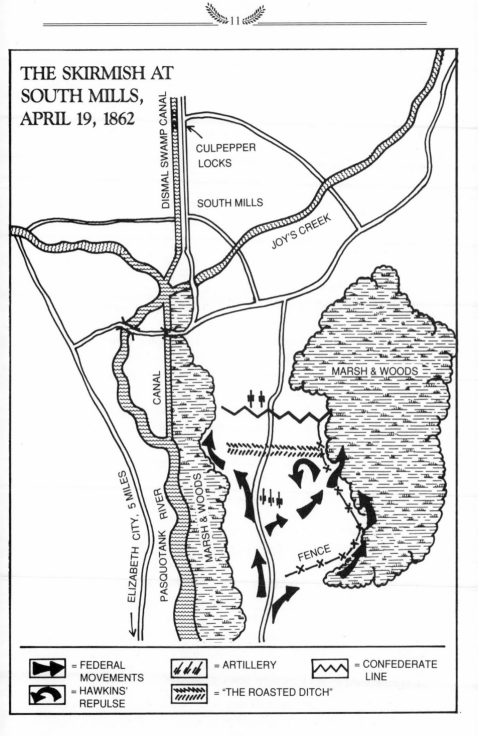

THE SKIRMISH AT
SOUTH MILLS,
APRIL 19, 1862

DISMAL SWAMP CANAL

CULPEPPER
LOCKS

SOUTH MILLS

JOY'S CREEK

MARSH & WOODS

CANAL

ELIZABETH CITY, 5 MILES

PASQUOTANK RIVER

MARSH & WOODS

FENCE

= FEDERAL
MOVEMENTS

= HAWKINS'
REPULSE

= ARTILLERY

= "THE ROASTED DITCH"

= CONFEDERATE
LINE

to escape. He didn't make it — Hawkins ordered him taken into the woods and shot.

Hawkins pressed his men ruthlessly now, marching them as fast as he dared, hoping to reach his objective before the rebels had time to concentrate superior forces in his path. The mulatto had lured them five miles down the wrong track, so the nocturnal detour had added a good ten miles to the already taxing marching distance. The men were dog-tired even before the sun rose -- "a great red ball of flame" which promised an unseasonably scorching day.

Meanwhile, Reno's missing regiments arrived and disembarked. Reno marched them up the main road, from Camden Court House, brushing aside another rebel cavalry picket in the process. He linked up with Hawkins and his hard-breathing men near Lamb's Corner, nearly halfway to South Mills.

All alone at South Mills were Colonel Augustus Wright and the 3rd Georgia Regiment. They had three cannon — one light rifled gun and two brass six-pounders — under the command of Captain W.W. McComas. Wright had quickly figured out what the Yankees were up to. There were two possible approaches to the South Mills locks: one from the west across the Pasquotank River from its southwestern bank, and the other up the opposite shore. Reno's force was taking the latter route. Sending two companies and one gun to cover the less likely route from the west, Wright concentrated the rest of his little force at a point about three miles south of the presumed objective.

He chose his ground with a remarkably keen eye. His men were positioned on the upper edge of a clearing, about a mile long and 600 to 800 yards wide, surrounded by virgin timber. McComas's little battery took up a position at right angles to the Camden Court House Road, and five infantry companies fanned out on either side of the battery, using an irrigation ditch for cover. About 300 yards in front of his line, Wright spotted another ditch which the enemy might be tempted to use as cover during their attack. To discourage them, he ordered his men to tear down hundreds of feet of fence rail from the boundaries of nearby fields, pile them in the ditch, and set them afire. In contemporary accounts of the engagement, this terrain feature was usually referred to as "the Roasted Ditch."

Once the rails were blazing, Wright's men settled down to await the enemy; 400 men to halt the advance of 3,000.

At about 11:30, the first of Reno's skirmishers appeared on the other side of the smoke from the burning ditch. McComas's guns opened up, bouncing roundshot down the road like murderous bowling balls. General Reno saw at once that a frontal attack would gain him nothing but casualties, so he ordered his men into the woods to outflank Wright. While the 21st Massachusetts and 51st Pennsylvania regiments moved off to the right side of the road, Reno's little boat howitzers unlimbered and tried to find the range of the rebel battery. Soon those regiments were joined by the 89th New York and Hawkins' Zouaves. The 6th New Hampshire moved to the left of the road to provide flank protection for the cannon. Getting to the woods was about all the 51st Pennsylvania could do; "totally fagged out" from the march and the unseasonable heat, the Pennsylvanians dropped down under the trees, panting like dogs, and refused to budge another inch.

Sensing the pressure growing on his left flank, Colonel Wright ordered one of his companies to change fronts, moving from the unthreatened right flank to the left. As this unit was crossing the road, a rifle ball struck and killed the gallant Captain McComas, whose artillery had been the heart of the Confederate defense for the past two hours. McComas's men panicked and started to leave the field. Colonel Wright rallied them and managed to get two cannon firing again, but during the time it took him to reestablish discipline, the volume of Confederate fire had slackened dramatically.

Observing this from his vantage point in the woods, Rush Hawkins decided the enemy was fading. It must have seemed like Roanoke Island all over again. Despite the fact that he was under orders to stay in the flanking column, Hawkins thought he could crush the rebel line with a bayonet charge. Turning to his men, "I described what I proposed to do, and asked them if they thought they were equal to the undertaking. Although greatly fatigued they answered: `We will try.'"[3]

While Reno gasped in disbelief, Hawkins led his men out of the woods and into the open, dressed their ranks, and marched them steadily up to the edge of the Roasted Ditch. There, Hawkins waved his sword and ordered a charge. Bellowing their customary war-cry, his men surged forward. Swept by a hurricane of gunfire from Wright's line, they reeled back about 90 seconds later. They had lost nine men killed and 58 wounded, and Hawkins himself took a ball in the arm.

Once the Zouaves had been repulsed, Colonel Wright brought up another company from reserve and put it in line on his still-threatened left flank. Despite mounting pressure, Wright's line continued to hold. But as his companies began running out of ammunition, just before 4 p.m., he gave permission for them to fall back toward some earthworks closer to South Mills.

Reno let them go. His men were played out. It would only be a matter of time before substantial Confederate reinforcements arrived from Norfolk, and his troops were in no condition to fight their way out of a trap. He let them rest a few hours, then marched them back to their ships. He never got close to the Culpepper Locks, and he had suffered 13 killed and 101 wounded. On the Confederate side, Wright suffered a half-dozen killed and 20 wounded.

A number of the most seriously wounded Yankees had to be left behind, under a flag of truce, for the Confederates to tend. One of the wounded men left behind was an old campaigner named John Dunn who had deserted from the British Army and enlisted in the U.S. Army. He had been brought up on charges several times for drunkenness, but he had proved fearless in battle. Now, as he lay mortally wounded among the men being left to the enemy's mercy, his company commander came by to bid him farewell. After shaking the old soldier's hand, the captain took out a canteen full of liquor and asked the attending surgeon if it was all right for the wounded man to have a drink. "Nothing can help him or hurt him," replied the busy doctor. "He can't last until morning." Dunn raised himself slightly on one elbow and croaked: "I've seen worse wounded men get well, but I thank you doctor, for your opinion, as long as it gives me the whiskey." Then he embraced the canteen and lay down with a peaceful expression on his face.

Small as it was, South Mills was a tonic little victory, raising Confederate spirits throughout that corner of the state. Wright had chosen good ground, energized his men, and led them well during a heated five-hour engagement against an attacker that outnumbered them almost nine-to-one.

Of course, no ironclad ever traversed the Dismal Swamp Canal, either, since none was ever designed to navigate such a narrow waterway. General Reno tried to write up the engagement as though it had been some sort of Union victory, but aside from forcing Wright off the field, he had not achieved his objective. And he had suffered galling casualties while inflicting little harm on the enemy. In a private memorandum to General Burnside, Reno blamed the failure on Rush Hawkins, calling him "a rascal" and claiming, with some justification, that Hawkins' grandstanding had wrecked any hope of regaining the initiative.

When the Reno expedition dragged into Elizabeth City later that night, the men felt they had been licked for the first time since coming to North Carolina. It was not a feeling they enjoyed, and many of them resolved not to feel it again.

THE SIEGE OF FORT MACON

Nowhere are the Outer Banks closer to the mainland than at the point where Bogue and Shackleford Banks guard the approaches to Morehead City and Beaufort. The waters of Bogue Sound at that point are only a couple of miles wide. From either port, it's a straight run to the open sea through Beaufort Inlet.

In the spring of 1862, the U.S. Navy had its eye on Beaufort as a satellite base to augment Port Royal. General Burnside had his eye on Morehead City, because it was the terminus of the Atlantic & North Carolina Railroad. Once the seaward approaches were in Federal hands, Burnside would have a first-rate supply line running from the sea to his main base at New Bern. In order to tidy up the situation, though, he would first have to subdue the last Confederate stronghold on the Outer Banks: Fort Macon, whose guns effectively closed Beaufort Inlet to Union traffic.

The need for some sort of military works on this part of the coast had been recognized since colonial times. As one of the first official ports of entry on the continent, Beaufort was a tempting target for raiders and other enemies. In 1747, the Spanish gave the place a good plundering. After several false starts, a permanent defensive structure was finally erected on the tip of Bogue Bank in 1809, a small masonry work known as Fort Hampton. It was manned for about a decade and then slipped into the sea as the fragile shoreline changed.

Following the War of 1812, when America's vulnerability to foreign attack became clear, Washington developed a comprehensive plan for seacoast fortifications. High on the list was a replacement for Fort Hampton. Plans and surveying work for the proposed Fort Macon were carried out between 1822 and 1824. Construction started in 1826 and continued, often in a fairly desultory manner, until 1834, when the fort received its first garrison. Regular garrisons manned the fort only during times of international tension, however. For long intervals, it was staffed only by an ordnance sergeant, with occasional inspection teams of engineers dropping by to make sure the place didn't fall into ruin. By about 1850, though, even the repair crews stopped coming, having apparently been trimmed from the federal budget. The fort was left entirely to its one-man garrisons. For a decade, Fort Macon slowly deteriorated, its woodwork rotting from exposure, its ironwork covered with rust, its masonry cracked and flaking, and its four operational cannon mounted on carriages so rotten that they would have collapsed after a single shot.

Nevertheless, when seen from a distance, it was a handsome and formidable-looking structure (and it remains so today, one of the finest surviving specimens of masonry fort design in the world). Since the late Renaissance, inland fortifications had not relied on masonry construction, because siege guns could readily hammer them down — although several days of bombardment might be required to do so. Seacoast fortifications, on the other hand, continued to be made of brick and stone until well into the 19th century. Masonry provided a simple, economical, and functionally elegant way of constructing a fort, and as long as the fort was not expected to come under fire from the landward side, it served well enough.

This was partly due to the more or less random quality of naval gunnery at the time. To punch through a stout masonry wall with smoothbore roundshot, it was necessary to hit the same spot over and over again until the brick was crushed and dislodged. But broadsides fired from moving wooden ships, their decks pitching and rolling, could be aimed only in a general way. Accurate fire against a small section of a wall was virtually impossible. Ships could neutralize forts only by ganging up on them in sufficient numbers to literally smother the walls with shot. As long as that equation held, masonry walls sufficed.

Then, in the mid-19th century, the introduction of rifled shipboard artillery changed the equation. Rifling -- the spiral grooving of a gun's bore to impart a stabilizing spin to its projectiles -- had long been used to increase the range and accuracy of small arms. It was not until about a decade before the Civil War, however, that the technology existed to apply this principle to heavy artillery.

Rifling made it possible to replace round cannonballs with pointed, elongated projectiles -- what we normally think of today as a "shell." This type of projectile has much greater mass than a spherical cannonball and encounters much less air resistance in flight, resulting in greatly increased range, accuracy, and force of impact. A fort that smoothbores could demolish only after a prolonged bombardment could now be knocked out rather quickly, and with much greater violence.

After the devastating effect of rifled shells against masonry had been demonstrated in a number of battles, field commanders began to rely instead on walls made of earth and sand, often backed with stout wooden timbers or, when available, sheet iron. Such defensive works tend to absorb, rather than transmit, the energy of rifled projectiles. But Fort Macon would have to endure its ordeal with defensive engineering that was a generation out of date.

Since September 1861, the fort had been under the command of a 27-year-old Vicksburg native, Colonel Moses J. White. A West Pointer (Class of 1858), White had considerable experience as an ordnance specialist, but little as a commander. Tall, beardless, and dark-complexioned, White wore his hair unfashionably short and was a strict disciplinarian, an inflexible by-the-book man. He was also an epileptic, given to seizures so severe and frequent that he was often rendered unfit for long periods of time. When Fort Macon came under siege, Colonel White commanded a garrison of 22 officers and 419 men.

Only during the period when Colonel Vance and the 26th North Carolina were stationed on Bogue Bank did Fort Macon have any adequate landward protection. The fort could adequately defend itself only against attacks from the sea. Without sufficient infantry to repulse a Federal assault along Bogue Bank, only one thing could protect the fort from being battered to pieces by land-based siege batteries: mortars. These high-angle cannon could shoot over sandhills and revetments to hammer the enemy gun crews sheltered behind them. But in spite of the obvious need, Wright had not received a single mortar from Richmond.

What he had instead were 7 Columbiads (2 10-inch and 5 8-inch), 19 24-pounders, 24 32-pounders, and half a dozen field guns. The field guns were of use only if the enemy tried to take the fort by storm -- something Burnside was not foolish enough to attempt. What Wright did not have, besides mortars, was sufficient ammunition to feed these weapons during a long period of intense combat. His magazine contained 35,000 pounds of gunpowder, sufficient for only three days of sustained firing. And much of that was substandard, of the same grade that had caused such vexation at Fort Hatteras. Although a few of the 32-pounders had been rifled since the war began, Wright's best pieces were the huge Columbiads -- 15,000-pound weapons with an effective range of more than 5,500 yards. Predictably, ammunition for the Columbiads was in shorter supply than for any of his other weapons.

When word of the fall of New Bern reached Colonel White, he understood that his turn would come next. He put his men to work filling hundreds of sandbags and piling them around the guns on the upper parapet of the fort. Gun drills were constant. On March 18, he also sent a detachment of men to the mainland to burn down the railroad bridge across the Newport River, an action which caused Burnside considerable bother in the days to come.

Burnside, too, was making preparations. He could afford to be methodical, because Fort Macon was isolated and contained the only significant Confederate force still operating on the entire coast between Wilmington and Norfolk. He selected his friend and trusted subordinate General John G. Parke for the assignment. Parke, in turn, picked two of his regiments, the 4th Rhode Island and the 8th Connecticut. Should it prove necessary to subdue the fort by siege, Parke put together a powerful artillery contingent, led by his brigade ordnance officer, Lieutenant Daniel W. Flagler. This battery consisted of a quartet of 10-inch siege mortars and a trio of 30-pounder Parrott guns. Parke hoped it wouldn't come to a siege; perhaps the hopelessness of the situation would compel Wright to surrender, or at least abandon the fort in an attempt to reach the mainland.

Parke set up headquarters in Carolina City, then a tiny village of about 100 inhabitants. On March 23 he dispatched a message to Colonel White:

Sir: In order to save the unnecessary effusion of blood I have the honor to demand the evacuation of the fort and the surrender of the forces under your command.

Having an intimate knowledge of the entire work and an overwhelming force at our command with the means for reducing the work, its fall is inevitable.

On condition that no damage be done to the fortification or armament your command will be released as prisoners of war on parole.

Very respectfully yours, &c.

Jno. G. Parke[1]

Colonel White responded: "Your request is received and I have the honor to decline...." When this reply was read to the garrison, they cheered.

A siege was now certain, and the Confederates seemed ready for it. As they went about their duties, some could be heard singing, to the approximate tune of "Dixie":

If Lincoln wants to save his bacon
He'd better stay away from ol' Fort Macon.

For the next week, Parke tightened the noose and consolidated his supply lines. He set men to work repairing the burned railroad bridge and sent troops to occupy Morehead City and Beaufort, from where the fort's garrison was still receiving supplies. Other detachments began hammering together rafts and flat-bottomed boats for the crossing to Bogue Bank.

A landing site had already been selected: Hoop Pole Creek, about four miles west of the fort, directly across the sound from Carolina City. On March 28, Parke established contact with the offshore blockade ships by means of small boats his men lugged across Shackleford Bank. And on March 29, when Parke learned that the damaged railroad bridge had been repaired, giving him secure communications with New Bern, he was ready to go. The first company went ashore on Bogue Bank, without resistance, that same night.

Colonel White and another officer named Pool were on the walls of Fort Macon when the first Federal campfires sprang up in the darkness, four miles distant. White pointed to the cluster of lights and said, "Do you see that, Captain? What is it and what does it mean?"

Pool sighed and said, "I see it, Colonel. It is the Federal anaconda of which we have read. Its folds encircle Fort Macon, and they must be broken or they will crush it. It means goodbye to outside friends and all news from this time to the end of the siege."[2]

While White was waiting for the shooting to begin, his new-found popularity with the men was all but undone by a casual decision that backfired, and by his stiff-necked refusal to rescind it. Among the commodities in short supply in the fort was flour. White had been permitting each company to draw a flour ration and use it as they chose. When he learned that one of the troopers had been a baker in civilian life, he promptly ordered that the fort's dilapidated Dutch oven be scoured out and the flour rations for all companies converted into loaves of bread -- a move which would stretch the flour supply considerably.

Unfortunately, either due to the age of the oven or the baker's incompetence, the first batch of loaves came out black, shriveled, and hard as bricks. There was at first much laughter, along with numerous proposals to add the loaves to the fort's supply of ammunition. When the second batch turned out even worse than the first, the hungry troops stopped laughing. The next day's food requisition chits from each company were accompanied by a letter respectfully urging Colonel White to go back to the old system. White refused. An order was an order, and it must be obeyed.

It was a measure of the tension everyone was under, expecting the first Federal shells to crash any hour, that the incident got out of hand. When the troops learned of White's refusal, they threatened to storm the commissary and seize the flour supply for themselves. The company commanders, having listened to nonstop griping for the past 24 hours, backed them up. White threatened to post armed guards over the food supply. The officers pointed out that there wasn't a soldier in the fort who would perform such guard duty. Backed into a corner, White snarlingly signed an order rescinding the "baked bread" directive, then retired to his quarters to sulk.

He didn't have much time to brood over the incident. On April 8 came the first skirmish between the Union landing force and picket detachments from the fort. As a result of this bloodless exchange of fire, White's men were driven back some distance from Parke's beachhead. While infantry kept the fort's patrols at bay, Lieutenant Flagler supervised the landing of his artillery. Getting the guns ashore proved to be no easy task. The Parrott guns weighed two tons without their carriages, and even the smallest weapons -- a newly arrived battery of 8-inch mortars that Burnside had sent down from New Bern just after the railroad bridge was reopened -- weighed 930 pounds each.

On the morning of April 11, General Parke, along with Flagler and several engineers, escorted by more than a battalion of infantry, made a reconnaissance toward the fort, looking for likely battery positions. White's picket force was a company of the 10th North Carolina, led by the same Captain Pool who had observed the enemy campfires spring up on the night of March 29. The Confederates withdrew in the face of overwhelming odds, but did turn several times and fire volleys at the Federal column, without hitting anyone. Undisturbed by some inaccurate shells from the fort, Parke and his aides surveyed the ground and quickly settled on three promising locations. The nearest site was a mere 1,300 yards from the walls.

Proceeding to develop the siege in a textbook manner, Parke next ordered infantry lines set up in front of the selected battery positions in order to protect them from Confederate counterattacks. This task was assigned to the 8th Connecticut. Again, Captain Pool's rebels disputed the terrain, and there was a hot exchange of musketry. The Confederates suffered one man wounded and hit two of the Connecticut soldiers in return. Pool's men showed a lot more spunk than marksmanship in this fight, standing up and taunting: "Come on, you damned Yankees! We're enough for you!"

But taunts and a ragged fusillade of musketry were not enough to stop the "damned Yankees" from accomplishing their purpose. By the end of April 12, the Connecticut soldiers had thrown up some breastworks only 2,000 feet from the fort and had manned them with five companies -- as many men as White had in his entire garrison. Work could now proceed on the batteries without fear of interruption on the ground. The siege had formally begun.

Sand dunes were excavated to build gun positions. The fronts of the dunes, facing the fort, were left intact, but the rear portions were dug out, floored with planks, and shored up with wired-together sandbags. This arrangement would protect the siege mortars from anything except plunging fire -- that is, shells fired from other mortars, of which White had none. The rifled Parrotts weren't high-angle guns like the mortars, so the Federals had to design a different kind of position for them. A thick hillock of sand was chosen, and firing embrasures were dug out along the top. The top and fort-facing surfaces were then revetted with squares of sod cut from nearby marshes.

It took a week and a half for the Federals to finish and stock the batteries. Closest to the fort, a mere 1,280 yards away, were the 8-inch mortars; 200 yards behind them were the Parrott guns; and 200 yards behind those were the big 10-inch mortars, commanded by Lieutenant Flagler. All three positions were connected with zig-zag trenches.

Observing all this activity from the fort, Colonel White had no doubt about what was going on. Unfortunately, there was little he could do about it. He ordered a few shots fired daily, partly for the nuisance value and partly to maintain his garrison's morale, but the only way he could damage Flagler's guns was to time the fuses on his shells so they would burst directly over the heads of the gun crews behind the sand dunes. Such precision was all but impossible to achieve with the crude fuses available at the time. The only alternative was to saturate a Union position with massed shellfire, on the theory that some percentage of the rounds would detonate where the gunners wanted them to. But White's ammunition supply was too limited for that kind of bombardment, so the Federals went about their preparations without serious interruption.

White did what he could to improvise. He dragged some older-model 32-pounders to a suitable location inside the lower walls and cobbled together some mounts that elevated their barrels to an angle of about 40 degrees. In effect, this crudely turned them into the mortars he needed. By experimenting with different powder loads, it proved possible to lob high-angle rounds into the general area of the Federal gun pits, although precise aiming was impossible. Again, the lack of ammunition limited White to firing 30 or 40 rounds a day, and the enemy crews were not seriously bothered by this random sprinkle of shells.

While Flagler's men were digging and White's gunners were improvising, General Parke put the finishing touches on a secure and reasonably efficient supply line that now ran all the way from New Bern to Bogue Bank. He also stationed Signal Corps officers along the coast, where they could use telescopes to observe and help him correct the fall of shot from his batteries. These observers could also report any surprise activity on the part of the besieged Confederate garrison.

One such surprise was a brave but futile sortie on the night of April 20, launched by Colonel White only hours after General Burnside had steamed away from Bogue Bank following a tour of inspection. Two companies from the fort attacked the Federal picket line under cover of darkness, but they were quickly driven back when Federal reinforcements converged on the spot. There was much flashing and banging in the darkness, but little damage done. White's men suffered no casualties; one of Parke's men was wounded in the leg, and an officer with a Rhode Island company managed to shoot himself in the arm with his own pistol.

There were additional casualties the next day, when Parke pushed his luck and tried to advance some of his rifle pits too close to the fort. The garrison had been praying he would try it, and the rebels met the advance with a burst of grapeshot that severely wounded two men. No more attempts were made to get closer to the walls.

A few days later, on April 24, Burnside himself tried, in a face-to-face meeting, to convince White to surrender. This time White had to think about it before once again refusing. His position was clearly hopeless, but he still had the power to resist, and he still concluded that resistance was the only honorable course open to him. Later that afternoon, word reached Burnside that Lieutenant Flagler's preparations were complete; the bombardment would open the next morning, April 25.

Dawn revealed a clear, mild day. Colonel White began the day as usual, with a roll call at 5:30 a.m. The numbers were not good. Out of the 450 men inside the walls, only 263 were fit for duty.

The rest were sick with fever, measles, diarrhea -- the usual list of field miseries that often decimated both armies. White had just finished toting up the roll call statistics when all hell broke loose.

One of the Union Parrott guns fired the first shot: a 30-pound, cast iron, shell-shaped bolt that blew a geyser of brick-dust from the upper parapet. After that, all of the Federal guns joined in, one by one. Within minutes, the fort suffered its first casualty. A 10-inch mortar shell dropped inside and rolled sputtering to the feet of a private named Combs, who stared at it in horror, unable to move. He only had time to turn around before it went off. A huge iron fragment struck him in the back, shattering his ribs and driving the jagged bones into his lungs. He screamed for three hours before dying.

At least now Fort Macon's gunners didn't have to ration their fire. With all of the 27 guns they could bring to bear, they replied thunderously. Great coils of flame and smoke spurted from the walls. The mainland shore was thronged with observers, both military and civilian, and what they saw was awesome. Even at a distance of three miles, the ground trembled as Union mortar shells traced sparkling arcs across the blue sky, then burst above the fort in dirty-snow puffballs. Roundshot from the fort struck the dunes, throwing big rooster-tails of sand into the air, then bounced along from hummock to hummock until all velocity was expended. By 7 a.m., the ramparts of the fort were obscured by billows of smoke. At odd moments the breeze would pick up, part the clouds, and reveal the Confederate "Stars and Bars" flag still rippling from the bastion's flagstaff -- a sight that always engendered cheers from the sympathetic civilians on shore.

Shortly after 8 a.m., four gunboats of the Union blockade fleet formed a battle line and added their broadsides to the weight of metal raining down on the fort. The sea was rough that morning, green water spiked with gnashing whitecaps, and the ships heeled over dramatically as they hauled into line, some of them rolling so violently that they shipped water through their gunports. Such conditions, naturally, were a hindrance to good gunnery, and most of the ships' firing was wild -- especially one shell from the USS *Chippewa*, which sailed completely over Bogue Bank and exploded close to a group of very startled onlookers about half a mile from Beaufort.

Fighting against ships was what Fort Macon had been designed for, and her gunners hauled their pieces around with considerable gratitude at having a chance, finally, to do that. At 9:20 a.m., the fort sent one shell through the American flag atop the USS *State of Georgia*. Ten minutes later, an 8-inch Columbiad round smashed into the USS *Daylight*, ripping through two decks and inflicting moderate damage on the engine room. The USS *Gemsbok* had one of its masts blown apart by roundshot from the fort. Near hits threw up waterspouts all around the rolling, staggering vessels. By 9:45, with two of his four ships damaged and the rough weather largely negating his gunnery, the commander of the naval squadron decided he'd had enough. He signaled for his ships to pull out of range and regain their normal anchorage stations. For the first and only time in the siege, as the Federal ships retired, the garrison of Fort Macon broke into cheers.

Thus far, Fort Macon had not suffered much damage, either structurally or to its armament. Most of the big mortar shells were overshooting the fort by 300 yards and dropping into either the sound or the empty sand on Shackleford Bank. Likewise, about 90 percent of the Parrott rounds were overshooting, while the 8-inch mortar shells were often dropping short. These "overs" and "unders" were now being corrected, thanks to signals sent from one of Parke's Signal Corps observation posts, located on the upper piazza of Beaufort's Atlantic Hotel. One by one, guided by the signals flashed from the mainland, Flagler's battery commanders augmented or decreased the powder charges in their weapons, until they found the proper range with deadly precision.

Mortar shells now rained on the parapets, throwing sandbags into the air and scattering the Confederate gun crews. Parrott rounds gouged great holes in the walls, spewing chunks of brick into the smoke-filled air. Other shells struck the lower, angled walls and ricocheted viciously into the fort's interior. White began to steadily lose men and guns. Shortly after the range corrections were made, a Parrott bolt slammed into one of the Confederate 24-pounders, breaking the elevating screw and killing the gunner who was sighting the piece when it was struck. By 1:30 p.m., three more 24-pounders, a 32-pounder, and two of the deadly Columbiads had also been knocked out. Casualties among the gunners had mounted and the Confederates' rate of fire had slackened drastically, to two or three shots every five minutes.

But Fort Macon's gunners were still shooting bravely and well. The protective sand around several Federal batteries was blown away by repeated strikes, and one of the Parrott positions sustained six direct hits. Miraculously, the only damage done to the Parrott was a wrecked sighting mechanism; it continued to fire nonetheless, for its range had long ago been set. Shortly after 2 p.m., the besiegers suffered their only fatality of the day — a Union soldier ran out from cover to replace some damaged aiming stakes, and he was struck squarely in the chest by a 24-pounder shot from the fort. The massive impact ripped out his heart, ribs, and breastbone.

At about that same moment, Flagler's gunners scored their most effective single hit of the battle. A Parrott bolt crashed into the carriage of an 8-inch Columbiad — disabling it and hideously wounding one of the rebel gunners — then glanced off obliquely and struck an adjacent 10-inch rifle, dismounting the gun and killing or wounding five of its crew. Its velocity not yet spent, the deadly Parrott shell then caromed off a brick wall and crashed into a 32-pounder with such force that the concussion knocked down every man within ten feet. Still moving, the shot finally hit the ground, rolled off the wall, and came to rest in a ditch.

At 3:30 p.m., White ordered the gunners to make a final all-out effort to silence the enemy batteries. Every gun still in commission began to fire as rapidly as its exhausted crews could load and point. The earth in front of the Federal gun pits suddenly seemed to boil with the impact of dozens of roundshot. As before, the fort's gunners were accurate, but they simply didn't have the right kind of weapons or shells to do much damage. The Confederates managed to disable one of Flagler's Parrott rifles, though only temporarily, and wound two of his men; but otherwise, the fort's last-ditch effort amounted to little more than a noisy display of fireworks.

By 4 p.m., it was clear that Confederate resistance could not be maintained much longer. Repeated strikes by the powerful Parrott bolts had opened a 12-foot crack in the wall shielding the fort's magazine, and it seemed only a matter of time before a shell would penetrate inside and detonate several tons of gunpowder. Looking around at the pitted, shell-scarred ramparts, the cracked and dismounted cannon, and the pools of blood where mangled men had fallen, Colonel White decided that honor had been satisfied and further resistance would accomplish nothing. The white flag was run up at 4:30.

General Burnside offered magnanimous terms of surrender, and after an evening's deliberation, White accepted. Burnside asked his subordinates to handle the surrender as tactfully as possible, and by all accounts they did. All who witnessed the scene were struck by the contrast between the ragged, motley dress and weaponry of White's men and the sharp uniforms and burnished weapons of the victors. White's men were paroled, not imprisoned, and were generously permitted to gather their personal belongings before being transported to the mainland to sign their parole documents.

As soon as the Confederate garrison evacuated Fort Macon, Flagler and his men swarmed over the place to evaluate their handiwork. They calculated that almost 600 projectiles had struck the fort during the bombardment. The parade ground was a blackened wasteland of overlapping craters; the outer face of the casements was pitted and scorched; dismounted cannon and smashed carriages lay strewn in all directions; and the walls were gouged with dozens of Parrott bolt strikes, some of which had penetrated two feet of solid masonry.

Considering the intensity of the firing, on both sides, casualties in the siege of Fort Macon were remarkably light. The garrison had lost seven men killed and 18 wounded, two of them mortally. Parke's force, in addition to the handful of men wounded in the preliminary skirmishing, lost one killed and two wounded.

On April 26, Ambrose Burnside held a victory parade through the streets of New Bern. All of his initial strategic goals had been accomplished; all that remained was some mopping up.

BURNSIDE DEPARTS

General Ambrose Burnside's subsequent Civil War reputation was checkered, to say the least, but with the capture of Fort Macon he emerged as the most successful Federal general then in the field. At a remarkably low cost in casualties, he had brought under Union control every major objective on the coast of North Carolina except for the heavily defended port of Wilmington. Now, Burnside felt, was the time to redouble success by driving inland on Goldsboro, perhaps even on Raleigh.

For a time it looked as if he might be able to do it. He received his first cavalry unit, the 3rd New York, just before accepting the surrender of Fort Macon. These troopers, in addition to the four regiments and several batteries that had already been shipped to North Carolina after the victory at Roanoke Island, gave Burnside a force of 17,000 men. This was a large enough force, certainly, to hold what he already had and to mount local operations to keep the rebels off balance. But it was not enough for a drive on Raleigh -- an offensive which would surely provoke the most desperate response from Richmond.

At the end of April Burnside suddenly found himself cut off from major reinforcements for an indefinite period. Not only men, but wagons and rolling stock were also being held back by Washington. The reason had to do with grand strategy. Despite Burnside's successes, his operations were now put on hold while the brilliant but impossibly pokey General McClellan opened his ponderous and ill-fated Peninsula Campaign. Indeed, Burnside was expected, from the middle of March until further notice, to subordinate his activities to McClellan's and not to make any moves inland until McClellan judged the moment to be ripe. Although

147

McClellan was all in favor of Burnside capturing Goldsboro and making at least a demonstration toward Raleigh, McClellan cautioned Burnside, in a message dated April 2, not to be overly bold:

> You will readily understand that if I succeed in driving the enemy out of Richmond I will at once throw a strong force on Raleigh and open communications with you via Goldsborough...Taking all things into consideration it appears probable that a movement in the direction of Goldsborough would be the best thing for you to undertake...Great caution will, however, be necessary, as the enemy might throw large forces in that direction...it would not do for you to be caught. We cannot afford any reverse at present.[1]

Less than a week after it began, McClellan's offensive was stopped cold on the Lower Peninsula, near Yorktown, and new orders reached Burnside: He was not to make any major moves in North Carolina until the situation on the Peninsula had been resolved.

So Burnside continued to do what he had been doing all along: sending out expeditions to probe for weak spots in the Confederate screen, keeping his opponents off-balance and making them respond to his actions rather than vice versa. On March 21, without resistance, his forces occupied the town of Washington, N.C., at the confluence of the Tar and Pamlico Rivers. About one-third of the town's 2,500 inhabitants were still there when troops of the 24th Massachusetts landed, and they met the invaders with an impressive display of Unionist sentiment. The New England soldiers behaved impeccably in response to this friendly reception.

Intelligence had also reached Burnside concerning Unionist feeling at the town of Plymouth, northeast of Washington on the south bank of the Roanoke River. Plymouth was first visited on May 1, then occupied on May 17. The town did seem pro-Union, and so vociferously did the citizens express their fear of Confederate retaliation that Burnside left a company of infantry and a gunboat stationed there for reassurance.

Contact between Burnside's patrols and the lurking Confederates was infrequent during this period, and fighting was desultory when it did occur. The Federals encountered little opposition, and much of this was offered by small detached cavalry companies and "partisan ranger" bands -- volunteer outfits that furnished their own mounts, guns, and uniforms, and which usually acted without supervision. Most of these units were militarily worthless, and their actions were usually limited to bushwhacking. Now and then, however, something like a real skirmish took place, such as the incident of April 7. Men from the Onslow County Dragoons, the Scotland Neck Mounted Rifles, and the 2nd North Carolina Cavalry divided into three 30-man platoons, charged out of the pine forest near Newport Barracks, and overran part of the 9th New Jersey, killing one man and capturing nine.

In Onslow County on the night of April 13, at a place called Gillett's Farm, a force of 200 German-speaking New York cavalry, led by one Baron Egloffstein, launched a sweep along the Morehead City railroad line. At first the expedition was successful. Without serious fighting, the baron's horsemen captured 23 rebel cavalrymen and 80 horses. Encamped at a farm that night, however, they were hit by three "rather desultory" charges by the 2nd North Carolina Cavalry. The attackers lost two killed and five wounded, while Baron Egloffstein's men suffered six wounded. The Tarheel cavalry's performance on this occasion was so lackluster that General Holmes ordered a formal inquiry. The panel's report, issued by General Robert Ransom, concluded that "ignorance, idleness and incapacity so strongly characterize a large number of the officers that a thorough purging is necessary."[2]

Part of the unit redeemed itself on April 27, near Pollocksville, when they again skirmished with Egloffstein. This time they wounded the baron and six of his men while suffering only a single casualty themselves.

There was another peppery little fight at Trantner's Creek -- about 12 miles from Washington, N.C. -- on June 5. The commander of the Union force in Washington, Colonel E.E. Potter, was informed by his scouts that a rebel regiment, the 44th North Carolina, was planning to assault the town as soon as their artillery showed up. On June 4, reinforcements were hurriedly shipped to Washington from New Bern, amounting to seven companies of the 24th Massachusetts and three pieces of artillery served by U.S. Marine gun crews. Potter devised a plan for striking the rebels first, and General John Foster, Burnside's deputy, approved.

At Grimes Mill, over Trantner's Creek, Potter ran into 400

Confederates dug in behind timber breastworks. The rebel commander, Colonel George B. Singletary, had ordered his troops to man the roadblock one company at a time. Each company would fire a volley, then fall back to allow another company to take its place. With several echelons of companies loading in turn, it was possible for the defenders to maintain uninterrupted fire against the road.

For awhile it worked splendidly. The hot musketry repelled the Federal infantry, killing seven men and wounding eight. But Singletary lacked artillery, and his breastworks were flimsy protection against Potter's roundshot and grape. One of the earliest rebel casualties was the gallant Singletary himself, killed by one of Potter's first cannon shots. The heart went out of the defense as the cannon fire struck home. After losing a few more men, the Confederates withdrew. The few survivors' accounts to reach print all speak of Trantner's Creek as a hot little fight. Three dead Confederates were found inside the mill, along with "an enormous quantity of blood," indicating that numerous killed or wounded men had been carried from the field.

Potter's men were glad to get back to Washington that night. The garrison thought the town was "a very pretty place," comparable in its appearance and amenities to the trim New England villages the soldiers had left back home. One participant in the Trantner's Creek fight, Colonel Francis Osborn of the 24th Massachusetts, wrote in a letter to his family: "There was one delightful feature connected with this affair which made it more pleasant than either Roanoke or New Bern. I mean that after it I returned to a first-rate supper in an elegant house, and after a bath went to sleep in a good bed. Was that not a pleasant conclusion to the day's work?"[3]

The late spring of 1862 was a busy time on the political front, too. On May 26, at New Bern, General Burnside turned over civil authority to Edward Stanly, the old-time Tarheel Whig who had been imported from California to become the new Unionist governor of North Carolina. Stanly soon learned that Unionist sentiment was not as great as his sponsors in Washington, D.C. had led him to believe. Stanly himself was regarded, even by many Unionists, as little more than a traitor.

He wasn't even an abolitionist, although he did implement effective measures to relieve the plight of the hundreds of Negro refugees who had flooded into New Bern. A man of good intentions and no small ability, Stanly lasted only until January 15, 1863, when he resigned in protest over the Emancipation Proclamation. In his letter of resignation, he told Abraham Lincoln that he could no longer, in good faith, tell North Carolinians that he was only trying to help them restore their status in the Union. "I fear it will do infinite mischief," Stanly wrote to the President regarding the Proclamation. "It crushes all hope of making peace by any conciliatory measures. It will fill the hearts of Union men with despair and strengthen the hands of detestable traitors whose mad ambition has spread desolation and sorrow over our country."[4]

In fairness to the unfortunate Stanly, his other reason for resignation did him more credit than his pro-slavery attitudes: He had become fed up with the looting and brutality that often accompanied Federal actions in the coastal counties, describing it as "the most shameful pillaging and robbery that ever disgraced an army in any civilized land." To another correspondent, Stanly voiced the opinion that if "the war in North Carolina had been conducted by soldiers who were Christians and gentlemen, the state would long ago have rebelled against rebellion."[5]

Late that spring there was some more reshuffling of Confederate commanders. First, General Robert Ransom was detached from duty in Virginia and sent to work under General Holmes. The thinking in Richmond was that since both men were native North Carolinians, their partnership ought to improve morale. This was a good choice. Ransom was a West Pointer (Class of 1850), and he had had lots of experience fighting Sioux Indians and carrying out police-action work during the partisan strife in pre-war Kansas.

On June 1, General James G. Martin left his post as state adjutant general, a job he had performed with brilliance, and took command of the brigade centered around Kinston. On paper, its strength was 5,300 men, but due to desertion and sickness, probably no more than 4,000 were present and fit for duty on any given day. To make matters worse, just two weeks after taking command, Martin lost three regiments to the defense of Petersburg. General Holmes was likewise called back to Virginia, and ordered to bring the best-equipped regiments with him. Holmes and his men were immediately plunged into the bitter fighting at Chickahominy. The campaign raging in Virginia eventually took General Martin's brigade, too, although Governor Clark parted with it only after desperate entreaties from Richmond. The total Confederate presence in eastern North Carolina then amounted to two infantry regiments at Wilmington and two at Kinston. Had the Federals chosen to advance any time in early July, Raleigh or Wilmington would have been theirs for the taking.

Burnside was ready to take the offensive by June 20. He had finally received some rolling stock -- two locomotives and 50 freight cars -- as well as enough wagons to sustain his army. Two other locomotives had gone down in bad weather off Cape Hatteras. Once again, the sea had done more to defend North Carolina than the Confederate government.

Finally, on June 25, Burnside received the marching orders he had been waiting for. He was to immediately advance on Goldsboro with all the forces he could command. Eagerly, Burnside fine-tuned his plans and issued orders to set the offensive in motion. He felt he was about to reap the full fruits of his earlier labors, and he entertained ideas (not too far-fetched) of being the man who would split the Confederacy in two.

But it was not to be. On June 28, President Lincoln sent a telegram to Burnside saying, "I think you had better go, with any reinforcements you can spare, to General McClellan." Burnside went, taking two divisions of troops with him. It was a panicky decision on Lincoln's part — Burnside's 7,000 men were a drop in the bucket on the Virginia battlefields, and they achieved little. Had they remained in North Carolina, they could have ended the war.

Indeed, for all the high hopes that Washington had placed on McClellan, it was not "Little Napoleon" who brought strategic victory, but Ambrose Burnside. As long as the Union maintained a strong presence on the North Carolina coast -- enclaves which could be reinforced very quickly by sea -- General Robert E. Lee's supply lines to Virginia were not secure. From June 1862 until the Confederate collapse in 1865, whenever Lee contemplated an operation in Virginia or elsewhere, he had to take into consideration the fact that large numbers of troops would have to be siphoned off to keep the Federals pinned down behind their earthworks at New Bern and elsewhere along the coast.

The other consequences of Burnside's expedition were similarly impressive:

— A total of 13 North Carolina counties, among the most agriculturally productive in the state, were now under Union control, or were lost to production due to the proximity of Union garrisons. Burnside conquered or removed from production almost 2.5 million acres, inhabited by 119,000 whites and 50,000 slaves. The antebellum productivity of this region had been great. In 1860 alone, it produced 5.2 million bushels of corn, $2 million worth of cotton, and vast quantities of naval stores.

— From this vast region, the Confederacy would not only get no more supplies, but would also collect no taxes and obtain no conscripts.

— Cities and towns lost to the enemy included New Bern, Plymouth, Morehead City, Beaufort, Edenton, Elizabeth City, Washington, and two dozen smaller localities.

— Blockade runners could no longer make for the safety of Beaufort or the sounds, but were forced to make Wilmington their only haven. This narrowing of options made the U.S. Navy's blockade much easier to enforce.

— Henceforth, large numbers of state militia and Confederate troops would be permanently tied down to protect Goldsboro and the vital railroad.

All things considered, Burnside's operations in North Carolina were the finest feat of arms yet accomplished by a Union commander. That his victories were won against demoralized, scattered, poorly armed, and often wretchedly led troops should not detract from the efficiency and intelligence of his leadership. He would also be missed, in a personal sense, by his men, for they had come to think of him as a father figure. He had looked after them, and had kept them well fed and warm — and had not squandered their lives in order to gain his victories.

PART 3

RAIDS AND
EXCURSIONS

GENERAL FOSTER TAKES COMMAND

When Burnside left, he turned over command to General John Gray Foster, who had led the Coast Division's First Brigade very ably since the start of the expedition. Foster was 39 years old, a large, burly, heavily bearded man with an honest, solid face. A native of Whitefield, New Hampshire, Foster had graduated fourth in his class at West Point in 1846. He had served on General Winfield Scott's staff during the Mexican War, had been gravely wounded at the battle of Molino del Rey, and had been compelled to accept light duties upon his return home. He taught engineering at West Point and served as an adviser in matters of harbor defense. The reason why Burnside's guns had been able to score direct hits on Fort Macon's ammunition magazine was that John Foster had told them exactly where to shoot -- he had inspected the fort several times before the war. Foster had been assigned to Fort Sumter at the time it came under bombardment, and his reports of the siege -- cool, detailed, precise, and keenly observant -- remain one of the most valuable firsthand accounts of the war's opening battle.

Burnside left Foster in command of a mere 9,500 troops -- scarcely enough for defensive security, and far below the number needed to conduct significant offensive operations. To maximize the effectiveness of his troops, Foster set to work, turning New Bern into an impregnable stronghold. His naval counterpart, Commodore Rowan, at first complained that Foster was spending entirely too much time and effort just digging. "He is an engineer,"

Rowan griped in one document, "and must build forts."[1] But future events would prove Foster correct. On at least two occasions, when New Bern was seriously threatened by powerful Confederate forces, it was the strength and depth of Foster's fortifications that discouraged the attackers and multiplied the effectiveness of the defenders. Much of the labor was done by hundreds of "contraband" Negroes. Foster organized the ex-slaves into quasi-military formations, gave them a fife and drum, had a special flag created for them, and saw to it that they were well fed and given medical treatment. In return for this unusual policy, the labor battalions worked diligently and in high spirits, fortifying, as it were, their own newly gained freedom.

Using all of his expertise as an engineer, Foster erected three strong earthen forts and lines of reinforced breastworks that stretched from the Trent River to the Neuse. The strongest work was Fort Totten, a star-shaped bastion centered between the two main roads leading into town. Across the Trent River, the rail line from the coast was protected by two smaller forts, entrenchments, and a series of stout log blockhouses placed at intervals along the track. Above the town, three separate strongpoints guarded the river approaches. On the New Bern side was Fort Stevenson, and across the Neuse were Forts Anderson and Chase. As a mobile battery, Foster designed and constructed a weapon christened "Burnside's Monitor" -- a blockhouse on a flatcar, armored with half-inch iron plate, and loopholed for rifles and a pair of six-pounder field guns.

Life in occupied New Bern, for both the occupiers and the citizens, was mostly rather pleasant. There was some spying, of course, and a small number of unconverted rebels still lurked among the population, but for the most part the townspeople who stayed behind had little to complain about. The Yankee soldiers felt secure behind Foster's earthworks and were generally on their best behavior. They lived in decent quarters, ate good food, worked reasonable hours, suffered much less disease than they would have out in the field, and had ample opportunity for recreation. Their recreation ranged from concerts to literary clubs, with an outside chance of enjoying female companionship now and again. All things considered, New Bern was a good place to pull duty. One

Massachusetts soldier recorded in his diary, in tones of some wonder, the details of his new quarters:

> Today the several companies of our regiment moved into the deserted mansions of the Confederate martyrs, which will be our quarters during our stay. Company B went into a two-story brick house on East Front Street. It has a pretty flower garden in front, with an orchard, vegetable garden and servants' quarters in the rear. The house is nicely furnished throughout; the floors, halls and stairs are carpeted, as are the chambers. The front parlor has upholstered furniture, center table, piano, lace curtains, ornaments, gas fixtures, etc...I don't see but we are pretty well fixed...this is one of the occasional sunny spots in a soldier's life.[2]

If the New England troopers had a high opinion of the antebellum standard of living enjoyed by the upper and middle classes of New Bern, they were often bemused and mildly repulsed by the quaint folkways of the lower classes, the so-called "poor white trash" that lived in the woods and along the tributary creeks all around the town. The same soldier quoted above recorded the following observations, a few days later, about the local poor whites:

> Nearly all of them are what is called poor white trash or clay-eaters. I am told they actually do eat clay, a habit they contract like any other bad habit. Now I cannot vouch for the truth of this, never having seen them eating it, but some of them look as though that were about all they had to eat. They are an utterly ignorant set, scarcely able to make themselves intelligible, and in many ways they are below the negroes in intelligence and manner of living, but perhaps they are not wholly to blame for it, the same principle that will oppress a black man, [will also oppress] a white one. They are entirely cut off from the means of acquiring land or an education, even though they wished to. Public schools are unknown here and land can only be purchased by the plantation. That leaves them in rather a bad fix; poor, shiftless and ignorant...you speak to one of them, and he will look at you in a listless sort of way as though unable or undecided whether to answer or not. Ask one of them the distance across the river and he will either say he don't know or "it is right smart." Ask one of them the distance to any place or house out in the country, and he will tell you "it is a right smart step" or "you go up yer a right smart step, and you will come to a creek," and from there it will be so many looks and a screech; meaning from the creek that number of angles in the road

and as far beyond as the voice will carry. They do not seem to have
any intelligent idea about anything, and in talking with the cusses,
one scarcely knows whether to pity them or be amused.[3]

Throughout the surviving letters and regimental histories, the
attitude of the occupiers toward the Negro population seems rather
contradictory. On the one hand, the Yankees enjoyed playing the
liberators and were sincerely compassionate toward those who had
lived in slavery. On the other hand, they were quite eager to obtain
for themselves the services of a low-paid "pickaninny" servant, and
apparently saw no contradiction. Negroes were also a constant
source of wonder and bemusement, which tended to express itself
in terms of utter condescension. They are often described in
minstrel-show terms, complete with all the eye-rolling-darkie
stereotypes, and their keen, completely natural, interest in their
new masters prompted the soldiers to think of the Negroes as "the
novelty-loving sons of Africa."

Sometimes the Negroes were nothing more than the butt of
amusement for bored soldiers, as this excerpt from the official
history of the 24th Massachusetts indicates:

> Late in the afternoon, the regiment was mustered for pay, and later
> still the men had a spell of that almost universal horse-play known in
> those days as "tossing 'niggers' in a blanket." While it was fun for the
> tossers, and very likely did not hurt the tossed, it was for the latter a
> period of intense fear, not to say horror. Of course the poor victims
> screamed and yelled, but the louder the cries, the greater the fun for
> the lusty fellows at the blanket's edge....[4]

Whether it was tossing Negroes in blankets or enjoying a
civilized tea with the town ladies, life inside the fortifications of
New Bern was certainly preferable to life in the field in Virginia or
Tennessee, and the Yankee soldiers appreciated their luck. Looking
back on his tour in North Carolina, one of them likened it to "our
summer vacation...it was a real treat not to be in the regular army,
where so much fighting was done...."[5]

Out on the picket line, beyond the main earthworks, duty was
somewhat more arduous, but still not without its charms:

> The general policy of the officers in command of the department was

a defensive one, and therefore invited attack or harassing demonstrations on the part of the enemy, which made outpost duty somewhat lively and often interesting. This was a novel experience [for the men of the 17th Massachusetts], who at first enjoyed it keenly, especially as the weather was mild and vegetation made the surroundings attractive, the deciduous trees coming into leafy and flowery luxuriance.[6]

The picket lines around New Bern were, of course, observed daily by the Confederates. Sometimes, cavalry and "partisan ranger" outfits bushwhacked Union patrols. On occasion, these little skirmishes -- though rarely mentioned in the *Official Records* -- turned into rather bitter engagements, especially considering the small number of men involved. On May 22, 1862, Company I of the 17th Massachusetts was involved in one such encounter while on a foraging patrol beyond Federal lines. The company commander, Captain Thomas Weir, had gained a reputation for being an aggressive leader. His "scouts," as these patrols were termed, often captured rebel prisoners and always netted some rebel property or food. Confederate units in the vicinity decided to make an example of Weir. They detailed 50 men, many of them armed with new breech-loading Harper's Ferry rifles, to set up an ambush on a heavily wooded bluff overlooking the road that Weir's men often took when leaving their lines at New Bern.

Weir's mission on that May morning was simple: to rescue some property belonging to a Unionist civilian who had requested protection against Confederate foragers. Weir left New Bern with 35 men. On the way back, most of his men were straggling at some distance behind the head of his column, leading cows and horses and nursing a wagon full of cotton. At the head of the formation, Weir had only about 15 men under arms -- too few for him to put out skirmishers. The Confederate party waited until Weir and his men were a mere 25 yards from their hiding place, then fired a murderous volley that struck down ten men, mortally wounding five of them. Federal reinforcements hurried toward the firing and quickly drove off the attackers, wounding one of them and capturing several of their fancy rifles. When General Foster learned of the ambush, he, too, chose to make an example of poor Weir. A court martial found Weir negligent in not putting out skirmishers, and his career was forever stained by the incident.

There were other perils on the picket line besides the occasional bushwhacker; perhaps the most dreaded was malaria. Men who came down with the disease were treated with so much quinine that their teeth came loose in their sockets and they were no longer able to eat hardtack. To ward off the disease, regimental doctors dosed their charges, every morning, with a grisly tasting cocktail compounded of whiskey and quinine powder.

Another plague, during warm weather, was the insects -- those winged serpents in the coastal Eden. The Yankees had to contend with clouds of huge mosquitos — great swollen-bellied monsters that left smears of blood when swatted — as well as sand fleas, ticks, chiggers, horseflies, and the omnipresent "grayback" lice. The coastal counties harbored a lot more snakes, too, in the days before highways and suburbs. Although the number of men who were actually bitten by a pinewoods rattler or a cottonmouth water moccasin was statistically insignificant, the number of men who were scared by them was legion.

'CLOSE ONE, SIR!' -- RAIDS ALONG THE RIVERS

General Foster may have lacked enough troops to undertake major offensives, but he had no intention of sitting idly behind his entrenchments at New Bern. One thing he did not lack was complete control of the water, and he encouraged his energetic naval counterpart, Commodore Rowan, to conduct armed reconnaissance patrols up the rivers and along the numerous inlets, searching for signs of Confederate activity. On July 9, 1862, a force of three Union gunboats, en route from Plymouth to Hamilton on the Roanoke River, found more activity than they bargained for.

Patrolling the riverbank, under orders to protect the vital railroad bridges at Weldon, was Company B, 1st North Carolina Cavalry, under Lieutenant Alexander B. Andrews. Andrews was not happy about being stuck with this dull, routine duty. Most of his regiment had been sent to Virginia, where they were riding hard with the glamorous Confederate cavalry commander, General "Jeb" Stuart.

Commanding the three Union gunboats was Lieutenant C.W. Flusser, one of Rowan's most aggressive skippers. The little flotilla had been spotted almost as soon as it entered the river, and word of its coming had been brought to Lieutenant Andrews. Andrews, with 41 men, rode swiftly to a wooded bluff called Rainbow Banks, about two miles downriver from Hamilton. There he ordered his men to dismount and spread out under cover. They were not to fire until Andrews opened up with his pistol.

At that point in the Roanoke River was a long, lazy bend. Judging from contemporary photos, Flusser's vessels could not have been more than 100 yards from Andrews's hiding place as they rounded the bend. Andrews waited until the lead gunboat, with Flusser clearly visible on deck, was directly opposite his troops. Then he emptied his pistol at the lead boat, yelling for his men to "rapid fire." Flusser's gunboats were riddled by hundreds of Minie balls. Their decks were torn up, their smokestacks pinholed, and their portholes blown out. Two Union sailors were killed and nine more wounded in the few minutes the ships were most vulnerable.

Once Flusser could bring his stern guns to bear, he cleared the bluff in short order, blowing large chunks of it into the water. Andrews and his men high-tailed out of range. Flusser may indeed have been contemplating a raid on the railroad bridges, but the heated reception made him think better of it, and his ships withdrew downriver. Andrews's cavalry followed them for miles, sniping at them occasionally, but Flusser's gun crews kept blasting shells into every concealed position on the banks, so there was no chance to repeat the original close-range ambush.

Andrews was duly promoted for this feat, one of the few recorded instances of cavalry repelling a naval force. A year after the ambush, Andrews survived a bullet through his lung in Virginia, and later became president of the Western North Carolina Railroad.

Unsure about Foster's real strength, the Confederate authorities in eastern North Carolina were still worried that he might try to break out of his enclaves and go for the jugular -- the Wilmington & Weldon Railroad. Throughout the summer, Governor Clark pleaded with Robert E. Lee to release additional forces for the coastal theater of war, but Lee, though sympathetic, felt that the situation in Virginia would not allow him to transfer any significant forces to North Carolina.

When it became clear that, once again, no help would be forthcoming from Richmond, some local Confederate commanders became determined not to let the Yankees grow complacent behind their fortified lines. They reasoned that an active and aggressive

Confederate posture would make Foster think twice before venturing toward the interior of the state.

One such Confederate officer was Colonel S.D. Pool. On the morning of September 6, he mounted a surprise attack on the Federal garrison at Washington, N.C. Under cover of thick fog, Pool's men hit the town at several points simultaneously while most of the Yankees were still asleep. After overrunning the Union pickets, the attacking Confederates charged wildly through the streets, uttering rebel yells and brawling with half-dressed bluecoats.

When the fog lifted, Pool's men came under fire from two Yankee gunboats out in the river: the *Picket* and the *Louisiana*. No sooner had the former vessel opened fire, however, than something -- most likely a stray spark -- touched off her powder magazine. The *Picket* was ripped apart by the explosion and 20 of her crew were killed. Observing the little warship going down, wreathed in flames, Pool's men cheered lustily, thinking the town was theirs.

It almost was, but the timely arrival of five companies of Yankee troops -- largely made up of Unionist volunteers from the coastal counties, as it happened -- shifted the tide of battle against Pool. After two hours of stubborn street fighting, he withdrew. All Confederate records of this engagement seem to have vanished, so the exact strength and composition of Pool's force, as well as his casualties, are conjectural. A dozen dead rebels were found in the streets, and other bodies were seen being carried off during the retreat. The Union garrison suffered fairly heavy losses; counting the sailors who died when the gunboat blew up, the defenders lost 27 killed and 58 wounded, making this affair one of the bloodiest raids of the year in coastal North Carolina.

During late October 1862, General Foster received substantial reinforcements. Most of the reinforcements, however, were newly raised volunteer regiments from Massachusetts, and some of the companies were so raw that the men didn't know how to load their rifles. Nevertheless, the added manpower gave Foster enough troops for some offensive action. When scouts brought word that three rebel regiments were foraging near Tarboro, Foster was determined to take to the field and either capture or destroy them. He assembled a 5,000-man expeditionary force, mostly comprised of green Massachusetts troops, and personally led them out of Washington, N.C., on the morning of November 2.

It was an unseasonably hot morning, although the sandy road on which they marched was covered in many places with deep pools of standing water. Foster's route lay through dense stands of coastal pine forest, where the air seemed suffocatingly close and humid. By mid-day, even the veteran units were staggering along with their tongues hanging out. By the time Foster encountered his first resistance, at about 4 p.m. at a muddy stream known as Little Creek, his whole command was exhausted, and the men's movements in the coming skirmishes would be sluggish in the extreme. A Confederate force on the opposite bank traded rifle fire with Foster's forward elements for about an hour, while the 5th Massachusetts prepared to cross the creek and have a go at them. The inexperienced volunteers prepared to face this minor water obstacle by carefully removing, folding, and piling their clothing. When the firing suddenly stopped -- the defenders having pulled back to another delaying position -- the new troops were left standing in the creek in various states of undress, presenting a sight which the advancing veterans found highly entertaining.

Things were not quite so jolly a mile up the road, at Rawl's Creek. The Confederates had burned the bridge and were offering stubborn resistance from some breastworks on the opposite banks. Skirmishing continued until nightfall, when the Confederates withdrew and Foster's engineers went forward to repair the bridge. By noon the following day, the Federal column had reached Williamston, about halfway between Washington and Tarboro. They found the town undefended, indeed almost deserted, and proceeded to make themselves at home, having located a good supply of poultry and sweet potatoes.

The Union expedition marched through Hamilton on November 4. Here, the foraging turned into outright looting, and Foster's men indulged themselves in a small orgy of pyromania -- fires lit up the night sky in all directions. Foster had issued orders to control this kind of behavior, but it is impossible to judge how serious he was about enforcing them. Even if he was serious, he couldn't be everywhere at once, and the green troops were proving quite undisciplined. Also, they were deep in enemy territory and getting nervous. It was reasonable for them to suppose that every Confederate unit within a hundred miles was converging on them, creeping closer in the dusky pine forests.

Indeed, when Foster received some fresh intelligence reports on November 5, it seemed to him that perhaps he really was pushing his luck. Scouts had moved close to Tarboro during the night and had heard the whistles of several locomotives pulling into town -- a good sign that Confederate troops were being rushed to the area. Foster was now less than ten miles from Tarboro, but his whole force was strung out in a vulnerable fashion along a single road, and his scouts had discovered more secondary paths in the vicinity than were drawn on his maps. There was a very real danger that the enemy, using routes Foster didn't know about, could concentrate to his rear and cut him off from his own base. He therefore chose to turn the expedition around and head back toward the coast. He marched to Plymouth, which was somewhat closer than his original starting point at Washington. From Plymouth, the faithful naval contingent transported the troops back to the comforts and amenities of New Bern.

Foster didn't accomplish much on this foray, and he had suffered some casualties -- six killed and eight wounded -- but it wasn't a complete waste of time. It had been a splendid shakedown exercise for his green troops, with just enough danger and hardship to get them into a soldierly frame of mind. He had also deepened his own "feel" for the terrain and for his opponents, though they had proven elusive. As one Massachusetts trooper expressed it in a letter: "We...burned their houses, stole their whiskey, and brought home their horses...[We got] the best of the country, especially as we left it when we got ready although our departure may have been somewhat hastened by the rebels."[1]

Foster's brief expedition was followed, on November 23, by a ship-to-shore engagement that was notable on several counts. For one thing, it resulted in the loss of a Union vessel to Confederate action -- the first time that had happened since the *Fanny* was captured. For another, the vessel in question was the USS *Ellis*, which had once been a member of the Mosquito Fleet. Most importantly, though, the battle marked another milestone in the career of William Baker Cushing, the most illustrious naval hero who ever fought in North Carolina waters.

Cushing was descended from a prominent Boston family, but was born in Delafield, Wisconsin. He gave evidence of being interested in a naval career from an early age and gained admission to the U.S. Naval Academy in 1857. He became something of an underclassmen's legend for his practical jokes and lack of scholarly application. A long series of disciplinary infractions culminated his senior year with his dismissal from the Academy. He was permitted to resign in March 1861. Six weeks later, he was in Washington, D.C., haunting the offices of the Navy Department and begging to be put on active duty. Cushing's zeal, and the reputation of his family, helped persuade the authorities to take him back — but not as an officer. He entered service only as an "acting master's mate."

While serving in this inferior capacity on the USS *Minnesota*, Cushing demonstrated a keen sense of duty and professionalism. He was duly restored to the U.S. Navy in October 1861 as a midshipman. Eight months later, he was made a lieutenant, in spite of the fact that he was only 19 years old.

Cushing shipped as executive officer of the USS *Commodore Perry*, serving under his old friend and patron, C.W. Flusser, who had been promoted to captain's rank shortly after his fight with the rebel cavalry on the Roanoke River. The *Commodore Perry* was a small side-wheeler with only four guns and a crew of 30 men, but with two hotspur officers like Flusser and Cushing, she was ready to take on anything the rebels might send against her.

Naval warfare in the sounds of North Carolina was not exactly the sort of thing men like Flusser and Cushing had in mind when they joined the service. Both were raised on the salty romantic traditions of John Paul Jones and Stephen Decatur. "...The lofty frigate shortening sail and clearing for action under the blue sky far out at sea," was the very emblem of that age of wooden ships and iron men, "but no such spectacle cheered the eyes and exalted the patriotism of the seamen [who patrolled the coastal sounds]...[Their] vessels were small and smokey, redolent of engine oil and innocent of snowy canvas and gleaming spars; instead of the bright blue sea of nautical romance, one saw the muddy, shallow flood of the far-reaching inland waters, stained and poisoned by the ooze and vegetable decay swept down by numberless rivers and creeks from the surrounding swamps."[2]

Since the Confederates rarely offered battle in the inland waters, men like Cushing and Flusser, whose vessels operated for long periods of time independently of higher command and supervision, had to go looking for trouble if they wanted real action. In Cushing, this aggressiveness, this compulsion to seek combat, verged on the pathological. There was a fire in his belly that only danger could calm, a restlessness in his mind that only action could soothe. One person who observed him at this stage of the war described him this way: "He was over six feet tall, straight as an arrow, a blonde, about twenty years old, and a bundle of nerves that it seemed to take the strain of furious combat to calm."[3]

Cushing distinguished himself in battle for the first time on October 3, 1862, when Flusser was ordered to lead a three-ship flotilla up the Blackwater River (which flows into the Chowan River, on the Virginia side of the North Carolina state line). This mission was part of a joint army-navy attack on the town of Franklin, Virginia. The land force assigned to the operation attacked half-heartedly, enabling the Confederate garrison to concentrate much of its attention on the three gunboats, which were forced to crawl slowly up a narrow, sandbar-dotted channel.

At one particularly narrow bend, Flusser's gunboat ran aground and came under fire from massed rifles and more than a dozen cannon. The situation went from grave to desperate when a mass of rebel infantry swarmed down the bank and charged the stricken ship. Seeing the danger, Cushing called for volunteers and led them to a wheeled howitzer on the afterdeck. He crammed the piece with canister shot and helped manhandle it to a point where it could fire at the attacking infantry. By that time, Cushing was all alone -- the other seven men with him had been either killed or wounded by the blistering fire directed against the gunboat.

By himself, Cushing aimed and fired the cannon, at a range of about 30 yards. The effect was devastating: "The troops, who had been cheering as they ran with their rifles held high over their heads, suddenly stopped and milled about in confusion, with surprised looks on their faces, stumbling over the bodies of their fallen comrades."[4] Cushing himself was almost killed at that moment, for one of the rebel officers had drawn a bead on him. Suddenly there was a musket-crack from behind Cushing, and the Confederate officer fell dead. Cushing looked around and saw one of his wounded gunners, standing in spite of his own pain, holding a smoking Springfield rifle in his hands. The man winked at Cushing and croaked, "Close one, sir!" Those words might well have been William Cushing's personal motto. They reflect not only his extraordinary personal bravery, and his luck, but also the unwavering loyalty he inspired in his men.

Flusser's after-action report credited Cushing with saving the ship. As a reward, Cushing soon found himself with his first command, the gunboat USS *Ellis*, captured by the Federals after the battle of Elizabeth City. An iron-hulled ship of 100 tons, the *Ellis* had been considerably upgraded since being taken into Federal service. Instead of the obsolescent 32-pounders she had carried when fighting with Commodore Lynch's Mosquitos, she now carried a potent 80-pounder rifle on her foredeck and a rifled 12-pounder howitzer aft. She drew only six feet of water, which enabled her to go far upstream on the inland waterways.

Cushing and the *Ellis* were given a kind of "roving commission"; they were to steam up and down the sound waters, investigate reports of Confederate activity, and make sure no Confederate shipping moved anywhere along the coast. Cushing got off to a fast start. He burned a large salt factory at New Topsail Inlet, then went to Jacksonville and burned another, and captured a pair of coastal schooners loaded with valuable naval stores. He also shelled, and actually captured, Jacksonville itself on November 23, 1862. But he ran into trouble two days later while attempting to take his prizes across the bar of the New River.

Hard aground, with Confederate forces gathering on the riverbank, Cushing tried desperately to free his vessel by using the anchor and engines as a winch. It didn't work. The tide was going down, and soon the *Ellis* would be virtually helpless until the next high tide. Cushing ordered one of the shallow-draft schooners alongside and lightened his gunboat of everything except the pivot gun, some small arms, and a couple of tons of coal; still the gunboat wouldn't budge.

Cushing called the men together and spoke to them. "I see no chance of getting this ship off," he began, "and we will probably be attacked in the morning...by an overwhelming force. I will try to get her off at the next high tide if I am not attacked in the interim. In the meantime it becomes my duty to provide for the safety of you all. If we are attacked by the enemy in the morning and he overpowers us, either by boarding or otherwise, the only alternative left is to go up with the vessel or submit to an unconditional surrender. To do the latter is neither my desire or intention. I will not do the former except as an absolute resort. I wish all the men, except five or six -- and these must be volunteers -- to go on board the schooner. I wish the schooner to be dropped down the river to a point without the range of the enemy's fire from the bluff. It is my intention, with the five or six men who may volunteer to remain with me...to work the pivot-gun in the morning and fight her to the last. I will not surrender [to] the enemy, while a magazine or a match remains on board."

As one, every man stepped three paces forward. Cushing grinned with the vulpine joy that lit his face every time he was going into battle. He cried: "By God, I won't forget that, men; I won't forget it as long as I live!" He selected six of his most experienced sailors and put the rest on the prize schooner, which dropped downriver and anchored a half-mile away.

The first cannon ball slammed into the *Ellis* before the dawn mist cleared, sending forth a crash that sounded like a giant gong struck with a hammer. Waterspouts from the following shots rose all around the gunboat. At first light, Cushing could see four fairly heavy guns, 24-pounders at least, firing on him from the rebel shore. Cushing replied with his own gun, but two of the rebel pieces were too far away for him to hit, and the two within range were well protected by breastworks. As visibility improved, the Confederates had no trouble pounding the little gunboat with accuracy. Her hull was dented and pierced, her smokestack turned into a sieve, her boiler ruptured. After continuing this one-sided fight for an hour or so, Cushing decided further resistance was futile -- the enemy would simply knock the *Ellis* to bits with impunity.

Cushing now turned his thoughts to saving his men. They all piled into a longboat and started rowing like devils toward the waiting schooner. But before leaving his ship, Cushing loaded the cannon, pointed it at the nearest rebel gun, and inserted a slow fuse, "so that the vessel might fight herself after we left her." He also set a few fires to render the ship unsalvageable.

Cushing and his men rowed for ten minutes under intense fire, at times hidden by the spray kicked up by near-hits. They had to bail water out of the boat a few times, and more than once they clearly heard the hiss of roundshot passing by their heads, but not a man was injured as they made their escape. The Confederates later attempted to salvage the recaptured *Ellis*, but her starboard magazine had blown up from the fires set by Cushing, and there was little of value left intact.

When Cushing was back aboard a Navy ship, he immediately turned himself in and requested a court of inquiry. Reports of his valor had already reached the Navy Department, however, and their verdict was a vindication: "We don't care for the loss of a vessel when fought as gallantly as that." The brave Cushing had only begun his career in North Carolina waters. Before the war was over, he would see more action, and win more honors, than any other naval officer who served in the state.

Confederate forces in the coastal sector mounted one more raid on the enemy in the closing days of 1862. The action had been planned by General Samuel French in October, and its main purpose was economic as well as military: to temporarily reassert Confederate control over Tyrell, Martin, and Washington counties, in order to bring in the harvest. As it happened, the operation didn't take place until December 10, too late to be of much good in that respect.

On that day, using troops from the 17th North Carolina Regiment, a small unit of cavalry, and a single battery of cannon, Lieutenant Colonel John C. Lamb attacked the town of Plymouth, taking its Union garrison completely by surprise. All of the Federal pickets save one were captured without resistance. The one man who got away, however, fired his rifle as he ran. This alerted his comrades in time for the Union commander, Captain Barnabas Ewer, to form his men in line across Main Street. Lamb unleashed his Confederate horsemen, who charged vigorously, screaming fearsome rebel yells. Ewer's men scattered in all directions. Part of the routed garrison took shelter in the dockside customs house and held off the cavalry with hot musket fire. Lamb ordered up one of his cannon; it threw nine shots into the building, blowing down one side of the upper story and killing one of the defenders. With the building crumbling around them, the rest of the Yankees hastily withdrew.

From locations overlooking the Roanoke River, Lamb could observe at close range on the town's sole naval protection, the gunboat *Smithfield*. Bringing up his artillery, Lamb brought the vessel under rapid and accurate fire. The first hit blew a ragged hole in her smokestack, and the second pierced her steamchest, bursting the boiler. Other rounds tore up her superstructure. Severely damaged and barely able to make headway, the Union gunboat upped anchor and headed downstream, out of range. Observing his naval support retiring, Captain Ewer seems to have lost his nerve. He abandoned his troops and hastened to the waterfront, where he managed to get aboard the departing vessel, much to the disgust of his witnesses. The Federals in retreat, Colonel Lamb burned down the garrison's headquarters, along with all of its accumulated paperwork, while his men burned down most of the buildings on Main Street. Whether this was part of a "scorched-earth" strategy or simple vandalism is unclear. After the incendiary work was finished, Lamb and his raiders departed, for they weren't strong enough to hold the town against a Federal counterattack.

Meanwhile, at about the same time Lamb had been planning his attack on Plymouth, Union General John Foster was preparing for his long-contemplated attack on Goldsboro. It would be the last Federal operation of the year in North Carolina, and the biggest since the siege of Fort Macon.

FOSTER'S MARCH ON GOLDSBORO

In early December 1862, General Foster was on the march once more, this time under orders to make a forceful demonstration to support General Burnside's attack at Fredericksburg. This expedition would be the largest Foster had yet mounted, consisting of 10,000 infantry, about 650 cavalry, and 40 cannon. As his main objective, he chose the vital railroad bridge over the Neuse River at Goldsboro, as sensitive a point for the Confederates as anything north of Wilmington. Foster also wanted to seize Goldsboro itself, if possible. Hence the large number of cannon he was taking the trouble to haul along -- they would be useful in fortifying the place, should he succeed.

It was "a splendid wintry morning, mild and serene" when the expedition moved out on December 11. Once the entire force was under way, it formed an ungainly column nearly five miles long. Foster's route of march followed the western course of the Trent River, skirting the vast Dover Swamp that lay between the Trent and the Neuse. On the first day, the expedition made about 14 miles, encountered no resistance, and was finally brought to a halt by a roadblock of felled trees. An attempt was made to outflank the obstacle, but the flanking routes ran into a maze of creeks and bogs. Foster encamped for the night while his soldiers, and their companies of Negro laborers, hacked through the roadblock.

Already, by the end of the first day, there were signs that the expedition might not be wholly a lark. The distance from New

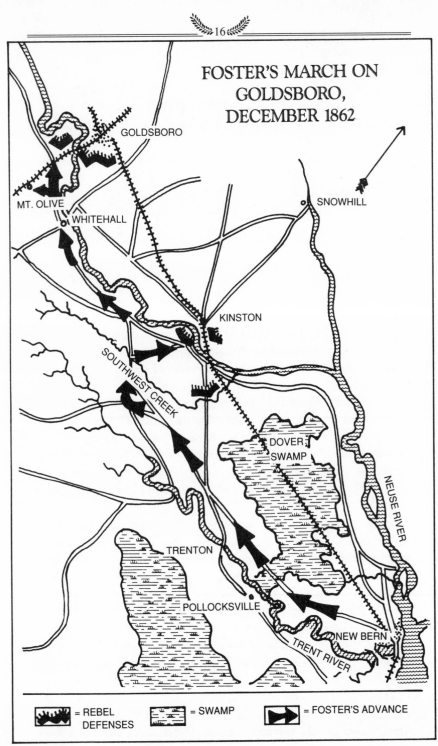

FOSTER'S MARCH ON
GOLDSBORO,
DECEMBER 1862

GOLDSBORO

SNOWHILL

MT. OLIVE

WHITEHALL

KINSTON

SOUTHWEST CREEK

DOVER
SWAMP

NEUSE RIVER

TRENTON

POLLOCKSVILLE

NEW BERN

TRENT RIVER

= REBEL
DEFENSES

= SWAMP

= FOSTER'S ADVANCE

Bern to Kinston looked deceptively short on the map, a mere 35 miles, and Foster's plan called for the march to be made in slow stages. Most regiments set out, therefore, with only a single day's rations in their knapsacks, assuming that the column's supply train would always be within hailing distance. No doubt it would have been, but for the fact that the wagons spent more time up to their axles in mud than they did actually moving. This situation got worse, not better, as the march progressed. Some units would march and fight for up to 24 hours without receiving any rations, which added plenty of incentive to do a little plundering along the way.

Nevertheless, for the as-yet-unbloodied soldiers of Foster's new regiments, the march started as a grand adventure. The mood was accurately reflected in this account by a young soldier in the 17th Massachusetts:

> After a tedious, plodding march of fourteen miles, the army bivouacked for the night on a plantation which seemed more fortunate than many others we passed. But its time had come, and as regiment after regiment arrived and stacked arms, it was a curious study to watch the rush they made for the nearest fence, as if by magic. As night darkened over the scene, the countless bivouac fires rose in all directions, casting a lurid glare up to the sky, and forming about as picturesque a scene as could possibly be imagined. And the sound of voices and laughter, the neighing of horses and the braying of mules, all combined to render...my first bivouac something to be remembered.[1]

The weather the next morning, December 12, was more seasonal. Overnight, the water had frozen in the men's canteens. There was more hard marching that day, and even a little fighting. The 9th New Jersey Regiment skirmished with some rebel pickets about three miles from Trenton, and a company of the 3rd New York Cavalry was bushwhacked, not very successfully, by some Confederate horsemen. After losing two men wounded, the New Yorkers charged their ambushers, killing or wounding several and capturing a few more, including the officer in charge.

There was more serious resistance the following day, December 13, when members of the 61st North Carolina Regiment opened fire from the north bank of Southwest Creek. The 3rd New York

Cavalry tried to take the bridge at a gallop, but found it partially destroyed and themselves under hot fire. After an hour of skirmishing, the 9th New Jersey fanned out on both sides of the bridge, outflanking the defenders, while one of Foster's batteries shelled them from the front. The North Carolinians retired in good order. Foster's men encamped that night about four miles south of Kinston.

A brisk little fight took place on the river that same Saturday afternoon, when the gunboat USS *Allison* got caught in a place where the channel was only 100 feet wide, and was roughly handled by a Confederate battery firing from a range of 1,200 yards. The top of her pilothouse was shot away, her smokestack was holed, and her decks badly chewed up. The *Allison* returned fire gamely with her forward gun, a 30-pounder Parrott rifle, and scored several hits on the rebel position. Then she retired out of range, her severed steam lines shrieking like a dozen banshees.

Two miles south of the Kinston bridge, the Confederates massed everything they had in Foster's path. Yet, even after the 61st North Carolina had fallen back and joined them, they still numbered only 2,014 men. Their commander, Brigadier General N.G. Evans, chose his ground with some skill. Evans established his line amid dense woods that formed a natural breastwork, with his right guarded by a swamp and his left anchored on a bend in the Neuse River. Having done that, however, Evans succumbed to funk. By the time Foster's column came into sight, he had managed to get staggering drunk -- but not too drunk, those around him were quick to observe, to neglect his personal safety. He stayed on the far side of the Neuse, near a 175-foot-long earthwork that had been thrown up behind the left flank of the main line on the south side of the river. His whiskey-addled slowness, compounded by his manifest cowardice, put the Confederates at as much of a disadvantage as Foster's superior numbers.

There was a lull between the time Foster's scouts located the rebel line and the start of the real fighting. While the artillery was skirmishing at long range, and while Foster's men were sweating it out waiting for the order to go forward,

...a negro teamster with his ammunition cart, was ordered forward to supply another battery on our right, whose caissons were running low on ammunition. The poor fellow thought he was going to his death, and if ever mortal fear displayed itself upon the countenance of any human being, it was upon that poor darkey's face. I shall never forget the wild rolling of his eyes, nor the frenzied and agonized expression of his face as he...guided his team in front of our regiment, urged on by our men with such encouraging remarks as "Go it, nig; don't be afraid!" -- "You're a goner, old darkey!" -- "Good bye!" -- "Won't the Rebs chew him up!"[2]

Foster deployed his men on both sides of the road, in concentric semicircles that matched the rebel line. Between the two forces on the west side of the road (Foster's left) was swampy ground, much of it impassable. On Foster's right, the two forces were separated by a swath of extremely dense woods, knotted with briar snarls and bogs. The 9th New Jersey moved in first. The foliage was so thick that the Confederates permitted the attacking companies to get as close as 75 yards before cutting loose with a sheet of rifle fire, supported by artillery fire from batteries on both sides of the river. The New Jersey regiment was pummeled to a standstill. When its ammunition ran low, the 85th Pennsylvania was hurried up to relieve it.

Cannon fire from the rebel line was severe. The 45th Massachusetts, attempting with little success to advance on Foster's left, encountered both dreadful terrain and fierce resistance. "The swamp was densely covered with huge old trees," wrote one survivor, "whose gnarled roots were twisted in all possible contortions beneath the slime and ooze of the bog." The massed fire of a Confederate battery to the regiment's front "cut a perfectly stripped path two rods [33 feet] wide through the forest."[3]

Over on the right, in the forest, conditions were even more chaotic. Visibility was so limited that some of Foster's units fired at each other, and his artillerymen unwittingly dropped dozens of rounds into friendly formations, causing great anxiety and resentment. A Massachusetts trooper recorded his baptism of fire in these words:

At about ten we left the main road and marched into a cornfield, crossing which we entered a swampy piece of woods where there was not the least vestige of a road. The swamp became deeper as we

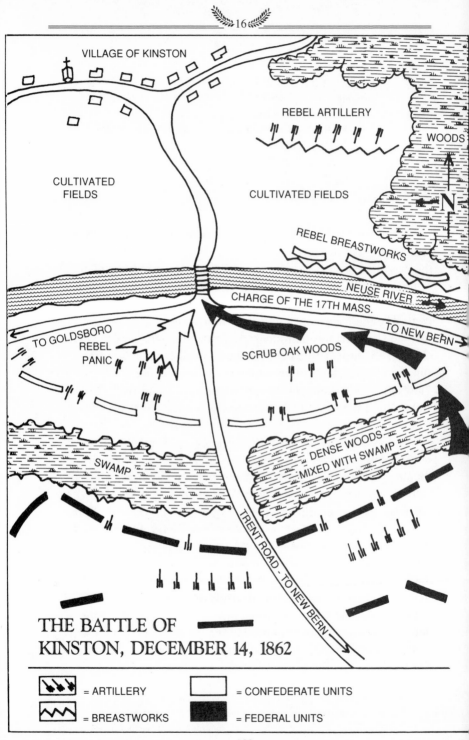

THE BATTLE OF
KINSTON, DECEMBER 14, 1862

advanced, until in many places it was up to our knees, in some cases waist deep. We had to struggle along as best we could; several times I became so enlaced in the vines and shrubbery that I found it almost impossible to extricate myself. We had not gone far in this way before we were obliged to pass under the fire of one of our own batteries; of course we felt perfectly safe in doing this, not supposing we would be shot by our own men, when to our unspeakable horror the first shot from the battery carried away half the head of a man in Co. D.[4]

Other young men found crystalline moments of near-poetry in their first combat experience. Another young New Englander wrote: "The music of rifle balls is in strange contrast to their deadly errand. It is a low, soft, singing tone, pleasant as a child's voice, almost like a loving sigh. It isn't a music that pays much attention to time."[5]

Eventually, despite the confusion and terrain, Foster managed to turn the Confederate left, manned mostly by some understrength regiments of South Carolina volunteers. General Evans — observing this movement through somewhat bleary eyes from his position on the far shore — assumed that all of his command was in retreat. It was not. The North Carolina regiments in the center and on the right flank were still closely engaged, and quite unaware that their whole left flank had already caved in. Evans ordered the bridge to be set afire, then, compounding the error, ordered his artillery on the far bank to begin shelling what he supposed were "abandoned" Confederate positions -- lines which were, in fact, full of his own soldiers.

Already under heavy fire from Foster's guns to their front, and now suddenly smitten with canister from behind, the North Carolinians quickly gave way. Their retirement was orderly at first, until they caught sight of the Kinston bridge slowly being engulfed in flames. Then panic set in. Men raced across the burning bridge with their hair curling to ashy dust. One poor fellow stumbled halfway across, causing a ghastly pileup. Scenting victory, Foster's men, spearheaded by the 17th Massachusetts, charged toward the crossing. The sight they beheld as they ran was unforgettable:

As we neared the bridge, we beheld a rout -- an almost indescribable body of men running for their lives. All discipline seemed lost, and casting aside guns, equipment and clothing, anything in fact that retarded their flight, they fled like a herd of deer, while close on their heels came...the charging columns of our men. It was a magnificent, and yet it was a pitiable sight...some of the poor fellows who had been wounded by our fire on the retreat, or who had been trampled down in the rush of the flying host, were burned to cinders, and I could actually see the fat seething and boiling in the hollow of the temple of one of the charred remains."[6]

Evans reformed his shattered little army on the outskirts of Kinston, got control of his own nerve, to some extent -- perhaps fear of a court martial had something to do with it -- and welcomed the addition of the 47th North Carolina Regiment. His men began urgently erecting breastworks. Foster sent a courier under a white flag to inquire if Evans wished to surrender. Evans snarled back, "You tell your general to go to hell!" -- brave words indeed for a man who had just finished shelling his own troops, and whose premature order to fire the bridge had resulted in the capture of 400 men.

Before Foster could call his bluff, Evans decided to withdraw rather than offer continued battle to Foster's aroused men. He did this rather dishonestly, by arranging for a truce to evacuate the women and children of Kinston, but actually to give his own force some breathing space. Foster was very annoyed when he learned of this dishonorable ruse, and he permitted his men to give Kinston a thorough sacking. "Feathers were seen all over the ground," wrote one trooper from the 3rd Massachusetts, "indicating that someone had been engaged in the poultry business on an immense scale."[7]

Foster's losses in the battle at Kinston were approximately 160 killed and wounded. Evans, whose men were under better cover, lost 125, plus the 400 men taken prisoner. One loss that hit Foster hard was that of Colonel Charles O. Gray of the 96th New York Regiment. A popular officer, Gray died not in battle, but rather as the result of a freak accident. Gray was leading a detachment of men who were trying to extinguish the burning bridge when a musket, dropped by one of the fleeing Confederates, ignited in the flames and fired a Minie ball into his breast.

Despite the intense fighting, there was one humorous incident that rapidly passed into legend among Foster's men. During the morning's fighting, the chaplain of one of the Massachusetts regiments, encountering an artilleryman being carried from the field on a stretcher, bent down to comfort the injured man.

"Were you supported by divine inspiration?" asked the chaplain.

"No," growled the wounded trooper. "We were supported by the 9th New Jersey."

On the Neuse River, below Kinston, the Union gunboats remained at anchor that night, their crews alert and armed to repel boarders. They had fired some long-range shells into Evans's position during the battle, but they weren't able to get close enough to materially contribute to the victory. They would have to return downstream on Sunday, for the river was getting dangerously low, and a drop of five more inches would leave them high and dry as prizes for the rebels.

Men described as "guerrillas" -- probably local "partisan ranger" companies out looking for easy pickings -- fired on the ships for 20 miles of their downriver voyage. They managed to kill one U.S. Marine gunner and wound three sailors, and to puncture the vessels' superstructures with hundreds of holes. The gunboats, of course, returned fire, and almost certainly inflicted much heavier losses on their assailants. Some of the Minie balls found embedded in the vessels looked like they had been dipped in verdigris, and others were tightly wrapped in copper wire -- the former designed to cause septic wounds, the latter to horribly rip the flesh when they struck. Both types of projectiles were variants on the dum-dum bullet concept, were against all "civilized" conventions of warfare, and prompted the Yankees to label the snipers as savages.

Late on the afternoon of December 14, Foster received news that General Burnside had been trounced at Fredericksburg. That meant there were sure to be heavy rebel reinforcements entraining for Goldsboro at that very moment. Nevertheless, Foster was determined to press on and at least burn the bridge, do what other damage he could, and then scoot back to New Bern before the enemy could concentrate sufficient forces to really threaten him. The relative ease with which he had broken Evans's formidable line must have encouraged him.

Foster marched his men back across the scorched bridge on December 15, heading once more for Goldsboro. He encamped that night a few miles below the village of Whitehall, and sent part of his cavalry to scout in that direction. The horsemen arrived in time to observe some Confederates setting fire to the Neuse River bridge. Foster's cavalry unlimbered the cannon they had brought with them and shelled the rebel positions until it was too dark to see. The cavalry commander thereupon decided to illuminate the scene. His men placed 2,000 barrels of turpentine along the south side of the river and ignited them more or less simultaneously. The resulting inferno was hard to match for sheer spectacle -- it lit up several square miles of countryside -- but was of value mainly because it enabled Foster's men to draw a bead on a partly finished rebel warship tied up to the opposite shore. It was, in fact, the first incarnation of the CSS *Neuse*, and if it wasn't destroyed on that night, it wasn't for want of trying.

First, a private from the 3rd New York Cavalry named Butler attempted to swim the river and set fire to the ship. He was driven back by "a perfect shower of bullets." The Yankees then fired canister rounds from the southern bank of the river, but this did little except chew up the vessel's timbers. Finally, the ship was pounded by solid shot and explosive shells. After this barrage, it was left in a derelict condition, low in the water.

Just as he had done by occupying Kinston for the night and then recrossing the river, Foster made another feint at Whitehall. The morning after the turpentine bonfire, he arrived on the scene personally, only to find the bridge burned and the enemy strongly entrenched on the far shore. He detached one brigade, with strong artillery support, to demonstrate noisily at the crossing, as though the whole army were trying to force its way across. The resulting engagement was more of a long-range rifle and cannon duel than anything else -- the two armies never actually came to grips -- but by all accounts it was an intense firefight. "A hornet's nest and no mistake" was how one participant described it. The North Carolina troops blocking Foster would have suffered severe casualties had they not thrown up a stout breastwork of saw logs. As it was, they suffered 10 killed and 42 wounded in the exchange.

Following this hotly contested feint, Foster resumed his progress toward Goldsboro. On December 16, Foster sent a raiding party of cavalry, five companies in all, to tear up any railroad tracks they could find in the vicinity. The horsemen elected to strike at Mount

Olive Station:

> On leaving the main column we pressed rapidly on, on regular and
> by-roads until we reached a swamp. Here we struck a turpentine path,
> and after a full gallop of over four miles, came out at this station at
> 3 PM. This action was a perfect surprise to the people of the place.
> The agent was selling tickets; passengers were loitering around
> waiting for the cars, the mail for Wilmington lay ready on the
> platform, and a few paroled prisoners were in readiness to go to
> Wilmington, probably to fight again.[8]

Foster's men arrested everyone, then cut the telegraph wires.
Two companies of cavalry were sent another seven miles southeast
to tear up some trestlework. Yet another company, with one
cannon rattling along for the ride, rode 3.5 miles toward Goldsboro
and managed to ambush the mail train just as it was leaving town.
The New Yorkers unlimbered their fieldpiece and put three shells
into the train before the engineer could back it out of range. Then
they rejoined the rest of the detachment at Mount Olive Station.
There, the main force had been busy building enormous bonfires of
railroad ties, using the heat to warp the rails. All this took place
under the dismayed and astonished eyes of their prisoners.

On the morning of December 17, Foster was ready to strike at
his main objective, the great railroad bridge at Goldsboro. Defending the vital crossing were three North Carolina regiments under
General Thomas Clingman. Again, as at Whitehall, the fight was
mostly conducted at long range, and mostly between the artillery.

The only Federal infantry regiment that really got mixed up in
heavy action near the bridge was the 17th Massachusetts, rapidly
becoming Foster's workhorse unit. As the regiment advanced,
using the elevated railroad embankment as a breastwork, they came
under hot fire. They pressed on gallantly, unfurling the regimental
colors "so the damned Rebs can see what we fight under!" As they
neared the bridge, they came under heavy volley fire from the
treeline on their left. To those watching the regiment's progress, it
appeared as though half the men had been struck down at once, but
actually they were all rolling for cover on the righthand side of the
embankment. They soon began to return fire. The rebels firing at
them, from a range of about 200 yards, seemed confused by the

height of the embankment, and consistently fired low. Soon Foster
sent a battery of artillery to support the 17th. It wheeled up into a
field on the right side of the railroad and opened a blistering
canister barrage on the treeline.

Finally the Bay Staters were close enough to try for the bridge.
The first group of men who rushed it were met with "a perfect
death-shower of bullets." One officer, who had dressed for the
occasion in a captured Confederate uniform, was driven from the
bridge, railroad ties splintering all around his flying feet, and was
heard to exclaim as he dove for cover: "No use! No use! It can't be
done!" Colonel Fellows, the much-admired commander of the 17th
Massachusetts, called for volunteers. A lieutenant named Barnabas
Mann and two privates named Edmands and Besse stepped forward. Equipping themselves with bundles of prepared combustibles, they ran forward to try their luck. This time, the bridge
ignited, although Mann was severely wounded in the stomach as he
tried to regain friendly lines.

Just as the bridge began to catch fire, cheers were heard from the
rebel side of the river. A train had just arrived, bearing part of
General James J. Pettigrew's brigade as reinforcements. The Union
battery supporting the 17th Massachusetts quickly repositioned
itself, and its captain stood boldly on the railroad embankment to
call out corrections to the fall of shot — the Confederate train was
the most tempting target they had ever seen, and for the moment all
danger was forgotten. A mood of high excitement seized the Union
gunners and the pinned-down men of the 17th. The rebel train
carried not only troops, but also an iron-plated "monitor" car that
began lobbing shells which burst over the heads of the crouching
New Englanders. But on this occasion the Yankee gunners were
better, and their third shot blew up the train's boiler. A fierce
geyser of white steam arched into the air, scalding several nearby
unfortunates.

With the railroad bridge blazing and Confederate reinforcements
already arriving, Foster decided not to push his luck. He ordered a
general withdrawal, protected by a rear-guard brigade under
Colonel H.C. Lee. Firing had just about tapered off, and most of
Foster's column was well on its way back toward New Bern, when
Lee's brigade was suddenly struck by a desperately brave Confed-

erate counterattack that materialized out of the woods without warning.

Every account of this incident differs as to the number of attackers -- there was probably a regiment, at least -- and as to the distance the attackers had covered before Lee's men opened fire on them. Some accounts say they got as close as 60 yards, but most put it at 200-300 yards, which is certainly close enough. All existing accounts, except a few superficial sentences, were recorded by Yankees, and all agree that the attack was pressed with "great dash and courage":

> Never did soldiers present better alignment than that rebel brigade; but when they saw that Belger's battery was supported by infantry, they made the fatal mistake of making a half right-wheel. "Aim! Fire!" commanded Captain Belger, when the rebel bayonets were not more than 200 yards from his battery. As the battery sent forth its deadly contents great gaps were made in the rebel ranks. Three times the colors were shot down and three times they were raised; but the fourth time they remained on the ground for want of any one to raise them. Some fifty of the men who had taken refuge behind a stack of fodder were served with grape and solid shot. It took but a moment to send both stack and men flying toward the woods; [another] fifty men became entangled by a fence and were treated to spherical case [projectiles], which bursting in their midst killed many of them.[9]

After this gallant but futile charge, the battle of the Goldsboro bridge came to an end. Foster could technically claim a victory in that he had, after all, burned the bridge, but that was an inconvenience to the enemy, not a catastrophe. Confederate repair crews had trains running across it again in about two weeks. The damage done to the Wilmington & Weldon Railroad was high-spirited but trifling.

Foster's own men had mixed feelings about the whole affair. Some found it an exhilarating experience; some came back convinced it had been an exercise in futility. As the men slogged back into New Bern, exhausted and hungry, all of them realized it had been the most costly Federal operation in North Carolina to date: 92 men killed and 487 wounded. Union losses would almost certainly have been greater had not the defenders been kept off-balance by Foster's rather elegant side-stepping maneuvers.

Confederate accounts of this little campaign are so skimpy that an accurate tally of casualties is impossible. Still, rebel losses must have been somewhat higher, even if one leaves out the 400-odd men captured at the Kinston bridge.

Union General Ambrose Burnside. Although Burnside's performance at Manassas/Bull Run and other battles was mediocre at best, he organized and led his expedition against North Carolina with consummate professionalism.

Typical of the converted civilian craft purchased at the start of the war was this former tugboat, the USS *Shawsheen*, armed with two 20-pounder rifled guns. She was part of Burnside's naval support and participated in the fighting at Roanoke Island.

The Mosquito Fleet's finest hour: the ambush and capture of the Federal gunboat *Fanny*, off Chicamacomico on the Outer Banks.

Civil War Naval Chronology

Burnside's ships steaming up the Neuse River before the attack on New Bern.

North Carolina Department of Cultural Resources

The bombardment of Fort Hatteras on August 27, 1861 by the Union fleet under Commodore Silas Stringham.

Sailors aboard the Union blockade ships fought boredom as best they could, often with their own musical ensembles.

The *Albemarle* as she looked after the war, just before being scrapped.

Commander Stephen C. Rowan's Union flotilla wipes out the valiant little Mosquito Fleet in the Battle of Elizabeth City. For the Confederates, the odds were suicidal: They had 5 ships mounting 11 guns against 14 Union ships mounting 40 guns.

Major General John G. Foster, who replaced Burnside as commander-in-chief of the Union forces on the coast of North Carolina.

A gun crew drilling aboard the USS *Miami* before the attack on Fort Fisher. One Yankee seaman is carrying a brush soaked in water to swab out the gun barrel between rounds. (This helped prevent stray sparks from accidentally igniting the fresh powder of the next charge.) Another sailor is adjusting the elevating screw at the rear of the piece.

Sometimes the Union blockade crews staged impromptu minstrel shows. One ship even had a trained bear that drank champagne.

The USS *Sassacus* is disabled after being rammed by the CSS *Albemarle*.

The USS *Southfield* is sunk by the *Albemarle*.

William Baker Cushing, "Lincoln's Commando." A man who thrived on danger and the excitement of battle, Cushing was happiest when leading a small band of hand-picked men deep into enemy territory.

The sinking of the *Albemarle*: Cushing detonates the torpedo while staring down the mouth of an eight-inch Confederate gun about to open fire.

A view of the torpedo launch used by Cushing and his men in their attack on the *Albemarle*.

Colonel William Lamb, the journalist-turned-soldier who led the Confederate defense of Fort Fisher with skill and great courage, only to be sacrificed by the inertia and incompetence of General Braxton Bragg.

The *Sassacus* plows into the *Albemarle*, pushing the Confederate ironclad's starboard side deep into the water and flooding part of her gun deck.

This view of the landface at Fort Fisher shows how well-protected were the Confederate guns between the mounts. Note the hunks of shrapnel littering the ground.

A contemporary view of the Mound Battery at Fort Fisher, sketched just after the battle. The debris in the foreground consists of cannonballs and shrapnel from the fierce Union naval bombardment.

A Confederate blockade runner is forced aground near Wilmington.

Admiral David D. Porter, commander of the Union naval forces during the attacks on Fort Fisher. Porter thought Union General Benjamin Butler was a fool and a poltroon, and gloated shamelessly at his downfall.

Admiral Porter's sailors and Marines assault the Northeast Bastion of Fort Fisher. Though bloodily repulsed, the attack did draw the Confederate garrison's attention away from the main Union thrust near the Cape Fear River, thus contributing to the Federal victory.

General Benjamin F. Butler, one of the most unsavory officers in the U.S. Army. The failure of his "powder boat" scheme, and the subsequent collapse of his attack on Fort Fisher, prompted General Ulysses S. Grant to sack him — something Grant was only too happy to do.

A damaged gun position at Fort Fisher. The weapon's muzzle was blown off by the Union naval bombardment and can be seen on the hillock just behind the emplacement.

PART 4

CONFEDERATE MOVES

D.H. HILL COMES...AND GOES

On February 25, 1863, General Robert E. Lee appointed Major General James Longstreet commander of the Department of Virginia and North Carolina. This move, undertaken as part of a general consolidation following Lee's impressive victory over Burnside at Fredericksburg, heralded a somewhat more aggressive Confederate posture in eastern North Carolina. Longstreet was keenly aware of how vital the agricultural products of those counties were to Lee's Army of Northern Virginia, and of how vulnerable the supply lines were because of their proximity to Union enclaves on the coast. Longstreet conceived of a major demonstration in front of New Bern and Washington, designed to pin the enemy inside his perimeters while Confederate supply convoys loaded up provisions in the surrounding counties, free from interference.

To run the show, Longstreet selected, with Lee's full agreement, General D.H. Hill. A North Carolinian with a reputation for being a fighter, Hill seemed a perfect choice. And indeed, his first proclamation to the North Carolina regiments under his command, issued on the same day he was appointed by Lee, promised vigorous action. On the whole, the troops greeted the change in command with enthusiasm. Perhaps, at long last, a serious campaign would be mounted to recapture the coast. One Raleigh newspaper greeted Hill's appointment with the following editorial comment:

> We have had vastly too much strategy, too much science, and too

much digging and ditching in North Carolina. Had we less of these
and more fighting, things might have been different than at present;
and as General Hill has established a reputation for being one of the
best fighting men in the service, we may expect a change in
management...in North Carolina.[1]

To augment Hill's striking power, Longstreet ordered 4,000 men
detached from the defenses at Wilmington, bringing Hill's total
force to about 14,500 men -- roughly comparable to the total Union
strength in the state, due to the fact that Foster had been ordered to
detach 10,000 of his 24,000 men to reinforce Admiral DuPont's
expedition against Charleston. That D.H. Hill had a sound strategic
grasp of the situation seems clear from the long, detailed memorandum he wrote Longstreet on the day he took command. In it, he
stated his belief that, if reinforced with "a single good brigade," he
could "drive the enemy to his strongholds" and restore confidence
among the planters in the eastern part of the state. He singled out
Pitt, Bertie, and Edgecombe as counties especially rich in crops
and direly in need of reassurance. He also believed that, by stirring
things up in eastern North Carolina, he could divert Federal attention and resources from the offensive against Charleston.

Longstreet's operational plan called for Hill to make a diversionary attack on New Bern and a surprise assault on Washington,
the weaker and more vulnerable of the two Union bastions. Meanwhile, Confederate supply trains would systematically take out all
the accumulated produce in the bountiful counties west of and
between those places. Bad weather, including heavy late-winter
rains that made the roads in several counties impassable, thwarted
Hill's plans to mount both operations simultaneously, however. He
chose instead to concentrate first on New Bern.

The resulting operation is still something of a puzzle. Bigger by
far than it needed to be for a "demonstration," Hill designed the
undertaking as though it were truly an all-out attempt to recapture
New Bern. Indeed, most of his commanders and men assumed
that's what it was. And yet it was conducted with a curious lack of
urgency that ultimately insured its failure. Hill himself seems to
have been in bad form. Ill, dyspeptic, in a perpetually scratchy
mood, he spent inordinate amounts of time venting his spleen in
sarcastic memoranda to Richmond and to his subordinate com-

manders. To General Pettigrew, for instance, he wrote: "...I have
been torturing my brain to devise a system by which our cavalry
can be got under fire. Can you help me?" Later on, he suggested
that if Pettigrew's "timid" horsemen gave him wrong information
one more time, he would "threaten them with death." These were
not the words of a commander who had faith in his troops.

Ironically, Hill's plan of attack was so good that it should have
worked, but he failed to light a hot enough fire under the officers
detailed to carry it out. The crux of the problem seems to be that
Hill himself was never sure, from one hour to the next, exactly how
far he wanted to push things at New Bern. His waffling attitude
trickled down to his subordinates and infected them with a bad case
of the "pokes." Were they supposed to risk it all and go for the
jugular, or just keep the Yankees occupied long enough for the
wagon trains to load up with corn in the interior?

Hill planned his attack to make use of the four roads that led
from Kinston to the coast, at various points around New Bern. One
brigade, under General Junius Daniel, advanced toward New Bern
via the "lower Trent Road." Hill's cavalry troops, most of whom
were quite aware that they were held in low regard by their commander, were to march along the south bank of the Trent River,
under the command of General B.H. Robertson. As they advanced,
they were to tear up the Atlantic & North Carolina Railroad near
New Bern. General Pettigrew, with most of Hill's artillery, under
Major John Haskell, was to attack Fort Anderson, across the Neuse
River from New Bern. They were to engage and if possible sink
any Federal gunboats that might be supporting the city's defenses,
and to seal off the river from any naval reinforcements.

General Daniel struck the city's defenses first, on March 13, and
enjoyed considerable success. Despite a strong Union counterattack, Daniel's fired-up troops overran and stubbornly held onto the
first line of entrenchments covering the rail line into the city, on the
peninsula formed by the Neuse and Trent rivers.

Across the river, however, things went rather strangely. Pettigrew showed every intention of sweeping into Fort Anderson. He
pushed his men hard on the approach march, and when he spoke he
seemed full of bellicose intent. But by the time his men got within
cannon range of the fort, they were so exhausted -- and so hungry,

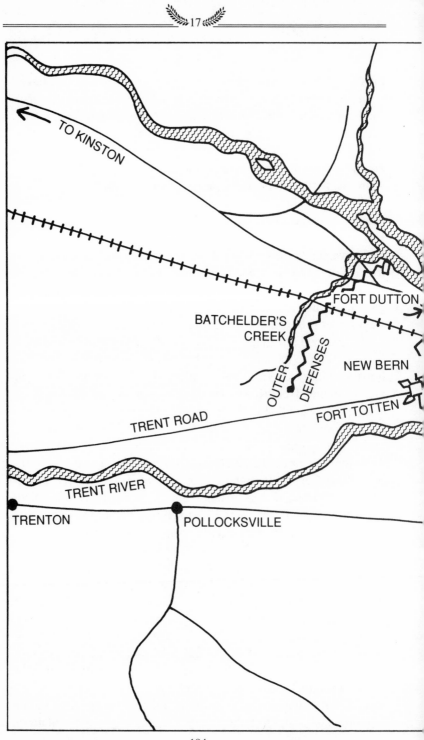

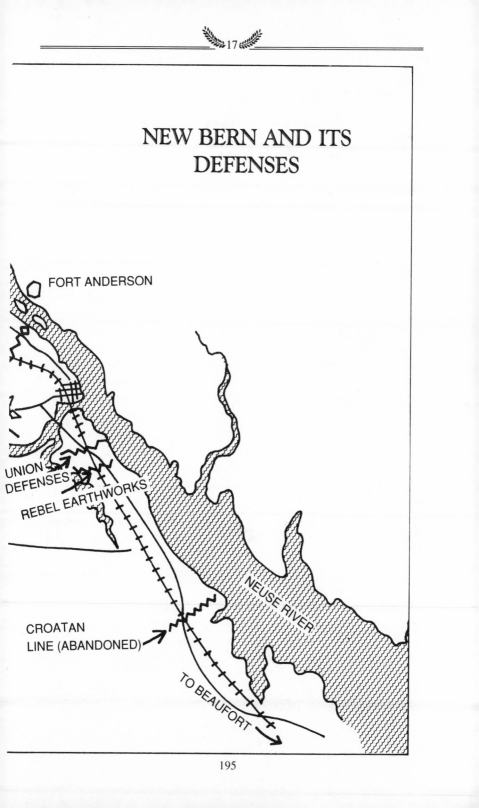

NEW BERN AND ITS DEFENSES

FORT ANDERSON

UNION DEFENSES

REBEL EARTHWORKS

NEUSE RIVER

CROATAN LINE (ABANDONED)

TO BEAUFORT

having outrun their supply train by a considerable distance -- that he was compelled to forget any offensive action for a full day and night.

Fort Anderson was a stout little earthwork bastion which could be approached, on its landward side, only by means of a slender causeway flanked by swamps. Storming it would have been costly. Pettigrew estimated he might have lost more than 100 men in the attempt. On the other hand, he might have won the battle, in which case 100 men made a pretty fair equation. If Fort Anderson fell into Confederate hands, New Bern would be cut off from outside help and the Union positions could be bombarded at leisure.

Pettigrew decided instead to draw up his guns and commence a methodical siege bombardment. After a brief demonstration of his firepower (and his gunners' accuracy, for by all accounts their shooting was very good), Pettigrew made a serious mistake: He ceased firing and began surrender negotiations with the fort's commander, Colonel Hiram Anderson of the 92nd New York Regiment. Anderson was not about to surrender, however. He was merely stalling for time so he could summon some gunboats. When Anderson requested a cease-fire, ostensibly so he could communicate with General Foster, Pettigrew naively agreed.

When it finally dawned on Pettigrew that he was being hood-winked, he ordered his cannon to recommence firing, which they did with some effect. Had Pettigrew launched an infantry assault under cover of this bombardment, Fort Anderson probably would have been his -- the 92nd New York was utterly pinned down, and the fury of the rebel cannonade was so great that the surface of the Neuse River just behind the fort was made to look like "a pond in a hailstorm." The regiment designated to storm the fort, the 26th North Carolina, under the valiant young Harry K. Burgwyn, was straining at the leash. Every man, from Burgwyn down to the lowliest private, was convinced they could carry the fort in short order (though less convinced that taking it would bring total victory).

As usual, Harry penned a vivid account of the incident while it was still fresh in his mind:

The plan was for the Brigade to go...immediately opposite New Berne [sic], take the fort there & then drive off or sink the Yankee gunboats, then shell & if possible dismount the guns on the Yankee intrenchments [sic] at New Berne while [Hill] attacked them in front. To do this we had infantry and smooth bored artillery enough to take the Fort but to sink the shipping & etc. we had 4 twenty pdr. Parrott guns and 5 or 6 light rifled guns [probably Whitworths]. These proved perfectly incompetent to damage the boats. One of the...Parrotts exploded killing & wounding 3 men and the men who manned the others were distrustful of firing them. Besides[,] the gunboats kept so far off that the light rifles could scarcely hit them & it was perfectly casual where and whom they hit. As the guns could not damage the boats there was no necessity to storm the fort.

My Rgt. was in front & was to do the storming. After driving in the pickets I advanced within from 540 to 600 yards of the fort & remained there 6 hours all the time being shelled upon an almost level plateau by the miserable gunboats. They had a man in the masthead who would direct their fire & they burst their shells amongst us, over us, & in front of us, with wonderful precision...I lost 17 men....[2]

Gradually, the initiative passed to the defenders. Gunboats gathered in the river opposite Pettigrew's position and hurled heavy fire at his men. As Burgwyn noted in his letter, one of Pettigrew's guns exploded, and shortly afterward another one broke down. Left with only four light-caliber guns capable of hitting the gunboats, Pettigrew passed the word to withdraw. Both Harry Burgwyn and Major Haskell, the chief of artillery, argued that it was not too late to storm the fort, and they assured Pettigrew that if they captured the work, they would be close enough to the gunboats to engage them on approximately even terms. Pettigrew rejected their arguments and started his men back.

The other major component of Hill's offensive, General Robertson's cavalry, contributed virtually nothing, as Hill had feared. Hill had been begging Richmond to loan him General Wade Hampton's cavalry, but he didn't get them. Robertson's units, which Hill described in one memo as "wonderfully inefficient," engaged in no significant fighting whatsoever. In fact, they did nothing at all except tear up a small stretch of railroad track. Robertson himself never went near the front, which rendered his part of the operation not only listless but leaderless.

With two of his three attacks nullified, Hill abandoned any

thought of pushing ahead, and meekly withdrew. Casualties were very light on both sides: about two dozen killed or wounded among Hill's men, perhaps half that many among the defenders. The whole display was more of a nuisance to the Yankees than a threat. Some Southern newspapers managed to claim this fiasco as a major victory -- many of them citing an utterly fabulous statistic of 1,500 Yankees taken prisoner -- but the men who had taken part knew better. Wrote one veteran, not long after the operation was abandoned: "No one down here knows what General Hill intended to do...these big generals don't always have such deep laid plans as people give them credit for."[3]

At least Hill's demonstration provided good cover for the foraging operations behind it. Equally successful was a secondary, and quite bloodless, operation in front of Plymouth, where a 2,500-man Confederate force effectively bottled up the Union garrison of that town long enough for the supply trains to round up an impressive amount of provisions from the countryside, including 35,000 pounds of bacon.

Whatever Hill had really intended to do at New Bern, he next turned his attention to little Washington, N.C., in Beaufort County. At first, Hill acted with much more energy than he had displayed at New Bern, and by April 1, Washington seemed seriously threatened. Hill placed batteries on the banks of the Pamlico River, drove pilings into the water, and sunk block-ships, all to prevent Foster from reinforcing the town by water. Two infantry brigades were positioned to intercept any overland relief attempt from New Bern, while a third brigade (Garnett's Virginians) besieged the town itself.

There were 1,200 Federal troops defending Washington, supported by three gunboats. General Foster himself went there as soon as he heard Hill was in the vicinity, and he implemented vigorous measures to improve the town's security. New forts were erected, blockhouses sited to cover road junctions, and the woods around the town were leveled, out to a distance of half a mile, so any assault would have to cross open ground.

The siege became a standoff. There were regular bombardments and counter-bombardments, almost ritualistic in their timing and duration. Out on the gunboats, the regular evening bombardments were turned into a kind of twilight concert: One of the sailors would play a recital on a calliope, then the guns would bark for an hour or so. It was all quite gentlemanly. General Hill kept suggesting to his artillery commander, Major Haskell, that he should drop a few shells on General Foster's headquarters, but since the idea was advanced as a suggestion and not as an order, Haskell demurred, fearing that misplaced projectiles would inflict civilian casualties. Aside from the usual skirmishing between patrols and pickets, there was no infantry action, and neither side's shelling did much physical damage.

Even so, the situation inside Washington was not pleasant. Hill had clamped a tight ring around the town, and while his quartermaster troops were stuffing their wagons with corn and bacon in the surrounding counties, food grew scarce inside Washington. By the end of the first week, Foster's men were forced to go on short rations, and their morale was appreciably lowered. Another two weeks of this treatment, and Hill could have taken the town.

Foster intended to break the siege by moving up strong relief forces from New Bern. He left it to his subordinate officers to decide how this should be done -- by an overland march, or by landing somewhere on the banks of the Pamlico River, below Hill's batteries and river obstacles. There were three generals in New Bern who were in line to handle this responsibility. Two of them, General Prince and General Palmer, were professional soldiers. The third, General F.B. Spinola, was a "political general" with no field experience.

General Prince drew the job first -- a logical choice -- but experienced a dire failure of nerve on his very first reconnaissance. "He took a steamer to the mouth of the Pamlico River, got a good look at [Hill's fortifications], became sick at his stomach, and retired ingloriously to New Bern."[4]

Next to try his luck was General Spinola. He chose to move overland, across Craven County. Hill had anticipated such a move, of course, and had positioned part of Pettigrew's brigade to block it. These troops were entrenched at a place called Blount's Mill, on a superb piece of ground: a fairly high (for the coast) ridge, terraced in appearance, overlooking a point where the road threaded along a narrow causeway flanked on both sides by impassable swamps. When Spinola's column drew up in front of this position, the Confederates unleashed severe and accurate fire. Pettigrew's gunners had measured the range to the foot and had pre-cut the fuses on their shells. One Union battery, firing in support of the doughty 17th Massachusetts Regiment, lost all of its horses and both of its officers.

Colonel Fellows, commander of the 17th Massachusetts, saw that his men were in a well-plotted bull's eye and resorted to a clever ruse to relieve some of the pressure. In his best parade-ground voice, he called out: "Seventeenth: *Fall back!*", certain that the command would be heard by the Confederates. After bellowing the command several times, he passed word in a much quieter voice for the regiment to halt and lie down. Due to the smoke and densely wooded terrain, Hill's gunners assumed what Fellows wanted them to assume and almost immediately began to raise their fire. Soon most of the Confederate shells were exploding harmlessly a hundred yards behind Fellows and his men.

To break this stalemate, the militarily ignorant Spinola ordered one company of the 17th to charge the causeway -- under the circumstances, the equivalent of a death sentence. Unflinchingly, the chosen men marched to their jumping-off point as though on a drill field, eliciting admiration from all who saw them. Once in position, they eyed the causeway nervously, knowing that, in addition to several hundred rifles, about a dozen cannon were going to sweep it with massed canister the minute anyone attempted to cross it. Not one man in the company expected to reach the far side of the causeway alive and unwounded.

At this tense juncture, a staff officer rode up and saw the company drawn up for the charge. He asked Colonel Fellows, "What is this company doing here?"

"They're going to charge the causeway," Fellows replied somberly.

"What? Who ordered it?" demanded the staff officer.

"General Spinola," answered Fellows.

With a scowl, the staff officer wagged his finger at Fellows and admonished, "Don't dare to move, sir, until I return." Then he rode off in search of Spinola. When he found the general, he told him he was lodging a formal protest against sending that company to certain death. "If you order it forward, I shall order it back, and will take the responsibility." Colonel Fellows joined the two men and the discussion became heated. Spinola wanted to save face, but his military reputation was already something of a joke, and he now began to envision a court of inquiry pitting himself against two experienced officers with sterling combat records. After arguing for a few minutes, he abruptly canceled his Charge-of-the-Light-Brigade order and commanded the whole column to return to New Bern. For the sacrificial company of the 17th Massachusetts, it had been a close call; Pettigrew's men had been praying that someone would be fool enough to try to storm that causeway.

By April 10, when General Foster received word of this latest fiasco to relieve his besieged town, he concluded that the only way to get the job done properly was to do it himself. He therefore proposed to leave Washington, run the river gauntlet back to New Bern, and take charge of the relief effort in person. On April 13, his mood was brightened by the arrival of the 5th Rhode Island Regiment. The steamer *Escort* had carried the new regiment past the Confederate river batteries unharmed, thanks partly to poor Confederate gunnery and partly to the fact that her machinery and crew spaces had been protected by stacks of wet hay bales. Confident that the regiment would enable Washington to hold out until he could return with a relief column, Foster resolved to take the same lucky boat back downstream on the night of April 15.

The ship's pilot, a gentleman named Pedrick, advised Foster to wait and make the run in daylight. Even without all the Confederate obstructions, he said, the river was too tricky to try at night. General Foster had heard rumors that Pedrick was secretly a Confederate sympathizer and suspected him of planning treachery. He agreed to the daylight run, but to make sure Pedrick didn't run the ship aground intentionally, Foster stationed himself in the wheelhouse with a revolver in his hand.

As soon as it was light enough to navigate, the *Escort* slipped her moorings and headed downriver toward Pamlico Sound. Captain Pedrick proved to be a man of iron nerve, coolly taking the ship past obstacles, keeping it off sand bars, and steering fearlessly through a forest of waterspouts as Hill's batteries, along with numerous sharpshooters, rained shots on the river. The *Escort* was struck by 40 artillery rounds, as well as hundreds of fragments and Minie balls, and the ship looked as if it had been mauled by a giant bear. One solid shot crashed into General Foster's stateroom and blew his bed to pieces; luckily, the general was elsewhere at the time. Another cannonball penetrated the galley and took off the cook's arm. On the whole, however, casualties were very light. As on the previous trip, the wet hay bales proved remarkably effective as improvised armor. General Foster began to feel a bit foolish, standing in the wheelhouse with his unholstered pistol -- clearly, Captain Pedrick was no traitor. Foster had reason to feel even worse a few moments later: "We were passing the last obstruction and Pedrick had just said to me: `I reckon we're all right now,' when he was shot. He exclaimed, `I'm killed, General, but by God, I'll get you through!'...I couldn't help it; I cried like a baby."

General Foster's dramatic getaway from Washington, the arrival of the 5th Rhode Island to strengthen the Washington garrison, and the successful completion of Confederate foraging operations in the nearby farmlands all convinced D.H. Hill that it was time to abandon the siege of Washington. He pulled his forces back before Foster could get a relief column into motion.

Hill wrote about the New Bern and Washington affairs as if they were major victories -- as indeed they could have been, had he acted with more determination and speed -- but the most they amounted to, really, were successful resupply operations. The situation in coastal North Carolina would never be quite so favorable for the Confederates again. Hill had enjoyed numerical equality with the Federals in the theater as a whole, and even enjoyed superiority at his chosen points of contact. Moreover, Hill had the initiative from the start. The Federals had been compelled to react to the Confederate moves, not the other way around, which was unusual in that region of the state. A better coordinated, more urgently led attack on New Bern would have had a better-than-fair chance of success, and Washington had been Hill's for the plucking. Moreover, Hill's troops, except for the cavalry, had felt themselves equal to the task.

Why Hill's performance was so uncharacteristically listless remains a mystery. Perhaps, like his patron Longstreet at the siege of Knoxville, he was just off his form; generals have bad days, too.

In any case, the window of opportunity closed soon after the siege of Washington was ended. Following his thundering victory at Chancellorsville in May 1863, Robert E. Lee began planning his biggest offensive of the war -- an invasion of Pennsylvania. Once more, the defenses of eastern North Carolina would be stripped bare to provide additional strength to the Army of Northern Virginia, and once again, General Foster would take advantage of the situation.

Yankee Raids

For a long time, General Foster had been irritated by the continuing presence of a rebel outpost at Gum Swamp, about eight miles below Kinston. His first attempt to clean out the place, on April 28, 1863, was only partly successful. He sent out more than 1,500 men, and they did succeed in forcing 180 men of the 56th North Carolina Regiment to leave the area, but only after an extremely hot skirmish in which four Confederates and ten Yankees were killed. General Hill reoccupied the outpost as soon as the Federal force retired to New Bern.

In late May, Foster tried again. He gave command of the expedition to one of his best officers, Colonel J.R. Jones of the 58th Pennsylvania Regiment. Jones's strike force consisted of five infantry regiments, a battalion of cavalry, and one three-gun battery of artillery. Jones sent three regiments, the guns, and the cavalry against the front of the Confederate position, while he personally led his own regiment, together with the 27th Massachusetts, along a neglected and overgrown path toward the Confederate rear. On the morning of May 22, both columns were supposed to strike at daybreak.

The frontal attack began as scheduled, but Colonel Jones didn't reach his jumping-off position until 9:30 a.m., due to the wild nature of the terrain. The delay didn't really affect the outcome, though. The Gum Swamp garrison, again the 56th North Carolina, was already under pressure from the front, and the sudden appearance of a strong force to the rear broke them quickly. Most of the rebels fled into the swamps, although 165 were captured.

Confederate reinforcements soon arrived from Kinston, how-

ever, and launched a counterattack that elicited rare praise from
D.H. Hill: "I never saw men behave better."[5] The attack's momentum drove the Federals back to the outer defenses of New Bern,
and during the final skirmishes, on May 23, the valiant Colonel
Jones was killed.

With the onset of hot weather, the fighting cooled down. June
saw little contact between the two armies, except for fairly regular
fraternization between the picket lines.

July 1863, however, proved to be a busy month in North Carolina (as it did elsewhere in the Confederacy). Action began on July
5 when a 650-man Union raiding party tore up some railroad track
near Warsaw, getting away unopposed. A bigger raid -- one of
Foster's more successful operations -- was launched a week and a
half later, this time using the largest cavalry force Foster had yet
employed, led by Brigadier General Edward Potter.

Potter's objectives were in Greenville, Tarboro, and Rocky
Mount: bridges, supplies, railroad track, prisoners -- whatever
damage he could do. He managed to do plenty. On July 19, he
captured Greenville without a fight, destroyed $300,000 worth of
supplies and property, looted the citizens, burned the Tar River
bridge, and rewarded his men by permitting them to drink their fill
from the local whiskey stocks. Thus fortified, they pushed on with
great energy and reached Sparta by midnight.

There, Potter detached one of his battalions, under Major Ferris
Jacobs, to strike out for Rocky Mount and destroy the railroad
bridge located there. Jacobs's column rode off at about 3 a.m. By 9
the next morning, after brushing aside trifling opposition by a
handful of pickets, Potter had captured Tarboro. There, he hit the
jackpot: a half-finished rebel ironclad was discovered, still on its
stocks. He burned the vessel, along with two steamboats, some
railroad equipment, 100 bales of cotton, and a considerable amount
of quartermaster goods. Late in the afternoon, learning that Confederate reinforcements were gathering across the Tar River, he
burned the local bridge and began retiring toward New Bern.

Major Jacobs rejoined the main column near dusk. He had been
wildly successful in Rocky Mount, capturing an entire train,
destroying 37 wagons full of supplies, and burning down a cotton
mill, a flour mill, a machine shop full of ironmongery, and 800

bales of cotton.

By now, however, the countryside was aroused, and little detachments of rebel horsemen began gathering near the wake of Potter's column and harassing his withdrawal. Potter's men had been in the saddle for four days with only a few hours' sleep, and the pace was starting to tell. Most of the 75 casualties Potter suffered during the operation were sustained after he passed through Sparta and finally made it back to New Bern on July 23. Toward the end, Potter's retreat became something of a scramble. As one member of the 50th North Carolina Regiment observed: "It is a wonderful thing to follow a retreating army in haste. So many things are strewn along the road; there were carriages that had been upset, throats of horses cut to prevent [their] falling into our lines...."[6] Potter would have suffered much heavier losses had the ill-disciplined Confederate pursuers not stopped so many times to do a bit of pillaging of their own.

The Yankees were not through with their raids. Perhaps the most sensitive target on the entire Wilmington & Weldon Railroad, except for the hub at Goldsboro, was the bridge at Weldon, not far from the Virginia state line. On July 26, Foster went after that too, disembarking with five regiments at what was left of Winton. His mission was to support a cavalry thrust from Virginia that was aimed at disrupting communications in the town of Weldon itself. Leading the advance were the 9th New Jersey and the 17th Massachusetts regiments, which were detailed to take a bridge over Potecasi Creek between Murfreesboro and Winton. The New Jersey troops disembarked first and marched off, but took the wrong road and had to retrace their steps. While they were getting oriented, the 17th Massachusetts took the proper road, not realizing that there were no friendly troops sweeping the path ahead of them. They were bushwhacked rather sharply by 200 men of the Murfreesboro Home Guard under Major Samuel Wheeler. This brave demonstration ended when the hard-breathing 9th New Jersey finally came trotting up the road and threw its weight into the attack.

With all his troops ashore and the valorous but hopeless resistance of the Murfreesboro men quashed, Foster spread out detachments to secure all the important road junctions in the area. Then he settled down to await the arrival of the Federal cavalry. His men foraged liberally in the countryside around Winton, and their appearance had an electric effect on the local slave population:

> ...Negroes by the hundreds followed us on our return march to Winton, with little bundles tied up and swung on sticks over their shoulders, shouting "We's gwine to liberty, hi-yah, gwine to liberty!" The Negroes would stop work in the fields, gaze at the Yankee column a few minutes, drop hoe or axe, and fling up their old hats and shout "Gwine to liberty!" Their day had come at last. At some plantations the mistress of the house would try to stop the slaves from leaving, but it was of no use. "Missus, we's gwine to liberty." On all the plantations no white men were visible -- the darkies said "All in the Rebel Army." A motley procession it was as we reached bivouac at Winton.[7]

In their leisure time, some men of Company C, the 9th New Jersey, discovered that there were some strange critters lurking in the murky depths of Potecasi Creek. One fisherman hauled in something "nearly two feet in length [which] propelled itself while on land with...six short legs, equidistant along its disgusting-looking body. It was a repulsive creature." It was also energetic and kept scrambling to get back into the water while the startled soldiers gathered around and tried to figure out what they had caught. It was not an eel, not a reptile, and didn't look like any amphibious lizard anyone was familiar with. Finally, wrote one eyewitness, "[We] had to kill it because of its intractability."

The Union cavalry force arrived on July 27, commanded by Colonel S.P. Spear. They were soon ferried across the Chowan River and set forth on their mission to Weldon.

This time, the Confederates reacted with alacrity. As soon as news reached Petersburg that Federal cavalry was across the Chowan, General Matt Ransom's brigade was immediately put into motion for the Weldon front. Ransom himself arrived at daybreak on July 28. He found a tiny army indeed: 200 men and two fieldpieces. There is some confusion about what unit these men were with. Several accounts say they were men from one of Ransom's own regiments, the 24th North Carolina. More recent research, based on local citizens' recollections and documents of General Ransom now in the hands of his descendants, indicates that perhaps the 200 men were local militia from the Weldon Provost Guards. Whatever unit they belonged to, on that day they earned a little glory, as did their energetic and resourceful commander.

After posting his men at Boone's Mill, Ransom rode out to reconnoiter. Not long after they started, Ransom and his escort heard "a great shout," turned in their saddles, and saw hundreds of bluecoated cavalrymen bearing down on them from a distance of 250 yards. Under fire all the way, Ransom led the Yankees on a two-mile steeplechase and made it back to rebel lines, winded but unhurt. Ransom was aghast to see that most of his soldiers had taken off their clothes and were placidly bathing in the warm waters of the millpond. Thundering commands in his best parade-ground voice, Ransom pointed behind him and let the sight of oncoming Yankee cavalry underscore the urgency of his words.

Most of the men in the water only had time to slip on their pants; some of them fought the ensuing battle stark naked. But within minutes, they tore apart the plank bridge over the millstream and armed themselves.

There was no reason why Colonel Spear's Yankee cavalry shouldn't have ridden over Ransom's minuscule force, but they didn't. Spear didn't like the look of the situation — the defending force appeared small, but the rebels weren't acting like outnumbered men. Instead, they seemed steady and full of fight. Moreover, Ransom's position was hard to get at, due to the millpond and the swamps that extended out from it. So Colonel Spear halted his attack, regrouped his men, brought up his artillery, and bombarded Ransom's entrenchments for about an hour before trying a dismounted assault. Ransom's men held firm and repulsed the attack.

When the Yankees got close enough, Ransom, who had taken cover behind a huge tree near the front lines, began bawling out loud orders to nonexistent regimental commanders, instructing them to occupy nonexistent positions. Spear got reports that there were many more rebels hidden in the swamp grass than the relative few who could be seen.

Midway through the battle, a cannonball smashed into the huge tree Ransom was hiding behind. He was momentarily stunned, but not hurt. The tree had saved his life. Years later, when he retired to this section of the state, Ransom had a fence erected around the tree to protect it from any molestation. He visited it often, as though it were an old comrade.

Spear made some rather feeble attempts to outflank Ransom's position, but Ransom's men moved smartly to dispute each one, pouring out a steady stream of fire and managing to further convince Spear that he was facing a much larger force than was actually the case.

After several futile hours of skirmishing, Spear gave it up as a bad day and ignominiously retreated, hauling six dead and about 25 wounded with him. Ransom's improvised stand had saved one of the most vital railroad bridges in the Confederacy. It was really one of the most remarkable feats of the war. Counting Foster's supporting infantry regiments, Ransom had repulsed an invasion of 5,000 men with a force of 200 barely trained yokels and two cannon. His own casualties amounted to one man wounded.

Nearly a year would pass before the Federals made another serious attempt to knock out the Wilmington & Weldon Railroad. For most of the rest of 1863, there would be no large-scale military action in the coastal region of North Carolina. But there would still be violence, and there would be a steady decline in living conditions, morale, and faith in the Confederate cause.

BUFFALOES
AND OTHER
SCOURGES

Whatever the Confederate quartermasters had overlooked during
D.H. Hill's "offensive" was fair game for Union foragers after the
coastal counties lost most of their regular troops to Robert E. Lee.
Defended only by small and poorly armed detachments of the
Home Guard, "partisan rangers," and a few second-rate companies
of regulars -- all of whom usually melted away whenever the
enemy came out of his entrenchments -- the eastern part of the state
was gradually stripped bare of anything edible or valuable. One
Confederate observer, reconnoitering in the Trenton area, penned
this description of a farm community recently visited by Federal
foragers:

> To cap all, really, they had killed all the stock on the farm, and the
> house and yard were full of buzzards, some of [them] regaling on a
> dead horse before the front door, and some...perching in the parlor
> and on the piazza. The walls of all the houses were scribbled on, and
> the writing generally was of a mean character...If every person in the
> South could witness the useless ruin that the Yankees have caused in
> Jones and adjoining counties, the name and sight of Yankee soldier
> would be hated throughout all eternity, and it would help to show
> what an abandoned and Godless foe we have to contend against.[1]

Things were the worst around New Bern, where the countryside
gradually took on an appearance of savage desolation, as though a
horde of Mongols had swept through. Barns, houses, and fences
had all been vandalized or burned to ashes within a 20-mile radius

of the town; all of the poultry, beef, and sheep had been consumed; and horses and mules were virtually an extinct species by the end of 1863. What had been prosperous farms were now weed-choked patches of wilderness. Even the occupying Union soldiers began to feel ashamed of the way this once-pleasant land had been laid to waste. Wrote one, in January 1863: "This whole country for purposes of maintenance for man or beast, for the next twelve months, is a desert as hopeless as Sahara itself."[2]

In the northeast corner of the state, north of the Chowan River, there had been little organized fighting, and there were no large or permanent Union garrisons. To a casual observer, this fertile part of North Carolina retained its bountiful and unspoiled appearance. Compared to the ravaged landscape around New Bern, it seemed like the Garden of Eden -- at least, that was how it was described in the spring of 1863, in this account penned by an Alabama soldier stationed in Gates County:

> The character of the country is almost level plain, thickly timbered with pine of a medium size, abounding in galberry swamp ponds, and blackish colored water courses of various sizes and depths, the latter being abundant in their supply of the finny tribe. Game of every kind is scarce, but of hogs, and corn and potatoes, there is the greatest abundance for home uses, and enough to feed our troops and animals for a long time ahead. The people are primitive in their habits -- hospitable to an exceeding degree, and bid you welcome to their fireside and table without the price of money. They have been largely robbed by the foe of their negroes, horses and grain, and they greeted us as their deliverers and friends.
>
> A great amount of land is being planted in corn, whilst the wheat is springing forth in the most beautiful proportions on every side of the splendid roads we traverse. At intervals there are elegant mansions, and between them the poorer classes live in one room houses which, though small, are generally neat and comfortable...Little or no attention is paid to the production of turpentine in this section -- grain being the chief product. Barns ten times the size of the residence are remarkable on every hand. The one-horse cart is the chief vehicle on the farms for pleasure use -- the buggies and carriages have been stolen and carried away by the thieves of Lincoln.
>
> The ladies, generally, are neat in their clothing, well behaved, and have none of those "highfalutin'" airs so common among the mushroom aristocracy further down South. What is more, they not only know how to cook, wash, spin, and weave, but take a pride in labor

of that kind. The best of the men in this section are away in our army, those remaining at home are being chiefly composed of old men and boys...I believe a more laborous and independent set of agricultural-ists do not exist in the South...Half you hear at home about the North Carolinians having rings about their legs from picking whortle berries in the flat ponds, and having no hair on their breasts from frequently climbing persimmon trees is "all bosh."[3]

Except for General Foster's occasional raids up the rivers, the Yankee invaders didn't disturb this part of the state. Nevertheless, they maintained an indirect, and on the whole quite nefarious, presence there. This presence took the form of companies of Unionists, armed and supplied by Foster's naval contingent. There were also partisan bands comprised of draft-dodgers and deserters from both armies — sometimes mixed together -- which operated under little or no higher supervision, and whose sole aim was survival.

There were no hard and fast lines between the "legitimate" Unionist companies and the outlier bands. Even the legitimate units rarely performed any conventional military service for the Union side, and the paramilitary groups were nothing more than gangs of outright brigands. Yet General Foster tolerated them, armed them, and, in the case of the formal units, outfitted them with uniforms. The Unionists provided him with information and formed a loosely knit network of outposts inside the no-man's-land north of Ply-mouth.

Whether they were regulars, deserters, or common bandits, all of these men became known to the fearful and unprotected civilians as "Buffaloes." Confederate authority was visible only in the scattered little towns set back from the rivers: Tiny companies of old men and boys, augmented by regular officers who were home recuperating from wounds. Now and then, in some of the county seats, Richmond's presence was betokened by a 50- or 60-man company of second-rate regulars. Considering how pathetic the Confederate resources were in this part of the state, it is not surpris-ing that the Confederacy "controlled" only a few towns and roads, and these only in the daytime.

Most Buffalo camps were deep in the swamps, where the ineffectual Confederate patrols scarcely dared to venture. In a land where game (other than fish) was not abundant, but where productive farmland was, the "Buffs" subsisted in the most logical way: by stealing. At first, they stole mostly food and a few horses. As the war grew longer and more bitter, they began stealing anything that wasn't nailed down, too heavy, or protected by well-armed men. If anyone betrayed them, or even stood up to them, they would come back one dark night and administer their own form of rough and bloody vengeance. One contemporary described the Buffaloes as "a foul and cowardly crew...[they] plundered alike the plate and pianos of the rich, and also the poultry and breadstuffs of the poor."[4]

The exact origin of the term "Buffalo" is murky. The earliest traceable reference is found in a Raleigh newspaper dated January 1856, which refers to Millard Fillmore's supporters in eastern North Carolina as "Buffalo Know-Nothings." Presumably, the bison had a common reputation for low intelligence. To the wealthy planters who pushed North Carolina toward secession, so did the lower-class whites in the eastern counties. "Radically mean and grovelling," wrote one secessionist, not to mention "lazy, sickly, poor, dirty, and ignorant."[5]

Another theory about the nickname can be traced in this description of one of the native Unionist companies (the North Carolina Union Volunteers): "The men look first-rate in their sky-blue pants and dark blue coats and caps...I believe that they make a better appearance than the Yankee soldiers do. Their uniforms make them appear so large that the people call them `Buffaloes.' I think that they like to be called buffaloes. They go about in gangs like herds of buffaloes."[6]

Whatever the origin of the term, it received only limited currency until late in the spring of 1862. Until that time, natives who sided with the Union were usually referred to, in polite society anyway, simply as "Tories," just as the Loyalists had been during the Revolution. But after the despised Confederate conscription laws were enacted in the spring of 1862, the number of deserters in the northeast corner of the state (and elsewhere, too) began growing dramatically. Very few Confederate deserters donned blue uniforms -- they merely hid out, formed bands with other outliers, and tried to stay alive. For awhile, some men continued to work their farms during the day, always with rifles stacked close by, and retreated to the swamps at night. Sporadic Confederate patrols eventually made this too hazardous, for it was easy to locate the deserters when they stayed near home. As things grew more brutal, these men were driven deeper into the swamps and forced to rely on outright theft in order to survive. Reviled by the wealthy planters, with no prospect of ever owning slaves themselves and no interest in fighting to protect the slavery system, they were men without anything to lose.

Most of these desperados were anonymous hard-scrabble farmers. Illiterate men surrounded by other illiterate men, they left no written accounts of their experiences, although some did gain local fame as bandit chieftains. Scattered accounts do exist of a few such men, enough to give us a glimpse of their brutality and of the fear they inspired in the general populace.

Here is an eyewitness description of a Buffalo chieftain named Johnson, who gained infamy by robbing and savagely beating an elderly grandmother who lived upriver from Winton. (He also tried to burn down the house, with the unconscious woman and her daughter still inside, but the fire only consumed part of one room):

> [His] face and features bespoke his bloodthirsty character. He had long sandy hair, skin a fiery red, and his face was covered with large freckles or spots the color of a three-cent piece of silver. He presented an indescribably savage appearance when sober, but now when inflamed by both whiskey and evil passions, he looked more like a fiery demon than a human being. When [his intended victim] informed him that he did not have any gold or silver in the house, the dreadful passions of this man appeared to be set on fire...his jugular vein seemed as large as a man's thumb. He began to pour out such horrible oaths and blasphemies as were enough to make the very hairs stand upon a man's head.[7]

Late in the war, as a result of a quarrel with another Buffalo leader -- over loot, naturally -- Johnson's career was ended by a bullet on a lonely backwoods road.

Another, rather more curious, figure who achieved some fame was a runaway slave of fairly advanced years named Gilbert Holloman. When an unkind master sold him away from his wife and children in late 1862, "Old Gilbert" ran off into the swamps of

Hertford County and established a camp next to a quicksand bog. The bog was known, and widely feared, by the name "China's Mash" -- reputedly bottomless, it was thought that anyone or anything that fell in would be sucked all the way down to China.

Old Gilbert had a talent for survival. With a few primitive tools stolen from his heartless master, he built a comfortable shed for himself. He crept into nearby plantations at night and recruited other slaves, who helped to keep him supplied with food. A few slaves actually ran off with him. After a few months, he had a small community going in the swamp, and his nocturnal depredations had of course enraged what was left of the local gentry.

Eventually, Old Gilbert was betrayed. Some accounts say by his son, whom he had offended in some way. Other tales insist it was a local white man named Napoleon Adkins. (In 1890, Adkins was murdered in his home by a Negro who claimed to have been motivated by vengeance; a mob dragged the Negro out of the county jail at Winton and lynched him.) In any case, a group of vigilantes tracked Old Gilbert to his lair and found him peacefully sitting on a log repairing a shoe. The posse confronted him and demanded his surrender. Game to the last, Old Gilbert dove for his cabin and came out with a gun in hand. He was cut down, along with two of his followers standing nearby. All three bodies, plus two cows and a dog, were thrown into China's Mash. Before marching their captives back to town, the posse members carved their initials on a tree near the bog. The tree was knocked down by a storm in 1900.

By far the most notorious of the Buffalo leaders was a "hard-drinking, fast-living Gates County farm boy" named Jack Fairless. Born in Mintonville in 1839, in a modestly prosperous farming family, Jack Fairless was a born hell-raiser. His first recorded brush with the law was in May 1861; his second was in October. Both times, he managed to get off lightly. On the latter occasion, it was partly because "his aged father sat...in the courtroom and excited the sympathy of many." He enlisted in the 52nd North Carolina Regiment in February 1862, and promptly got into trouble again for stealing from another soldier. This time he was given a light but extremely humiliating form of "field punishment" of the type regimental commanders were wont to hand out in those days:

He was sentenced to wear the "barrel shirt." A head-hole was cut in a flour barrel, the barrel was jammed down over Fairless, and he was pulled through the streets of Gatesville three or four times, while the rest of his company ran alongside, beating on the barrel with sticks. After the barrel was removed, half of his head was shaved, to mark him as a miscreant and insure some lingering embarrassment.

Jack repaid this treatment by immediately deserting. He made his way to the coast and eventually presented himself to the Federal command on Roanoke Island. He worked for some time as a pilot on one of General Burnside's steamers, and during the course of several operations he befriended the hotspur Colonel Rush Hawkins. Hawkins seems to have liked Fairless -- perhaps sensing, in Jack's rebellious independence, something of a kindred spirit. When Hawkins learned that Burnside was forming a regiment of North Carolina Unionists, Hawkins put forth a good word for his young friend, and Fairless was duly commissioned a lieutenant.

Fairless went ashore in August 1862 and began recruiting dissident citizens. He raised about 25 men in the vicinity of Mintonville, where he knew who to look for, then expanded his efforts to neighboring communities. His recruits were fugitives from conscription, Confederate deserters, and genuine Unionists. When they enlisted, he arranged for them to receive new uniforms, good rifles, decent food. He also promised that they wouldn't have to serve more than a day's march from their homes.

By mid-August, Jack had set up headquarters for his Buffalo company at Wingfield plantation, the stately home of Dr. Richard Dillard, Sr. It was located on a stretch of elevated land beside the Chowan River. Dr. Dillard and his family were living in Virginia at that time, so the place was Jack's for the taking. Doubtless he enjoyed the fact that Dr. Dillard was a passionate secessionist. The house, which dated back to 1762, consisted of a big, square central building flanked by two wings, all harmoniously built of brick and wood. A spacious, white-columned portico faced the river, and the high bluff leading to the dock was gracefully terraced. The estate was bounded by rustic old-English styles, and the drive which led to the main county road was lined, for nearly a mile, with stately imported Lombardy poplars. Dr. Dillard's son, writing after the war, remembered Wingfield with aching nostalgia: "[It was] an idyllic spot; the sunshine spilled in diapered patterns of light and shadow upon the lawn through the rifts of the foliage of the stately ancestral trees, and the ancient river lapped the shore at the back of the beautiful old garden."[8]

This was a pretty fancy bivouac for the poor farm boys Jack Fairless commanded. When they got their first look at the new encampment -- a place they had heard about all their lives, but which few had actually seen -- they were impressed, and Jack's prestige rose. Aside from its physical comforts and beauty, Wingfield was a practical location as well. It was easily defensible on the land side, and its riverbank location gave the Buffaloes a safe, reliable avenue of communication with their Yankee masters.

Through September 1862, Fairless and his band gave the Yankees their money's worth in terms of information, prisoners, and regional influence. They also freed numerous slaves in the vicinity, as the following letter from an Edenton man recounts:

> ...it would be difficult indeed to record the evils which these ruffians have inflicted upon the people of that neighborhood and the surrounding country. I believe that they were stationed here for the purpose of decoying off our slaves, who have been going boldly to them in large numbers since first they came here. They have allured off hundreds of our Negroes and they continue to steal them. This notorious "Fairless," the leader of this band of thieves and robbers, has boldly asserted that it is his intention to clear the county of every slave.[9]

For more extended raids, both up and down the river, Fairless and his boys were transported by one or another of Foster's gunboats, which served tours of duty at Wingfield on a rotating basis. None of the skippers liked the duty. Lieutenant Flusser, even in his official reports, bluntly described the Wingfield irregulars as "thieves," although he dutifully protected and transported them, as his orders required.

By October, the quasi-military activities of Fairless and his band had been largely usurped by simple robbery and intimidation. The Buffaloes were drawn from the lowest rungs of the social and economic ladders. Now they were equipped with things none of them ever had before: uniforms, modern guns, and authority. It was a perfect opportunity to settle a lot of old scores, and to rob, bully, and intimidate the better-off citizens who had always looked down on the "clay-eaters." By mid-October, Fairless and his men had established a reign of terror. And Fairless himself was losing his grip as a leader. As long as he was fighting against authority, Fairless had radiated a certain amount of gang-leader charisma; now that he himself was authority, his worst traits took command of him. He drank copiously, even during missions, and began treating his own men almost as badly as he treated their victims.

Fairless was still a conduit for useful information, but most of the Federal officers who dealt with him had started to become a little queasy about it. Reports of the Buffaloes' outrageous behavior began to reach General Foster. Foster conferred with Flusser, who dispatched the USS *Shawsheen*'s commander, Lieutenant Thomas J. Woodward, to make a firsthand report on conditions at Wingfield. Not good, Woodward reported back. When he arrived, he found Fairless "in a state of intoxication, threatening to shoot some of the...men, and conducting himself in a most disgraceful manner."[10]

The company was rapidly losing what little coherence it had as a military unit. Some of Fairless's men, fed up with his drunken bullying, had picked up their brand-new Springfield rifles and had walked away from Wingfield — deserters first from the Confederacy and now from the Union. Much of the costly ammunition stocks given to the Buffaloes had been smuggled into town and exchanged for whiskey.

Despite these transgressions, Fairless continued to act as the Union's eyes and ears in that part of North Carolina. And as long as that held true, the Federals were reluctant to put him out of business. But Jack's own bad habits eventually spared them the trouble. About a month after Woodward's report on him, Fairless got into an argument with a deserter named Wallace. The two men eventually drew their revolvers on each other. Fairless was so drunk he couldn't aim properly, and Wallace killed him with one shot.

With the embarrassing Fairless out of the way, a proper Federal officer was dispatched to whip the Wingfield "wild bunch" into some kind of paramilitary shape. The Federal officer was Joe

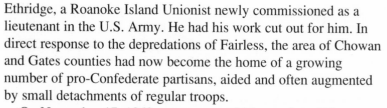

Ethridge, a Roanoke Island Unionist newly commissioned as a
lieutenant in the U.S. Army. He had his work cut out for him. In
direct response to the depredations of Fairless, the area of Chowan
and Gates counties had now become the home of a growing
number of pro-Confederate partisans, aided and often augmented
by small detachments of regular troops.

On November 17, 1862, a company of 20 men from Edenton
under Captain Ned Small attempted to sneak up on Wingfield. A
Unionist sympathizer tipped off the sentries, however, and Small
was compelled to withdraw under a barrage of shellfire from the
gunboat stationed in the river.

Following this incident, the plantation was fortified. Labor was
provided by the large number of Negroes who had settled on the
grounds. Breastworks were thrown up starting at the top of the
river embankment and running 200 yards southeast, then due south
for another 400 yards. At the angle where the two lines of entrenchments came together, a square-sided fort, measuring 75 feet
per side, was erected on a mound of earth 15 feet high. A small,
bronze Napoleon fieldpiece, dragged through the woods from
Edenton, was mounted there. The third landward side of the estate
was secured by building two dams across a small creek, creating a
moat 10 to 15 feet deep. The riverbank ends of the breastworks
were anchored by two stout log blockhouses.

In early March 1863, 150 men of the 42nd North Carolina
Regiment, led by a Charlotte native named Jonothan Brown,
crossed the Chowan River in small boats and almost got the drop
on the Unionist garrison. They were spotted by a picket just before
starting their attack, and once again, shellfire from Union gunboats
in the river forced the attackers off.

Brown tried again about three weeks later, taking advantage of
the fact that, for a brief interval, the gunboat usually stationed at
Wingfield had been dispatched elsewhere. In a bold charge through
the early morning fog, Brown's men broke through the breastworks
in a matter of minutes. The Buffaloes' cannon was fired twice,
without hitting anyone, before it was spiked and abandoned. All
but about two dozen of the Buffaloes fled into the woods, many of
them escaping down to Plymouth in small boats. The rest took
shelter in one of the blockhouses, from which Colonel Brown

could not dislodge them, as he had no artillery. As soon as word spread about the attack, three of Flusser's gunboats steamed up to Wingfield, forcing Brown to withdraw. He pulled back only after reluctantly setting fire to the mansion and all of its outbuildings except the occupied blockhouse -- nobody could figure out a way to get close enough to ignite it. One eyewitness never forgot the sight of a Confederate soldier sitting in the parlor of the great house, flames taking hold all around him, nonchalantly playing "Home Sweet Home" on the Dillards' piano. There was only one casualty, a Buffalo who was killed during the Confederate charge; Brown had him buried in the Dillard family graveyard, with respects.

Wingfield may have been cleaned out, but the Buffaloes were not. As the war ground on, and desertions increased, their numbers grew, and so did the terror and violence. By the autumn of 1864, conditions in the Roanoke-Chowan corner of North Carolina were as chaotic and frightful as they were in many mountain counties. Buffalo bands preyed on anyone they liked, and were in turn ruthlessly hunted down by vigilantes and Confederate irregulars. Atrocity begat vengeance, and by the last spring of the war, the region had sunk into bloody anarchy.

The violence got so out of hand, in fact, that Robert E. Lee and the Union commander at Norfolk, General Benjamin F. Butler, actually made a bizarre agreement to mount a joint cavalry expedition into the region to put down the outlier bands. Despite the fact that Lee was fighting his own last-ditch battle for survival, he managed to send a column of horsemen as far as Gates County. In a series of vigorous sweeps, aided by intelligence provided by the long-suffering civilians, Lee's men killed 22 Buffaloes, captured dozens more, and dispersed many of the bands. Butler tried to keep his end of this strange bilateral arrangement, but the war was over before his men got into the field.

Benjamin Butler, nicknamed "Beast" Butler, was one of the least-liked officers in the U.S. Army. In early autumn, 1863, the popular and respected General Foster was transferred to another command and was replaced by Butler. One of Butler's first acts, upon taking command of the department, was to invite General Edward A. Wild and two regiments of his Negro brigade to come into the northeastern corner of North Carolina and do whatever they liked with it. Officially, Wild's orders were to clear some Confederate guerrillas from the area of the Dismal Swamp Canal, to free whatever slaves in the area still remained in bondage, and to comb through the Negro population to find new recruits. Unofficially, Wild gave the inhabitants of northeastern North Carolina a foretaste of the kind of warfare that General William Tecumseh Sherman would visit on the state in 1865.

Following the Dismal Swamp Canal road from Norfolk to Elizabeth City, Wild and his 1,800 black troopers misplaced their supply boats after taking a wrong turn in the swamps, and almost immediately had to start living off the country. Wild's columns came and went like a cloud of locusts. From December 9 to December 16, Wild made his headquarters in Elizabeth City. For the white citizens of that town, the specter of armed Negroes was an almost archetypical nightmare, and they felt that Beelzebub himself had taken up residence.

Wild's patrols scoured the countryside in all directions, looking for provisions and "guerrillas." Twenty suspects were brought in, clapped in irons, and put on trial. Nine were found innocent, eight were convicted and packed off to jail in Norfolk, two were retained as hostages, and one fellow -- Daniel Bright of Pasquotank County -- was hanged for bushwhacking while the other prisoners were forced to watch.

Edward Wild was not the sort of man one would expect to find in the role of a ruthless anti-partisan commander. He was, in fact, a Harvard College graduate and a practicing physician in civilian life. Nevertheless, he seems to have quite enjoyed the task. In reporting his severe actions to his superiors, he advocated "a more rigorous style of warfare...Finding ordinary measures of little avail...I burned their houses and barns, ate up their livestock, and took hostages...."[11]

Even General Butler, no softie himself, felt that Wild was doing his job with "perhaps too much stringency." One Confederate officer, upon learning of the events in Pasquotank County, wrote to General Wild directly:

Probably no expedition, during the progress of the war, has been attended with more bitter disregard from the long established usages of civilization or the dictates of humanity than your late raid into the country bordering the Albemarle. Your stay, though short, was marked by crimes and enormities. You burned houses over the heads of defenceless women and children, carried off private property of every description, arrested non-combatants, and carried off ladies in irons, whom you confined with negro men.

Your negro troops fired on Confederates after they had surrendered and they were only saved by the exertions of the more humane of your white officers. Last, but not least, under pretext that he was a guerrilla, you hanged Daniel Bright...forcing the ladies and gentlemen whom you held in arrest to witness the execution. Therefore, I have obtained an order from the General commanding, for the execution of Samuel Jones, a private from Company B. Fifth Ohio, whom I hang in retaliation. I hold two more of your men -- in irons -- as hostages for Mrs. Weeks and Mrs. Mundin. When these ladies are released, these men will be...treated as prisoners of war.[1]2

It is not likely that this letter would have deterred Wild from his more zealous actions, but a stern word from General Butler did. Before leaving North Carolina, Wild sent his men on a sweep through Currituck and Camden counties, where they fought a number of minor skirmishes with Confederate partisans and regulars, and liberated anywhere from 2,000 to 2,500 slaves. (Wild himself never got an accurate count because people were constantly joining and leaving his columns, and a head count taken at breakfast was meaningless by suppertime.) After that, with Confederate reinforcements hurriedly converging on that part of the state, Wild prudently retired to Norfolk. He had been dramatically successful in quelling Confederate sympathies in the region -- rebel partisan activity dropped off to almost nothing, and stayed that way until the end of the war.

However, Wild was hotly pursued on the last leg of his withdrawal almost as soon as he crossed the Virginia state line. Captain Henry A. Chambers, a member of Ransom's Brigade, which had been hurried into the area in an effort to trap Wild's retreating column, described in his diary the breathless final laps of the chase:

We now began to double-quick and the nearer town [Suffolk, Virginia] the faster we were required to go. We did not understand the object of this until we were rising over the hill just this side of town when we were met by a little Franco-Louisiana Zouave who had been sent back to urge us on. He was in a perfect fever of excitement and, rising in his stirrups, with his sharp stirring voice, he would cry, "Colonel, for God's sake hurry your men on or you will be too late." Turning on the men he would rush along with "Run, boys, run, and we will catch the G--D-- niggers yet!" We were nearly exhausted with our long double-quick, but when told that "the hated negroes had been encountered," we received as it were renewed vigor, and on we pushed."[13]

As Ransom's men jogged through the streets of Suffolk, the townspeople ran out and brought them cups of water to drink on the run. Most of Wild's column did escape, but several stragglers were surrounded in a house on the far side of town, and one of Ransom's men was killed in an attack on the building. It was then set afire with the black soldiers still inside.

Accounts of the Negro troops' behavior vary dramatically, as might be expected, depending on who wrote them. The white inhabitants and Confederate soldiers viewed them as fiends incarnate and ascribed all manner of outrages to them. Because this was the first all-black expeditionary force sent into Confederate territory since Congress had authorized Negro regiments, it attracted a lot of attention from the Northern press. Several newspaper correspondents tagged along, and according to their reports, there was no significant difference between the behavior and discipline of the Negro soldiers and those of the average all-white unit. The two verdicts were not necessarily mutually exclusive.

PICKETT DOES NOT CHARGE

As the war dragged on, the importance of North Carolina as a source of supply increased. The situation in the state had been nagging at Robert E. Lee for a long time, but crisis after crisis on the main front in Virginia had made it imprudent at best for him to spare the troops or the attention to do anything about it. He had, however, spent a good deal of time conferring with Brigadier General Robert Hoke, the intelligent and combative young North Carolinian who had become one of Lee's most trusted subordinates. On the second day of 1864, Lee sent a memorandum to Jefferson Davis setting forth his thoughts on the strategic possibilities in North Carolina. The plan Lee outlined was Hoke's:

> The time is at hand when, if an attempt can be made to capture the enemy's forces at New Berne, it should be done. I can now spare the troops for the purpose, which will not be the case as spring approaches...New Berne is defended on the land side by a line of intrenchments [sic] from the Neuse to the Trent. A redoubt near the Trent protects that flank, while three or four gun-boats are relied upon to defend the flank on the Neuse. The garrison has been so long unmolested, and experiences such a feeling of security, that it is represented as careless. The gun-boats are small and indifferent and do not keep up a head of steam. A bold party could descend the Neuse in boats at night, capture the gun-boats, and drive the enemy by their aid from the works on that side of the river, while a force should attack them from the front. A large amount of provisions and other supplies are said to be at New Berne, which are much wanted for this army, besides much that is reported in the country that will thus be made accessible to us.[1]

Clearly, Lee understood there was much to be gained by even a single success on the North Carolina coast. By now (a couple of years too late to do much good), so did Jefferson Davis. The Confederate President even suggested that Lee himself could travel south and temporarily take command of the operation. But Lee felt a native North Carolinian should have the responsibility, and he counterproposed the name of Robert Hoke, whose plan he had just submitted to Davis. Hoke would have been the perfect choice. He knew the terrain well, knew how to motivate his troops, and was an aggressive, imaginative tactician. Davis, however, felt it would be unseemly to give that much responsibility to a young man of such relatively low rank. In typical fashion, therefore, he passed over a brilliant brigadier and selected a mediocre major general, George Pickett.

Pickett assembled his forces at Kinston. By the time he was ready to move, on January 30, 1864, he had 13,000 ground troops and a supporting naval force of 14 small wooden vessels, ably led by Commander John Taylor Wood. After studying Hoke's plan, Pickett wisely concluded he could not improve upon it. Pickett assigned his strongest column to General Seth Barton, consisting of Barton's, Kemper's, and part of Matt Ransom's brigades, supported by 14 cannon and 600 cavalry. This column would strike the New Bern defenses at Bryce's Creek, take Forts Gaston, Spinola, and Amory, and then assault the city itself across the railroad bridge over the Trent River. A weaker column, under Colonel James Dearing, consisting of three infantry regiments, 300 horsemen, and a battery of artillery, was assigned the task of neutralizing Fort Anderson. Robert Hoke's division, with Pickett himself tagging along, would attempt a surprise attack on New Bern's inner ring of fortifications, north of the city along Batchelder's Creek.

All three operations were to be launched simultaneously on the morning of February 1. To further support the attacks, a diversionary thrust would be launched, under the one-armed but stouthearted General James G. Martin, by part of the Wilmington garrison. By striking at the Newport Barracks, Martin would pin down the attention and resources of the Federals in Morehead City. The one wildcard in the picture was the constantly fluctuating number of Union gunboats docked in or anchored near New Bern. These gunboats gave the enemy a powerful reserve of mobile artillery. To eliminate them, the Confederates planned a daring naval operation -- a commando raid, really -- under the leadership of Commander John T. Wood.

If there was anyone in the Confederate naval service who compared with William Cushing, it was John Wood. Born in Louisiana, Wood belonged to an exceedingly well-connected family: his mother was the daughter of President Zachary Taylor and the sister of Jefferson Davis's first wife. A career Navy man since 1847, Wood had resigned his commission to fight for the South, and he had seen much action. He commanded a party of sharpshooters that wrought havoc on the decks of Union ships at Drewry's Bluff, won plaudits for his courage and skill as one of the gunnery officers on the ironclad *Virginia*, and led successful small-boat operations against the enemy on Chesapeake Bay and the Rappahannock River. Now he was about to lead one of the most daring Confederate naval attacks of the war.

Ten small wooden cutters arrived by train in Kinston on the morning of January 31. The crews were made up of veteran tars from the James River Squadron, commanded by Lieutenant Benjamin P. Loyall. From Wilmington came two heavier launches, a pair of rowboats, and another 135 men to comprise the strike force. By late afternoon, the entire force was embarked on the Neuse River: 285 officers and men, including 25 Confederate Marines, distributed in 14 boats. The waters of North Carolina, for a brief and glorious hour, experienced a resurgence of Confederate naval vigor; Wood's little flotilla might almost have been a diminutive reincarnation of the Mosquito Fleet.

Midshipman J. Thomas Scharf, who would later write the first complete history of the Confederate States Navy, was a participant in this mission, and he left a vivid recollection of the voyage down the Neuse:

> The distance between Kinston and Newberne by rail is about thirty miles, but the torturous and circuitous course which the river takes, makes the journey by water at least twice that length. Bending silently to the muffled oars, the expedition moved down the river. Now, the Neuse broadened until the boats seemed to be on a lake; again, the tortuous stream narrowed until the party could almost touch the trees on either side. Not a sign of life was visible, save

occasionally when a flock of wild ducks, startled at the approach of the boats, rose from the banks, and then poising themselves for a moment overhead, flew on swift wings to the shelter of the woodland or the morass. No other sound was heard to break the stillness save the constant, steady splash of the oars and the ceaseless surge of the river. Sometimes a fallen log impeded the progress, again a boat would run aground, but as hour after hour passed by, the boats still sped on, the crews cold and weary, but yet cheerful and uncomplaining. Night fell, dark shadows began to creep over the marshes and crowd the river; owls screeched among the branches overhead, through which the expedition occasionally caught glimpses of the sky.[2]

Navigation became trickier as they neared New Bern, for the river widened until the opposite shoreline vanished, and a bleak winter fog rolled in from the swamps. Just before dawn, Commander Wood steered his little navy into hiding in the marshy maze of blackwater streams near the mouth of Batchelder's Creek.

While the sailors rested during the daylight hours of February 1, Wood and Loyall reconnoitered the river and discovered that only a single Federal gunboat was currently anchored off New Bern. She was the USS *Underwriter*, and as the ironies of history would have it, she was the ship that had fired the first Yankee gun at Roanoke Island. She was a side-wheeler, mounting four guns, including an 8-inch Dahlgren, and she was the largest of the vessels currently on duty in the New Bern area. Since the ship was alone, it suddenly seemed feasible to Wood to capture her intact, use her cannon to support General Pickett's attack, and then brazenly sail her back to Kinston, where she would be a welcome deterrent to any Yankee moves later in the year.

The approach to the vessel would be tricky, for the *Underwriter* was anchored a mere 500 yards from a fortified battery known as Fort Dutton, and was directly in line with the guns across the river at Fort Anderson. If Wood and his men were detected during their approach, they would be blown out of the water.

As darkness fell, Wood divided his force into two sections. Lieutenant Loyall would lead one, and Wood himself would lead the other. The men were heavily armed with revolvers, carbines, and cutlasses. At least one of the boats (the one containing Midshipman Scharf) also mounted a small howitzer crammed with canister. In addition, each boat was equipped with grappling hooks attached to stout lines. Each man in the raiding party wore a white patch on his left arm so he could tell friend from foe in the dark. As a final precaution, Wood issued a password: "Sumter."

Silently, the two little squadrons rowed downriver, passing Fort Anderson at 2:20 a.m. At first they couldn't spot their target, so dark was the surface of the river. Then, just as they passed the silent ramparts of Fort Dutton, they heard a ship's bell toll faintly in the distance. Following the sound, the men bent to their oars and altered course.

Now they could make out the *Underwriter*. It was a small warship, to be sure, but it dwarfed their own little cutters and mounted four guns that could sink one of their boats with a single shot. Not long after the commandos spotted their objective, a sharp-eyed Union lookout aboard the *Underwriter* also spotted them. Alarmingly loud came the cry: "Boat ahoy!"

Wood and his men kept rowing. The challenge came again: "Boat ahoy! Boat ahoy!" This time, when a moment went by and there was no reply, the sentry sounded a rattling alarm, and the approaching Confederates clearly heard the shuffle and clatter of the gunboat's crew turning out of their bunks and pounding to their battle stations.

There was no point in stealth now. "Give way, boys, give way!" shouted Wood and Loyall, and the cutters shot ahead through the black water. Rifle and pistol fire flashed on deck, Minie balls hummed past like lethal mosquitos, and the rowers were splashed with water from near-hits. The Union vessel slipped her cable and got into motion, but the range was too close to bring her big guns to bear. The raiders' boats crunched into the hull; grappling hooks sang in the air and bit deep; the Neuse echoed as more than 200 throats cut loose the rebel yell. It was the kind of melee that had not been seen in North Carolina waters since the days of Black-beard the pirate.

Midshipman Scharf fired the boat howitzer, which seared the darkness like a strobe light. Canister balls splattered into the pilothouse, shattering glass and throwing out a hailstorm of splin-ters. The first Confederate aboard the *Underwriter* was Lieutenant Loyall, cutlass in one hand, Navy Colt in the other, followed

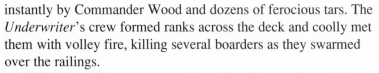

instantly by Commander Wood and dozens of ferocious tars. The
Underwriter's crew formed ranks across the deck and coolly met
them with volley fire, killing several boarders as they swarmed
over the railings.

Wild cannon fire now opened from Fort Dutton. One shell
landed squarely amidst the swarm of grappling men, but the fight
continued savagely. Slowly, the raiders gained control of the
blood-pooled deck, driving the gunboat's crew down into the
wardroom and eventually into the coal bunkers. In such close
quarters, there was little time to reload. Men used their rifles as
clubs, their pistols as bludgeons. It was a brawl fought with cutlass
and dirk and belaying pin, an alley fight in a confined, flame-lit
chamber.

When it was all over, the captain of the Union gunboat and fully
half of his crew lay dead or wounded. Six of Wood's men died and
22 were wounded. To his disgust, Wood found there was not
enough steam in the boilers for him to get up speed right away. Nor
was there time to stoke the fires — Fort Dutton was getting the
range, and now Fort Anderson, too, was lobbing shells at the
helpless vessel. By the time Wood reemerged on deck, solid shot
from across the Neuse was raising plumes of water all around the
gunboat. Reluctantly, Wood set fire to the *Underwriter*, then led
his victorious swashbucklers back upstream on the first leg of their
laborious but triumphant return to Kinston.

Wood's exuberance wouldn't last long once he learned what had
happened to General Pickett's main effort, the three-pronged land
attack. General Hoke made first contact with the Federals, attempting to storm the Batchelder's Creek bridge around 2 a.m. on
February 1. He was brought up short when shots from some
Federal pickets alerted the defenders — and when he discovered
the bridge had already been demolished. A controlled attack
against prepared defenses at night was beyond the tactical abilities
of most 19th-century armies, so Hoke had to cool his heels until
daybreak. He knew the routine of the New Bern garrison well, and
he fully expected the Federals to send reinforcements across the
creek by train. Therefore, he planned to ambush the train, seize it,
and simply ride it back into the city. But the train crew, alerted by
telegraph, hastened back to New Bern, and Hoke missed capturing

them by about five minutes.

Hoke resumed his conventional attack as soon as it was light enough to see what was going on. Despite the fact that the Federal line at Batchelder's Creek had been reinforced in the pre-dawn hours by fresh troops from New Bern, Hoke broke through and drove the Federals from their trenches in disorder. He was now within one mile of the city itself, but he didn't think his column, unsupported, was strong enough to penetrate the city's formidable inner defenses, which were designed by that crack military engineer, John Foster. Besides, Hoke's orders were to coordinate his attack with that of General Barton. Any minute now, Hoke supposed, he would hear the rumble and crash of battle to the south, across the Trent River. Minutes turned to hours while Hoke, with growing apprehension, waited for some sign of Confederate activity on his right. Instead, he finally heard two trains pull into New Bern and assumed -- correctly -- that they were bringing reinforcements from Morehead City. That meant something was very wrong with Barton's attack.

What had happened was a signal failure of nerve, all the more lamentable because Barton conducted the preliminary moves of his attack with competence. His approach was a model of discipline and stealth; several Federal outposts were taken without a shot being fired. But then, at about 8 a.m., Barton got his first glimpse of the main enemy defensive line, and it unnerved him. It was too bad, really, for he had the advantage of surprise, and if he had attacked with all available resources at once (as Robert Hoke would surely have done), he probably could have carried the earthworks after a sharp but brief encounter.

Instead, he halted. Barton brought up his artillery, started a cannon duel with the defenders, and sent out patrols to find a weak spot. There wasn't one; the Union garrison had spent two years fortifying this terrain, and John Foster knew what he was doing.

Of course, every hour that passed saw the enemy breastworks manned by more and more troops. The attacking spirit of Barton's men began to melt under the hot shelling they received from the defenders' well-sited guns. And the more time Barton spent studying the fortifications, the lower his courage ebbed. He wasted the entire day stewing and fretting and sending out cavalry patrols

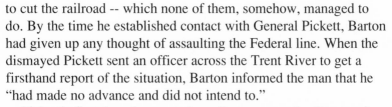

to cut the railroad -- which none of them, somehow, managed to do. By the time he established contact with General Pickett, Barton had given up any thought of assaulting the Federal line. When the dismayed Pickett sent an officer across the Trent River to get a firsthand report of the situation, Barton informed the man that he "had made no advance and did not intend to."

Pickett's first thought was to have Barton cross the Trent and join Hoke for a massed attack on the one front where Confederate land forces had enjoyed some success. It might have worked. There was only one mile between Hoke and the streets of New Bern, and the Union garrison, even with its reinforcements, was stretched very thin. But before Barton could cross the river, Pickett sent him new orders, directing him to withdraw to Kinston. The attempt would not be made after all. Robert Hoke was beside himself with frustration, anger, and disgust.

The third Confederate column, the one directed against Fort Anderson, made even less headway than Barton's force. Its commander, Colonel Dearing, did not even pretend to attack the position. By the morning of February 4, all of Pickett's units were in retreat toward Kinston. The march was memorable because of the black mood of the men and the abominable condition of the road. Heavy winter rains had turned the road into "one vast mudhole the consistency of batter."

Pickett's failure at New Bern stands out even among the other sad examples of thrown-away chances and missed opportunities that mar the record of Confederate actions along the North Carolina coast. He had inherited a fine plan from Robert Hoke, one that would have stretched the Union defenses to their limit and offered the Confederates a reasonable chance of a breakthrough. He had been superbly supported by Commander Wood's naval raiders. But he had failed to infuse his subordinates with the attitude of urgency, the simple emotional drive, needed to make the daring plan work. Of the three army commanders involved, only Robert Hoke emerged from this operation with his reputation untarnished -- indeed, Robert E. Lee pointedly singled him out for commendation. About the only consolation Pickett could take was the fact that he had inflicted greater loss on the defenders than they had inflicted on him: about 100 killed and wounded and 300 prisoners, compared to 45 Confederate casualties.

The feint from Wilmington, under James G. Martin, was a smashing little success. Martin moved fast, struck hard, and routed the garrison of Newport Barracks. He drove the Yankees back into Beaufort, killing and wounding 17 and capturing about 80. He also bagged an enormous amount of urgently needed booty, including ten cannon, 200 crates of artillery ammunition, several hundred stand of small arms, and a dozen wagons full of victuals and other supplies.

Perhaps the most disturbing footnote to Pickett's failed offensive concerns the Federal prisoners. Among the 300 Yankees captured were the gallant Colonel Fellows of the 17th Massachusetts and 69 of his men. Fellows and all but 11 of his men later died at the dismal Confederate prison camp in Andersonville, Georgia. Also among the prisoners were some natives of eastern North Carolina who had enlisted in the U.S. Army. Some were Unionists at heart, while others were deserters who had simply changed sides. Pickett held a tribunal and had 22 of them hanged. Pickett wasn't cleared of Federal charges for this act until 1866, when General Ulysses S. Grant intervened on his behalf — largely to spite his old nemesis, General Ben Butler, who was beating the drum to have Pickett brought to trial.

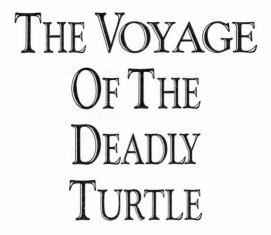
THE VOYAGE OF THE DEADLY TURTLE

If the Union's early amphibious victories in North Carolina taught the Confederates anything, it was that shallow-water naval power could not be maintained — much less regained once lost — by using old tugboats, passenger steamers, and canal barges for warships, particularly if they were armored with cotton bales and armed with one or two puny fieldpieces. One of General Burnside's gunboats could have outfought any three such vessels the Confederates ever sailed in North Carolina waters.

After studying the early coastal campaigns, committees of Confederate engineers and ordnance experts emerged with a radical design for more-or-less standardized shallow-draft armored rams. These vessels would be cumbersome and slow, and they would sacrifice armament in favor of protection -- each would carry only a pair of heavy-caliber rifled cannon. The theory was that these hulking ironclads could withstand dozens, maybe hundreds, of hits, yet could disable the Yankee gunboats with a few powerful shells and then finish the job with their armored rams.

As it happened, wartime shortages and the usual Confederate administrative incompetence combined to keep all but one of these vessels from ever seeing real action. But the short, victorious career of this lone ship — the famous ram CSS *Albemarle* — proved the soundness of the design. The only Federal ships that might have stood a chance against the *Albemarle* were the mighty steam frigates out in the blockade line, and they drew far too much water to pass safely from the sea into the shallow sounds. The Confederacy originally planned to build five such ironclads (and possibly more; records are very fragmentary for ships other than the *Albemarle* and the *Neuse*). If all of them had actually gone into service, Federal naval power would have been swept from the coastal waters of North Carolina in a matter of days.

Contracts were let for three ironclads in the fall of 1862. These were intended as replacements for the vessels burned on the stocks in Norfolk when the pathetic General Benjamin Huger abandoned the city. A New Bern shipbuilding firm was commissioned to build one ironclad at Whitehall, on the Neuse River, but that project suffered a drastic setback when General Foster's artillery pummeled the half-finished vessel during his Goldsboro campaign. A second ironclad was supposed to be built at Tarboro, but little if any real work appears to have been done on it. The third ship, destined to be known as the CSS *Albemarle*, was to be laid down at a place called Edward's Ferry on the Roanoke River, about halfway between Hamilton and the Weldon railroad bridges.

The *Albemarle*'s general specifications were drawn up by the best naval engineer in the South: John Porter, the man who had made naval history by converting the captured USS *Merrimac* into the famous ironclad CSS *Virginia*. The actual design and construction contract was awarded to an amazingly precocious marine engineer named Gilbert Elliott, a native of Elizabeth City who was but 19 years old when he got the job. Jefferson Davis's secretary of the navy, Stephen Mallory, was one of Davis's better appointments -- a man of imagination, drive, and ability -- and Mallory did everything in his power to expedite the ironclad projects. To oversee the construction of the *Albemarle*, he dispatched Porter himself to Edward's Ferry.

Porter was ordered to proceed to a place identified in his orders as the "Edward's Ferry Shipyard." When he arrived at Edward's Ferry, he was flabbergasted to discover that the "shipyard" was nothing more than a big cornfield next to the river. The cornfield's owner, a resourceful man from Scotland Neck named Peter Smith, nevertheless became fired with enthusiasm for the project. Smith set to work creating a shipyard out of thin air. He imported lumber mills to cut and finish the heavy beams needed for the ironclad's framework, and set up a blacksmith's forge to make whatever tools were lacking at Edward's Ferry. (Virtually all of the tools were missing, it turned out, beyond a few simple hammers and saws.) Smith even invented a new drill that cut the time needed to pierce holes in the iron plate by about 80 percent.

Young Elliott, meanwhile, ranged all over North Carolina trying to find iron. He collected old railroad iron, broken boilers, even buckets full of rusty bolts, and sent the scraps to the Tredegar Iron Works in Richmond, where they were melted down and rolled into plates. "The entire construction was one of shreds and patches; the engine was adapted from incongruous material, ingeniously dove-tailed and put together with a determined will that mastered doubt, but not without some natural anxiety as to derangements that might occur from so heterogenous a combination."[1] In the summer of 1863, the project received a boost from Governor Vance. After much prodding by Secretary Mallory, and after assurances that the ironclads would be used solely in state waters, Vance released 400 tons of reserve railroad iron from supplies held by the Atlantic & North Carolina Railroad Company, a firm in which the state enjoyed the status of majority stock holder. Nevertheless, so overburdened was the Tredegar Iron Works that almost a year passed before the iron came back to Elliott in the form of armor plate.

Up where the *Neuse* was being built, its future commander, Lieutenant Benjamin Loyall, was not so lucky. Several boxcars of iron from Georgia were waiting on a railroad siding in Wilmington, but the city's naval commander thought the whole ironclad scheme was idiotic and did little to expedite shipment. This naval commander happened to be William F. Lynch (now promoted to flag officer, the Civil War equivalent of rear admiral), who had commanded the Mosquito Fleet earlier in the war. Loyall fumed in one letter, dated February 6, 1864: "You have no idea of the delay in forwarding iron to this place -- it may be unavoidable, but I don't believe it. At one time twenty one days passed without my receiving a piece...every time I telegraph to Lynch, he replies, `Army monopolizing cars.' It is all exceedingly mortifying to me...."[2]

Elliott, too, had his troubles with Lynch. In a letter to Governor Vance, Elliott once described Lynch as "incompetent, inefficient, and almost imbecile...." The crew and carpenters, often idle for weeks at a time while waiting for construction material to arrive, began calling their half-finished behemoth the CSS *Neuse-ance*.

The man who really got the *Albemarle* finished was its future captain, Commander James W. Cooke, who replaced Porter in late 1863. With him, Cooke brought from Richmond some additional engineers and a load of urgently needed tools and equipment. What drove the project forward was largely Robert E. Lee's desire to have the ironclad finished in time to support General Pickett's attack on New Bern. Cooke couldn't work miracles, but he did work a series of slow improvements. Infuriated that the ram was not finished in time to support Pickett's operation, Cooke became obsessed with completing the vessel. He finally took the drastic step of organizing armed patrols which fanned out across the eastern third of North Carolina and collected every hunk of scrap iron they could find, at gunpoint if necessary. These tactics earned Cooke a nickname: "The Ironmonger Captain." He was proud to accept it.

The finishing touches were put on the ironclad in late March 1864, at a docking facility at Hamilton. Except for her fragile engines, the finished *Albemarle* was as formidable as her designer had hoped. She was 45 feet wide and 152 feet long, sheathed in yellow pine four inches thick. There were two layers of armor covering her turtle-backed superstructure, each two inches thick. The iron-covered prow, the actual ram, measured 18 feet long and was layered over a framework of oak. There were six gunports — one each fore and aft, and a pair on either side — and the armament could be pivoted quickly from one port to another, as needed. The ram was intended to be the real ship-killer, but the battery, too, was powerful: two eight-inch Brooke rifles.

When General Robert F. Hoke was appointed by Lee to lead an all-out effort to wrest the coast from the invaders, one of the first things he did was travel upriver to Hamilton and inspect the ironclad. When Hoke met with Cooke and explained his plan to attack Plymouth, Cooke at first demurred, insisting it was impossible for the *Albemarle* to be ready in time. Hoke made it clear that the window of opportunity in North Carolina would be open only as long as the front in Virginia remained quiescent; he could not wait. He finally wore Cooke down with his entreaties, and Cooke promised to have the ironclad in action to support Hoke's attack on Plymouth, whatever it took.

Hoke made another visit on April 16, just one day before his attack was scheduled to begin. Cooke promised him that the ironclad would be there. The following morning, as Hoke launched his operations, the CSS *Albemarle* was formally commissioned, slipped her moorings, and started downriver on her maiden voyage. Few of her crewmen were trained sailors. Most appear to have been volunteers from Hoke's brigade — "long, lank Tar Heels...from the Piney woods."[3]

As it made its torturous way downstream, the great iron turtle towed a launch carrying a blacksmith's forge, just in case anything broke down. Almost immediately, something did: the engines. Not long afterward, part of the rudder control failed. The *Albemarle* was forced to anchor for the night and make repairs, which turned out to require ten hours of hard labor.

The next day, progress downriver resumed. As viewed from the banks, the passing vessel presented a spectacle that cried out for the pen of a Mark Twain. As the massive ironclad churned along, carpenters and blacksmiths swarmed over her, hammering and tightening bolts. Brawny crewmen, precariously balanced on swaying construction stages hung out over her sides, clanged on her with sledgehammers, trying even now to get everything to fit properly. Inside the armored shell, gun captains bawled orders to their crews: "Port side! Drive in spike! On nut below and screw up! Vent and sponge! Load with shells! Prime!"

To the curious and incredulous citizens who watched the armored monster drift by, accompanied by all this banging and babel of tongues, the *Albemarle* seemed both outlandish and wondrous. Wrote one local farmer, recalling the incident many years later: "I never conceived of anything more perfectly ridiculous than the appearance of the critter as she slowly passed by my landing."[4]

THUNDER ON ALBEMARLE SOUND

After General Pickett was recalled to Virginia, tactical command of Confederate forces in eastern North Carolina passed to Brigadier General Robert Frederick Hoke. He would now show what could be done -- indeed, what could have been done long before the spring of 1864 -- by an energetic and imaginative commander, given a single division of good troops.

Hoke was 27. A native of Lincolnton, he came from a prosperous middle-class family whose assets included a cotton mill and a small iron foundry. A handsome, dark-haired man with deep, rather poetic eyes, Hoke was educated at local schools, then attended Kentucky Military Institute. He fought, as a lieutenant, in the early battle at Big Bethel. Later, as second-in-command of the 33rd North Carolina Regiment and colonel of the 21st North Carolina, he participated in nearly every major engagement in Virginia, from the Seven Days Battles to Chancellorsville. In the latter campaign, he was severely wounded while fighting with Jubal Early at Marye's Heights. He was promoted to brigadier general in January 1863. In terms of all-round professional competence, Hoke was one of Robert E. Lee's finest subordinates — the compleat soldier. And now, in the spring of 1864, in his home state, he would reach the zenith of his career with a small but brilliant triumph at Plymouth.

Hoke's plan encompassed nothing less than the total expulsion of the enemy from North Carolina. He chose to strike first at

Plymouth for two reasons: It was the key to Federal control of the upper Albemarle Sound region, and it was an important supply center for all of the Yankee enclaves. Plymouth would be easier to overcome than New Bern, and a victory there would boost the morale of the Confederates and shake the resolve of the remaining enemy garrisons.

Defending Plymouth was Brigadier General William H. Wessells and about 3,000 men, including two companies of native Unionist volunteers from the coastal counties. The little city was protected by a formidable system of earthworks, starting with a detached diamond-shaped redoubt called Fort Grey, located on the south bank of the Roanoke River west of town. Its purpose was to oppose any rebel attack on the river. The fort was augmented by rows of obstacles placed across the river both upstream and downstream from its guns, stretching from the south bank to Tabor Island. A mile southwest of Plymouth rose another detached earthwork, Fort Wessells.

Following the general line of the city limits was a continuous line of strong breastworks, reinforced at several points with earthen redoubts. In the center of this line was Fort Williams, the strongest single work in the system. Due to the swampy and broken nature of the ground, fortifications on the extreme eastern and western sides of town were not continuous. Between Third and Fourth Streets was a strong earthwork called the Conaby Redoubt, and between the Columbia Road and the Roanoke River was a somewhat larger work dubbed Fort Comfort. Scattered breastworks had been erected on vulnerable pieces of ground on the flanks of those two works, but on the whole it was considered unlikely that an assault would be delivered across that ground. Not only was the terrain boggy and treacherous, but it was wide open, and any attack mounted there could be raked mercilessly, at close range, by canister from Lieutenant Commander Flusser's gunboat squadron.

Flusser had four warships stationed at Plymouth: the *Miami*, *Southfield*, *Ceres*, and *Whitehead*. Together they packed eleven 9-inch rifles, two 100-pounder Parrotts, a dozen or so 20-pounder Parrotts, and numerous 24- and 12-pounder howitzers for shore bombardment. In a pinch, Flusser could also call on fire from the armed transport USS *Bombshell*.

Flusser had been receiving intelligence reports about the Confederate ironclad *Albemarle* for months, and he was ready to do battle with it. His problem was that he didn't know exactly what he was up against -- each report attributed different armament and design to the *Albemarle*. Flusser felt safe in assuming that whatever kinds of guns she was mounting, the ironclad would be heavier and less maneuverable than his own ships. The best bet might be simply to immobilize the behemoth, then pound her to scrap iron at short range. To this end, Flusser had linked together his two strongest ships, the *Miami* and the *Southfield*, with a wide web of spars and heavy chains. He hoped to lure the Confederate ram between the two ships, snare it in the chains, and then hammer it to pieces, relying on his big Parrott rifles to shatter the heavy armor.

Sunday, April 17, 1864, dawned as "an ideal spring day...neither too warm nor too cool for comfort." The men in Wessells's brigade, Pennsylvanians mostly, were in good spirits. Word had just come through that about two-thirds of them were about to receive their first furloughs after two years of active service. At about 4 p.m., a routine cavalry patrol, a company strong, rode out of town on the Washington Road. A short time later came the sound of a "murderous volley" from the distant woods south of town. Soon afterward, the Union cavalry detachment came galloping back into Plymouth with several empty saddles. At points around the perimeter, drummers sounded the long roll, and the Federal garrison took up arms. The siege of Plymouth had begun.

Hoke began by using the remaining hours of daylight to pound the isolated Fort Grey with strong artillery fire. Armed with a 100-pounder and a pair of 32-pounders, Fort Grey was equipped to duel with ships, not land-based attackers. As darkness ended the preliminary bombardment, its garrison felt little reason for optimism.

During the night, the Union steamboat *Massasoit* docked at Plymouth to evacuate the remaining women and children, along with a number of sick and disabled soldiers -- "the `impedimenta' of the garrison." Word spread through town that the dreaded rebel ram *Albemarle* was on its way, and rumor enlarged the mysterious ironclad to gigantic proportions and equipped it with fearsome powers. Flusser shepherded the refugees aboard the steamboat and did what he could to calm their fears. To a group of women whose

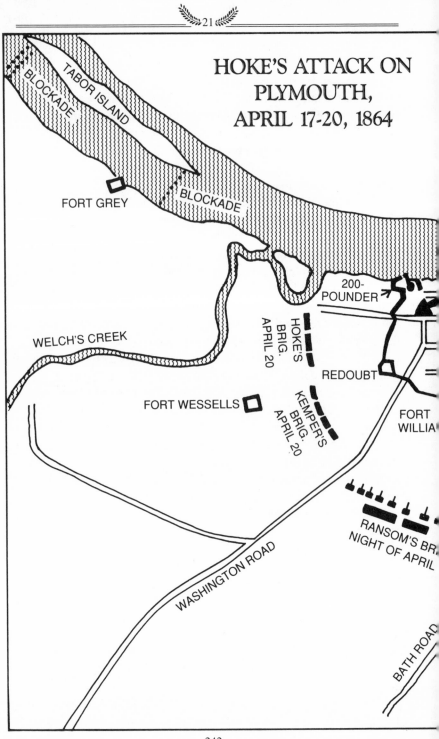

HOKE'S ATTACK ON PLYMOUTH, APRIL 17-20, 1864

TABOR ISLAND

BLOCKADE

BLOCKADE

FORT GREY

200-POUNDER

WELCH'S CREEK

HOKE'S BRIG. APRIL 20

REDOUBT

FORT WESSELLS

KEMPER'S BRIG. APRIL 20

FORT WILLIA

RANSOM'S BR. NIGHT OF APRIL

WASHINGTON ROAD

BATH ROAD

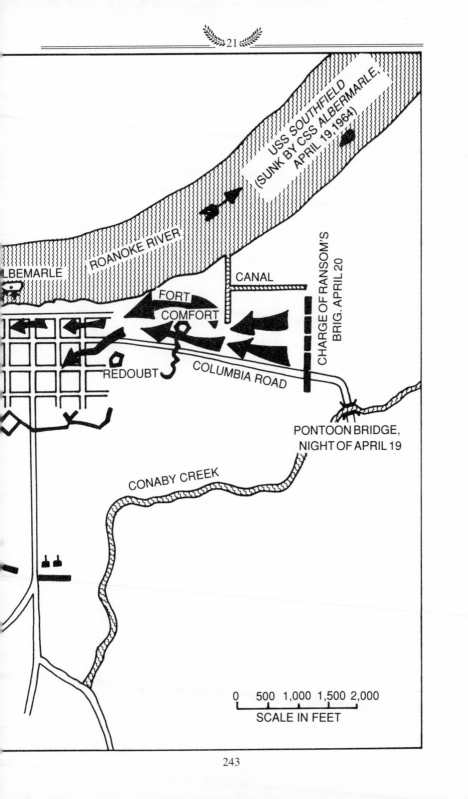

USS SOUTHFIELD
(SUNK BY CSS ALBERMARLE,
APRIL 19,1964)

ROANOKE RIVER

LBEMARLE

CANAL

CHARGE OF RANSOM'S
BRIG. APRIL 20

FORT
COMFORT

REDOUBT

COLUMBIA ROAD

PONTOON BRIDGE,
NIGHT OF APRIL 19

CONABY CREEK

0   500 1,000 1,500 2,000
SCALE IN FEET

fear of the rebel ironclad verged on hysteria, he calmly, and prophetically, said: "Ladies, I have waited two long years for the rebel ram. The Navy will do its duty. We shall sink, destroy, or capture it, or find our graves in the Roanoke."

Anticipating a daybreak assault, the entire Federal garrison stood ready at dawn on Monday, April 18. But Hoke was methodical, and he intended to reduce the outer defenses first. The Confederates rained intense fire on Fort Grey, inflicting some casualties on its defenders but doing surprisingly little harm to the work itself. Hoke's gunners had better luck with the steamer *Bombshell*, which attempted to open contact with Fort Grey and received for its trouble several holes below the waterline. She made it back to the wharf at Plymouth, but sank almost as soon as her moorings were fastened. The Union gunboat *Ceres*, too, came under fire as it tried to support Fort Grey, principally by a 32-pounder Parrott that Hoke had emplaced overlooking the river. The *Ceres* was severely damaged, and nine of her crew were killed or wounded.

Brisk skirmishing flared all morning, about 1,200 yards in front of Fort Williams, with both sides swapping barrages of rifle and cannon fire. The Union gunners in Fort Williams kept up hot fire until a hideous accident marred their rhythm in mid-afternoon. A gunner named Hoyt from the 24th New York Battery was ramming home a shell when an over-excited comrade accidentally discharged the cannon. Shell, rammer, and powder charge all struck the unfortunate Hoyt, ripping off one arm, shattering the other, and charring the upper half of his body. He lingered, suffering terribly, until April 26, and died as a prisoner of war.

Late in the afternoon, General Hoke sent Matt Ransom's brigade, supported by 14 cannon, to make a strong demonstration-attack against Fort Williams. Ransom's men advanced with their usual elan and came within 300 yards of the fort. They didn't actually assault it, but pressed hard against the Federal line, driving in Wessells's skirmishers. Ransom traded intense fire with the defenders until 1 a.m. Then, figuring he'd done enough "demonstrating" for one day, he withdrew his men to their jumping-off line.

While Ransom was pinning down the Federal center, Hoke launched his own brigade against Fort Wessells. Fighting was fierce. Both Colonel John T. Mercer, who was leading Hoke's brigade while Hoke himself supervised the overall operation, and Captain Nelson Chapin, leader of the 85th New York inside the fort, lost their lives. Several times, Hoke's men surged forward and got to the foot of the earthwork, only to be repulsed by a hailstorm of Minie balls and showers of sputtering hand grenades. Finally, after the fourth or fifth attack, the Yankee garrison of Fort Wessells was overwhelmed and abandoned the position. Hoke immediately brought up some 32-pounders and trained them on the town itself. Half of Plymouth now lay open to him from the elevation provided by the captured earthwork.

Meanwhile, on the night of April 18, the *Albemarle* had dropped anchor about three miles upriver from Plymouth. Ahead of her lay the obstacles and block-ships sunk by Flusser to prevent her from pulling within range. Commander Cooke was worried that the behemoth might not be able to join the fight after all; there was nothing to do but wait until daylight.

But young Gilbert Elliott was too nervous about the debut of his creation to sleep. At about midnight, he went out in a small boat and discovered that an underwater current had deepened the channel to such an extent that the ram could squeeze through the obstacles after all. He rowed back to Cooke, who was delighted at the news and promptly ordered steam to be raised in the boilers. Shortly before 3 a.m., the *Albemarle* threaded her way through the obstacles. As the first light of dawn began to thin the darkness, she went into battle.

Her dim, hulking shape was spotted through the pre-dawn murk by the alert Federal gunners at Fort Grey. She immediately came under heavy and accurate fire, but the shots -- even the 100-pounder projectiles -- glanced from her armored sides like so many pebbles. In a matter of moments, the *Albemarle* was out of range and loosed among her enemies.

Flusser was waiting for her east of Plymouth, where the Roanoke River makes a northeastward bend. He watched her coming in the growing light, and for awhile it looked as if the Confederate ironclad would steam right into his trap.

But Commander Cooke, observing the peculiar additions of woodwork and ironmongery festooning both the *Miami* and the

Southfield, figured out what Flusser had in mind. He avoided the trap by throwing the ironclad's helm sharply to the south, then suddenly reversing course and approaching the flank of the two tied-together Union ships, aiming his reinforced prow at the *Southfield*. When the massive *Albemarle* struck, the impact was strong enough to jar teeth loose from several jaws. The iron-sheathed ram tore a gaping hole in the *Southfield*'s hull. Indeed, the two vessels were locked, by the force of their contact, in a mutually deadly embrace, their spars, lines, and chains all intermingled. As the *Southfield* went under, she almost took the Confederate iron-clad with her. Huge columns of water poured in through the ports in the *Albemarle*'s bow. Only the shallow river saved her, for when the *Southfield*'s keel touched bottom, the stricken Union gunboat turned turtle. The *Albemarle* popped loose with a great tearing of wood and a volcano of foam. Ponderous as a dinosaur, the great ironclad returned to an even keel, her inner decks awash ankle-deep in water, but otherwise undamaged and still full of fight.

Flusser's vessel, the *Miami*, had meanwhile closed on the Confederate ram until the two ships were within grappling distance of one another. When the two ships jammed together, the *Miami*'s crew made an attempt to board the ram. Cooke had anticipated this, however, and had ordered as many men topside as the narrow superstructure would hold -- about two dozen. These men maintained a blistering fire with rifles and revolvers at anyone showing himself aboard the Union vessel. As the Confederates atop the *Albemarle* emptied their weapons, they passed them down into the casemate and exchanged them for freshly loaded arms. The Union boarding party never got past the railing of the *Miami*, and several of Flusser's men were struck down. A Confederate was killed, too — a curious gunner who stuck his head out of a gunport to see what was going on. He fell back inside the ship with a Minie ball in his brain, the only Confederate fatality of the battle.

While the two ships were pressed together, Commander Flusser himself pulled the lanyard of his most powerful weapon, the ten-inch 100-pounder Parrott rifle, loaded with a high-explosive shell. The massive cannon was aimed directly at the *Albemarle* at point-blank range. Unfortunately, the ten-second fuse on the projectile was much too long for this range. The huge shell struck the Confederate ironclad, bounced high into the air with a shower of sparks, and — incredibly — landed back on the deck of the *Miami*, a few feet away from Flusser. Dumbfounded, Flusser stood there, still holding the lanyard in his fist, as the powerful shell detonated.

The surgeon's assistant on board the *Miami* described the disaster in a letter:

> Our 100-lb. rifle was fired at her and struck her plumb, but the shot...produced no more effect than one of those little torpedoes we have Fourth of Julys...They killed our commander, C.W. Flusser, and wounded Ensign Harris, Engineer Harrington, and ten men. Capt Flusser was awfully mangled had 19 musket balls and pieces of shell in different parts of his body, one arm was blown off. Dr. Mann and I looked like butchers, our coats and vests off, our shirt sleeves rolled up and we covered with blood. O it was an awful sight. God grant that I may never witness the like again. As fast as the men were wounded, they were passed down to us and we laid them one at a time on the table, cut their clothes from them, and extracted the balls and pieces of shell from them. The blood was over the soles of my boots, all over the berth deck, and the shrieks and groans of the wounded were heartrending. The ram kept butting us, and when Capt. Flusser fell, the men seemed to lose all heart.[1]

The *Miami* also took several punishing hits from the *Albemarle*'s cannon, and as soon as the executive officer could take the con, he steered the battered Union vessel out of the fight. The *Miami* headed for the open waters of the sound at full speed, trailed by the smaller Federal gunboats, whose 32- and 24-pounder shot would have been about as effective against the Confederate ram as golf balls.

Having cleared the river of Federal naval power, the victorious *Albemarle* steamed back to Plymouth and spent the remainder of the afternoon hurling eight-inch shells at the town's defenses.

Hoke spent April 19 further softening up the town with artillery and repositioning Ransom's brigade to hit the defenders from the east, along the axis of the Columbia Road. To aid Ransom's assault, a pontoon bridge was constructed across Conaby Creek during the night. Ransom's men were in position by midnight and were able to get a few hours' rest before forming up for the attack at daybreak.

The attack crossed a cow pasture north of the road. Ransom's men charged with great vigor, filling the air with rebel yells, while Hoke's artillery thundered in support. The charge collapsed Wessells's whole left flank. Ransom's men swept over the Union defenses and just kept going, into the town itself. By the end of April 20, the landward defenses of Plymouth, just like the naval defenses, had been swept clean. Only Fort Williams now remained in Federal hands. One fired-up regiment, the 8th North Carolina, made a valiant, unsupported attack that rolled right up to the earthworks, but the Confederates were thrown back with heavy losses.

On learning about this impulsive and reckless charge, Hoke issued orders that no more assaults were to be launched, figuring that the trapped garrison inside Fort Williams could be beaten by artillery fire alone. He sent a courier to General Wessells, who was holed up inside the walls, and asked for an honorable surrender to end the bloodshed. Wessells, himself an honorable fellow, of course refused the first appeal. Hoke thereupon opened a savage and punishing bombardment, vividly described by General Wessells himself:

> I was now completely enveloped on every side...a cannonade of shot and shell was opened upon [the fort] from four different directions. The terrible fire had to be endured without reply, for no man could live at the guns. The breastwork was struck by solid shot on every side, fragments of shells sought almost every interior angle of the work, the whole extent of the parapet was swept by musketry...this condition of affairs could not be long endured without reckless sacrifice of life....[2]

At 10 a.m. on April 20, 1864, General Wessells surrendered. As he handed his sword to General Hoke, he remarked, "General, this is the saddest day of my life." Hoke responded, "General, this is the proudest day of mine!"

Robert Hoke had just won the cleanest, most competent victory ever gained by the Confederacy on North Carolina soil. It had been a North Carolinian's show, too, since Hoke was a native of the state and most of his regiments were Tar Heels as well. So, as it happened, was Commander Cooke, whose resolute handling of the

248

Albemarle had, in the space of a few hours, unlocked the whole defensive scheme of Plymouth. Hoke had inflicted 300 casualties on the Federals, captured 2,500 men, and taken as booty 500 horses, 28 cannon, and 5,000 stand of small arms, to say nothing of an immense amount of provisions, medical stores, clothing, and gunpowder. Had Hoke, rather than D.H. Hill or George Pickett, been in charge of the earlier rebel offensives on New Bern, the whole coast might have been under Confederate control months earlier, with incalculable consequences for the South's fortunes elsewhere.

As it was, there was no stopping Hoke now. On April 27, he laid siege to the little town of Washington. There wasn't much fighting, and the Federal defenders abandoned the town on April 30 — but not until they subjected the place to three days of the most brutal and wanton pillage, capped by a fire which left half of Washington in ashes.

Leaving one regiment behind to garrison Washington, Hoke pushed on for the big prize, New Bern, determined that this time, with such momentum behind his offensive, the place would fall. It almost did.

Once again, Hoke called on the valiant Cooke and his ironclad to furnish the naval power, hoping to repeat his successful tactics at Plymouth. Cooke was certainly game, but could make no promises about his vessel's ability to complete the long journey from Plymouth down the length of Pamlico Sound -- after all, she had barely been able to make it 20 miles downriver from Hamilton to Plymouth.

Federal naval authorities at New Bern fully expected the *Albemarle* to put in another appearance, and they were devoting considerable time and thought to figuring out a way to overcome the rebel Goliath. The task of intercepting and neutralizing the *Albemarle* was assigned to Captain Melancton Smith, who had arrived in late April. Smith had four large double-ended steamers, well armed and considerably more maneuverable than the Confederate ram. These ships consisted of the refurbished *Miami*, the *Sassacus*, the *Mattabesett*, and the *Wyalusing*. Supporting them were three smaller gunboats whose job was to attack the ram's handful of escorts. The *Miami* had been rigged with a powerful torpedo at the end of a long boom. Smith hoped to place this weapon under the ram's keel as it was attacking, and then detonate it, ripping out her bottom. Nets would also be available to foul the *Albemarle*'s propellers, should the chance arise. Once she was motionless, she could be boarded. Furthermore, Smith had drilled his ships to encircle the ram, as though dancing "a terrific grand waltz" with her, using their superior mobility to maintain an incessant drum-fire barrage at the closest feasible range. These preparations were barely in place before the great ram was sighted once more, on the afternoon of May 5.

Smith's flotilla was drawn up across the entrance to Albemarle Sound. At 5 p.m. the *Albemarle* opened fire. Her second shot drew blood, shearing off much of the *Mattabesett*'s rigging and wounding six Union crewmen. Next, she tried to ram the Union vessel, but missed. The *Sassacus* took advantage of the moment to fire a full broadside at the *Albemarle* at point-blank range, using nine-inch guns and its heaviest weapon, a Parrott rifle loaded with 100-pound solid shot. None of these projectiles penetrated the Confederate ram's sloping armor. Indeed, Lieutenant Commander F.A. Roe of the *Sassacus* watched in horror as some of his 100-pound cannonballs broke in two like melons. He did score one lucky hit, however: a roundshot crashed into the muzzle of one of Cooke's eight-inchers, breaking off some 20 inches of the barrel. Amazingly, the *Albemarle*'s gunners continued to serve and fire the shortened weapon. At this range, the damage hardly mattered.

A score of brave Union sailors, leaning out from the rails and lower rigging of the *Sassacus*, attempted to pitch casks of gunpowder down the Confederate ram's smokestack. Others chucked sputtering hand grenades at the gunports. The *Sassacus* then passed out of range and subdued one of the ram's escorts, a little armed launch, raking her with a broadside that prompted a white flag to go up almost immediately.

Commander Roe of the *Sassacus* now thought he was in a good position to gain speed and ram the *Albemarle*, which was broadside to him about 400 yards away. He ordered emergency speed, and to give it to him the engine crew fed the fires with oily rags. "Give her all the steam she can carry!" cried Roe as the vessel leaped forward. He aimed the *Sassacus* at the seam between the *Albe-*

marle's hull and armored casemate, expecting this to be one of the few relatively vulnerable points on the vessel. With her throttle wide open and her steam gauges trembling dangerously "in the red," the *Sassacus* shuddered, throbbed, and shot through the water as if she had come alive.

It didn't take long to cover the distance to the Confederate ship, but the *Sassacus* was gathering speed so rapidly that it worked up tremendous momentum by the time it struck. The impact was bone-cracking and spilled crewmen all over the decks of both vessels. The damage, however, was mostly to the Federal ship. The *Sassacus*'s bow was torn, and its underwater timbers were seriously weakened by the force of the collision. There was a bad moment for the *Albemarle*, too, as she was thrown into a list and several tons of seawater roared in through her ports. But even though his face was pale with fear, Cooke's voice was steady as he called out: "Stand by your guns -- if we must sink, let us go down like brave men."

The *Sassacus* was now wedged firmly into her target, but because of the angle was unable to bring her full broadside to bear. Inside the ovenlike casemate of the *Albemarle*, the sweat-lathered Confederate gun crews pivoted one of their Brooke rifles toward their trapped adversary and fired the single most devastating round of the battle: a 100-pound rifled shot that punctured the Federal ship's starboard boiler. Instantly, the *Sassacus* was filled with live steam, and the shrieks of scalded crewmen could be heard above the blasts of cannon fire. The impact of the shot was so great that it jarred the Union vessel free of the *Albemarle*. The *Sassacus* slowly drifted away, still gamely and futilely firing at the Confederate ram until she was out of range. Her chief engineer, a man named Hobby, was cited for gallantry for staying by his one functioning engine until the ship was out of danger, despite being blinded and all but flayed alive by escaping steam from the ruptured boiler.

Both the *Miami* and the *Matabesett* also took damaging hits from the *Albemarle*'s guns. The former vessel's smokestack was shot nearly in half, and its superstructure was severely damaged; the latter was swept by a single shot that tore off all the legs of three crewmen.

Tactically, this engagement was another clear victory for the

Albemarle, but strategically, the victory turned out to be Commander Roe's. The concentrated fire of the Federal squadron, coupled with the ramming, had inflicted enough damage on the Confederate vessel to make it impossible for her to continue toward New Bern. Her smokestack was like Swiss cheese, so riddled with holes that her speed dropped to almost nothing. Her steering apparatus, too, had sustained severe damage. Commander Cooke was able to nurse her back to Plymouth only by cramming lard, bacon, and tubs of butter into his boilers.

Meanwhile, General Hoke's attack on New Bern had begun, and he achieved some significant early victories. Striking hard at several points along the defensive lines south of the Trent River, Hoke's forces drove in all the Union pickets and swiftly overran several of the same fortified positions that General Barton, back in February, had considered impregnable. With such momentum behind him, Hoke figured he could carry New Bern with a general assault, with or without the *Albemarle*.

Then, only one day after the attack began, Hoke received urgent orders from Richmond. He was to withdraw his army, turn it around, and entrain for Petersburg, Virginia, where Lee needed every available man in the trenches.

Were it not for this order, New Bern almost certainly would have fallen to the Confederates within 48 hours. Hoke would have virtually eliminated the Federal presence on the North Carolina coast, opening up additional ports for the blockade runners and guaranteeing the safe passage of supplies to Lee on the coastal railroad. A strategic victory of this dimension would have been worth the gamble. And then, after taking New Bern, Hoke could have come north to help Lee, his army flushed with victory. As it was, he abandoned the attack with a heavy heart, knowing somehow that the Confederacy had lost its last, and best, chance of regaining the coast.

Cushing's Torpedo

William Cushing and Charles Flusser had been friends for a long time. Together, they had dreamed about the days of great white-sailed frigates breasting the open seas, and about the heroic deeds men could perform aboard such graceful ships. Flusser had stood loyally with Cushing when Cushing was in disgrace after his expulsion from the U.S. Naval Academy at Annapolis. There was no man in the U.S. Navy whom Cushing admired more deeply, no man anywhere for whom he felt deeper affection. In time, both men had risen to command and had performed valiantly aboard the small, oil-reeking steamers that plied the shallow waters of North Carolina's coast — a world apart from their youthful dreams of Nelsonian glory on the high seas.

But now one of them was dead. Flusser had been ripped to pieces trying to lead his wooden ship against a mighty ironclad. For Cushing, the *Albemarle* became more than just another Confederate opponent — it was a personal enemy. And Flusser's death was not merely a tragedy of war, but instead was an affront to all that Cushing held sacred and honorable about the naval profession. When Will Cushing was told of Flusser's grisly fate at Plymouth, his mouth compressed into a thin white line, and he vowed: "I shall never rest until I have avenged his death."

Cushing had not participated in the second battle with the Confederate ironclad in Albemarle Sound. Following his exploits with the *Ellis*, Cushing had been given ships of his own to command — first the *Commodore Barney*, then the *Shokoken*, and finally a full-fledged ship of the line, the *Monticello*. Most of his time aboard these vessels was spent in the blockade line off Wilmington. But Cushing, even more than most men, was driven half-mad with boredom by the routine of blockade duty. Before long, he was going off on his own again, in small boats with picked crews of volunteers, raising hell up and down the whole Cape Fear coastline. Several times he led raiding parties ashore on the beaches north of Fort Fisher and on the islands below Confederate Point. He captured Confederate outposts, tried to seize cargo from blockade runners that had run aground, and in August 1863, with 20 men, he even overran an artillery battery. Nearly everyone thought he was crazy, and in a way he probably was, but even the superior officers who railed at his independence had to admit that his exploits raised morale in the offshore squadron. Those who wanted to chastise him for insubordination were restrained by the knowledge that his deeds made great newspaper copy in the North, and consequently endeared him to the naval establishment in Washington, D.C.

In February 1864, Cushing managed to top himself. On the last day of the month, at about 8:30 p.m. -- without permission, of course -- Cushing set out in two small boats with 20 of his faithful buccaneers. With muffled oars they rowed between Bald Head Island and Fort Caswell, then crossed the Cape Fear River and landed, without being detected, near Smithville. Leaving a dozen men to guard the boats, Cushing led the rest through the darkened streets of the little town until their progress was blocked by two Negro men sitting at a campfire.

Scuttling like a crab, Cushing crawled to within three feet of the two men, then suddenly rose to a crouch in front of them, his big Navy revolver pointed right at them. He motioned for silence and they complied. Back in the shadows, the two captives gladly agreed to help Cushing. Indeed, they could hardly contain their delight when they learned what he intended to do: capture the Confederate commander of the town, General Louis Hebert, and then hijack a steamboat from the wharf and brazenly sail out to rejoin the Union fleet. Alas, one of the black men told him, there were no steamers in town just then. Never mind; Cushing would abduct the general anyway.

Taking three men and one of the Negroes to act as a guide, Cushing crept ahead. General Hebert's headquarters -- a large, white, antebellum structure with a handsome veranda -- was situated about 50 feet from a barracks containing several hundred Confederate soldiers. To Cushing, that only meant his coup would be all the sweeter.

After positioning his three men, and permitting the helpful black man to return to his campfire, Cushing crept onto the porch and tried the front door. It was open. He went in. The house was dark and silent, save for the ticking of a clock in one of the rooms off the main hall. Not knowing for certain where General Hebert slept, Cushing decided to try the most logical places, the upstairs bedrooms. Noiselessly he ascended the stairs. At the top landing, he found himself engulfed in utter darkness. He was too close to give up now, so he did the next logical thing: he struck a match.

In front of him were three or four doors, all closed. With a mental shrug, he chose the middle one. He opened the door and peered in; more darkness. Suddenly he heard a loud noise outside, and one of his men calling out: "Captain! Captain!" Cushing bolted down the stairs and followed the sound into a darkened front room. Inside, he found a tall man in a sleeping gown struggling to raise a heavy chair above his head. Hurling himself at the man, Cushing knocked him down and clamped one hand around his throat, simultaneously cocking his pistol and pressing the front blade-sight against the shaking man's temple.

Dizzily happy at the thought that he had captured General Hebert, Cushing lit a candle and asked a few questions. His joy was soon compromised. The man he had just taken prisoner was Captain Kelly, chief engineer for the Smithfield garrison. A decent catch, but not the prize; General Hebert was away for the night in Wilmington. Moreover, Cushing soon learned, Hebert's second-in-command, Adjutant General W.D. Hardman, had fled the house, clad in his nightshirt, and was even now rousing the men in the nearby barracks.

While the still-befuddled Kelly donned a pair of pants, Cushing stuffed his pockets with all the loose documents in the room. Then he jammed his pistol into Kelly's side, collected his three men, and calmly walked down the main street of town. Confused and alarmed rebel soldiers swarmed all around them. Several armed Confederates even banged into the little party, but not a man stopped them, questioned them, or even seemed to notice them.

With magnificent insolence, Cushing even paused long enough to collect the two helpful Negroes, both of whom were delighted to make a break for freedom.

Cushing's boats were just pulling away from the harbor when the first shots rang out behind them. Soon, however, they were hidden by the darkness. By 3:30 a.m., Cushing and his party were safely back aboard the *Monticello*.

The next day, Cushing sent one of his subordinates, Ensign J.E. Jones, under a flag of truce to Fort Caswell. Ensign Jones was met by the fort's commander, a colonel also named Jones. Colonel Jones asked Ensign Jones about the purpose of his mission. Ensign Jones innocently and courteously replied that he had come to fetch clothes and money for the hapless Captain Kelly, so that his sojourn in a Federal prison might be as comfortable as possible. Colonel Jones had heard all about the night's escapade, of course -- the telegraph wires had been humming with it all morning -- and at first he merely looked woodenly at Ensign Jones without saying a word. Then he studiedly turned his back on his guest and looked out the office window, pretending to study his troops while they drilled on the parade ground. The strained silence continued for a moment, and then Ensign Jones saw an unrestrainable grin start working at the corners of the colonel's mouth. Finally, unable to contain himself any longer, Colonel Jones turned around, shook his head, and chuckled: "That was a damned splendid affair, sir! Damned splendid!"

Before taking his leave, after a half-hour of pleasant conversation, Ensign Jones handed the colonel a message. It was from Will Cushing, addressed to General Hebert, and it read: "My Dear General: I deeply regret that you were not at home when I called. Very respectfully, W.B. Cushing."

Cushing embarked on another "splendid affair" in June 1864. Ostensibly, his mission was to gather intelligence about the Confederate ironclad *Raleigh*, which had made an unsuccessful sortie against the Union blockade line some weeks earlier. Rumors had reached the Federal fleet that the ironclad had run aground on her way back up the Cape Fear River and was no longer operational. Cushing's objective was to verify the status of the ram and then get back in one piece. Cushing being Cushing, however, he chose to interpret his orders rather liberally.

Just after sunset on June 23, Cushing shoved off in one of the *Monticello*'s cutters, commanding a party of 15 men. They carried two day's rations, 18 pistols, and a half-dozen breech-loading Sharps rifles. Cushing himself was armed with a pair of beautifully inlaid dueling pistols. The boat followed the same basic route Cushing had used on the night of the Smithfield raid, passing the silent cannon of Forts Caswell and Holmes, then passing the small rebel bastion on Zeek's Island. They rowed almost 15 miles, all the way to the outpost line around Fort Anderson, where they were finally spotted and taken under heavy fire. By conning the ship from one patch of reflected moonlight to another, Cushing managed to get away without losing a man, although nearby splashes from cannonballs drenched the boat's occupants as they zig-zagged out of range.

Still, they had seen no sign of the *Raleigh*. Cushing figured the Confederates would now be looking for them downstream, near the mouth of the Cape Fear River, so after what he thought as a reasonable interval, he ordered the men to come about and resume their course toward Wilmington. At first they looked at him incredulously. Then, as they realized what he was planning, they grinned and put their backs into the oars once more. This time, the Yankee cutter made it past Fort Anderson, and by dawn they were only seven miles from Wilmington. Along this stretch of the river, the trees grew right to the water's edge. Cushing's men pulled their boat ashore and took cover in the foliage. For the rest of the day, Cushing took copious notes on the traffic he saw on the water, both civilian and military, while the men took turns napping and keeping watch.

The only rations they had brought were hardtack and salted meat, and by evening their supplies were about gone. They decided to search the vicinity for food, but before anyone could set out, two small boats were spotted heading directly for their hiding place. The occupants turned out to be fishermen, not Confederate soldiers, and they surrendered meekly when suddenly confronted with a dozen desperate-looking Yankees brandishing weapons. Cushing questioned the men closely, and they were not reticent. Yes, they told him, the *Raleigh* had run aground and was a total wreck.

Cushing thought they were lying. He resolved to stick around until he could verify the ironclad's status to his satisfaction.

After dark, Cushing took his cutter upstream and inspected the inner defenses of Wilmington: ropes, chains, submerged logs, block-ships, pilings, and at least ten heavy cannon. Having obtained this valuable intelligence, he headed the cutter downriver until he reached the area of Cypress Swamp, about four miles from the city. The crew poled their way up a shallow creek until they came to a log road. After hiding the boat, Cushing led a patrol down the path. After a two-mile hike, they came to a bigger, better-maintained thoroughfare. This, the helpful fishermen informed him, was the main route between Wilmington and Fort Fisher.

Cushing's ears pricked up at that news: Here was a good place to lie in wait. For what, he was not yet sure, but he was convinced something would turn up to make it worthwhile.

Something did. Just after daybreak, an armed Confederate courier appeared on horseback, whistling carelessly as he rode right into Cushing's ambush. He was carrying the morning mail, and it included documents that listed in detail the armament and condition of the great fortress.

All rations were now exhausted and the men's stomachs were rumbling. One of Cushing's men exchanged clothes with the crestfallen courier, stuffed his pockets with a wad of Confederate money taken from the mailbag, and sauntered off to Smith's general store, a couple of miles away. The proprietor, Mr. Smith, happened to be one of the fishermen Cushing had captured, so Cushing's man had no trouble finding the place. The Yankee engaged in a cordial conversation with Mrs. Smith, who sold him a basket full of eggs, milk, and chicken. These comestibles were added to the quart or so of ripe blackberries Cushing's men had located near the creek, and a luxurious repast was enjoyed by all, including the captive fishermen.

By mid-afternoon, Cushing and his men had captured 26 prisoners, both soldiers and civilians. By talking to them, Cushing had learned when the evening courier was due. He resolved to stay until he had added that fellow's mailbag to his booty, but this courier wasn't alone and was sharp-eyed enough to spot a bluecoat in the bushes. Cushing chased him on horseback for two miles, but couldn't catch him.

By now, even Will Cushing thought it was time to leave. In an hour, the whole region would be swarming with Confederate patrols, and in all likelihood the river would be sealed tight. Before leaving, he cut the telegraph wire from Fort Fisher.

Cushing planned to leave his prisoners on a small island in the Cape Fear River, except for one man whom Cushing kept on board to act as pilot. The sudden appearance of a rebel steamboat interrupted that plan, but again, the Yankee raiders escaped detection. Cushing now figured he didn't have time to unload two dozen people. Instead, he deposited them in a couple of derelict canoes and set them adrift, keeping only the pilot and a couple of the more important prisoners. The pilot proved faithful -- no doubt the presence of Cushing's pistol in the small of his back gave him incentive -- and even steered the cutter past the spot where the *Raleigh* lay on a sandbar, a rusting and useless hulk.

Although they had been rowing for five hours, Cushing's men steered the cutter boldly through a swarm of rebel picket boats, regained the open sea, and made it safely back to the *Monticello*. Cushing made his report, delivered his documents and prisoners, and then fell into his bunk. He had not slept for 68 hours and had pushed his luck beyond all rational limits, but he had tweaked the rebels' noses, stirred up a veritable hornet's nest ashore -- Confederate companies were running up and down the peninsula looking for a Yankee invasion force -- and had verified the status of the *Raleigh*. All things considered, he was pleased with the results of his little excursion.

Next Target: The *Albemarle*

June 1864 also marked the first Union attempt to blow up the *Albemarle* as she lay at anchor near Plymouth. A five-man team, using stretchers, lugged two 100-pound bangalore torpedoes through the swamps behind Plymouth, tied the weapons together, and then tried to float them on the current so they could be exploded simultaneously on both sides of the ironclad's bow. The Yankees were spotted, however, and repulsed by small-arms fire.

There was no question that the *Albemarle* had to be destroyed.

The mere fact that she was still afloat, lurking up the Roanoke River, forced the U.S. Navy to keep a powerful squadron of ships across the mouth of the river — ships that were urgently needed elsewhere. The Federals made a detailed study of various ways to attack the ram, and a list of qualified naval officers was drawn up as candidates to lead the effort. John Ericsson, the inventor of the Union ironclad *Monitor*, was brought in as a consultant. He studied the charts and announced that all of his designs drew too much water to even get into the sound from the ocean, much less up the Roanoke River to Plymouth. As scheme after scheme was discarded, the options narrowed down to one: a small boat raid designed either to board and capture the ram, or to blow her up at her moorings. There was one significant drawback to this option: the men who went on the mission would almost certainly die.

Career Navy officers are not supposed to balk at such missions, of course, but the Navy Department couldn't find anyone who was available, healthy, and qualified by virtue of both skill and zeal. Finally, in July 1864, the commander of the North Atlantic Blockade Squadron, Admiral Samuel P. Lee, read the report of Cushing's incredible reconnaissance behind Confederate lines near Wilmington. When he had finished reading, he summoned an aide and said: "Get Lieutenant Cushing...of the *Monticello*. I've got some work for him."

Cushing had already decided what he wanted to do: board the ram, overwhelm her crew, and then brazenly sail her downriver under a Union flag. During a trip to the Brooklyn Navy Yard, he selected two 30-foot steam launches with screw propellers, and had a 12-pounder howitzer mounted in the bow of each. One of the craft, however, was lost on the voyage south, so Cushing had to proceed with a single vessel. While he was in Brooklyn, Cushing also took delivery of the boom-torpedo that was supposed to strike the fatal blow, should it prove impractical to capture the ram. It was an incredibly complicated, Rube Goldberg-type device, the brainchild of an engineer named John L. Lay. The shell-shaped warhead was attached to a 14-foot boom that was securely bracketed to the side of the launch. The spar could be lowered or raised until the weapon was in position. Then, when a lanyard was pulled, a pin was released, and a heavy ball of grapeshot fell onto a nipple on top of a percussion cap on top of the powder charge. Cushing tested several of these bizarre contraptions in the Hudson River, and found that if the operator had enough presence of mind to pull both the aiming lanyard and the trigger-line at precisely the right instant, the device worked as advertised. The fact that he would have to jiggle the thing into position while presumably under murderous close-range fire seems never to have bothered him.

In September 1864, while final preparations were being made, Cushing took a brief leave of absence to visit his family in upstate New York. He wanted to tell his mother about the mission in person; she still hadn't fully recovered from the death of Will's brother at Gettysburg. They walked into the hills together on a crisp wintry day, and while his mother sat beneath a tree, Will knelt beside her and told her everything: the *Albemarle*'s great strength, the ram's early victories, the slaying of Charles Flusser, and the plan that had been devised to destroy the rebel giant.

"I don't understand all this," Mrs. Cushing said, after a long silence. "I don't see how you can succeed. If this ship is so strong that a thousand men and nine ships could not destroy it, how can they expect one man to do it?"

"I will succeed, Mama, or you will not have any Will Cushing."

"But I don't understand...why you?" she pleaded.

"There is no one else, Mama," he replied.

On October 12, Admiral David D. Porter relieved Admiral Lee as commander of the North Atlantic Blockading Squadron. Porter considered Cushing a reckless and insubordinate daredevil, and he was tempted to cancel the mission, especially after Cushing was forced to proceed with only one steam launch. Ultimately, under intense pressure from Washington, he allowed the mission to go forward. To Commander W.H. Macomb, now the officer in charge of all Union naval vessels in the North Carolina sounds, he sent a memo outlining Cushing's mission. It concluded with these words: "I have no great confidence in his success, but you will afford him all the assistance in your power, and keep boats ready to pick him up in case of failure."

After a difficult journey down the Chesapeake and Albemarle Canal, Cushing and his steam launch arrived at Roanoke Island on October 23. Word had already gone around among Macomb's

crews that "Cushing was going to lead an expedition," and —
although no one knew what the mission might be — there were ten
times as many volunteers as Cushing needed. Cushing had no
trouble selecting the best men from a half-dozen ships. He warned
them that "not only must you not expect, but you must not hope to
return. I can promise you nothing but glory, death, or possibly a
promotion."

Macomb made available to Cushing the latest intelligence
reports concerning the *Albemarle*. She was moored eight miles
upriver at a point where the channel was 150-200 yards wide.
About a mile downstream from the *Albemarle* was the superstructure of its first victim, the USS *Southfield*, still protruding above
water and now inhabited by a Confederate picket detachment.
Moreover, the rebels had anchored a small schooner close to the
wreck and had equipped it with a fieldpiece, two dozen soldiers,
and some signal rockets. Cushing decided to tow a cutter of extra
men to deal with that outpost.

Everything was ready on the evening of October 27. It was a
brisk autumn night, about 65 degrees; the sky was streaked with
heavy clouds and the waters of the sound were pimpled with
intermittent showers. Just before he shoved off, Cushing turned to
the men standing on the deck of Macomb's flagship and waved
farewell, laughing, "Another stripe or a coffin!" Will Cushing was
in his element.

At about 11:30 p.m., its crew of determined volunteers wrapped
in a shivering, rain-soaked silence, the launch entered the mouth of
the Roanoke River. The boat's engine had been muffled with a
wooden box and a thick tarpaulin, so their passage was marked
only by a soft and rhythmic chuffing sound. Cushing rehearsed his
moves. Some rehearsal was necessary, for in addition to the two
lines in his left hand, which controlled the torpedo, Cushing held
three more lines in his right hand. One led to the engineer's ankle
and could be used to signal speed; one led to the sailor in charge of
"lowering the boom" with the torpedo attached; and the third led to
the 12-pounder boat howitzer, which had been double-charged with
grapeshot. How any man could expect to keep track of all five lines
in the midst of a close-range nocturnal firefight is something which
transcends all logic and reason, but Cushing was certain that, when

the time came, he would be able to pull the right line at the right time.

Shortly after 2 a.m., the launch passed the wreck of the *Southfield* and the fortified schooner. Cushing was about to wave a white handkerchief, signaling the men in the towed cutter that he was about to cast them off, but then thought better of it. Although the launch was passing the schooner at a distance of no more than 60 feet, there was no outcry from the Confederate pickets, no sign that they were detected. So the launch chugged on, the cutter still in tow. Cushing was still determined, if possible, to take the *Albemarle* by boarding her from the landward side -- and if he succeeded, he would need every man to overcome the *Albemarle*'s crew.

He very nearly got away with it. Ten minutes after passing the schooner, the launch rounded a bend, and there she was — "a dark mountain of iron" looming dead ahead. Cushing steered for the wharf. Just as the launch cut toward shore, a sharp-eared dog began to bark, alerting the half-asleep picket on top of the Confederate ironclad. "Who goes there?" came the challenge.

No need for silence now. "Ahead fast!" cried Cushing, redundantly jerking on the line attached to his engineer. The launch dug into the river with an audible crunch. Cushing turned toward the stern and yelled to the leader of the men in the cutter: "Cast off, Peterkin, and go down and get those pickets on the schooner!" Freed of the tow, the launch leaped ahead.

Already the first shots were peppering the water around them, wild at first, but sure to get closer. Muzzle flashes were leaping from the top of the ram's casemate and flaring from her gunports. There were cries of alarm and a sudden racket of movement on the shore. Fifty yards to go.

Suddenly, a prepared bonfire burst into flame on shore, bathing the scene in lurid, flickering light. The great Confederate ram seemed enormous, and its shadow upon the river was gigantic. Peering at the vessel, Cushing now observed that it was protected by a torpedo screen of floating logs, a semi-circular shield designed to protect the behemoth against just the sort of attack Cushing was about to execute. With icy determination, Cushing actually slowed down the launch and took a moment to examine the protective screen. All the while, Minie balls were zinging past his head like angry wasps. Then, to the amazement of his engineer, he ordered the launch to turn away. He took the boat across the river, turned around, and aimed her at the ram again.

If he worked up enough speed, he calculated, he would hit the logs with sufficient momentum to ride over them and bring his bow within range of the spar-torpedo. Of course, once over the logs, there would be no escape — no way to cross back over the obstacle and regain open water. Yet his mind was clear and remarkably calm; if anything disturbed the smooth, hot flow of adrenalin throughout his body, it was a passing reaffirmation of his vow to avenge the death of his friend Charles Flusser.

Cushing's launch tore across the river at flank speed, straight into a storm of bullets. Forty yards. Thirty. The *Albemarle* was sparkling with musketry and the air was alive with bullets. Cushing ignored everything but the point he was aiming for. A rifle ball clipped off the sole of his left shoe. Twenty yards. Now the rebels were firing shotguns at them. A charge of buckshot tore out the back of Cushing's coat.

Now, rather incongruously, came a hail from the Confederate ship: "What boat is that?" Cushing yelled back: "We'll soon let you know!" Then he fired the boat howitzer, raking the *Albemarle*'s sides with a hundred balls from the double charge of canister. The powerful discharge made a fearful clanging, banging, pots-and-pans racket against the ironclad's armor. Cushing ordered the torpedo-spar swung into position just before the launch struck the logs.

There was a terrific, grinding crash. The little steamboat's bow rose into the air, and it shuddered to a halt. The flame-lit darkness was treacherous, but to Cushing it looked as if the distance was just about right. He leaned forward to make sure the torpedo was in place. Satisfied, he raised his head and experienced the first real lurch of terror he had known that night. Directly in front of him, about ten feet away, was the muzzle of one of the *Albemarle*'s eight-inch cannon. Cushing knew all about eight-inch guns. He did some rapid mental calculations as he listened to someone bawling commands to the gun crew inside the armored casemate: He had about 20 seconds until the gun would be ready to fire.

Cushing gently pulled on one of the lines in his right hand, freeing the torpedo from its rigging and enabling it to float upward under the edge of the ram's hull. Two bullets fluttered through his clothing. Another pulled at his sleeve. A fourth ripped off part of his collar. Yet another skimmed his left hand and drew blood, although he didn't realize it at the time. He forced himself to pull the remaining line ever so slowly, making sure it wouldn't break. The pin came free, the heavy ball of grapeshot dropped, the percussion cap fired, and the torpedo detonated almost beneath his feet. At that exact instant, the *Albemarle* fired its eight-inch gun.

The force of the torpedo explosion, combined with the powerful vacuum created at the muzzle of the eight-inch gun by its shot, flattened out the steam launch "like a pasteboard box." A boiling pillar of water shot skyward, then fell, cold and crushingly heavy, upon the launch and the now-desperate men within it. When Cushing could hear again, he heard cries from the ram and from the shore: "Surrender or we will blow you out of the water!" Cushing was already peeling off his shoes, sword, shot-torn coat, and sidearm. He paused long enough to scream back: "Never! I'll be damned first!"

Then he shouted, "Men, save yourselves!" He dove into the river and began swimming. As he recovered from the shock of the cold water, and as the hammering of his heart began to ease, he wished more than anything he could hang around long enough to make sure the torpedo had done its job. But the confusion, the darkness, and the need to put as much distance as he could between himself and the enemy made that impossible.

The skipper of the *Albemarle* on that dramatic night was Commander W.F. Warley. (Commander Cooke had been relieved, his nerves shot and his health in tatters, shortly after the battle with the *Sassacus*). As soon as the concussion from Cushing's torpedo subsided, Warley sent his chief engineer below to inspect the damage. The engineer reappeared a moment later and announced that there was a hole in her bottom "big enough to drive a wagon through." Warley had begun to suspect as much -- already he could feel the ironclad settling lower into the Roanoke River.

Cushing's crewmen, meanwhile, were swimming for their lives or surrendering, depending on how much they feared incarceration in a Confederate prison camp. The men in the cutter easily managed to subdue the garrison aboard the fortified schooner, but in time some of them, too, surrendered.

Will Cushing had no intention of rotting in Andersonville. Despite his appetite for violent action, he was a man of precarious health, and he probably wouldn't have survived incarceration until the end of the war. He paddled out to midstream, found the current, and swam with it.

He was cold and tired now, and his injured hand had started to throb like the devil. He drifted until he found a region of relative silence and darkness, then headed for shore. Before he had gone far, he heard one of his men splashing anxiously nearby. Cushing turned around, swam to the man, and found him in the last stages of exhaustion, about to go under. Summoning his own reserves of energy, Cushing hooked his uninjured arm around the sailor and swam one-handed for 15 minutes. Then, without either a warning or so much as a murmur, the man slipped from his grasp and vanished beneath the black water. Cushing kept going, very close to the end of his strength, until his feet touched the blessed ooze of the bottom. He hauled himself a few feet out of the water, knelt for a few minutes in a pool of mud, and then passed out, unable even to drag himself to the riverbank proper.

He woke to the delicious touch of sunlight, to warmth, and to the alarming realization that he had become disoriented in the dark and had landed on the Plymouth side of the river, not far downstream from the town's outer defenses. Rebel patrols were everywhere -- one passed so close to Cushing that he could tell the colors of the men's eyes. Yet his luck held, even now. Only later, when he thought back on it, did he realize that the mud he had slept in had coated him with a perfect layer of camouflage.

With the aid of a friendly Negro, who verified for him that the *Albemarle* was "dead gone sunk," Cushing eluded all of the Confederate searchers. At mid-afternoon, he emerged with torn and bleeding feet from the briar patch where he had been hiding and stole a flat-bottomed boat from a rebel squad that had stopped for a picnic lunch nearby. He reached the open sound and was eventually hauled aboard the gunboat *Valley City*, whose skipper, J.A. Banks, had heard reports that Cushing and most of his men were dead.

Cushing was barely conscious when he was carried aboard "like a sack of meal." Banks bent over the still unidentified castaway, peered through the mud, whiskers, and blood-caked scratches, and breathed: "My God, Cushing, is this you?"

A feeble smile appeared on Cushing's cracked lips. "It is I," he whispered.

"Is it done?" asked Banks.

"It is done," answered Cushing.

Indeed it was. Commodore Macomb wasted no time capitalizing on the victory. The very next day he sailed his flotilla up the river and shelled the Confederates out of Plymouth.

Several of Cushing's men managed to get away, but most were captured. The only fatality among the raiders was the man who had slipped from Cushing's grasp in the river. Cushing's daring exploit made headlines, of course, in both the North and the South. Congress voted its thanks, and the Navy Department awarded him a commendation and another stripe. The public showered him with honors. But of all the accolades, the one that probably meant the most to Will Cushing came from the Confederate officer who was his adversary on that tempestuous October night. Writing about the incident a few years later, Commander Warley said simply: "...a more gallant thing was not done during the war."

PART 5

RUNNING THE BLOCKADE

THE NOOSE TIGHTENS, THE PREY ELUDES

The Confederate attitude summarized by the phrase "King Cotton" was a belief, seemingly supported by hard evidence, that the entire British economy depended upon an uninterrupted supply of that commodity arriving at the textile mills of Liverpool and Manchester. On paper, statistics seemed to confirm this notion. At the time the war began, almost five million British subjects depended on jobs in the cotton-based textile industry, whose output, in 1860, was valued at 60 million pounds sterling. Almost 80 percent of the South's cotton crop in 1860 had been exported to Great Britain. Deprive the English of their raw cotton, Confederate economists theorized, and Britain would face economic ruin.

But such arguments looked at only one side of a much more complex trade equation. On the other side was the South's chronic need for imports — most importantly, manufactured goods. Before the war, nearly all such goods, even those manufactured in England, had entered the South via internal transportation routes from the North. Very little had been imported directly to the South from Europe.

As a result, the Confederates had few merchant ships when the war started, and the vast majority were sailing vessels instead of steamships. At first, that didn't seem unfortunate, for in 1860 the big sailing ship was still the unchallenged queen of overseas mercantile trade. Steamships, although faster, made second-rate cargo carriers for the simple reason that so much of their space was occupied by the bulky engines and coal bunkers. Yet from the very start, it was the steamships — and only the steamships — that had a chance of outrunning or outmaneuvering the Union blockaders.

Five days after the Union evacuation of Fort Sumter, President Lincoln proclaimed a blockade on all of the Southern states that had seceded. Eight days later, after Virginia and North Carolina left the Union, Lincoln's proclamation was extended to include the coastlines of those states as well. But the blockade existed only on paper, for the U.S. Navy was woefully unprepared to police a shoreline anywhere near that vast. From Cape Henry, Virginia, to the Texas-Mexico border in the Gulf of Mexico, there was more than 4,000 miles of shore to patrol. In May 1861, the total number of vessels on blockade duty off the coast of North Carolina was two. No wonder the Confederates sneered at the blockade proclamation and waited a dangerously long time before taking it seriously. They also assumed that if the Union's ships started cutting off the flow of commerce between the King Cotton states and their British markets, the Royal Navy wouldn't hesitate to intervene.

The Union blockade was something of a hybrid strategy. It was partly a throwback to the rational "chessboard" warfare of the 18th century — in that it was essentially a passive, siege-like operation — and partly a step toward the "total war" concept familiar in modern times, in which the enemy's economy and civilians are considered targets equal in legitimacy to the battlefield armies.

Rules for wartime blockades had been codified and internationally ratified in the late 18th century, and Lincoln's aides formulated their blockading strategy to conform to those principles. Chief among these rules was this key phrase: "Blockades, to be binding, must be effective, that is to say, maintained by a force sufficient really to prevent access to the coast of the enemy." Instead of scattering its ships on the high seas, blindly sailing about in hopes of spotting a contraband sail, the U.S. Navy intended to enclose the Confederacy at close range.

At the start, most of the Union blockade ships were hastily converted merchantmen, fast and maneuverable, but poorly armed. As it turned out, massive broadsides were not often necessary. The

Confederate blockade runners depended on stealth and speed, not armament. Resistance on their part would have changed them from contrabands into "pirates," and their fate, should they be captured, might have been hanging rather than a few weeks or months in jail.

Although most European naval experts doubted the Union's ability to seal off the Confederate coast, they gave tacit recognition to the blockade by declaring their neutrality in the late spring of 1861. Although disappointed, Confederate leaders remained unruffled. It was too late to withhold the cotton crop of 1860 — all but a fraction of it had already been shipped — but the belief persisted that, by holding back the crop of 1861, they could force European, and specifically British, intervention.

Overall coordination of the blockade was developed by a deliberative body called the Blockade Strategy Board, which held its first meetings in June 1861. Once the problem was studied rationally and methodically, the length of the Southern coastline didn't seem unduly worrying — there just weren't that many Southern ports with deep enough channels, adequate docking facilities, and sufficient inland rail connections to qualify as international ports. Two of the best Southern ports, Richmond and Norfolk, were accessible only through Hampton Roads, anchorage of the U.S. Navy's Home Squadron and dominated by the huge seacoast guns of Fort Monroe. No blockade runners could hope to succeed there.

More problematic were the Outer Banks of North Carolina, which began just south of Hampton Roads at Cape Henry and stretched for 200 miles, a complex system of barrier islands sheltering a vast network of shallow inland waterways. During colonial times, the ports of New Bern, Washington, Edenton, and Elizabeth City had enjoyed a flourishing overseas trade. But by the time the Civil War broke out, three of the main outlets to the Atlantic Ocean — Ocracoke, Hatteras, and Oregon Inlets — had become so silted up that they were no longer passable by transatlantic merchantmen. All four North Carolina ports had become, by 1860, secondary centers for light intracoastal trade, but nothing more.

Beaufort, North Carolina, was therefore the first deep-water port south of Norfolk, although by 1860 Morehead City had taken the

lion's share of transatlantic trade, thanks to its connection with the
Atlantic & North Carolina Railroad. Ninety miles south of
Beaufort, and 28 miles upstream from the mouth of the Cape Fear
River, lay North Carolina's premier deepwater port: Wilmington.
Wilmington enjoyed excellent connections to the South Carolina
cities of Charleston and Columbia via the Wilmington & Manchester Railroad, and westward to the interior of North Carolina via
the (incomplete) Wilmington, Charlotte, & Rutherfordton Line.
Coastal steamboat lines made the city a regular stop on their runs
to Charleston and New York, and by 1860 there was a thriving
export business in tar, turpentine, resin, and agricultural products.

Nature herself seemed to have designated Wilmington as a sally
port against the blockade. Surrounded by a veritable maze of
channels and tributaries, some of them at least partly navigable by
larger vessels, the city had not one but two outlets to the sea. The
main channel, called the Old Inlet, led to the Atlantic in a southwesterly direction. It was suitable for larger vessels, although the
bar separating the channel from the open sea was notoriously shifty
and might change its depth by as much as five feet, up or down,
following a storm. In 1761, when a monster hurricane had
slammed ashore, a second passage had been cut to the sea in a
northeasterly direction, between Confederate Point ("Federal
Point" before the war) and Smith Island. This somewhat shallower
channel was known, logically enough, as the New Inlet.

Geography also favored Wilmington. The city was 674 nautical
miles from Bermuda and 570 miles from Nassau. The trip to
Nassau was the most favored by blockade runners, for it could be
made in three days, and it consumed less than 200 tons of coal,
thus freeing more space for valuable cargo.

Norfolk was the first Confederate port blockaded, on April 30,
1861, followed in subsequent weeks by Charleston, Savannah,
Mobile, and New Orleans. Wilmington was officially blockaded,
more symbolically than anything else, on July 21, by a single,
small converted merchantman named the USS *Daylight*.

Almost immediately, trade declined. Between June and August
1861, not one steamship entered or left a Confederate port, and
only seven sailing vessels arrived from overseas ports. Although
this might seem alarming, it didn't unduly disturb the Southern

merchants, bankers, and planters who put their faith in the King Cotton theory. All the South had to do, they reasoned, was let its cotton crop sit idly in the warehouses until there were food riots in Manchester. Then the Royal Navy would blow its way through the blockade. Months of precious time were lost to this illusion — months in which the blockade was easily penetrated, and in which a systematic plan for overseas trade could have been worked out. As a result, the various blockade-running schemes were put into effect long after they should have been.

Wilmington's golden age as a blockade-running port began in April 1862, when the *Thomas L. Wragg*, coming from Nassau, found the New Inlet unguarded and sailed in, close to the protective Confederate batteries of Fort Fisher. She ran aground, but was partially unloaded by tugs from the city, lightening her enough to float free again. Three Federal warships hovered nearby, but were unwilling to come within range of the fort's guns. In addition to 6,420 stand of arms, the *Thomas L. Wragg* brought in hundreds of cases of blankets, boots, and medicine.

By the end of 1862, it became clear that King Cotton rested on a shaky throne indeed. Simply keeping the cotton off the European markets had not been enough to push the British to intervention. The textile industry in Great Britain was in a severe depression, and thousands of people were out of work, but there were no riots in the streets, and it was clear the British government didn't consider cotton worth waging war over.

At the same time, circumstances were forcing the blockade runners to become much more systematic and practical in their endeavors. Gone were the big deep-draft steamers that had sufficed in the early months, when the blockade line was porous and inefficient. Gone, too, were the flat-black paint jobs that had proven disconcertingly easy to spot against a background of surf and mist. The new generation of blockade-running vessels was low, sleek, and lean, with powerful engines and freeboards just high enough to keep them stable in rough seas. All superfluous cabins had been removed to provide more cargo space, all masts had been lowered to reduce the ships' silhouettes, and mottled, neutral paint schemes — dove-gray, gray-green, or light blue — had been introduced as nocturnal camouflage.[1]

Most successful of the new designs were the "Clyde Steamers," a type of vessel that had been introduced on the Clyde and Mersey Rivers and on coastal runs between Ireland and England in the late 1850s. They had proved so efficient that by 1860 they had swept their competition from the seas. The Clyde Steamers were low, narrow, iron-hulled packets, shallow of draft, and they mounted state-of-the-art steam engines. These sleek side-wheelers were stripped down to the essentials for blockade running. Their funnels were rebuilt so they could be "telescoped" down to the deck — or even lower in some ships — to reduce their silhouette to a minimum. Cabins and staterooms were removed to make even more space available for cargo. Masts and spars were hinged or mounted in sockets so that they, too, could be lowered when not needed. As a final measure, the fuel bunkers were stocked with anthracite coal, which was virtually smokeless when burned in the ships' furnaces.

There were two types of blockade-running operations: runs sponsored by the Confederate government, and those undertaken by private companies, often in the form of partnerships between Confederate and English businessmen. By the end of 1862, this peculiar kind of business was booming, and there was never any shortage of men willing to officer and crew the blockade runners.

Captains and pilots engaged by the Confederate government could expect to earn a handsome wage of $200, plus a bonus of $200 if they succeeded. This pay scaled down to $25 plus $25 for the mess boy. At first, Richmond reserved the right to pay in Confederate money, but the crews demanded, and eventually got, gold instead. Richmond-licensed ships used Confederate officers for their captains whenever possible, which saved the government considerable money, since the going wage for a Confederate officer was much less than that for a freelance skipper.

Those were decent enough wages for the times, and most men would have been content with them under ordinary circumstances. But Richmond couldn't match the compensation offered to privately hired blockade runners. A successful captain working for a private firm could clear $5,000 per voyage. His chief engineer took home $2,500, and even the lowliest member of the crew could expect to pocket $250 from a successful voyage.

Ship owners hired the most experienced men they could find,

usually merchant seamen or former navy tars, English and Irish for the most part. Companies which ventured into the blockade-running business competed eagerly for the services of former steamboat captains with experience in piloting along the Southern coastline. Captains with good reputations and long experience could virtually command their own salaries, for they were always the objects of competitive bidding. If a Southern skipper were unavailable, the companies could take their pick of Englishmen — both civilians and furloughed Royal Navy officers. These men were attracted to the venture by its excitement and potential for enormous profits.

With few exceptions, the first-person accounts written by successful blockade runners convey an impression that every voyage was a thundering, swashbuckling adventure. It's true that some voyages had moments of high drama, and some skippers almost seemed to generate dramatic episodes. But the public's perception of the blockade runner as a daredevil buccaneer, cheating death on every passage, was somewhat exaggerated.

One giveaway clue to the reality of blockade running is the simple fact that hundreds of women and children booked passage on the runners, both to and from Wilmington, and apparently did so with no more than the normal misgivings of transatlantic travelers in the mid-19th century. To be sure, it was risky. But then, a career at sea has always been risky, and the statistics prove beyond any doubt that the greatest risks to a blockade runner were the traditional hazards of a seafaring life: storms and shallow water. (However, there was the sinister possibility of contracting yellow fever, which was never far away in Nassau during the mosquito season.)

In their confrontations with the Union blockading squadron, the runners enjoyed a clear advantage. They picked the time and place for their runs, and they were faster than any ships in the picket line — except for the captured blockade runners which had been converted into warships. Even if they were spotted, they were almost impossible to hit. And even if the runner's ship were trapped or disabled, the men aboard had little to fear — there was good prize money to be shared for capturing a runner, but only a nominal bounty for sinking one. Federal captains usually fired only to warn or disable, not to cause serious damage.

Union incentives and international law helped create a strange environment in which these adventurers, even by their own occasional admission, escaped the "excitement" or hazards of fighting. For the most part, blockade running was a chess-like form of warfare, quite like the old 18th-century ideal of scientific military maneuvering which culminated in surrender with no real loss of persons or valuable goods, and with none of the indiscriminate violence associated with total war. Vessels jockeyed for position, but when one was outmaneuvered, a warning shot or an order shouted from the patrolling vessel's quarterdeck — "Heave to, or I'll sink you!" — usually sufficed to end the encounter.[2]

Runs going out of Wilmington were much safer than runs going in. Spotters on the beaches signaled the departing skippers when the coast was clear. With engines straining and nobody in her immediate path, a blockade runner darting through the New Inlet on a moonless night was across the bar, through the picket line, and on the high seas in a matter of a few hours. Of the 168 steamers that departed Wilmington and Charleston during all of 1863, only 11 were intercepted. Of the 204 ships that tried to enter those two ports during that same period, only 36 were caught. Given the enormous profits to be made, most speculators and skippers considered those odds quite attractive.

The aura of blockade running derived less from its danger of "combat" (there was no real fighting as such) than from the sport-like excitement of matching wits with the Union blockaders. Now and again, of course, one of the "warning shots" would strike a runner, and if anyone was standing in the way, he was in no less peril than someone under fire at Gettysburg. Violent death or dismemberment happened just often enough to add a dash of excitement to the adventure, but not often enough to be statistically significant. The memoirs of the English captains — and of hot-blooded young romantics like North Carolina's own dean of coastal historians, James Sprunt — give the impression that blockade running was not really a military experience at all, but rather a combination of cricket, fox hunting, and a big-game safari (the prize being a fortune in gold rather than a set of tusks or a leopard-skin rug). The odd cannonball flying by now and then added a voluptuous rush of adrenalin.

Beginning in midsummer 1862, the odds off Wilmington were tilted even more in favor of the blockade runners. In late June, the steamer *Modern Greece* was spotted by the picket ship USS *Cambridge* about three miles north of the batteries at Confederate Point (a series of detached earthworks which had not yet taken the shape of Fort Fisher). The *Modern Greece* hoisted British colors, which fooled no one, and raised steam to make her final lunge for the New Inlet, running parallel to the shore and as close to the surf as she dared. Only three-quarters of a mile from safety, she was struck by shells from the *Cambridge*'s Parrott rifle, and her captain was forced to run her aground. Due to hazy weather conditions, and the proximity of the powerful rebel batteries at the Point, the Union ships retired without finishing off the grounded runner.

The Confederates ashore knew that the *Modern Greece* was carrying a huge shipment of gunpowder, and they were afraid the ship would catch fire from the smoldering Union shells. To prevent this, they opened fire on their own ship, blasting solid shot into the *Modern Greece*. By knocking holes through the hull, enough water poured in to keep the grounded runner from burning. A portion of the ship's cargo was therefore salvageable, including 1,000 tons of powder. More important was the discovery of four 2.75-inch Whitworth rifled guns.

The Whitworth was a state-of-the-art breech-loading weapon, a product of the latest metallurgical and ballistics technology. It featured hexagonal rifling, was made of steel, and the three-inch model could throw a shell almost five miles with pinpoint accuracy. Colonel Lamb, commander of Fort Fisher, organized the Whitworths into the "Flying Battery," horse-drawn and escorted by a company of cavalry. Whenever a blockade runner looked to be in trouble, the Flying Battery would gallop out of the fort along the firm-packed, gently sloping beach, duck into one of the thick-walled revetments Lamb's engineers had constructed at suitable intervals along the shore, and open fire on any Union naval vessel that came too close. As a tradeoff for their range and accuracy, the small-caliber Whitworths fired a rather light 12-pound projectile that had a small bursting radius and rarely did more than tear up some woodwork when it hit a Union ship. On the other hand, the little rounds arrived with tremendous velocity and were known, on occasion, to punch clean holes through both sides of a wooden ship. No Union skipper could afford to treat them too lightly.

The Flying Battery did heroic work in providing covering fire for endangered blockade runners, and in keeping blockade ships at a safe distance from grounded runners so their cargo could be salvaged. Lamb's Whitworths became famous throughout the South, so much so that Richmond, in its customarily heavy-handed manner, demanded that three of the four guns be sent to Virginia for field service, leaving Lamb with but a single weapon. Richmond should have left well enough alone; in regular field service, the Whitworths proved much too delicate and temperamental to be worth the trouble of maintaining them. When a couple of Whitworths were captured by the Yankees, they were tested and found too complicated for the average soldier to operate under combat conditions. The captured weapons ended up playing a static role as part of the defenses around Washington, D.C.

Typical of the blockade-runners of this period was the *Banshee*, constructed and maintained by the Anglo-Confederate Trading Company, organized in the spring of 1863 by a prominent Liverpool shipping firm. The company's first venture, in the early days of 1862, had been aborted because the ship employed was an old cattle boat, much too stout and deep of draft to make it through the blockade or the inlets. The cargo had been sold in Nassau in July, making just enough money to cover expenses. The firm tried again a year later, this time with the *Banshee*, a vessel specifically designed for the purpose: steel-hulled, a side-wheeler, 220 feet long, and flat-bottomed. A product of the latest Clyde Steamer design concepts, the *Banshee* drew only eight feet of water and had watertight compartments.

After completion of her trials on the Mersey River in England, the *Banshee* became, in April 1863, the first steel ship to cross the Atlantic Ocean. The engineering skills required to build steel-hulled ships were still in their infancy, and it was discovered, well out on the high seas, that the engines were too powerful for the structure — their vibrations were buckling the steel plates, and the hull was leaking badly. After repairs in Nassau, the *Banshee* took aboard one of the most experienced English runner skippers, a gentleman with the appropriately ringing name of Jonothan Steele.

He was accompanied by a veteran Wilmington pilot named Tom Burroughs.

Departing Nassau on May 9, 1863, the *Banshee* took three days to reach the coast of North Carolina. Burroughs took the con and steered the vessel for New Inlet. He evaded detection, thanks to his skill, the ship's new camouflage paint, and her low silhouette. At daybreak, however, Burroughs had to steer the ship back out toward the blockading squadron to avoid a shoal that had formed since the last time he had sailed these waters. Shell-spouts began to straddle the sleek steamer as she came into view, but the range was long — the Union ships stayed beyond the range of Fort Fisher's protective batteries. With a final burst of speed, the *Banshee* thundered across the bar and pulled into safety in the waters of the Cape Fear River. Her arrival inaugurated the busiest and most successful year of blockade running in North Carolina waters.

The *Banshee* was quickly unloaded and refilled with tobacco and cotton, and the return voyage to Nassau was uneventful. The profits from this single voyage were huge. On the inner leg, the *Banshee*'s backers received a return of 50 pounds profit for each ton of war material the ship carried; the cotton and tobacco yielded a profit of 32,000 pounds on top of that. The total was more than enough to repay the investment in the vessel itself, and its subsequent successful trips were consequently even more profitable.

Although private ventures like this did import a great deal of military supplies, they also hindered the Confederate government's efforts to get the South's economy on a sound footing. Faced with private competition, Richmond could never be entirely successful in ordering the priorities and cargoes of a comprehensive blockade-running campaign. Moreover, the appearance of consumer goods imported by the privately owned ships helped fuel the fires of inflation and speculation, and there was no way to curb the practice. When a skipper could purchase corset stays in Glasgow for pocket change and resell them in Wilmington for a profit of 1,100 percent, Richmond's disapproval was no deterrent.

Private companies were also a source of competition for scarce wharfage, coal, railroad capacity, and the costly services of good skippers and pilots. By the end of 1862, the Confederate government therefore concentrated most of its official blockade-running ventures at Wilmington, leaving Charleston and the gulf ports to the private adventurers. Before the end of the year, however, Charleston was closed to the runners, and Wilmington became the most important destination in the South for both government-sponsored and privately owned blockade runners alike.

During the first half of 1863, Wilmington recorded 76 entrances and clearances of blockade runners; during the same period, Charleston recorded 81. Until the middle of that year, Charleston was the busiest port in the South — so busy that at times the Cooper River was too crowded to allow another ship to squeeze through, and collisions were a constant hazard. Of course, the North, too, realized Charleston's importance as a blockade-running port. To halt this activity, Union forces besieged the city in the summer of 1863. Although the siege failed to take the city proper, the Federals managed to emplace powerful guns on Morris Island and Cummings Point, guarding the entrances to Charleston. Coupled with gunboat patrols, backed by powerful armored monitors, the Union effectively put at end to blockade-running operations to and from Charleston. A few small boats continued to scoot in and out, but the larger steamers were choked off for good. Between July 10, 1863, when the Federal siege began, and March 1864, only five sea-going vessels managed to enter or leave the port. The focus of all blockade-running activity on the eastern seaboard then shifted north to Wilmington.

THE STATE GOES INTO BUSINESS

If the odds of success were so favorable and the need so great, why didn't the Confederate government enter the blockade-running business earlier and more systematically than it did? Probably for the same reasons it didn't fortify Roanoke Island: confusion, inexperience, bureaucratic myopia, and political fragmentation. Long after the blockade runners had proven their value as a source of everything from surgical instruments to coastal artillery, the Confederate government remained stubbornly, irrationally inert. Worse, its minions, taking their cue from President Davis and Secretary of War James A. Seddon, seemed bent on obstructing the successful work going on at the state and departmental levels.

The Confederate chief of ordnance, the very able Josiah Gorgas, working without War Department approval, bought five vessels and used them successfully to import cannon, munitions, and spare parts. Other, lesser figures implemented more limited programs — a vessel or two, perhaps — but without government approval and financial support, the results were meager.

North Carolina got into the blockade-running business at the end of Governor Henry T. Clark's administration, at the suggestion of then-Adjutant General James G. Martin. Clark left office, however, before anything more than some studies could be worked out. The proposal was one of the first matters to land on the desk of Governor Zebulon B. Vance after his election in 1862. The young governor hesitated for awhile — some of his close advisers thought the idea was unconstitutional — but it didn't take long for him to become a passionate convert. The scheme fitted perfectly into his strategy for making North Carolina militarily self-sufficient, and no doubt it appealed to his own streak of buccaneering bravado. When the ships finally did put to sea, there can be little doubt that Zeb Vance, in spirit, sailed with them.

Vance polished the basic plan Martin had submitted to Clark, then went before the state legislature in secret session and used his great powers of persuasion to enlist support. The state appropriated $2 million for the scheme. The economic basis for the plan was sound: The state would buy cotton grown within its borders, sell whatever the market would bear, and then warehouse the rest. Certificates would be issued against this stored cotton, and these would be used as the medium of exchange on European markets for the purchase of needed supplies.

Once the financing was in place, the next obvious step was to find a ship. On the recommendation of several advisers, Vance selected as his purchasing agent a 48-year-old Scot named John White. A resident of Warrenton, White had emigrated to North Carolina as a teenager and had over time become one of the most successful merchants in the state. He was an excellent choice, honest and shrewd, and he turned out to have a keen eye for ships.

White sailed through the Union blockade for the first time in November 1862, and by year's end he had purchased, for $190,000, a fast and rakish Clyde Steamer that had seen service on the Dublin-Glasgow run. Command of the ship was given to Thomas Crossan, a veteran of both the U.S. Navy and Confederate States Navy. The ship was rechristened the *Ad-Vance*, both as a toast to the governor (*ad* in Latin, of course, meaning *to*; hence *To Vance*) and as a symbol of the state's progressive strategy. The vessel departed Cardiff on its maiden voyage under the state flag on May 30, 1863.

The business part of the plan was worked out in partnership with the prominent London firm of Alexander Collie & Co., which had already reaped considerable profits from earlier blockade-running enterprises, and which had efficient and dedicated representatives in Wilmington. Bermuda would be the *Ad-Vance*'s main port of call. She would carry cotton to Bermuda, and then for the return trip be loaded with supplies and hardware already shipped over by Collie & Co.

Back in North Carolina, the state was offering top dollar for locally grown cotton and was enjoying considerable success. Most of the crops were stored in warehouses in Graham, between Chapel Hill and Greensboro, convenient to the railway system and beyond the reach of the Federals on the coast. The operation even netted some surplus cotton, which Vance had turned into cloth and yarn, which was then exchanged in Virginia for leather. The whole scheme was benefitting the state even before the blockade runner completed its first voyage.

The *Ad-Vance*'s initial crossing terminated in Wilmington on Sunday, June 26, 1863. Vance, of course, came down from Raleigh to greet the ship and revel in the hoopla. Upon his arrival, he dutifully obeyed regulations and applied for permission to board a steamer down to the Wilmington quarantine station, near Smithville. All incoming vessels were required to stay at the quarantine station until they were certified free of yellow fever carriers — a process that usually required 15 days. Vance had already obtained a waiver for the vessel; its crew had been examined and declared free of the dreaded disease. The *Ad-Vance* sailed happily upriver and docked at the main wharf in Wilmington. General William Whiting, commander of the Wilmington district, happened to be away on business that day, so he wasn't there to greet the ebullient Vance as he loped up the gangplank, glad-handing, back-slapping, and thoroughly enjoying himself.

He was still basking in the moment, standing at the head of the gangway, when an officious young lieutenant colonel named Thorburn, in full dress uniform with a sword, stationed himself near the ship and proclaimed in a bombastic tone that the vessel was in violation of regulations and must return to the quarantine station for two weeks. All aboard her must remain where they were.

Zeb Vance was barely able to get along with Whiting, whom he regarded as a petty despot and a drunk, but that was nothing compared to the emotions aroused in the fiery governor by this young popinjay Thorburn. Not only was Thorburn rude and overbearing, he was a Virginian. Vance peered over the railing and

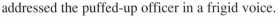

addressed the puffed-up officer in a frigid voice.

"Do you dare to say, sir, that the governor of the state shall not leave the deck of his own ship?"

Thorburn swelled with authority and replied: "I shall let no one off this ship, be he Governor Vance or Governor Jesus Christ." He then ordered a detachment of soldiers to shoot anyone who tried to disembark.

Vance had to be restrained. He was a vigorous and fairly emotional young man, and this arrogant officer seemed to embody everything about the Richmond government that drove him to fury. Here was a huge ship loaded to the gunwales with urgently needed military supplies, already given clearance to dock, and this fool wanted to quarantine it for the next two weeks in the Cape Fear River, with the governor of North Carolina incommunicado on the quarterdeck.

Someone had the good sense to fetch the official who had final authority over the clearance of vessels in port. Summing up the crisis at a glance, he quickly issued the required permit and stationed himself to greet the seething governor when he stormed down the gangplank. Upon reaching the wharf, Vance thundered to the assembled crowd: "No man is more prompt to obey the civil authorities than myself, but I will not be ridden over by epaulets or bayonets!" The crowd gave him three lusty cheers, and Vance hurried back to Raleigh to dash off another fire-and-brimstone letter to President Davis. General Whiting later wrote Vance a fulsome letter of apology, once he learned what had transpired in his absence, and Lieutenant Colonel Thorburn ended up resigning from the Confederate Army about six weeks after the incident.

The *Ad-Vance* was as beautiful as she was successful, and as powerful as any ship in the trade. She cruised at 17 knots, but when pursued — as she often was — she could do 20 knots without undue strain. When spotted, she simply "showed a clean pair of heels" to the pursuers and usually got away without even getting splashed by a near-hit. She was renowned for her punctuality; people passing on the streets of Wilmington would commonly remark to one another, "Tomorrow the *Ad-Vance* will be in," and most of the time she would arrive right on schedule. She came to symbolize the proudest aspects of North Carolina's devotion to the war effort, as well as Governor Vance's iron-willed determination that North Carolina's soldiers would be the best-clad, best-armed, and best-fed troops in the Confederacy.

The crew of the *Ad-Vance* was mostly British, although there was a minority of more exotic types. All were veteran sailors attracted to some degree by the adventurous life of the blockade runner, but attracted much more by the prospect of earning more money in one trip than a sailor might hope to earn in three or four years of normal employment. The officers, with the exception of the sailing master, a Scotsman named Wylie, were all Southerners.

In any undertaking sponsored by Zeb Vance, there was likely to be a touch of eccentricity. Aboard the *Ad-Vance*, that quality was most dramatically evidenced by the ship's petty officer, James Fauntleroy Taylor II, the son of the state solicitor general. Nearly everyone regarded Petty Officer Taylor as being but one step from a madhouse. Taylor affected a style of pronunciation that was patently ridiculous, and demanded that his underlings on board mimic it to the last absurd syllable. He could often be found patiently correcting some poor sailor as to the proper pronunciation of words such as "alligator" ("ah-li-GAH-tor") and "toad" ("TOW-ad"). Once, when the *Ad-Vance* was under rather brisk shelling by some pursuing Union gunboats, Taylor turned to the white-faced officers gathered around the wheel and lectured them for being tense. "A bullet, gentlemen," he assured them, "has a path called a *line of trajectory*. All you have to do to insure safety is to stand to the left or right of this line." But for all his colorful dementia, Taylor performed his duties well enough. Before the year was out, the *Ad-Vance* had proven itself one of the most successful ships in the runners' trade.

She also had some extremely close calls. Her first one came at the end of the summer of 1863. At St. George's, Bermuda, she had picked up a cargo of cloth, blankets, shoes, drugs, and sundry military goods. For two days and three nights out of St. George's, the sea was smooth and empty. The *Ad-Vance* simply altered course whenever smoke was spotted, and her speed served to take her out of sight very quickly.

Aboard was a raw young lad of 19 named Smith, who had signed on as the ship's signal officer. He was befriended by the

Wilmington pilot, an old sea-dog named Kit Morse. If ever the
need came to scuttle the ship to avoid capture, Morse confided to
the boy, "You just step into my boat, take a seat by Kit Morse, and
if any boat can live through the surf, I will land you safely on
North Carolina grit."

Captain Crossan's strategy was to reach the coast some 25 miles
north of Fort Fisher, steam carefully south while hugging the
shoreline, and then make the final, most dangerous part of the run
into Wilmington at about 2 a.m. — floodtide across the bar, the
only dependable moment in which the heavily laden ship could get
across. But in her approach to the coast, the *Ad-Vance* was forced
to dodge several suspicious-looking steamers, and her timetable
was upset. She passed the Cape Hatteras lighthouse at about 1 a.m.,
but at dawn she was near Masonboro Sound, still almost 25 miles
from the protection of Fort Fisher. The fresh daylight revealed the
presence of five Union warships, lined up abreast about three miles
out to sea.

Through his spyglass, Captain Crossan could observe no sign of
life aboard the blockaders, but it was common practice for the
picket ships to maintain a full head of steam, and they might spring
to life at any moment. Crossan decided to stay calm and try to
sneak past them, using for cover the surf mist and the smoke from
the coastal salt works, now hanging in shrouds over the beach.
Quickly he gave his orders: "I am going to take the risk of running
by them." To his chief engineer, he said: "Mr. Morrison, be ready
to give her all the steam possible." To his teenaged signalman, he
said: "Mr. Smith, stand by to signal Colonel Lamb to man his guns
to protect us." And finally, he stepped aside from the helm and
gestured to Kit Morse. "Pilot, take charge of the ship. Put her in if
possible, if not, beach her."

As young Master Smith took his post on the starboard side of the
quarterdeck, at the pilot's right hand, Morse muttered from the
corner of his mouth: "Old boy, we are in for it." The *Ad-Vance*
steamed at moderate speed, hugging the surf as close as she dared,
wrapping herself in the line of fog and smoke which "hung like a
veil" along the beach.

All went well until she got past Masonboro. Suddenly, the
blockade ships showed signs of life. Steam was vented and men

could be seen scurrying on their decks. They moved quickly to trap the runner. One Union ship closed in from astern, three came in obliquely off the port bow, and one — the fastest of the lot, the USS *Connecticut* — rushed ahead to cut off the fugitive. Crossan ordered "Full speed ahead!" and "Run up the colors!" The Southern cross whipped taut in the wind as "the bonny ship bounded forward like a racer."

Twenty miles from Fort Fisher, the *Connecticut* fired a round of solid shot that flew across the wavetops and sank well short of the blockade runner. The *Ad-Vance*'s crew cheered, but the demonstration was short-lived, for the *Connecticut*'s second shot screamed directly overhead, right between the runner's smokestacks. Now the other pursuing ships opened fire, ripping the air and splattering the water all along the *Ad-Vance*'s port side.

At last, one of Colonel Lamb's signal stations at Fort Fisher came into sight. Young Smith braced himself and tried to ignore the shells filling the air around him. To the lookouts on shore he waved: "Col. Lamb: have guns manned to protect us. Signed, Crossan, Captain, *Ad-Vance*."

From the shore came a businesslike: "O.K." The runner was now 15 miles from the arc of the Confederate fort's big guns. Fragments of bursting Union shells began to rain on her decks, and the pilot, standing unflappably at his post, shoved the young signalman under cover. By now, however, the *Ad-Vance* was at full speed and had outdistanced every pursuer save the dogged *Connecticut*. Now was the moment of greatest peril, for as she neared New Inlet, the runner would have to make a broad turn to starboard that would bring her within 100 yards of the Union warship. Kit Morse glanced calmly at the flame-belching *Connecticut*, then over to the sandy ramparts of Fort Fisher, and said: "I wonder why Lamb doesn't fire?"

At that exact instant, one of Lamb's Whitworths banged from the beach and put a shell into the hull of the nearest ship astern of the *Ad-Vance*, prompting the Union vessel to break off the engagement and retire seaward.

The *Connecticut*, meanwhile, was now so close that Smith could see her gun crews at work, and actually saw the nearest gunner's mate pull his lanyard. At point-blank range, the Yankee projectile was intercepted by a sudden crest of seawater that rose about 20 feet from the *Ad-Vance*'s waterline. The pilot yelled "Hard over!" and the sleek rebel steamer bounded "with the speed of a chased stag" from the open sea into New Inlet. As she cleared the bar, a massive Confederate salvo crashed out from the walls of Fort Fisher, raising a forest of waterspouts around the *Connecticut*. "Safe, thank God!" cried someone on the *Ad-Vance*'s quarterdeck. Smith faintly heard a sportsmanlike cheer from the Yankee sailors aboard the *Connecticut*, even as the thwarted Union ship came about and retired at flank speed beyond the range of Fort Fisher's artillery.

One account of this close escape, which appeared in a New York newspaper, described the Confederate vessel as the "Saucy Block-ade-Runner" and praised the coolness of the Confederate crew under fire. Colonel Lamb, who had watched the last half-hour of the chase from his command post (known as "the Pulpit") atop the seawall of Fort Fisher, was astonished to learn, after inspecting the *Ad-Vance* later, that the only damage it had sustained from that hurricane of shellfire was a single dent in one smokestack, caused by a shell fragment. What had saved the vessel this time, as much as Lamb's cannon or Kit Morse's calmness at the wheel, was the condition of the sea: rough, with heavy, sudden, swells. The *Connecticut*'s gunners, in accordance with standard tactics, had concentrated their fire on the waterline of the fleeing ship — the surest and quickest way to seriously wound her — but the rising waves had deflected or diminished the force of every shot.

The *Ad-Vance* was as successful as she was lucky. By January 1864 she had made eight runs to Bermuda, bringing in tons of munitions, 40,000 pairs of shoes, 40,000 blankets, vast quantities of high-grade woolen cloth from British mills, and more than 300,000 pounds of bacon.

One of the smallest but most vital items shipped on the vessel were "cotton cards," devices that made it possible to turn raw cotton into yarn. Governor Vance encouraged a cottage industry throughout the state by importing and distributing 112,000 sets of cotton cards. This enabled thousands of families to clothe them-selves. It also created a large surplus of cotton yarn which the state bought for uniforms. Eventually, Vance had the state-owned blockade runner bring in machinery to manufacture the cards.

North Carolina cotton bonds had become highly profitable for overseas speculators. A pound of cotton could be obtained for six pence, then resold in Liverpool for 24 pence, a profit of 400 percent. The whole enterprise became so profitable and efficient that in the spring of 1864, Governor Vance entered into a new agreement with Alexander Collie & Co. to bring additional steamers under state contract.

The governor sold half of the state's interest in the *Ad-Vance* and used the proceeds to purchase one-quarter interest in four steamers owned by Collie. Two of the vessels, the *Don* and the *Hansa*, would come under state control when they entered Wilmington on their next run. The third ship, a new vessel called the *Annie*, was still on the stocks in London, and construction on the fourth hadn't started yet. The deal was secured with 20,000 pounds' worth of cotton bonds for each ship. For this, Vance was entitled to claim the total cargo space on inward voyages, and one-fourth of the space on outward trips. His first priority was to eliminate a backlog of warehoused goods in Bermuda, especially some high-priority railroad iron and equipment.

During the rest of the spring season, the arrangement went well, with both the *Hansa* and the *Don* bringing in valuable cargoes and going out with state cotton in their holds. Mr. Collie found Governor Vance "a meddling and bothersome partner,"[1] but on the whole, both men had reason to be satisfied with their arrangement.

The Confederate administration wasn't happy with it, however, for the deal put North Carolina in the awkward position of competing with the Confederate government for docking facilities, cotton, railroad space, and even coal. Richmond finally insisted that state-owned ships comply with the same regulations as ships that were owned by the Confederate government or private parties. Anticipating Governor Vance's likely response to this action, Richmond wisely decided not to exercise its claim on the *Ad-Vance* as long as the ship was entirely state-owned. As soon as Vance sold off part of the state's interest, however, the Confederate government insisted on claiming space on the vessel, and aboard the other two as well. When Vance protested, in his usual blunt manner, Secretary of War Seddon coolly reminded him that other states that owned blockade runners were complying with the rules, and he pointedly suggested that North Carolina stop going its own way and fall into line.

Vance, of course, bridled at that kind of language, and fired back a suggestion that the War Department purchase its own ships, if it was so keen on getting into the blockade-running business. Seddon's frigid reply stated that he had no intention of permitting North Carolina to compete with the Confederacy; for the common good, Vance must comply. Vance tried to maneuver, offering Richmond a percentage of the cargo space in his little fleet, but Seddon wouldn't compromise, and eventually Vance had to back down.

While all this bickering was going on, the ships themselves continued to do well. The *Ad-Vance* made six successful trips between January and April 1864, then had to cross the Atlantic to Liverpool for some much-needed repair work. In May, the *Hansa* also went into dock, but not before completing seven good runs. The *Annie*, when she finally entered service, enjoyed a streak of 13 profitable runs before grounding on a sandbar off the Cape Fear River. Only the *Don* had bad luck, completing just three trips before she was taken, on March 4, by the USS *Pequot*.

The end for the *Ad-Vance* came in September 1864. She tried several times to get out of Wilmington, but each time was thwarted by the increased number of Union picket ships lined up off the coast. Finally, on September 9, she crossed the bar, outran a Union vessel that tried to chase her, and reached the open sea. At first, it seemed to be a clean getaway. Then her lookouts spotted smoke. It was the USS *Santiago de Cuba*, one of the swiftest ships in the blockade. She hadn't been looking for the *Ad-Vance*, but spotted the Confederate blockade runner anyway, thanks to the telltale plume of smoke created by the soft bituminous coal the *Ad-Vance* was burning on this voyage. The chase lasted until 8 p.m., when the *Santiago de Cuba* finally pulled into range and started plowing up the sea with heavy-caliber shells. The career of Governor Vance's proud flagship was over — or at least, the Confederate part of her career was over. The captured blockade runner was taken North, renamed the USS *Frolic*, armed with a few cannon, and returned — a bitter irony indeed — to join the Union blockade off Wilmington.

Vance blamed the capture of his beloved ship on Confederate Secretary of the Navy Mallory, who was at that time hoarding a couple of commerce raiders in Wilmington. All of the clean-burning anthracite coal, Vance asserted, had been commandeered by the Confederate Navy for use by those two ineffectual warships — vessels that Vance had always maintained would be of more use if they were lightened, disarmed, and used as blockade runners, not as commerce raiders. Vance may have had a point about the ships, but he was wrong about the coal. Mallory didn't start impounding anthracite until several weeks after the *Ad-Vance* was captured. Exactly why the blockade runner was loaded with coal that one engineer described as "little better than slate" remains unclear to this day, but Vance harbored a grudge about it for the rest of his life.

Sadly, there are no reliable surviving statistics to prove how successful North Carolina's blockade-running program really was. Vance spoke about it often in speeches, but each time quoted different, and obviously estimated, sets of figures. That it was a success cannot be doubted. The state-owned vessels brought in everything from lubricants to overcoats to Enfield rifles. It also netted the state a handsome profit. The surplus goods sold to Richmond reaped as much as $2.5 million. No other state had a blockade-running program to match North Carolina's, and the Confederate government's own system — belated, inefficient, and beset by the usual bureaucratic bungling — didn't even come close.

WILMINGTON AT WAR

In the years preceding the war, Wilmington was one of the busiest and most cosmopolitan cities in North Carolina. It was well connected with the outside world, thanks to new railroad lines, the Fayetteville and Western Plank Road, another plank road to New Bern, and regular packet-boat service to Charleston, Baltimore, Philadelphia, and Washington, D.C. All of these connections made Wilmington a vital crossroads community that bustled with commerce. Quite naturally, Wilmington achieved a level of cultural sophistication unmatched by any other city in the state.

Although the city's population was not large in 1860, even by 19th-century standards, it had grown 100 percent in a period of 20 years. According to the last prewar census, there were 9,552 people living in Wilmington in 1860. Of that total, 4,350 were Negroes, 13 percent of whom were free. This unusually high ratio of free Negroes to slaves reflected a tiny but lively community of black craftsmen and artisans -- carpenters, brickmasons, shipwrights, and sailors — that emerged as a direct result of the great economic opportunities found in a thriving coastal town.

Cotton was not king in the Cape Fear region; little was grown in the immediate vicinity of Wilmington. Rice was far better suited to the local climate than cotton, and vast rice plantations dotted the tidewater fields in all directions. The great rice-planting clans lived a baronial existence. They organized seasonal bird hunts (as much to keep the birds from eating the crops as for sport) and marked holidays and important social occasions with lavish dinners of turkey, duck, roast pig, roast beef, ham, tongue, puddings, potatoes, rice dishes, coconuts, oranges, and table wines as fine as any served in America.

The greatest source of Wilmington's prosperity was not the rice crop, however, but the somewhat grubbier treasures generically called "naval stores." These consisted of resin, tar, and various grades of turpentine, as well as wood products, such as timbers and shingles, all produced from the vast pine forests that covered the land to the west of the Cape Fear River. In the last year before the war, Wilmington exported eight million feet of lumber, much of it to the deforested islands of the West Indies.

Few steamships could pass the shallow bar into the Cape Fear River, but prewar Wilmington's harbor was always crowded with sailing ships. From November 1860 until the outbreak of war in April 1861, more than 600 sailing vessels registered to dock at the city's wharfs. During the busiest weeks of the trading season, an average of more than 30 ships a day could be seen loading and unloading at the docks, their officers and crews adding to the waterfront bustle and color.

When Mrs. William Lamb first arrived in Wilmington, fresh from her sophisticated hometown of Providence, Rhode Island, she was surprised to find "...a pretty place...and the people are very refined and polite."[1] Indeed, it was a pretty town, laid out in an orderly rectangular style, with main thoroughfares more than 60 feet wide and surfaced with gravel, sand, or stone. Sidewalks were well lit, by the standards of the time, with gas or kerosene lamps. The houses were handsome, and most were surrounded by attractive little gardens.

On the other hand, there was no sewage system — even the richest merchant in town still had a backyard privy. Nor was there a municipal water system, beyond a few pipes that carried water downhill into the wealthier neighborhoods. Most citizens drew water from public springs. The town was cursed with poor natural drainage, and certain neighborhoods turned into quagmires during the spring and autumn rains. Worst of all, when the wind blew from an inland direction, it brought the acrid stench of the turpentine distilleries. At times this gave the city a severe air pollution problem, particularly on hot, humid, summer days.

Culturally, Wilmington surpassed any other city in the state. It boasted an opera house, several musical societies that gave concerts, and a significant percentage of the total number of bookstores found in North Carolina. Jenny Lind, the most famed singer of the time, stopped there briefly in 1850, with P.T. Barnum and her entire entourage, and was welcomed so warmly by a passionate crowd of 700 Wilmingtonians that she changed her itinerary in order to schedule a concert there the following year.

If there was one cultural passion that ruled all others in Wilmington, it was a love of the theater. The theatrical tradition dated back to the era of fabled Royal Governor Tryon. One young player of antebellum days, a girl named Elizabeth Hopkins — said to have "great wide mysterious eyes [and] the face of an elf" — enjoyed a number of stage triumphs in Wilmington. Before dying at the age of 20, she married and gave birth to a son, Edgar Allen Poe. (Another famous Wilmington mother lived much longer — Anna Mathilda McNeill, whose son was the painter James McNeill Whistler. During the war, when James was living in Liverpool, Mrs. Whistler employed her immense personal charm to prevail upon Governor Vance to give her passage on a state-run blockade runner to Nassau. From there she made her way to Liverpool, where she enjoyed a reunion with her hot-tempered son. It is to these circumstances that we owe the existence of the famous "Whistler's Mother" painting.)

Wartime conditions did nothing to dampen enthusiasm for the theater. The Thalian Hall did a booming business. Doors to the 950-seat auditorium opened at 7:30 and performances began a half-hour later. The bill of fare usually consisted of one fairly heavy work — Shakespeare and Victor Hugo were the favorites — followed by a chaser of musical comedy or farce. Box seats went for 50 cents; floor seats for a quarter. "I go to the theater occasionally," wrote one Wilmington merchant in 1862, "to cease thinking...the playhouse is reeking with the foul crowd. It is difficult to say which is more farcical, the stage or the pit."[2]

The war enhanced the popularity of the Wilmington Library Association, too, as well as several industrious women's groups that organized extensive programs to aid the rebel war effort. Food, blankets, clothing, and Bibles were distributed to troops throughout the Cape Fear vicinity. A more direct contribution to the war effort was the manufacture of items needed in the forts. General William Whiting prompted this program, and he mentioned it, rather patronizingly, in a report to Richmond: "I have started all the ladies to making cartridge bags and sand bags, and that keeps their little hearts quiet."[3]

Once Wilmington became a major blockade-running port, however, the city's character changed. It became a frantic, hard-edged place, filled with soldiers, speculators, high-rollers, and freelance buccaneers. But the fact that the city had become the central focus of contraband trade meant little in terms of the average citizen's lot. Very few of the goods brought in ever made it to the local open markets. However, there were numerous private deals and arrangements, and the wealthy and influential continued to enjoy their coffee, fresh fruit, and corset stays. But for the citizen of modest means, Wilmington became a city of scarce provisions, high prices, and boisterous, sometimes dangerous living conditions.

The moment a blockade-running steamer docked, the wharf was mobbed with people anxious to bid on whatever consumer goods would be auctioned off, invariably at wildly inflated prices. Much of this "gray market" business was conducted by speculators, who bought items by the box or by the dozen, then resold them at profits that sometimes shamed even the runners themselves. Many otherwise honest and patriotic citizens also indulged in some small-scale speculating, when the chance came their way. As one man rationalized, "There is no harm in a trifling investment now and then; whenever the opportunity is an innocent one, I must embrace it."[4]

As acute as the city's economic problems became, however, the blockade runners brought something even worse than inflation to Wilmington in the autumn of 1862: yellow fever. The disease came into town aboard the steamer *Kate*, and its first victim was a young German who managed a shipyard near the dock where the vessel had landed. He was diagnosed, at first, as having jaundice. When numerous other cases were discovered, spreading in a discernable radius from that same point, the authorities were forced to consider the possibility that something more sinister was stalking the city. By the time 15 people had keeled over dead, the citizens of Wilmington comprehended, to their horror, what was happening. From October 20, when the first cases were diagnosed, to November 15, when the cold weather put an end to new cases, the epidemic claimed 710 lives — about 15 percent of the population.

In those days no one knew, that the plague was carried by mosquitos from Nassau. The epidemic was attributed merely to some pervasive and mysterious airborne contagion ("nocturnal vapors"), and countermeasures were not much more sophisticated than those practiced during the Middle Ages. Tar pots were ignited on every street corner in the vain hope of purifying the air and driving away the contagion. All that the tar pots did, of course, was fill the air with a charred stench and make the city appear from a distance as if it were covered with a pestilential cloud. "Plague soil" from the municipal gas works was dumped in heaps at intersections, because of the widespread belief that gas-impregnated dirt would absorb the contagion and disinfect any clothing it was rubbed on. Between gas-flavored laundry and tar fumes, the citizens of Wilmington must have become a fragrant lot. "Business men, whose interests compelled them to keep up their affairs, moved to the sounds and came up to town late in the morning and left some time before sundown. Their great concern was to avoid the vapors of the cool air of the earlier and later daylight hours. And the night air was considered deadly."[5]

Everyone who could get away fled the town for a safer refuge inland; those who couldn't leave stayed indoors. Wilmington became a ghost town. An editor for the *Wilmington Journal* reported: "We have gone all over town in broad daylight without meeting a vehicle, save a doctor's buggy or a hearse." During the height of the epidemic, a contingent of nuns arrived from a convent in Charleston and heroically assisted the city's handful of overwhelmed physicians. The disease didn't abate until mid-November, when a providential and most unseasonal snowstorm chilled the city and killed the mosquitos.

There were other perils, too. In the summer of 1863, a dangerous fire — quite possibly the work of an arsonist — destroyed part of Wilmington's waterfront, burning docks, storage buildings, and more than a thousand bales of contraband cotton. A later, accidental, conflagration destroyed $700,000 worth of valuable cotton. Following that disaster, General Whiting ordered that all departing steamers had to be towed into the river before they were allowed to

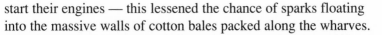

start their engines — this lessened the chance of sparks floating into the massive walls of cotton bales packed along the wharves.

From most accounts of the period, it seems clear that 1863 was a kind of "golden period" in Wilmington's wartime history. Tight new quarantine regulations made a recurrence of the plague unlikely, the runner trade was booming, and the city had a wide-open, boisterous vitality that reminded many visitors of San Francisco during the days of the gold rush.

Things were at their liveliest during the height of every monthly blockade-running cycle: the nights of little or no moon. Footloose young adventurers involved in the runner trade would pool their pocket money and rent, at deflated rates, the stately homes of prosperous merchants who had fled inland to escape the inflation, the plague, and the rowdy living conditions. Parties lasted long into the night, replete with minstrel shows, ladies of easy virtue, marathon card games, and cock-fighting arenas. Much of the roistering was done by hot-blooded young Englishmen, many on long-term leave from the Royal Navy.

Typical of these characters was a gent known as Captain Roberts, who was actually the Honorable Augustus Charles Hobart-Hampden, son of the Earl of Buckinghamshire, on leave from Her Majesty's Navy. After five enormously profitable and adventurous runs on the steamer *Don*, Hobart-Hampden returned to England, his leave expired, and wrote a colorful, salty book about his Confederate escapades. For some years he served as captain of the royal yacht, the *Victoria and Albert*, before the urge for adventure seized him again. He wound up as "Hobart-Pasha," admiral-in-chief of the Turkish Navy during that nation's bitter war with imperial Russia.

If Wilmington was sometimes scandalized by the unbuttoned lifestyle of the swaggering blockade runners and their new-rich mercantile backers, it was also fascinated by their Bohemian ways. Here is a contemporary account, written shortly after the war's end:

> At every turn you met up with young Englishmen dressed like grooms and jockeys, or with a peculiar coachman-like look, seeming, in a foreign land away from their mothers, to indulge their fancy for the outre and extravagant in dress to the utmost. These youngsters had money, made money, lived like fighting cocks, and astonished

the natives by their pranks, and the way they flung the "Confederate stuff" about. Of course, they were deeply interested in the Confederate cause, and at the same time [they] wanted cotton.

They occupied a large, flaring yellow house at the upper end of Market Street. There these youngsters kept open house and spent their pa's, and the company's money, while it lasted. There they fought cocks on Sundays, until the neighbors remonstrated and threatened prosecution. A stranger passing the house at night, and seeing it illuminated with every gas jet lit (the expense, no doubt, charged to the ship), and hearing the sound of music, would ask if there was a ball going on. Oh, no! It was only these young English Sybarites enjoying the luxury of a band of Negro minstrels after dinner. They entertained any and everybody.

But, alas, there came a day when these Masters Primrose, with brandy-flushed faces, faded away, and were scattered like their namesakes before a chilling northeast wind, and Wilmington knew them no more. We...miss and mourn them sadly.[6]

Economic conditions worsened during 1863. Wilmington depended on the railroads, not the blockade runners, for most of its own provisions, and all available freight space on the trains was monopolized by businessmen trying to get their cotton crops into town so they could be exported by a runner. Even the Confederate government had a hard time shipping its cotton, because private speculators consistently outbid Richmond for scarce railroad space. Speculation was feverishly heated by an atmosphere of rampant financial gambling. Men thought nothing of running up enormous debts, since the safe arrival of a single runner could turn them from debtors into rich men in an hour.

Things got worse in the latter half of 1863, when firms operating out of Charleston moved north to Wilmington. The atmosphere in town became more raw, less genteel. Many large and financially powerful English firms were represented by their sailors, hard-bitten tars from the Royal Navy or the overseas merchant trade. Many were "bluff, coarse...and vulgar" men who offended the town's gentler traditions by first generating and then openly patronizing a number of waterfront establishments that combined the services of saloons and bawdy houses. On any given day or night, when the runners were in, swarms of these men could be seen disdainfully and drunkenly swaggering along the town's streets, arm in arm with their "quadroon" hussies. Not since the days of the Spanish Main had the coast of North Carolina been as salty. By November 1864,

> ...the frivolity of the war's early days was gone, replaced by a crueler lifestyle. The city had developed a worn, neglected look. Paint peeled from formerly well kept homes and businesses, missing shingles were left unreplaced, streets were dotted with potholes, garbage lined the avenues, and municipal government had practically ceased to exist. Most local citizens, like the city's numerous soldiers, had become seedy-looking, dressed in worn, patched clothing...Lean, half-starved dogs roamed the streets and troops had to patrol the docks around the clock to prevent deserters from stowing away on outbound ships.[7]

As prices soared and food became scarce, and as the rumors of a Union attack grew more persistent, most of the city's inhabitants — those who had not already fled because of the yellow fever epidemic — departed inland, where conditions were more settled and the necessities of life easier to come by. Between the mass exodus of the upper and middle class, and the loss of population from the epidemic, there was never any shortage of housing. Rents, however, inflated like food prices. By the summer of 1864, an ordinary hotel room was renting for $1,200 per month in Confederate money, and food prices were going through the ceiling:

Commodity	1860 Price	January 1865 Price
Eggs	15 cents/dozen	$10/dozen
Bacon	15 cents/lb.	$7/lb.
Sugar	12 cents/lb.	$10/lb.
Chicken	25 cents $12[8]	

Robberies and assaults were up dramatically even by the end of 1862, when the *Wilmington Journal* advised its readers: "It behooves citizens to keep ready some loaded weapon and when such persons force or attempt to force themselves into respectable houses with insulting purposes of plunder, to draw trigger without hesitation. An example will be wholesome."[9]

By mid-1864, shootings and knifings were an everyday occurrence, either as part of a robbery attempt or as the result of some drunken altercation on the waterfront. Nearly every Sunday morning, the body of at least one murdered sailor would be found floating in the river. One such incident was described in a letter written by Wilmingtonian James R. Randall:

> Last night we were treated to a murder right under our windows. One of the *Lynx*'s crew went into a bar kept by a notorious fellow named Kelly. Soon after, the man emerged closely pursued by Kelly who fired at him as he ran. Kelly was suddenly apprehended, and his victim removed to his ship, where, after lingering until morning, he expired...I saw the murdered man on the forecastle of the *Lynx*. He looked like a dead tiger. His comrades were munching their breakfast around him with the most perfect indifference.[10]

Members of the Confederate States Navy were accorded surprisingly little respect by either the inhabitants of Wilmington or by General Whiting and his staff. One of Whiting's men referred to the entire Navy establishment, in a letter dated April 1864, as "those drones in Wilmington," and accused them of spending all their time "sporting their gold braid and lace...in houses of prostitution...." while contributing nothing material to the defense of the city.[11]

There was some truth in that accusation. All of the wooden ships under the rebel flag in the whole Cape Fear region probably couldn't have bested one small Union gunboat in an open fight. Nor was the program of ironclad construction, begun with much optimism in the spring of 1862, much of a success.

The first such vessel to be completed was the CSS *North Carolina*, a 150-foot-long armored ram mounting four guns and carrying a crew of 150. She looked formidable enough, but her engines — one of them salvaged from a tugboat — were junk. Her speed was so pathetic that no one dared send her against the Union fleet. Instead, she was anchored as a floating battery, downriver from the city. She saw no action, and her fate was both ignominious and absurd: Sea worms ate out the bottom of her hull, and she sank at her moorings in September 1864.

The ironclad CSS *Raleigh* at least made one sortie against the enemy, after she was commissioned in early 1864. She went out on the night of May 6 and boldly steamed toward the nearest Federal blockader, the USS *Britannia*. The only damage done during the brief exchange of fire was when a near-hit extinguished the *Britan-*

nia's binnacle light.

Striking out like a blind man, the CSS *Raleigh* sailed aimlessly through the Union blockade lines, causing a great stir and prompting an hysterical discharge of signal rockets, but doing no harm. By dawn, seven Union warships had boxed in the ironclad, which retired to the safety of the Cape Fear River after perforating the smokestack of one Federal gunboat. Just after passing through the inlet, the ironclad ran aground on a sandbar. When the tide went out, her keel straddled the hump of sand. As the water receded, the strain of the ship's enormous weight slowly pulled her apart from each end until her back was broken. The Confederates salvaged her armor and cannon, but the vessel itself was reduced to scrap — and with it any hopes of offering a credible harbor defense. It was folly to send such a deep-draft ship over the bar, but indications are that it was done to still the voice of public ridicule and thus redeem the honor of the Confederate Navy.

There was one other ironclad under construction, the CSS *Wilmington*, and she was the best-designed, most potentially useful, of the lot. Had General Braxton Bragg been smart enough to hold onto the outer Cape Fear defenses until the ironclad was launched, Admiral Porter and General John M. Schofield might never have taken Wilmington, even after the fall of Fort Fisher. As it was, the vessel was burned on February 21, 1865, when Bragg's men evacuated the city. She was about 95 percent finished at the time.

Interservice rivalry at Wilmington was bitter, and on occasions it verged on the confrontational. The local citizens gave their allegiance to the army, which was obviously better able to protect them. Consequently, General Whiting always enjoyed a tactical advantage over his naval rival, Flag Officer Lynch.

Whiting's and Lynch's respective services almost came to blows in March 1864. The Confederate government's representative at Wilmington, enforcing the new policy requiring government-owned cotton to be included in the cargo of every runner that left port, held up the departure of the *Hansa*. Lynch backed him up, with a vengeance, by ordering the CSS *North Carolina* to make one of its rare voyages upstream. She anchored next to the impounded runner, and aimed and loaded her cannon. Lynch also sent a detachment of Confederate Marines to take possession of the ship.

Not to be outdone, Whiting sent a larger detachment of Confederate Army soldiers to take possession back from the Marines. The commander of this detachment stationed armed guards around the dock to make sure no Navy personnel came close. The first man to try the sentries was Flag Officer Lynch himself. When a "brute" with a musket tried to stop him, Lynch stared him down with a commanding glare and shoved the man's rifle aside with his walking stick.

When word of these undignified squabbles reached Jefferson Davis, he summoned both officers to Richmond and let them know of his acute displeasure. He placed a naval officer aboard the *Hansa*, and the vessel cleared port with its governmental cargo intact. That much was a victory for Lynch. On the other hand, Lynch himself was recalled to other duty before the war's end and was replaced by Flag Officer Robert F. Pinckney. Whiting may have been a prima donna, and much too fond of the bottle on occasion, but the Cape Fear defenses were largely his creation, and he was more valuable at Wilmington than Lynch with his impotent little naval squadron.

Another controversy erupted in September 1864, centering around the two commerce raiders *Tallahassee* and *Chickamauga*, which were using Wilmington as their home port. The former ship enjoyed a spectacularly successful maiden cruise, destroying 29 Federal merchant ships before returning to Wilmington for refitting. The *Chickamauga* was being readied for her first voyage.

The raiders' very success seemed guaranteed to bring renewed Federal clamor for an attack on Wilmington. At the very least, their presence would force the Union to tighten the blockade. In the opinion of local military commanders, and of Robert E. Lee as well, the two raiders were nothing more than a gallant gesture, and both of them together were not worth the closing of Wilmington for even a single month. Whiting felt so strongly about this matter that he asked Governor Vance — not one of his close political allies — to pressure the Confederate government into turning over the two vessels for use as transports within the Cape Fear defensive perimeter. Their powerful guns could be used to augment Colonel

Lamb's firepower at Fort Fisher. To support his argument, Whiting cited statistics to prove that the number of blockade runners captured off Wilmington had risen alarmingly since the *Tallahassee*'s raiding spree. Vance, on this occasion, agreed with Whiting, and he was still angry at Richmond over the loss of the *Ad-Vance*.

But Richmond disagreed with the plan. Taking a different perspective, Navy Secretary Mallory argued that by raiding Union merchant shipping on the high seas, the two ships would in fact draw Federal vessels away from the blockade and into pursuit. Therefore, the two Confederate raiders were permitted to leave. The *Tallahassee* slipped through the blockade on the night of October 29, 1864, and in a very busy week destroyed six Union merchant ships before scooting back into Wilmington on November 7. The *Chickamauga* made only one cruise before Wilmington fell to the Federals, but she too scored well, taking four enemy ships.

Of course, a Federal expedition against Wilmington was inevitable whether or not the raiders were sent out, so the whole squabble over their proper deployment was academic. Yet it provides a vivid illustration of how the Confederacy was hamstrung by its lack of naval resources.

In realistic terms, the only role open to the Wilmington naval contingent was that of harbor defense. Gallant as the *Raleigh*'s sortie may have been, it accomplished nothing except the ventilation of one enemy smokestack. Had it been retained on the Cape Fear River, Admiral Porter's Union ships would have faced a very difficult tactical problem when they attacked Wilmington, because they would have been forced to fight the ironclad in waters where an ironclad had all the advantages.

Similarly, the fate of the *North Carolina* was not predestined. Had the ship not been left to rot at anchor, the sea worms wouldn't have eaten through her bottom — a few cruises into fresh water, in fact, would have killed the tiny saltwater worms boring into her hull. If both the *North Carolina* and the *Raleigh* had been intact and operable when Porter's Union fleet arrived, the Confederates could have sealed off the Cape Fear inlets almost as effectively as Fort Fisher itself. This would have allowed at least some blockade-running traffic to continue to enter Wilmington. That two such valuable ships could be destroyed by a sandbar and some sea worms — before either fired a single effective shot — reveals much about the unfocused and mismanaged nature of Confederate naval strategy.

'A Parcel Of Cats Watching A Big Rathole'

It has been estimated that the total amount of ship-to-ship naval combat in the Civil War amounted to about one week's time out of a four-year conflict. For the overwhelming majority of U.S. Navy personnel, the war was blockade duty and nothing but blockade duty. The blockade was, of course, a vital component in the North's victory, but to the officers and men who manned the picket ships, it was a purgatory of boredom and discomfort. "When breakfast's done," wrote one terminally bored sailor, "the next thing I look forward to is dinner, and when that's done, I look for supper time."[1] Considering the quality of fare at all three meals, this statement indicates true spiritual and mental desperation.

One of the best descriptions of the blockade came from Admiral Porter, who said it was "very much like a parcel of cats watching a big rathole; the rat often running in where they are expecting him to run out and vice versa."[2]

The U.S. Navy began the war without any coherent doctrine of blockading tactics. It was all very much hit or miss during the first year, mostly miss because of the small number of ships available. Due to the particular conditions of the Confederate coastline, and the aggressive, entrepreneurial spirit of the blockade runners, the Napoleonic precedent of blockading — a few big frigates leisurely patrolling near or even beyond the horizon — soon gave way to a closer, tighter formation comprised of smaller, faster steamers working as close to the inlets and harbor channels as they dared.

Commanding the North Atlantic Blockading Squadron, and responsible for blockading the shoreline from the Piankatank River in southwestern Virginia to the South Carolina line, was Admiral Samuel Phillips Lee. Lee had spent most of his life at sea, first serving as a midshipman aboard the *Hornet* in 1827. He was born in Fairfax, Virginia, but chose to remain faithful to the Union when war broke out. Prior to his assignment off the coast, he had taken part in the capture of New Orleans and had commanded the first Federal naval offensive up the Mississippi River. He was well qualified for the blockading job not only because of his experience, but also because he had spent eight years working for the U.S. Coast Survey. There were few men in the U.S. Navy who knew the Atlantic shoreline as intimately as Admiral Lee. Shortly after his promotion to the blockade squadron, an old friend wrote him a note of congratulations: "I am thankful that I live to see the day when only old age...rank and imbecility are no longer the sole qualifications for command."[3]

Lee demanded, and got, more ships. When he took command on September 4, 1862, the squadron numbered only 48 vessels. By the end of 1863, he had almost 80, and when he was finally relieved by Admiral Porter in October 1864, the North Atlantic Blockading Squadron was the largest unit in the U.S. Navy, averaging between 90 and 110 vessels at sea on any given day.

He also tightened up the whole system, which he found incredibly slack and haphazard. He insisted that all ships keep up steam at all times, ready to move at a moment's notice. He also shifted his picket lines as close to shore as the water and sea bottom allowed — so close, in fact, that collisions were frequent until proper drill and communications procedures could be worked out. Almost immediately, the Confederate blockade runners noticed the difference.

The Cape Fear entrances were Lee's biggest tactical problem. The two inlets were only six miles apart on the map, but the irregular bulk of Smith Island, and the deadly extended elbow of Frying Pan Shoals, made the traveling distance between the inlets almost 50 miles — a six- or seven-hour voyage for most of Lee's ships. Wilmington, then, presented Lee with not one, but two distinct fronts. After personally sailing up and down the coast and inspecting the situation, Lee requested a vast amount of information from his former colleagues in the Coast Survey bureau — charts, hydrographic data, weather records, and anything else that might aid the blockaders.

Lee was methodical. First, he closed off the secondary inlets of Shalotte and New Topsail, neither of which were continuously picketed before. Then he refined his tactics near the two Wilmington inlets. Closest to shore, Lee stationed his oldest, slowest, least seaworthy vessels. Although they were incapable of chasing the swift blockade runners, they were under orders to shoot at the Confederate ships if they got the chance, and to signal the course and location of the runners to the faster, more powerful blockading ships stationed in two concentric outer lines further offshore. To sharpen the skills of the crews (and to keep them busy), Lee made each vessel conduct regular training drills in small-boat handling, amphibious landings, boarding, repelling boarders, and basic gunnery.

But no amount of drill could offset the weariness of blockade duty, which combined the need for constant vigilance with month after month of stupefying boredom. Watches were taut and tiring for those who kept them. The daily routine began at 5:30 a.m. when the petty officers came around, booting and shaking and cursing the men out of their sea hammocks and onto the deck. Between reveille and breakfast at 8 a.m., the crew took care of routine maintenance: sweeping, washing, and holystoning the decks, polishing the brass fittings until they glowed, splicing ropes, and sewing clothes. Once the ship was properly cleaned, the men had a brief period of time to attend to their own toilette. Small wonder that so many men wore beards aboard Lee's ships: Anyone who wanted to shave had to use a bucket of cold salt water.

Since steam had to be kept up 'round the clock, heat from the boilers filled much of the vessels' interior. That was agreeable enough in winter, but in hot weather the atmosphere below decks was thick and oppressive. It was worse at night, because the ships were battened down tight to prevent any light from showing. If conditions were uncomfortable on the wooden steamers, they were very close to torturous aboard the iron-walled monitors. In cold, damp weather, serving in a monitor was "like living inside a well" — condensation ran in streams down the bulkheads, and it made everything from beds to shoes damp and mildewed. In summer, serving aboard a monitor was more like living inside a Dutch oven. Morale was so bad aboard the ironclads that the Navy Department eventually raised the pay-scale for that duty.

Nothing much ever happened during daylight hours, although once in a great while a blockade runner might heave into sight because of bad timing or some mechanical emergency. Still, watches had to be stood, if only because of the remote chance that a Confederate ironclad might suddenly appear. The men stood their time, scanning the sea, waiting for something to happen, cursing under their breaths, bored to the point where boredom became a physical sensation rather than a state of mind.

One sailor aboard the USS *Florida* summarized in his diary a recent letter to his mother:

> I told her she could get a fair idea of our "adventures" if she would go to the roof of the house on a hot summer day, and talk to half a dozen hotel hallboys, who are generally far more intelligent and agreeable than the average "acting officer." Then descend to the attic and drink some tepid water, full of iron-rust. Then go on to the roof again and repeat this "adventurous process" at intervals, until she was tired out, then go to bed, with everything shut down tight as not to show a light. Adventure! Bah![4]

Supper finally came at 4:30, and from sunset to 8 p.m., the crews enjoyed what limited recreational opportunities their ships could provide: whittling, tale-telling, sewing, sketching, reading, writing letters, making music. Mindful of the evils boredom could breed, most captains did whatever they could to enliven the dreary routine. Many ships had their own minstrel bands comprised of crewmen in blackface, sometimes augmented by real Negro contrabands. Some ships even mounted elaborate music hall shows, often featuring material which today would be regarded as forbiddingly racist — such as the comic opera "Ethiopiana," which proved a huge success on one frigate. On rare but cherished occasions, a real band would be brought on board to give concerts.

The officers had more leeway to amuse themselves, of course, and some of them responded to the tedium by concocting eccentric forms of entertainment. The officers of the USS *Wabash*, for example, kept a trained bear who loved to guzzle champagne.

Drunkenness was as common as the men could arrange for it to be. Homemade hootch, most of it fairly gruesome, was brewed in hidden mess kettles and surreptitiously consumed. Extra grog rations were the currency of a barter economy. Inebriation became such a problem that, in late 1862, Congress decreed an end to the U.S. Navy's sacred grog ration — a move that brought howls of protest from enlisted men and officers alike. The abstemious navy secretary, Gideon Welles, suggested in one memorandum that iced coffee or a gruelly concoction of water and oatmeal could be an acceptable substitute. Far more practical was the approach of Admiral DuPont. Upon taking command, one of his first acts was to order some barrels of whiskey from the army and shipped to the fleet under the heading of "medical stores."

Food aboard the Union blockade ships was both monotonous and unappetizing. It mostly consisted of sea biscuits, salt pork — sometimes arrayed in very un-pork-like colors and textures — and beans, which invariably turned moldy after about two weeks at sea. Some of the older ships were infested with rats, and men in the lower berths would sometimes be awakened by rodents nibbling on their toes or clawing at their hair.

Scurvy was always a hazard, as were eye infections, diarrhea, and a wide assortment of fevers. Sooner or later, nearly everyone had trouble with hemorrhoids as well. There were a dozen or so suicides recorded, including that of a boatswain's mate who cut his throat with a straight-razor. Homosexual relationships were formed, for the most part fleeting and mechanical, although there were some fairly durable affairs, including a few between officers and enlisted men. Most sailors didn't get to see a woman more than once a year. All in all, duty aboard a blockade ship differed remarkably little from doing time in a penitentiary.

About the only thing that kept the Yankee sailors from going completely crazy was the prospect of actually bagging a blockade runner. It happened seldom, but when it did, the excitement was more than just a release of tension and adrenalin. The monetary rewards for capturing a runner were impressive, even if half the proceeds were claimed by the U.S. government. The squadron commander got a five percent skim off the top, whether his ship had any part in the capture or not; after that, the blockader's share was split into 20 equal portions and divided among the crew according to a formula. The ordinary seaman, of course, got the smallest cut, but even so, these bonuses, for a 19th-century working-class fellow, were enough to give some promise of security in the years after his service. In one typical capture — of the runner *Hope* by the armed tug *Aeolus*, in October 1864 — the skipper took home $13,164, the engineer $6,657 (about what he would make in five years on his Navy salary), and the ordinary deckhands slightly more than $1,000 each. Even the cabin boy got $532.

Back at the Navy Department, there was a lot of huffing and puffing about the "prize system," as it was called, because it tended to make each skipper think about his own ship rather than the operation as a whole. But to have mandated the system out of existence would have been to deal a deathblow to the already fragile morale of the men on the ships. Besides, the staff officers in Washington got their cut, too. Admiral Porter, for one, used to complain long and loud about the detrimental effects of the prize system on discipline, but that didn't prevent him from enriching his own bank account with nearly $100,000 in prize money.

The blockade-running trade continued to thrive until the late summer of 1863, but after that, the Confederacy started absorbing supplies much faster than they could be smuggled in. Immense quantities of munitions, equipment, and supplies had been consumed or lost in the defeats at Vicksburg and Gettysburg, and the siege operations at Charleston were draining off an alarming amount of the European ordnance that did get through.

In Wilmington, August 1863 was considered the month that the blockaders' luck started running out. Many citizens attributed it, superstitiously, to a local feud between a prominent Wilmington lady and the local representative of the Alexander Collie Company, whose name was Crenshaw. Crenshaw was a brusque and unpleasant man, and he managed to rouse the ire of Miss Mary Ann Buie, a Wilmington belle who had risen to the top of society — what was left of it — by virtue of her indefatigable efforts on behalf of the soldiers' aid society. Most of Miss Buie's funds came from subscriptions she sweet-talked, cajoled, or shamed out of the pockets of successful blockade runners, mostly by pointing out to them that, after all, it was the gun crews of Forts Fisher, Holmes, and Caswell who protected them as they scuttled into harbor with their profitable cargoes. For whatever reasons, Mr. Crenshaw and Miss Buie developed an intense dislike for one another, and in June 1863 Miss Buie publicly declared that she hoped Crenshaw's next ship would be lost. It was. The next one was, too. From then on, Miss Buie became an object of intense, almost fetishistic, superstition among runner captains.

Crenshaw's two losses, and others which followed with alarming frequency, were actually due to new Union tactics and ships. Admiral Lee's efforts were paying off. New, faster ships were arriving, including a number of captured blockade runners. The two Wilmington inlets were now guarded, in the first rank of picket ships alone, by eight or nine vessels, instead of the five or six stationed there previously. Additional ships in the outer lines also meant that blockade runners were being intercepted further and further out at sea. The trend was not in the runners' favor, as the following table indicates:

Losses of Blockade Runners at Wilmington

April 1862 - December 1862: 1
January 1863 - July 1863: 4
July 1863 - January 1864: 14[5]

The worst week was in early November 1863, when three of the finest ships in the trade — the *Robert E. Lee*, the *Ella and Annie*, and the *Cornubia* — were all taken within 48 hours. On November 21, even the fabled and hitherto lucky *Banshee* was captured, towed north, and eventually recommissioned as a Federal gunboat.

These severe shipping losses, coupled with the battlefield defeats of that bloody summer, helped turn the Confederacy's overseas financial system into a shambles. Cotton bonds depreciated dramatically. To avert collapse of the whole rickety structure, Secretary of War Seddon took the unprecedented step of clamping strict government controls on the entire blockade-running system.

From August 1863 onward, all runners leaving Southern ports were required to reserve half of their cargo space for government cotton. Failure to comply could mean seizure of the ship.

These changes had been a long time coming. For the first two years of the war, the Confederate government's trade policy had been virtually unrestricted. Exceptions were few and obvious — cotton, naval stores, and a handful of other valuable commodities could not be exported to any destination from which they might end up in Northern markets. By the end of the summer of 1863, however, Richmond's hand was forced, not only by military reverses, but also by the blockade runners' increasing allocation of cargo space for outrageously profitable consumer goods at the expense of urgently needed military supplies.

The government's program got off to a shaky start. Lines of authority were unclear, especially with regard to vessels already subject to Confederate contracts. Foreign shippers, and their Southern business partners, disliked having the Richmond administration infringe on what they regarded as their right of free trade. On the whole, however, most people agreed that some kind of government regulation over the runners was only sensible, and indeed was overdue. The regulations of August 1863 were amended in February 1864 by legislation that forbade the import of space-consuming luxury items, from wallpaper to carriage parts.

The final piece of legislation in the new trade system was passed on March 5, 1864. According to this bill, all shipping operators, before clearing a Southern port, had to declare the names of the vessel's owners, officers and crew, passengers, port of destination, value, and amount of cargo. Ships operating under the cotton bond program, or under actual contract to the Confederacy, wouldn't have their cargo space commandeered, but up to half of the space on all other vessels could be taken by the government, on both inward and outward voyages. And before any ship could clear a Confederate port, the operators were required to post a bond equal to double the stated value of the ship. This was viewed by the Confederate government as an incentive to the skippers not to dawdle. But given the profits most of them stood to make from even a single successful run, such a spur would seem superfluous.

A separate bond also had to be posted on the cargo, providing that half of the net proceeds from the outward voyage would be reinvested in goods that would be shipped back to the Confederacy within 60 days. If the ship's operators chose not to bring cargo back to the South, they were required to hand over half of their proceeds in gold or pounds sterling to a Confederate agent, who would then arrange for government cotton to be allocated at a fixed rate. The bonding rates were lenient, in order to make the whole package go down more easily.

All of these new regulations struck the runner trade like a salvo of Parrott shells. Many merchants, investors, and captains predicted the end of the whole business. "Unjust and extortionate!" thundered one large British investor. But in the end he, like almost everyone else, realized that even the sternest of the new rules was merely a nuisance, compared to the profits that could still be made by a lucky ship. A brief slowdown followed each new set of regulations, particularly the ones passed in February 1864, but by mid-spring, things were as busy in Wilmington as they had been in the summer of 1863. In one typical transaction from this period, the *Banshee II* left Wilmington carrying 100 bales of cotton, which were sold in Liverpool for 4,616 pounds sterling. Expenses for the shipment, including the new bonding fees and wharfage, amounted to 1,695 pounds. The Confederacy made a profit from this single voyage of more than $14,000 in gold. (In Confederate money, it was more like $300,000.)

By early summer, reports from Confederate agents in Europe indicated the new system was having a positive effect. Confederate credit was firmed up again by July 1864, and the appearance of new, faster, more spacious vessels was spurring further investment. Part of the proceeds from these regulated voyages was used to commission the building of a new class of fast, powerfully armed, and partially armored commerce raiders. These handsome and potent ships were designed either to challenge the blockaders broadside to broadside, or to force the blockading ships to disperse in order to protect Union merchant shipping. But diplomatic pressure from the North — now so clearly the side to bet on, in military terms — prevented any of these British-made vessels from entering Confederate service. Only one of the new cruisers, the CSS *Stonewall*, which was constructed in France, actually got to sea, and that was only in the closing days of the war.

Two factors served to increase the importance of the blockade runners' activities in late 1864. One was General Grant's strategy of unceasing pressure against the main rebel armies. The other was the Confederacy's loss of resources and territory resulting from the loss of several major battles. In previous campaigning seasons, the South had enjoyed some moments to catch its breath after each major clash. Now the battles were happening continuously, on both Grant's and Sherman's fronts, and the Confederacy was steadily losing territory that contained valuable resources and industry.

After the Atlanta campaign, for instance, the Army of Tennessee needed 58,000 pairs of shoes, 55,000 pairs of pants, 38,000 weapons, and 21,000 blankets. Virtually all of this now had to come through the blockade. After the bloody failure of the Franklin and Nashville campaign, when the Army of Tennessee dwindled to only 25,000 effectives, the Confederate War Department still estimated it needed 100,000 pairs of pants, 108,000 sets of underwear, 60,000 shirts, and 45,000 jackets. Again, all of the raw material had to pass the blockade — which meant, almost exclusively now, it had to come through Wilmington.

Still, the blockade-running system continued to work, even though only one major port remained open, and despite increasing losses, tighter regulations, and more strain on personnel. Food, munitions, cloth, leather, medicines, even paper, were all coming through in enough quantities to keep the Confederate armies in the field and the bureaucracy functioning. From mid-spring to mid-autumn of 1864, for example, blockade runners arrived in Wilmington with 290,000 pairs of shoes, 275,000 blankets, 27,000 European rifles, a million pounds of saltpeter, 3,500 pigs of lead, and substantial amounts of steel, leather, copper, industrial chemicals, and medical supplies.

It was hoped that, by the start of 1865, these supplies would increase beyond the subsistence to the surplus level. There was a new generation of ships coming off the ways in Europe, and blockade runners were increasingly using ports on the Gulf of Mexico. (These ports had not been used to their fullest capacity, mainly because of the lack of railroad connections with the eastern part of the Confederacy.)

But then, in late September 1864, word reached Liverpool of the falls of Atlanta and Mobile, and the whole Anglo-Confederate trade system was convulsed by panic. To compound the problem, outbreaks of yellow fever in Nassau and Bermuda kept ships in quarantine for three weeks, and supplies were backing up the pipeline. Especially affected were the shipments of meat which the Confederate Subsistence Bureau now depended upon to supply three-fourths of the meat consumed by the Army of Northern Virginia. (Ironically, much, if not most, of this meat originated in the North. It was shipped to the islands by merchants working both sides of the conflict, and then reshipped to the Confederacy. Beef that was tinned in Cleveland, and pork that was salted in Cincinnati, arrived daily in Halifax or Liverpool, then was rerouted to Nassau and Bermuda.)

By the end of 1864, Wilmington was the most important city in the Confederacy. If Richmond were lost, the cause could still live. If Wilmington were lost, "the aorta of commerce" would be severed and the South's armies would wither. Arms, saltpeter for making gunpowder, lead for casting Minie balls, cloth for uniforms, leather to shoe the soldiers' feet, steel to make cannon shells and bayonets, chloroform to ease the pain of the wounded — all but a small trickle of these goods came in through Wilmington, and then were shipped to the battle fronts on the rapidly crumbling North Carolina railroad system. And still, the Union had not tried to capture Wilmington, thanks to the fierce bluff maintained by Colonel Lamb inside his vast sand castle, Fort Fisher, and to the fact that heavy warships could not cross the bars and get close to the city.

All of that was to change in January 1865, when Fort Fisher was overwhelmed. The last blockade runner to clear Wilmington was the *Wild Rover*, belonging to the Anglo-Confederate Trading Company, which slipped out on the night of January 2. Ships continued to try to sneak in, even after the fort had fallen, but it didn't take long for word to get around that disaster had struck. Several veteran runner skippers, in fact, sensed trouble even from the sea. The captain of the *Rattlesnake* thought there were just too many campfires on shore, and turned back in time to avoid capture. Signals from shore tried to lure him in, but he signaled back that the tide was too low for him to cross the bar and he would return the next night. He thereupon threaded his way back through the Union blockade and returned to Nassau, where the news of Fort Fisher's fall struck like the thunderclap of commercial doom. One merchant who was in Nassau when the news came remembered that "upon receipt of the information...business was nearly suspended, and had they known that the islands were to sink in 24 hours, there could hardly have been greater consternation."[6]

The state of North Carolina began closing the books on the blockade-running trade in February 1865, when Governor Vance ordered all accounts settled. It had been a magnificent effort, and as colorful an episode as any in the state's history. Fully 60 percent of the Confederacy's infantry weapons, and about half of its coastal artillery, came through the blockade. So did one-third of the lead its armies fired during the war, and enough saltpeter to make millions of pounds of gunpowder.

From 1861 to 1865, there were 2,054 runs in and out of blockaded ports in North and South Carolina; 84 percent were successful. As long as even one port remained open, and as long as there was at least a reasonable chance of getting through, the blockade could be judged only a partial success. On the last day of 1864, the Richmond newspapers printed part of a Confederate Treasury report listing the goods that had come in during the previous two months alone:

- 6 million pounds of meat
- 1.5 million pounds of lead
- 2 million pounds of saltpeter
- 316,000 blankets
- 69,000 rifles
- 43 cannon

When Fort Fisher capitulated, the Army of Northern Virginia had about one month's supply of food on hand. Reserves of all critical military supplies and equipment were sufficient to last only two or three months. That, as it turned out, was about how long the war itself would last — as clear an instance of cause and effect as history provides. The fall of Wilmington was the final nail in the Confederacy's coffin.

PART 6

THE GUNS OF FORT FISHER

The Sand Castle Of Colonel Lamb

All of the rivers that begin in the central Piedmont region of North Carolina trace a southwesterly course which gives them the shape of inverted commas. The reason for this lies in prehistoric geology. Before the coming of the last ice age, a warm, shallow, primordial sea extended inland as far as the Appalachian foothills. When the sea retreated, it left an immense plain of sand called an overburden. When rainfall in the western half of the state sired streams, and the streams came together to form rivers, each body of water cut its own meandering channel through the sand-plain. The parabolic curve traced by their modern-day courses is the result of interaction between the waters' flow and the force of the Earth's rotation. When, after eons of time, the overburden itself had been washed away, the rivers stopped pushing in a southwesterly direction and headed more directly for the sea. The overburden was pushed out to form the great Atlantic Shelf, and the surplus sand humped above water to form the Outer Banks. Of all the major rivers thus formed, only the mighty Cape Fear River broke its way free to the open sea; the others empty into the shallow sounds between the mainland and the Outer Banks. The final push of up-country sand into the sea left behind a deadly, hidden sandspit extending more than 20 miles out into the Atlantic Ocean. Early sailors would learn to fear and respect it under the name Frying Pan Shoals.

After passing through Wilmington, the Cape Fear River broadens greatly, doubling and then tripling its width. By 1862, there was no estuary in the Confederacy more heavily fortified. The west bank of the Cape Fear River was guarded by Fort Anderson and its smaller auxiliaries, Forts Lamb and Pender. The river entered the sea about 28 miles south of the city. Directly in its path was the porkchop-shaped hump of sand and bog known as Smith Island. The southern exit of the river, Old Inlet, was guarded by Fort Holmes on Smith Island, and by the powerful Fort Caswell, directly across the inlet from Holmes. And Fort Holmes was itself supported by a pair of powerful satellite redoubts: Fort Campbell and Fort Shaw.

The eastern bank of the river below Wilmington was a long, tapering, triangular peninsula that had been known since Revolutionary War days as Federal Point, but which had naturally been rechristened Confederate Point at the start of hostilities. The channel into Wilmington was guarded, on the river side of the Point, by no less than four earthworks: Forts Stokes, Lee, Meares, and Campbell (yes, there were two Fort Campbells). Down at the narrow end of Confederate Point, where the sandspit bent westward, lay the blockade runners' favorite channel, New Inlet. Guarding New Inlet was the "Gibraltar of the South," Fort Fisher.

To this windswept jut of strategic land, on Independence Day 1862, came a young man in his mid-20s named William Lamb. Lamb had graduated from William and Mary College with a law degree in 1855, when he was only 19. Too young to join the bar, Lamb found employment as a journalist for a newspaper in Norfolk, a town where his father was mayor. Young William was a competent journalist, but his background in the legal profession — not to mention his family environment — inclined him toward politics. He attended the Democratic National Convention in 1856, and if the Civil War had not cut like a canyon across his youth, he almost certainly would have gravitated toward a political career. He probably would have done well; by all accounts, he had great natural tact and charm as well as inordinate good looks. His warm eyes, wavy hair, and neatly trimmed beard offset a profile that looked as though it were waiting to be stamped on a Roman coin. In 1857, he married a lovely young woman named Sarah Anne

Chafee, who was from one of the most solid families in Providence, Rhode Island. He called her "Daisy."

Lamb's first taste of military adventure came in 1859, when he and his militia unit were mobilized during John Brown's raid at Harper's Ferry. When war broke out, he was ordered to Wilmington, where he spent some months as district quartermaster, dull but necessary work which he performed capably. More congenial duty came along when he was appointed to command a small earthen battery on the western bank of the Cape Fear River known as Fort St. Phillip.

Lamb discovered, quite to his surprise, that he harbored a passionate natural genius for defensive engineering, a field in which he had absolutely no formal training. During his tenure at Fort St. Phillip, he transformed a nondescript cluster of weak gun emplacements into the first version of the massive earthwork which would later be renamed Fort Anderson. His labors and accomplishments were noted with approval by General William Whiting, overall commander of land forces in the Wilmington district, who was a superb engineer himself. In the early summer of 1862, Lamb was appointed colonel of a regiment, the 36th North Carolina, which had been assigned to guard Confederate Point. To streamline the organization of the defenses, Lamb was also named, on July 4, 1862, the commander of the Point's straggling line of batteries, known as Fort Fisher. These batteries were named after Charles F. Fisher, a Salisbury native who had died heroically at the Battle of First Manassas/Bull Run.

When Lamb arrived for his first inspection, he found six semi-detached earthen batteries, mounting 17 guns, connected by some rather perfunctory entrenchments. With his keen eye for terrain, Lamb saw at once that the fort was nowhere near as strong as it needed to be if it were to succeed in keeping the New Inlet open. That very day, he resolved to embark on a vast construction project. "I determined at once to build a work of such magnitude that it could withstand the heaviest fire of any guns in the American Navy."[1]

The day after he arrived, Lamb spotted a Federal gunboat only two miles from the beach. He asked a staff officer why the enemy vessel had been permitted to get so close. The officer shrugged and replied that orders forbade the gunners from firing unless fired upon. Lamb thought that was idiocy and promptly started creating Fort Fisher's reputation for bellicosity by ordering one of his Columbiads to have a crack at the blockader. Within moments a column of water boiled up close to the Union ship, and it quickly hoisted anchor and retired from range.

Lamb himself sketched out the fort's basic design, although he consulted his new friend, General Whiting. Both men consciously modeled the fort after the world-famous Malakoff works in Sevastopol, which had withstood tremendous punishment during the Crimean War. Lamb employed as many as 1,000 men per day, including every slave he could get, usually working them seven days a week. Much of the work involved long circular lines of wheelbarrows, pushed and pulled on wooden scaffolding. "It was very interesting to see two or three hundred wheelbarrows rolling in unison from the points of loading to those of dumping, returning in a circle and passing the loaders who shovel in hand threw sand in the barrows as they passed without stopping."[2]

What finally took shape was the largest earthwork in the world. It was configured like an enormous and inverted L, with the long stem facing the sea and the short one crossing the peninsula at right angles. Fort Fisher eventually mounted a total of 44 cannon, not counting its field artillery. The landface consisted of 15 huge earthen mounds, 20-25 feet high and 20 feet thick, with 45-degree slopes on both sides. Between each mound (or *traverse*, as they were known in the military parlance of the day) were sunken, sandbagged gun emplacements. While working in those positions, the gun crews were protected, from the neck down, against anything but an incredibly lucky direct hit.

Stairs and ladders led from the gun mounts down to the interior of the fort. The base of each mound was hollowed out to provide bombproof shelters for men and ammunition. A tunnel, half a mile long, complete with air shafts, connected each mound. North of the landface, Lamb ordered all foliage cleared from the beach out to a distance of half a mile. To further discourage an infantry assault, a nine-foot palisade of sharpened stakes was erected from the river to the beach, and even extended into the surf itself. A sally port, protected by howitzers and loopholed for riflemen, allowed Lamb to rush field artillery into the open space between the mounds and the palisade, should an enemy force breach the latter.

To complete the defenses on the landface, Lamb also took pains to lay out one of history's first minefields. This consisted of two dozen powerful "torpedoes" stuffed with 100 pounds of powder, buried 80 feet apart, and ignited — it was devoutly hoped — by a galvanic battery apparatus housed in a dugout inside the walls. At a signal from Lamb, so the plan went, the battery operator would trigger all the mines at once, with presumably dire consequences for an attacking mass of infantry.

At the angle where the land- and seafaces came together, Lamb constructed the Northeast Bastion, a strongpoint which mounted an 8.5-inch English Blakely rifle and a big smoothbore gun. A hundred yards south of the Northeast Bastion was Lamb's command post, known as the Pulpit, an immense crescent-shaped mound some 30 feet high. From the sandbagged top, he could see most of the fort in both directions. Inside the Pulpit was the fort's hospital, as well as storage space for small arms and ammunition. Below the Pulpit was another sally port that led to the beach. It was protected by a ten-inch gun which was sited low, as were several others on the seaface, so its projectiles could be ricocheted across the water to strike Federal ships at their vulnerable waterlines.

South of the Pulpit, the rest of the seaface stretched for about a mile. One hundred yards south of the sally port was Fort Fisher's proudest weapon, a huge, hulking, 150-pounder Armstrong rifled cannon, reputedly a personal gift to Jefferson Davis from the legendary British industrialist, Sir W.J. Armstrong. The Armstrong was a handsome weapon, mounted on a carriage of mahogany and decorated with brass fixtures which its crew kept polished to a high gloss. Ammunition for the Armstrong was scarce, however, so Lamb kept it in reserve, for use only against a direct naval attack. Not once did he permit it to be fired at blockade ships, although he was fiercely tempted, knowing what kind of damage it could do to a wooden-hulled frigate.

To the south of the big Armstrong were carefully spaced batteries of Brooke rifles and columbiads. The seaface terminated in a massive earthwork known simply as the Mound Battery, a 60-foot-high artificial mountain that loomed over the beach and utterly dominated New Inlet. It took three months to construct the Mound Battery. An old lighthouse had been dismantled to provide lumber for the scaffolding, and a wall of underbrush had been planted at the mound's base to retard erosion. To hasten completion of the mound, Lamb built a small inclined railroad, on which a steam-powered mining cart rolled back and forth from dawn to dusk, carrying tons of sand to the top. Once the base was complete, Lamb designed a gun pit for the top, mounting a 10-inch Columbiad and a rifled 32-pounder. Both weapons were on movable carriages and were capable of sustained plunging fire onto the decks of any Union ship foolish enough to come within range. Finally, Lamb hollowed out the base of the Mound Battery to provide a bombproof shelter for its crews, then added a signal light on top as a marker for the blockade runners. Offshore, of course, the Federal ships' crews watched all this activity on a day-by-day basis, and most of the Union sailors eventually came to regard the Mound Battery with almost superstitious awe.

The final bastion in this enormous fortified complex was a detached, two-tiered, oval-shaped earthwork known as Battery Buchanan, located on the Cape Fear shore of Confederate Point's tip. It commanded not only the interior of New Inlet, but the actual mouth of the Cape Fear River. Battery Buchanan really qualified as a small fort itself, and Lamb's plans called for using it as a kind of castle keep, a final redoubt the garrison could fall back to if the main walls were breached. Here, they could hold out until reinforcements arrived via the river. There was a steamboat landing at Battery Buchanan, although the primary docking spot for the defensive complex was at Craig's Landing, north of the fort.

Once the walls were up, all the angled surfaces were sodded with sea grass to prevent erosion. The dugouts inside the mounds provided about 14,000 square feet of protected storage space. The fort's main magazine — an enormous mound 60 feet wide and 20 feet tall — was large enough to hold 130,000 pounds of powder.

Lamb's headquarters was in a three-room shack that before the war had belonged to the Federal Point lighthouse keeper. Lamb's family shared the building with him until the soldiers finished building a cottage about one mile north of the landface. It had three rooms clustered around a great central chimney and was heated entirely, as Colonel Lamb nostalgically recalled in his postwar accounts, "by North Carolina pine knots." Throughout the war, his wife Sarah was able to correspond regularly with her family in Providence by means of letters taken by the blockade runners to Bermuda and mailed from there. In one of these letters she described the final stages of outfitting the cottage:

> I can get no furniture for my house either old or new — so am going to have some made at the fort, or course of pine and very rough, but I presume the place will look real neat and comfortable when it is all done. I take a great deal of pleasure in it, it will certainly be cool and comfortable.[3]

Indeed, she made the little house quite comfortable. The lack of tall trees at first bothered her, but the view over the river was lovely and there was usually a breeze that close to the water. The interior was finished, and furnished, with varnished pine, which made it seem a warm place. It was airy, clean, and pleasant, shaded by wide verandas and awnings. The cottage became an oasis for Lamb, although during times of peak blockade-running activity he was seldom home long enough for more than a catnap.

Soldiers and blockade runners soon referred to the colonel's residence simply as "the Cottage" — everyone knew what they were talking about. Sarah held dinners there for visiting sea captains, and many of them wrote fondly about these evenings in later years. In return, the colonel's lady received a steady stream of presents from the runner captains, including such delicacies as fresh fruit and real coffee.

> Let me tell you the presents I had from Captains in two days — a large bag of white sugar — four bottles of rum, two jars of pickles, a large cheese, six boxes of sardines, a quantity of limes and two pineapples — a box of toilet soap — half a dozen bottles of claret — one dozen bottles of port — two bottles of brandy and two of Madeira — and two beef tongues, isn't that doing very well?[4]

Sarah Lamb kept enough on hand for official functions, and made sure her family was well fed. She donated the considerable surplus to sick and wounded soldiers, and on numerous occasions was observed taking baskets of food to the Negro laborers who comprised about one-third of her husband's construction force.

Lamb might have wished daily for more Armstrongs and fewer obsolete smoothbores, but as the earthworks grew and grew, and as the layers of sandbags doubled, tripled, and quadrupled, he became confident that Fort Fisher could take anything the Union fleet could hurl at it. The focus of his concern now shifted to the landward approaches. He worried for two years about the fort's ability to withstand a determined amphibious assault. The bulk of his garrison consisted of his own regiment, the 36th North Carolina, which totaled only about 500 men, and a fluctuating but never very large number of miscellaneous troops, some of them naval. Lamb's men were untested in battle, but at least they seemed willing enough — after months of piling up sand, the prospect of action must have seemed fairly attractive. Morale always improved noticeably after an artillery skirmish with a blockader.

Quarters for the garrison were spartan indeed: pine-plank huts that were both cramped and drafty. Daily life at the fort was monotonous, toilsome, and uncomfortable. Food was mostly poor and unappetizing, and the drinking water was foul-tasting and probably contaminated. Exposed on their open peninsula, the soldiers sweltered in the humid days of summer, and shook with cold during the gale-blasted months of winter. Sand fleas and biting flies were a persistent source of irritation whenever the sea breeze faltered, and in season the mosquitos "could cover arms and legs like thick gray blankets."[5] In time, the men grew to hate the very sand from which the fort was made. The stuff blew in stinging sheets across the parade ground, and it got into eyes, shoes, and hair. It made the already vile food downright gritty, and when it sifted into their clothing, it gave many men a painful and persistent skin rash.

The garrison's day began before dawn. Most of the time, the men filled and tarred sandbags, or shoveled sand, or drilled at their cannon. When they were given free time, they played cards, fished, swam in the ocean, or held impromptu musical sessions with whatever instruments were on hand.

Given the conditions of hardship and boredom, it was a tribute to Lamb's leadership that so few men from the 36th tried to desert. Even so, there were three executions for desertion at Fort Fisher during the war, and Lamb found that duty hard to bear. The executions were staged for maximum impact on the garrison. The condemned men rode in the same wagon with their own coffins while the band played the "Dead March." Then they were tied to stakes and offered blindfolds. "All three were farmers," wrote Lamb of this sad business, "and were married, and doubtless the condition of their families at home had much to do with their crime. They had not deserted from my command but when captured their companies were stationed at Fort Fisher, and it was my painful duty to see the sentences of the court martial enforced. They all died fearlessly."[6] What Lamb modestly refrained from mentioning is that he sent each man's family a generous donation, using his own money.

As the months went by, General Whiting developed an almost paternal affection for Colonel Lamb. Unfortunately, Lamb's immediate superior was not Whiting, but General Louis Hebert (whose headquarters in Smithville had been so dramatically infiltrated by Will Cushing). Lamb's relations with Hebert were intensely strained. Whiting had requested Hebert's services, for Hebert was an experienced coastal defense expert, but he sometimes wondered if Hebert was not more trouble than he was worth. Exactly why Lamb disliked Hebert so intensely is not clear; in his gentlemanly fashion, Lamb was reticent about the matter in his postwar writings. A good deal of Lamb's animosity seemed to focus on Hebert's drinking habits. Lamb was neither a teetotaler nor a prude, but thought it was disgusting for a general to drink himself into oblivion as often, and as publicly, as Hebert managed to do. Matters between the two men came to some sort of head about 18 months after Lamb took command at Fort Fisher, for he requested a transfer. Whiting turned him down, and thereafter ran what interference he could between Hebert and the young colonel. Whiting knew that sooner or later Fort Fisher would have to fight for its life, and he needed William Lamb right where he was.

Whiting, too, was worried about a possible amphibious attack on Fort Fisher. He was genuinely, though prematurely, alarmed in August 1863 when the blockade runner *Hebe* ran aground after a hot chase by the USS *Niphon*, a heavily armed screw steamer. The *Hebe* struck the beach about nine miles north of Fort Fisher and precipitated an energetic little skirmish.

First, the *Niphon*'s crew came ashore with a tow line, in case they could get the prize afloat again, and combustibles, in case they could not. But their boats were swamped in the heavy surf, and before they could launch one of the runner's boats, three Confederate cavalrymen rode up and took them prisoner.

Both sides now sent reinforcements. Another gunboat, the *Shokoken*, came to assist the *Niphon*, while Colonel Lamb dispatched more cavalry and the Flying Battery of Whitworths. Both sides banged lustily at one another, but did no damage, because the rough seas made aim impossible from the gunboats and made the gunboats just as hard to hit from the shore. The original Union boarding party was trapped aboard the grounded blockade runner, and several Yankees who came to rescue them were either drowned or taken prisoner. Finally, the trapped prize crew abandoned the *Hebe*, and the two offshore gunboats began firing at her. So wild was the shooting on both sides that it took three hours for the Union gunboats to set the grounded runner ablaze. Although the Whitworths kept firing during that entire time, all they managed to do was tear up a little rigging.

During the next few days, work parties from Fort Fisher labored to unload the *Hebe*'s cargo, shielded by the Flying Battery, which had been dug in behind a sand redoubt not far away. After watching this in frustration for several days, Admiral Lee's sailors decided to teach the cheeky rebels a lesson. On the morning of August 23, five Federal warships mounting a total of 68 guns, and this time sailing on calm seas, closed in and opened a tremendous barrage. The little battery of Whitworths bravely returned fire — and did so with some effect, scoring five hits on two Union vessels — but the storm of shot and shell ripped across the sand dunes like a series of tornadoes. In a matter of minutes, one Confederate gunner was killed and four wounded, and one of the Whitworths was disabled. At that point, flesh and blood had stood all it could stand, and the rest of the little Confederate force took to its heels. A little later, the Federals came ashore unopposed and captured the Flying Battery's guns.

The Whitworths were eventually replaced by new weapons brought from England, and neither the casualties nor the material losses from the incident amounted to much. Nevertheless, General Whiting was alarmed by this demonstration of the power of naval gunfire. What the Yankees had done on a small scale on August 23, they could easily repeat on a scale vast enough to overwhelm the beach defenses manned by Whiting's small infantry contingent.

It was not long before Whiting had other, more personal things to worry about. It was ironic that Whiting should finish his military service under a growing barrage of criticism, for his prewar career had been without blemish and his future at one time had seemed bright. Born in Biloxi, Mississippi, the son of a career army officer, Whiting had graduated from West Point in 1845 with the highest grade-average yet recorded at that institution. His specialty was engineering, and he was involved in a number of coastal fortification projects, from San Francisco to Baltimore. During a tour of duty at Fort Caswell, the bastion that guarded the Old Inlet of the Cape Fear River, Whiting married into a prominent Wilmington family. He was serving in Savannah when the war broke out. A month later, he resigned his commission in the U.S. Army and entered the Confederate States Army as a major of engineers.

Whiting was a short man whose rather delicate features were offset by a moustache that drooped at both ends. He dressed well, carried himself with grace and dignity, and usually made a favorable impression on those he met, professionally and socially. He was well educated, having completed a four-year course of study — in only two years' time — at Georgetown University, prior to his admission to West Point. He was an avid reader and a conversationalist of wit and eloquence.

If ever a man seemed destined for an outstanding career in the Confederacy, it was William Whiting. His first assignment in the Wilmington area lasted only a month; he was transferred to Virginia, where he served as chief of staff to General Joseph E. Johnston. He received a battlefield promotion to brigadier general at First Manassas, fought at Seven Pines, and rode with Stonewall Jackson in the Valley Campaign. In his official file were letters from Jackson, Johnston, and General Pierre Beauregard, all praising his skills as a military engineer and his conduct under fire. His star ascended, at first, as rapidly as any man's in the Confederacy.

Then, in late 1861, he ran afoul of "someone who lacked the will to forgive and possessed the power to punish: Jefferson Davis."[7] President Davis had come away from an inspection tour of Johnston's army with a harebrained scheme to reorganize the whole force by grouping its troops into brigades, according to their state of origin. Evidently, Davis believed this would instill a healthy spirit of competition in the ranks. General Johnston thought it was lunacy to impose a change of such magnitude on an army that was still in the field and still threatened by a strong enemy. He delayed implementing the directive as long as he could. Impatient to see his pet project put into motion, Davis finally issued a direct order to start the process by grouping all the Mississippians into one brigade. He gave command of this brigade to William Whiting.

Whiting refused to comply and sent a strongly worded memorandum to the War Department in Richmond, in which he labeled Davis's scheme "foolish" and "suicidal." To break up existing regiments and regroup troops according to their home states, he concluded, was "inconceivable folly...[undertaken] solely for the advancement of logrolling, humbugging politicians and I will not do it." When this memo was passed on to Jefferson Davis, the Confederate President became enraged. He tried to have Whiting sacked, and surely would have succeeded if Johnston had not intervened.

As was his wont, Davis never forgave Whiting. He nurtured his grudge and scanned every report from or about Whiting, looking for something to criticize; usually he found it. When Johnston wanted to promote Whiting, Davis angrily denied the request, labeling Whiting "insubordinate" — one of the Confederate President's favorite terms for someone who did not agree with him.

Once Davis singled out a man for this kind of treatment, he never wavered, even if the exercise of his spite conflicted with the best interests of the Confederacy. He refused to forgive Whiting, even after Whiting actually saved him from either death or imprisonment. It happened during the Seven Pines engagement, when Davis, riding around in search of General Lee's tent, took a wrong turn and headed off toward Federal lines. Whiting rode frantically after Davis, caught him, and turned him around only minutes before he would have ridden straight into the hands of the Yankees.

A man of ordinary grace might have displayed some gratitude.

Not Davis. He continued to make disparaging remarks about Whiting, claiming that Whiting had been incapacitated by drink during the battle. He also repeated a ridiculous rumor that Whiting was plotting to overthrow the Confederate government and install Joseph Johnston as military dictator (which may not have been such a bad idea). When one of Whiting's friends had the temerity to question Davis about the source of his information, Davis turned on him and snapped: "I am not on a witness stand!" A few days later, the questioner found himself demoted.

General Lee had watched this pathetic feud develop long enough. In October 1862, he decided to intervene. He wrote the secretary of war and suggested that Whiting might be able to realize his full military potential in a "sphere of action" far removed from Davis. Whiting hoped for a command near Charleston, where he could work with his old friend Pierre Beauregard. Instead, on November 8, Richmond ordered him to Wilmington.

Whiting arrived in Wilmington just as the city was recovering from its yellow fever epidemic. He found the city's defenses — all except for Fort Fisher, where Lamb at least had made an energetic start — to be in poor condition. The number of infantry in Whiting's new command was absurdly small. He wired Richmond for 10,000 men and six batteries of field artillery. He might as well have asked for Lee's entire army. All he got, after much delay, was a little infantry and a few additional cannon, mostly old smoothbores of limited worth. He augmented these forces as best he could with an extensive system of well-designed fortifications, but he never felt that Wilmington was really secure, and his constant, sometimes ludicrous, exaggerations of earlier Federal threats no doubt put him in a position of crying wolf when the real crisis loomed.

Once settled in the city, Whiting made his headquarters on the corner of Market and Second Streets, in a building owned by the deRossett family. He established a good personal and professional relationship with Colonel Lamb almost from the day he arrived, but otherwise the next two years were a time of endless aggravation and frustration. He longed for a chance to redeem himself on the battlefield, but there was no combat in his district, save for the odd exchange of fire with a Union blockader, or, rarely, a skirmish with

Federal patrols probing at the railroad line in the northernmost reaches of his district.

Whiting became fretful and his drinking did increase, although never as much as his enemies declared. His pleas for reinforcements and modern artillery were ignored, and therefore grew more shrill and frantic as time went by. He railed at the War Department for not sending him cavalry, and at state and local authorities for a wide variety of reasons.

One major source of contention was the state-run salt works on Masonboro Sound. The factory was staffed by half-hearted conscripts who made no secret of their joy at being out of combat. Whiting suspected, probably with good reason, that some of these men were not just slackers, but were actual traitors who regularly exchanged information with the blockading Yankees. Governor Vance was willing to tolerate the conscripts' lack of enthusiasm in return for their steady production of salt, a commodity needed desperately in the hungrier sections of the state, so he refused Whiting's request that the salt works be dismantled. Vance's growing distrust of Whiting probably dated from this incident.

Finally, in May 1864, Whiting got his chance to return to Virginia and fight. His old friend Beauregard, recently appointed commander of the Department of North Carolina and Southern Virginia, summoned him. Whiting left Wilmington with no regrets and went north on the train to win glory.

He won nothing. At the Battle of Drewry's Bluff, Whiting failed to carry out his part of Beauregard's carefully drawn plan. Had Whiting not been so slow, a large Union force probably would have been trapped. Once again, Whiting was accused of being too drunk to command. This time, the stories reached the newspapers, and of course they pilloried Whiting. Whiting denied he had been drinking during the battle, and he was backed up by the testimony of his second-in-command, who swore the general had consumed nothing stronger than coffee on the day in question. To explain his failure, Whiting said he had not been given sufficient time to familiarize himself with the ground or the tactical situation; it was only prudent to move cautiously. Moreover, he had gone straight to the front after arriving to take command, and he had had no sleep for more than 24 hours. Unfortunately, Whiting's failure had taken place on the very day Jefferson Davis had chosen to visit the battlefield. Humiliated, Whiting asked Beauregard to relieve him. Beauregard did, and Whiting dejectedly returned to Wilmington.

He arrived just after Lieutenant Cushing had stirred things up with his daring reconnaissance of the Cape Fear defenses. Such bothersome Federal activity, Whiting believed, was a sure sign that the enemy was finally going to attack Fort Fisher. Nor, during Whiting's brief absence, had more troops been sent to Wilmington. Whiting continued to demand veteran troops for his region, because the men he had were, in his opinion, "...the poorest in the world...I have nothing but a few hundred boys and old men, utterly inefficient and unreliable...." Whiting was resolved to do the best he could, but there was no denying that the prospects were grim. In a letter written in the fall of 1864, he lamented to one friend: "It's an ungrateful duty, this, and no bed of roses...."[8]

Relations between Whiting and Governor Vance deteriorated badly in the autumn of 1864. Vance had come to believe that Whiting was too sunk in alcoholism to perform his duties, and the young governor was tactless enough to say so one day within the hearing of people who made sure the remark got back to Whiting. Whiting demanded an explanation from Vance, and Vance replied with remarkable, even brutal, frankness, informing Whiting that this "general impression" of drunkenness had grown during the two years Whiting had been in command.

Vance also believed that Whiting was too authoritarian, and that his job might be handled better by someone with more tact. Vance believed Whiting had seized state-owned property, had intimidated numerous civilians, and, last but far from least, that Whiting had been altogether too public in voicing his distaste for the governor of North Carolina. "I have even," wrote Vance, "swallowed in silence some very rough and discourteous remarks of a personal character, more than once reported as having fallen from you."[9]

This unflattering little tussle between Vance and Whiting turned out to have extraordinary repercussions. Vance finally got so irritated that he wrote to Jefferson Davis and begged to have Whiting replaced by General D.H. Hill. Instead, Davis, from the depths of innermost perversity, sent General Braxton Bragg to supersede Whiting. Poor Whiting was not even relieved of command, but would have to remain in Wilmington as the subordinate of a man whom he, and nearly everyone else except Jefferson Davis, regarded as disastrously incompetent.

The day after Bragg's appointment was announced, an editorial comment in one of the Richmond newspapers summed it up: "Bragg has been sent to Wilmington...Goodbye Wilmington."

BEN BUTLER
AND HIS PET

In August 1864, Rear Admiral David D. Porter happened to be in Washington, D.C. attending to some routine duties when he received an invitation to dine at the home of Postmaster Montgomery Blair. Also attending were Secretary of the Navy Gideon Welles and his able assistant, Gustavus G. Fox. Porter was surprised to find these gentlemen clustered around a table covered not with hors d'oeuvres but with nautical charts and coastal maps. Porter bent over and instantly recognized the outline of the Cape Fear estuary. His pulse began to beat a little faster, for he suddenly realized why he had really been invited to dinner. Sure enough, Gideon Welles announced that Porter had been chosen to lead the long-contemplated expedition against Fort Fisher. Porter accepted without hesitation.

David Porter was 51, powerfully built, and somewhat ferocious looking, thanks to his long, black beard. He was a career U.S. Navy officer who came from a seafaring family. For four generations, his ancestors had served as merchant captains, privateers, and career naval officers. Porter himself had gone to sea on a man-of-war at age 13, as a midshipman. He had served with distinction in the Mexican War, and after a peacetime decade of stagnation without promotion, he had risen steadily following the outbreak of hostilities with the South. He ran the forts at New Orleans with Admiral David Farragut, and later commanded the Mississippi Squadron.

Farragut, in fact, had been the Navy Department's first choice to lead the Fort Fisher operation, but he had declined, stating reasons of ill health. It's true that Farragut was worn out after the Mobile Bay campaign, but it wasn't the only reason why he declined. For one thing, Farragut disapproved when the Navy Department relieved the conservative but staunch old Admiral Lee. Farragut was reluctant to take Lee's place because he didn't know Lee's men or ships, and he didn't have Lee's intimate knowledge of the Cape Fear region. Nor was Farragut happy about the Army's reluctance to provide a land force large enough to crush the expected opposition. Farragut thought he could smell the ingredients for a first-class disaster, and he saw no reason to finish his Civil War career with a debacle.

Porter knew he had received the assignment by default, but that didn't dampen his enthusiasm. A restless, glory-hungry man, Porter saw in Fort Fisher his last and greatest opportunity to leave his mark on history.

For two long, frustrating years, the Navy Department had been wanting to take Fort Fisher, but each time plans were drawn up and an expedition tentatively scheduled, something went wrong. The first attempt, in 1862, was scuttled when it was learned that the ironclads designated to lead the bombardment couldn't get through the shallow inlets. Later attempts were postponed, time and again, for a single common reason: the reluctance of General Grant to detach the number of troops needed to guarantee the mission's success.

Finally, in August 1864, Grant agreed, but under two conditions: The Navy had to appoint someone Grant approved of to head the expedition, and the number of troops earmarked for the operation could not exceed 10,000. Grant thought Porter was a good choice to command the naval contingent. To command the land forces, Grant selected 28-year-old Major General Godfrey Weitzel, an experienced and able career soldier. Unfortunately, Weitzel was then serving under General Benjamin Butler, and when Butler got wind of what was happening, he came forward and insisted that he be given command instead. Weitzel could still lead the landing force, but Butler, as Weitzel's superior and as the senior Army officer in line, felt he had a perfect right to tag along. And if he did, his orders would be final.

Ben Butler had done well enough on the North Carolina coast early in the war, when he led the troops who captured Forts Hatteras and Clark. Since then, his reputation had taken a nosedive. As

military governor of New Orleans, he had captured national
attention (and earned for himself the everlasting nickname "Beast
Butler") by hanging a man whose only crime was tearing up a U.S.
flag. A while later, after a woman emptied her chamber pot on
Admiral Farragut's head, Butler issued an order that any woman
who behaved "disrespectfully" toward the occupying troops could
be jailed as a prostitute. This slander on Southern womanhood
generated choleric outrage throughout the Confederacy. Jefferson
Davis had Butler officially declared an outlaw, and vowed to hang
him without trial if Butler ever came under his hand.

In addition to stirring up resentment, Butler managed to acquire
a sudden personal fortune while ruling New Orleans. So much
looted silverware found its way into Butler's private vault that even
his own men started calling him "Spoons Butler." Nakedly ambitious, often flagrantly incompetent as well as greedy, Butler was
nevertheless protected by powerful political cronies. Whenever he
was sacked from one post, his friends in the Democratic Party
managed to get him appointed to another. Many of his associates
found him loathsome — not just morally and professionally, but
personally as well. Indeed, he was no dashing cavalier. In Washington, Ben Butler was considered the ugliest officer in the U.S.
Army. He was obese and nearly bald, with two quivering fleshy
dewlaps that hung low from his mottled cheeks; he also had puffy
and dissolute-looking eyes, fat lips, and was cursed with a muscu-
lar tick that frequently made him appear cock-eyed.

Porter later voiced such contempt for Butler that historians have
always assumed that Porter detested Butler from their first meeting.
Actually, the two men seem to have gotten along amicably enough
at first. In Porter's dispatches, one can even find genuine enthusiasm for Butler's vigor and a certain shared enthusiasm for some of
Butler's unconventional ideas.

Whatever Porter's feelings about having to work with Butler, he
was driven to fits of exasperation by Grant's reluctance to part with
his infantry. The naval part of the expedition had essentially been
ready to go as early as September, but Grant kept postponing it.
Porter tried to keep his sailors busy, overhauling boilers, staging
mock amphibious landings, and holding endless gun drills, but
their fine edge was dulling day by day while Grant procrastinated

over his infantry. Secretary Welles tried to get President Lincoln to issue a simple presidential edict to start the operation, but Lincoln was reluctant to interfere with Grant — it had taken him too long to find such a general. As the days dragged by and autumn waned, David Porter stalked the deck of his flagship, wrote vitriolic letters to his friends, smoked hundreds of cigars, worked his way through several cases of expensive champagne, and cursed the Army.

Porter's opinion of Ben Butler began to change as a result of an incident that happened in November aboard Butler's headquarters ship, a former blockade runner now armed and rechristened the USS *Greyhound*. They were steaming down the James River, having just completed a planning conference. Porter couldn't help noticing how slack the general's security seemed to be, especially in view of the top-secret nature of their business. For one thing, there was a group of suspicious-looking civilians on board who seemed to have no reason to be there. After spotting these people loitering in the ship's lounge, Porter went topside to tell Butler that he appeared to have some stowaways. Just before he reached the bridge, however, Porter was thrown to the deck by a violent explosion. The stern of the *Greyhound* erupted in flames, and the ship sank in about five minutes. An investigation blamed the explosion on a Confederate bomb, shaped and painted to look like a lump of coal, which had been planted in the ship's coal bunkers by rebel saboteurs — probably the very men Porter had spotted.

In late November, Grant finally acted. He had received intelligence reports that indicated General Braxton Bragg was withdrawing men from the Wilmington garrisons and moving them south to oppose General Sherman near Savannah. Where before he had urged caution, Grant now urged audacity and speed, hoping that Fort Fisher could be captured while some of its troops were still in Georgia. Grant's orders to Butler, however, were compromised by a degree of ambiguity uncharacteristic of Grant. Apparently Grant envisioned a swift operation, not a prolonged amphibious campaign. Grant wanted his troops returned to the main front the moment Fort Fisher was taken. Although Butler deserved most of the criticism he later received after his attack on Fort Fisher, the criticism should be interpreted in light of the pressure Grant had put on him and of Grant's reluctance to provide troops in the first place.

In truth, by the time Grant issued his directive on November 30, Fort Fisher was, for all practical purposes, at his mercy. Half of Lamb's garrison had in fact been withdrawn and sent to Georgia by Braxton Bragg, leaving the crucial fort defended by a garrison only one-tenth the size of the force Grant was preparing to send against it. General Whiting himself estimated that without massive reinforcements, an amphibious attack could wrest the fort from him in less than 24 hours. And Whiting, too, was receiving intelligence reports — alarming ones about the size and strength of the Federal force being assembled at Hampton Roads.

Whiting did what he could. He erected field artillery emplacements and sent out cavalry patrols along the beaches north of the fort, and ordered the men still under his command to work feverishly to strengthen the existing earthworks.

The troops sent to Georgia did not arrive in time to help defend Savannah, a city that General Sherman took in a depressingly short time. The troops began returning to the Wilmington area on December 18. On that same day, Robert E. Lee received a report that the Federal armada had sailed from Hampton Roads. He knew it could have only one destination. As it happened, Lee was at that moment mulling over reports that the Army of Northern Virginia had less than a month's worth of rations. If Fort Fisher fell, Lee's most important artery of supply would be severed. Bowing to the inevitable, Lee withdrew General Robert Hoke's brigade — 6,155 men, all veterans — and ordered them entrained for Wilmington. But the Confederacy's rail network had become so fragile by this time that it would take Hoke's men several frustrating days to cover the distance. At one point on the trip, when the brigade was strung out along the rickety stretch of new line connecting Danville, Virginia, and Greensboro, the trains were moving so slowly, with so many stops, that Hoke took his men off and marched them to the next junction. They beat the train by a couple of hours.

At Fort Fisher, on the morning of December 20, Colonel Lamb was awakened by an orderly. He stumbled outside into a cold, gray, overcast dawn, his hair blown wildly by a fierce northeast wind. His heart beating faster, he climbed the ladder into the Pulpit and stared out at the lead-colored Atlantic. Starting at one end of

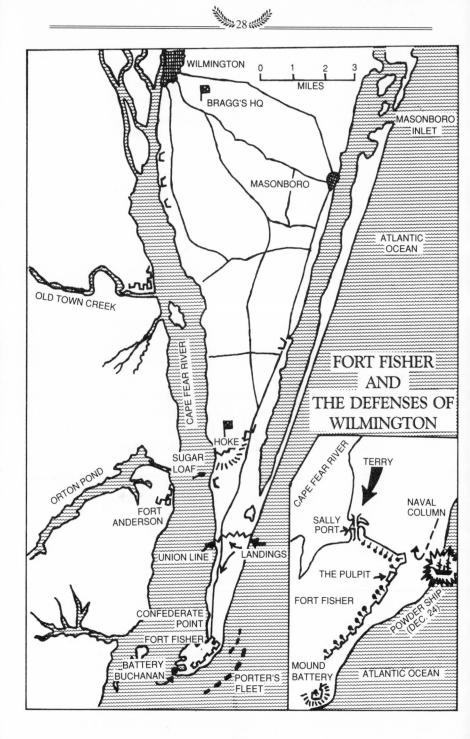

FORT FISHER
AND
THE DEFENSES OF
WILMINGTON

WILMINGTON

BRAGG'S HQ

MASONBORO INLET

MASONBORO

ATLANTIC OCEAN

OLD TOWN CREEK

CAPE FEAR RIVER

HOKE

SUGAR LOAF

ORTON POND

FORT ANDERSON

UNION LINE

LANDINGS

CONFEDERATE POINT

FORT FISHER

BATTERY BUCHANAN

PORTER'S FLEET

CAPE FEAR RIVER

TERRY

SALLY PORT

NAVAL COLUMN

THE PULPIT

FORT FISHER

POWDER SHIP (DEC. 24)

MOUND BATTERY

ATLANTIC OCEAN

the horizon and working toward the other, he counted the masts of 30 ships. It was happening at last.

Lamb rushed back to the Cottage and woke his family. Tearfully, Daisy and the children took their belongings and made ready to depart for the mainland. Once he had seen them off, Lamb returned to the earthen ramparts and stood huddled in his greatcoat against the icy wind, counting and recounting the probable number of guns arrayed against him. He might have felt somewhat better if he had known that the actual attack was not underway — first there would be a prelude that smacked of farce.

Butler Drags His Feet

Despite the fact that Grant had ordered General Butler to make "a bold dash" against Fort Fisher, Butler took his time getting underway. Not until December 7 did the troops receive their orders to prepare for embarkation. The main landing force was comprised of the 2nd Division, 24th Corps — four brigades of veterans from New Hampshire, Indiana, Pennsylvania, and New York — commanded by Brigadier General Adelbert Ames. Supporting them would be a division of Negro troops, the 3rd Division of 25th Corps, commanded by Brigadier General Charles J. Paine.

Boarding started on December 8 and continued all day. Then the transports, along with two hospital ships, sailed out to join Admiral Porter's fleet. Porter assumed Butler would be ready to get underway immediately, but he was not. Not, in fact, for another five days, during which Butler fussed over the details of his "Pet."

For such a mediocre soldier, Butler had a passion for military experiments and off-the-wall schemes. Some of his ventures made unusually good sense — such as his purchase of a battery of Gatling guns, and his use of captive hot-air balloons for reconnaissance — but others verged on the ridiculous. An example of the latter was his bizarre scheme for digging an immense tunnel under Richmond in order to take the Confederate capital from below ground.

About two months before the Fort Fisher expedition sailed, Butler happened to read a newspaper account about the explosion of some gunpowder barges at a dock on the Thames River near

345

London. The barges had touched off a couple of nearby ammunition magazines, and the force of the blast had caused a wide radius of destruction, leveling buildings and inflicting hundreds of casualties. Animals and birds, it was luridly reported, had been struck senseless, and upon recovery, had foamed at the mouth. Human remains had rained from the sky miles away, and paintings had been knocked from the walls of the Crystal Palace, more than ten miles away. This newspaper account rekindled Butler's interest in big explosions. Earlier in the summer, a clockwork bomb planted by rebel agents had blown up a Union ordnance ship at City Point, Virginia, setting off a chain reaction that touched off a number of ammo dumps. Among other things, General Grant's headquarters had been destroyed. (Fortunately for the Union, the general was not occupying his headquarters at the time.) For a few days afterward, Butler had buttonholed every superior officer within reach, imploring them to let him detonate in the middle of Charleston harbor a vessel crammed with 1,000 tons of powder. No one seriously listened to Butler, but his enthusiasm was rekindled by the conjunction of the Fort Fisher operation with the newspaper accounts of the Thames accident.

Even so, the spark for the scheme may not have come directly from Butler, but from Assistant Navy Secretary Gustavus Fox. Like Butler, Fox was an innovator and a firm believer in radical experiments. He appears to have discussed some sort of powder-boat scheme with Butler in early November. Whoever broached the subject initially, Butler soon embraced it with hearty, almost messianic zeal. He christened the powder-boat "my Pet" and referred to it as if it were some kind of large, faithful dog.

In essence, the idea was simple. Just take an old, worn-out vessel, pack it with explosives, and set it off one night as close as possible to the walls of Fort Fisher. If it worked, it would enable his men to capture the place with fewer casualties — and would certainly garner banner headlines and more political clout for Butler. Butler wasn't deterred even when subsequent newspaper accounts stated that the damage caused by the Thames explosion was about ten percent of what had originally been described. Butler plowed right ahead, unveiling the particulars of his scheme at a secret shipboard conference. He proposed to detonate 200 or more tons of powder as close to the base of the walls as possible. The resulting shock wave should level the sod-covered ramparts — they were, after all, nothing but sand — and either kill or stun most of the garrison. Those still standing after the blast would probably suffocate, or at least be incapacitated, by the toxic gases released by the blast. After that, Butler's troops could walk ashore and plant the flag without resistance.

Admiral Porter was impressed. He never believed the blast would be as lethal as Butler claimed, but even a small breach in the fort's wall would make the expedition's task much easier. After obtaining Porter's concurrence, Butler returned to his ship, enormously pleased with himself. But not everyone in the room greeted the scheme with as much enthusiasm as Porter. After Butler had gone, one of Porter's aides quietly remarked: "Butler has about as much chance of blowing up that fort as I have of flying." When General Grant revealed the scheme to General Richard Delafield, the Army's chief of engineers, Delafield snorted that blowing up the powder-ship would have about as much effect on the fort "as shooting feathers from a musket."

Porter agreed to furnish the ship to be sacrificed. He selected an elderly flat-bottomed steamer that was docked at Beaufort, N.C., the *Louisiana*. In early December, the *Louisiana* joined the Union fleet at Hampton Roads, where the work of converting her into a floating bomb was led by Major Thomas Casey, reputedly the U.S. Army's best explosives expert. Casey removed the masts, added a fake smokestack, and painted the whole ship a dull, chalky gray. On a dark night, he hoped, she would look just like a blockade runner. Once the *Louisiana* was converted, Casey anchored the ship a safe distance from the rest of Porter's fleet and began packing it with 250 tons of powder. His workers started at the waterline with barrels of the stuff, then worked their way topside, stacking 60-pound sacks of powder on the deck and superstructure.

Even that much powder, however, would not do the job if the whole load didn't go off simultaneously. Casey rigged timing devices from percussion caps and clockwork, then connected them with a veritable spider-web maze of fuses that snaked over the decks and through the hatchways. As a crude but reliable backup system, the fuses were also connected to a box of candles and to a length of slow-burning fuse that could be safely ignited by hand. As a last resort, resinous pine was piled against the ship's cabin so the vessel could be set afire quickly if necessary.

Butler hovered over the project like an anxious parent, constantly nagging Casey with questions. Butler also bragged, to everyone who would listen, how the bomb-boat was going to revolutionize naval warfare. Finally, on December 13 — two full days after he had received a strongly worded order from Grant to proceed "immediately" — Butler gave the order for the expedition to proceed. The armada sailed south in three columns, with the transports in the center and the warships on the flanks. It was, by all accounts, a magnificent sight, the greatest display of naval power on the high seas since the war began.

It was magnificent, that is, if one happened to be in good health and out in the fresh air on the open decks. For the long-suffering infantrymen crammed below decks, the voyage was an ordeal. One soldier wrote to his family:

> Day after day we have been tossed drearily on the waves off the bleak coast, out of sight of land, living on raw pork and hardtack, and crowded almost without breathing room into the filthy old transport...this completes the fifteenth day aboard. The lower decks and hold are so confined that it is wonderful how the men have thus far escaped pestilence. Had our soldiers been so roughly treated by the rebels, there would be no end to cries of "shame" and accusations of "barbarity" from the enlightened press. Probably a more mismanaged expedition never left our ports. As yet nothing has been accomplished beyond testing uselessly the endurance of the troops, and this two long weeks of seasickness and suffering had undoubtedly harassed and worn them out more than six weeks of active campaigning could have done.[1]

Porter led his fleet into Beaufort on December 15 to take on ammunition and supplies. Butler conferred with him that night and agreed that the Army's part of the flotilla should continue on to Fort Fisher, anchor at a point some 20 miles offshore, and await the arrival of the naval contingent. Porter estimated he could rejoin Butler in about 24 hours, but it took much longer to refuel and reprovision than he had expected. The fleet was not able to rejoin the transports until after sundown on December 17.

It was Porter's plan to explode the *Louisiana* that night, then commence the bombardment and landing operations the following morning. Typically vile Atlantic weather prevented him from doing so. Even before the final planning conference began, Porter's flagship, the USS *Malvern* (formerly the North Carolina-owned blockade runner *Ella and Annie*), had begun to roll sickeningly in the heavy seas. By the end of the conference, both the wind and seas had become so stormy that Porter was forced to abandon any idea of carrying out the powder-boat attack that night. And by now, to confuse matters still more, Butler's ships had started to run out of fuel and provisions. Butler elected to take them back to Beaufort for replenishment.

While the transports embarked on their 80-mile voyage to Beaufort, conditions worsened at the anchorage. The tempest grew in strength until the night of December 21, when it reached gale force and smote the wallowing vessels with powerful winds and enormous green-water waves. One soldier, who rode out the storm aboard the transport *Weybosset*, described it this way:

> Last night was the roughest we have experienced at sea. The vessel rolled terribly. Everything movable was dashed and slammed around in the most confused manner. The officers rushed across the cabin like locomotives off the track. One shut the door of his stateroom on his coattails, and then pitched forward and tore those tails clean off. The poor darkies dove around, butting their hard heads through the panels and howling like demons.[2]

The expedition's horses, all quartered aboard two transports, became so terrified during the storm that they stampeded and kicked holes in the woodwork. The soldiers eventually had to shoot the crazed animals and throw the carcasses overboard. Porter's ships, still anchored at the rendezvous point off Cape Fear, suffered just as terribly. The admiral was especially worried about his ironclad monitors. Repeatedly during the height of the storm, those low-lying and barely seaworthy vessels simply vanished beneath mountainous waves. (The original ironclad after which they were patterned, the USS *Monitor*, had of course sunk in a similar gale off Cape Hatteras a year before.)

When the storm subsided and daylight finally came, it came

sickly and gray, with pale sunlight that gave no warmth. Amazingly, the monitors were all accounted for. Bravely riding out the last swells, their seasick crews were no doubt convinced that storming Fort Fisher would be infinitely preferable to one more night spent half-submerged in icy water.

On December 22, Butler's transports steamed into Beaufort. The troops on board hoped they could get off, stretch their legs, and enjoy a few hours' respite from the smell of vomit, but Butler kept them cooped up in the interests of security. It was, however, much too late for that. Every newspaper from New York to Richmond had already printed speculative stories about the expedition, and most of those stories had already drawn the logical conclusion that Fort Fisher was the target. Some accounts had even mentioned rumors about a top secret "fire ship" that would be sent against the fort.

The morning of December 23 dawned clear, calm, and cold. Porter decided he had no choice but to begin the attack while the weather held, even though Butler had not yet rejoined him. He could at least set off the powder-ship and begin the bombardment. He sent Butler a message to that effect and ordered the powder-boat scheme put into motion.

At dusk, unsure about what sort of explosion would be unleashed, Porter prudently withdrew his fleet far out to sea and ordered the steam released from all the ships' boilers. That way, if the shock wave proved strong enough, even at that distance, to rupture the steam engines, at least his crews wouldn't be scalded to death. The *Louisiana* remained closer to shore, just beyond sight of the fort, along with her escort, the gunboat USS *Wilderness*. The gunboat's job was to beat off with grapeshot any rebel attempt to board the *Louisiana*.

Commander Alexander Rhind had been chosen to lead the powder-boat sortie. Rhind was cut from the same cloth as Will Cushing. He had led several raiding parties against Confederate targets near Charleston and had proven himself fearless and aggressive. Although this newest and most dangerous mission had been described only in the most general terms, Rhind still obtained hundreds more volunteers than he could use. He picked the best men, including a dozen from his own ship. At the last minute,

Rhind and his volunteers told Admiral Porter that they had come to a serious decision. If the fuse systems didn't work, or if the rebels overwhelmed the ship in a boarding attack, they would point the *Louisiana* for the fort, sail her as far as she would go onto the beach, cut open a powder bag with a knife, and thrust a lighted candle into the grains. Porter at first refused to sanction this last-ditch plan for self-immolation, but grimly agreed to it when Rhind insisted that every man in his crew had sworn to carry it out.

At 10:30 a.m., the *Wilderness* began towing the *Louisiana* on her final voyage. Five hundred yards from the beach, the tow line was cut. Rhind started the powder-ship's engines and tenderly felt his way along the coast. He was resolved to get as close as possible to Fort Fisher, preferably to within 150 yards. He was pondering how he might best accomplish this when, at about 11:30, he spotted another vessel hugging the shoreline and steering for New Inlet. It turned out to be the Confederate blockade runner *Little Hattie*.

Porter had chosen well when he selected Rhind for this mission. Instantly making his decision, Rhind swung the *Louisiana* into line behind the blockade runner and followed her through the shallows at a distance of about 300 yards.

If the *Louisiana* was spotted by Confederate lookouts that night, no alarm went up. The ruse of disguising her like a blockade runner paid off handsomely. When Rhind estimated he was 300 yards from the earthen ramparts of Fort Fisher, he stopped the engines and dropped anchor. Then he and two volunteers began igniting the various fuses. They triggered the clockwork mechanisms, lit the box of candles, and started the slow-burning wick. For good measure, they also set fire to the resinous pine on deck. Meanwhile, the rest of the skeleton crew piled into longboats and rowed like galley slaves for the open sea. The *Wilderness* waited for them, anxious to put as much distance as possible between itself and the massive time-bomb the *Louisiana* had become.

It was almost midnight when Rhind and his two brave companions were finally able to leave the ship. The great explosion was timed to begin in less than 90 minutes. Rhind rejoined the rest of his crew aboard the *Wilderness*, which instantly steamed at flank speed to rejoin the fleet. Out on the anchored Union ships, Admiral Porter and his staff, along with dozens of newspaper reporters and

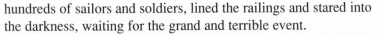

hundreds of sailors and soldiers, lined the railings and stared into the darkness, waiting for the grand and terrible event.

At 1:30 a.m., the *Louisiana* appeared wrapped in flames. From time to time, the fire would ebb to a dull glow, then suddenly brighten, so that on several occasions during that tense period the onlookers braced themselves for the big blast, only to be frustrated when it didn't happen. Ten more minutes crept by. Then, in the words of a reporter from *The New York Times*, "the heavens were electrified into one vast sheet of flame." There were three distinct and massive explosions, followed by dozens of smaller airborne bursts as flaming bags of powder were blown into the air and detonated like shells. The immediate after-effects were even more impressive:

> A few minutes after the explosion a dense black smoke rose rapidly on the horizon and stood out in sharp, well-defined outlines against the clear starlight [sic] sky. The cloud was of huge proportions, and it rose rapidly in the air, and came swiftly toward us on the wings of the wind, presented a most remarkable appearance, assuming the shape of a monstrous waterspout, its tapering base seemingly resting on the sea...In a few minutes it passed us, filling the atmosphere with its sulphurous odor, as if a spirit from the infernal regions had swept by us.[3]

Other onlookers were not as impressed. Rhind himself merely shook his head and muttered: "There's a fizzle...."

It certainly looked impressive from a distance, but in truth the only things destroyed were two glasses aboard one of the Union ships, and the only things killed were some Confederate fish. The rebel soldiers nearest the blast were a unit of Junior Reserves camped out on the beach directly opposite the explosion. The shock wave tumbled them out of their blankets, recounted one of their officers, "like popcorn from a popper," but otherwise did them no harm. The reverberations from the blast were felt as far away as Wilmington, but didn't shatter so much as a pane of glass. Most of Fort Fisher's garrison was awakened by the explosion, but they speculated that it was probably a boiler blowing up on one of the Union blockade ships, and they went back to sleep.

General Grant later summed up the episode this way: "It would seem from the notice accorded it by the Southern newspapers that the enemy were never enlightened as to the object of the explosion until they were informed by the Northern press...."[4] The main response in Confederate circles, once the origin of the mysterious explosion was known, was an expression of envy for an opponent who could afford to waste so much gunpowder. Perhaps the last word came from a Confederate deserter who was questioned by Admiral Porter himself a few days later. Be frank, Porter had encouraged the fellow, and tell me what effect that powder-boat explosion really had on the garrison. With a straight face, the rebel replied: "Why Admiral, it was dreadful — it woke everybody up!"

What went wrong? There was nothing really faulty about the idea itself, but inefficient planning, interservice rivalry, and a ludicrous effort by some of Butler's people to save money by buying second-class gunpowder had guaranteed its failure. All of the elaborate fuses apparently failed, so the blast was finally set off by the bonfire. This in turn meant that each layer of powder went off in succession, not all at once, starting with the bags on deck and working down to the waterline. Finally, due to enormous last-minute confusion, not only was some of the gunpowder substandard, but there was only 215 tons of it instead of 300 tons. Therefore, the explosives were not confined tightly enough to generate the maximum potential blast. In fact, it was later estimated by ordnance experts that as much as 80 percent of the explosive force was directed straight up into the air, not outward.

At first light the next day, the USS *Rhode Island* went in to evaluate the damage to Fort Fisher. There was none. The sod grass covering the walls wasn't even disturbed. No traverses had been blown down, no barracks reduced to matchsticks, no cannon dismounted. The Confederate flag still flew, untattered. Fort Fisher looked exactly as it had the day before the explosion. Admiral Porter sadly concluded that the fort would have to be reduced the hard way, by bombardment.

On the Confederate side of the walls, Colonel William Lamb had awakened that morning without any knowledge of what the explosion really signified. It had cost him a little sleep, but like everyone else he had attributed the blast to some mechanical catastrophe in the Federal fleet — a magazine exploding, or a boiler bursting. Doubtless he would have felt encouraged if he had known that the enemy's dreaded secret weapon had done its worst, without any more effect than a clap of thunder over the Atlantic.

But Lamb was preoccupied with too many problems to give more than a passing thought to the nocturnal explosion. He wasn't sure why the enemy had remained inactive offshore for four whole days, but he had tried to make use of every hour of time allowed him by their inaction. He had issued rifles and pistols to the garrison, evacuated all the civilians, including his own family and all the Negroes, and had worked his men hard, filling thousands of sandbags and placing them around the gun positions, strengthening the fort even more.

Other Confederate authorities in the region hadn't made the same good use of the lull, however, and that worried Lamb. He had sent desperate pleas to General Hebert in Smithville, asking for men, ammunition, and food. Hebert, though, had sunk into alcoholic despondency at the news of the Federal fleet's arrival, and consequently was even more useless than usual. General Whiting had at least managed to round up a ten-day supply of rations — by commandeering hardtack from less-threatened units that barely had enough to eat themselves — and had shipped it to the fort. Whiting had also purchased, with his own money, calcium flares to be used in the event of a night attack. However, these had not yet arrived on the blockade runner that was carrying them.

But no one seemed able to get more men to Lamb. The 500-odd soldiers he had were barely adequate to keep the guns firing and to maintain minimum security on the walls. They were hopelessly inadequate to repel the kind of massive amphibious assault Lamb suspected was about to be hurled at the fort. Lamb knew, of course, that Hoke's division was on its way, somewhere between Wilmington and Petersburg, but given the condition of the railroads, there was no guarantee they would arrive in time. Moreover, given Braxton Bragg's reputation for generalship, there was no guarantee that Hoke's men would be put to good use once they did show up.

On December 20, Governor Vance issued a windy proclamation urging everyone who could shoulder a musket, regardless of age, to join him in the defense of Wilmington. "Your Governor will meet you at the front and will share with you the worst," Vance promised. His intentions were no doubt good and his courage beyond reproach, but the proclamation was just so much hot air. Nobody showed up, including the governor.

When Lamb wired Whiting that he had no men inside the fort who knew how to fire the two rifled Brooke guns on the lower seaface — weapons originally mounted on a now-sunken Confederate gunboat — Whiting drafted 32 men from the CSS *Chickamauga*, a commerce raider then riding uselessly at anchor in Wilmington. Whiting sent the sailors to Fort Fisher to man the Brooke battery. He also rounded up two companies of regulars from the 10th North Carolina Regiment, and a battalion of Junior Reserves (beardless and ill-prepared youths no more than 16 years old). Whiting managed to get these meager reinforcements into the fort before Butler's attack. Lamb held the teenagers in reserve, stationing them on the beach north of the fort.

With these reinforcements, Lamb's garrison now totaled about 650 men. And with these men — all of them already exhausted from poor diet and lack of sleep, and virtually all of them lacking experience, and poorly armed to boot — Lamb was expected to withstand an assault by more than 6,000 hardened veterans, supported by what was then the most powerful naval force ever assembled by the United States.

THE FIRST
ATTACK

At first light, on Christmas Eve 1864, Admiral Porter scanned the southern horizon and beheld no sign of General Butler and the transports. He was heard to grumble, as he had on several occasions during the past few days, that maybe it would be a good thing if Butler had gone down in the recent storm. Those around him were beginning to suppose the admiral was not kidding. Porter decided to open the bombardment anyway. This should soften up the target sufficiently to allow Butler's men to go ashore almost as soon as they arrived.

No one who witnessed Porter's armada assemble its formation that morning ever forgot the sight. Old men, recounting the story 50 years later, still felt a chill coursing down their spines at the recollection. The sun rose moltenly in a clear winter sky. The morning was mild, the temperature about 50 degrees, with a light wind from the east, and the sea was smooth and glossy. Fifty-seven vessels of war executed a graceful preliminary ballet, followed above by clouds of screeching gulls. It took several hours to get the ships sorted out and in motion, but by 11:30 a.m., they began assuming their assigned positions for the bombardment.

Through the clear, almost-still air came the rattle of drums as the U.S. Navy crews were "beat to quarters" aboard each warship. Cooking fires were extinguished in the galleys. Deep below decks, in the ships' lazarets, surgeons washed down plank tables with cold water and laid out their gleaming probes, bone saws, and brass-handled tourniquets. Above them, sailors traversed the length of the gun decks with buckets of ashes, spreading a gritty layer on the wooden surfaces so that men wouldn't slip in the blood of their injured shipmates.

From his post in the Pulpit, William Lamb watched Porter's fleet deploy with mingled feelings of awe, dread, and resolution. Behind him, drums snarled on the parade ground, and on both sides of Lamb's position the garrison of Fort Fisher went to their battle stations calmly and in good order. They may have been inexperienced — probably four out of ten were too young or too old — but Lamb noted with pride that they readied themselves with the coolness of combat veterans. He knew they were in for one of the longest and most powerful bombardments in history, and he had planned accordingly.

There was too little ammunition for him to allow his gunners to fire at will. For all calibers and types of weapons, Lamb had a total stock of only 3,600 rounds — an average of 80 rounds per gun. Fire would have to be rationed and disciplined. Only the long-range guns would fight the ships, and no piece was permitted to fire more than once every half-hour. To spare the men from unnecessary exposure, the gun crews were to remain inside the bomb-proof dugouts until the time came to fire their half-hourly shot. Crews would be rotated on a regular basis, so the danger would be spread evenly among all the men. For his deadliest weapon, the gigantic Armstrong cannon, Lamb had only 13 rounds; that particular piece could not be fired without his direct order.

Porter's ships came into range about noon, led by the frigate USS *New Ironsides*. The mass of ships steered to port, moving into final formation from the north. As planned, they took station in three lines, with a fourth, smaller line in reserve. Nearest the fort, only three-quarters of a mile from the beach, opposite the Northeast Bastion, were the heaviest warships and the ironclads. One mile to the east was the second bombardment line. The third anchored one-and-a-quarter miles from the Mound Battery. The first line had been ordered to concentrate its fire on the landface and the Northeast Bastion, while the other two were to hammer the seaface. The reserve ships were held about a half-mile behind the firing lines, and would be sent forward individually if any ship were forced to withdraw because of damage. Admiral Porter's swift flagship, the USS *Malvern*, roamed freely from one line to the next so he could keep an eye on the whole operation.

On shore, as the Union ships made their final maneuvers, Lamb found he was breathing shallowly and that the men around him were talking in whispers, oppressed by the strained silence that throbbed over the majestic and terrible scene. Aside from the shrieking seagulls, the loudest sounds were the crash of the restless surf at the foot of the ramparts and the bullwhip thud of the Stars and Bars as it snapped taut in the freshening wind. Lamb glanced at his watch: 12:40 p.m.

The powerful broadside of the *New Ironsides* began the fight with a roll of thunder. The battle's opening shot — an 11-inch shell — was clearly visible as it arced over the beach and exploded with a flash above the Northeast Bastion. Lamb turned and signaled the 10-inch Columbiad near the Pulpit to make reply. It was a beautiful ricochet shot, smacking across the smooth water like a well-skipped stone. It took a perfect bounce in front of its target and tore a gaping hole through the smokestack of the USS *Susquehanna*. Now, all along the mile-and-a-half barricade of earthen ramparts, the guns of Fort Fisher spoke as one. Several more of Porter's ships were hit. The USS *Minnesota* was struck four times in that first salvo, losing her anchor cable and sustaining damage to her masts.

So good were Lamb's gunners that, had their ammunition supply been lavish enough to permit them to fire at will, the battle might have gone quite differently. Throughout the day, a fairly high percentage of rounds fired from Fort Fisher found their targets, but the fleet's expenditure of ammunition was so profligate that Lamb began to lose guns before any of them had been able to fire more than five or six shots.

Now all three lines of the Union warships fired simultaneous broadsides, sending a wave of smoke rolling toward the shore, pushed by the sea wind. As Porter's gun crews worked up to tempo, their rate of fire grew until an estimated 115 shells per minute were landing in or exploding above Fort Fisher. The seaface boiled and heaved as shell after shell plowed into those great sandy mounds. The air above the traverses rippled with flashes as whirling iron shells exploded and showered their deadly fragments on the terrain below. The wooden buildings inside the walls took hit after hit, sending clouds of splinters into the air.

Yet, Lamb lost his first cannon not from Union gunfire but from
mechanical failure. One of the eight-inch Columbiads on the
seaface tore loose from its mounting by the force of its own recoil,
tumbled backward, and toppled into the sand while the gun crew
scampered wildly to get out of its way. Not long after this, the
garrison suffered its first casualty. A young courier was running
toward the seaface Brooke battery when an 11-inch shell from one
of the monitors exploded just above his head, ripping him to
shreds. The Brooke battery itself took a hit some moments later,
and a shell fragment sheared off the left leg of one of the *Chickamauga* sailors.

But as the engagement reached its peak of intensity, there was
spectacle as well as horror. The lines of Union ships, now anchored
firmly to provide steadier gun platforms, were wreathed in great
billows of smoke. Periodically, long spears of fire lanced outward
from their sides. The air above both fort and fleet was filled with
shrieking, whistling, whirring projectiles, and flocked with the
sharp flash-bang detonations of time-fused shells. Cotton-balls of
smoke hung in the air following each burst, then dissipated in the
breeze, drifting like veils above the masts of Porter's ships and the
huge upturned breasts of sand that marked the walls of the fort. By
2 p.m., fires inside the walls of Fort Fisher had rolled a vast,
flaming pillar of smoke over the whole scene, casting an immense
and sinister shadow that darkened not only the peninsula but part of
the Cape Fear River itself. Skipped shots from the fort kicked up
evenly spaced lines of waterspouts across the surface as they
sought their targets' waterlines. The ramparts of the seaface
seemed to turn almost liquid as hundreds of shell strikes blew
spurts of sand and sod into the air, adding a gritty haze to the
smoke from the fort's batteries. Thunder rolled over the beach in
stupefying crescendos.

From across the river, on a bluff near Smithville, Mrs. Lamb
watched it all through binoculars and thought it "an awful but
magnificent sight." At the height of the bombardment, when the
thunder had turned to one continuous roar, Lamb's little boy Dick
ran over to his mother, a "grave and thoughtful" expression on his
face, clasped her around the knees, and said: "Momma, I want to
pray to God for my papa."

In Wilmington, Christmas church services were accompanied by the rumble of the bombardment. The irony was not lost on most worshippers:

> The thunder of the guns, distinctly audible and shaking the atmosphere like jelly, had been irregular until the Litany was read, when from the beginning of that solemn service to its conclusion almost simultaneously the responses from the congregation and the roar of the broadsides united. "From battle and murder, and from sudden death," read the minister, "Good Lord deliver us," prayed the congregation, and simultaneously "Boom-boom-boom," answered the guns until the situation was almost intolerable.[1]

Aboard the USS *Powhatan*, a young seaman named Evans was high on the mast, spotting for the guns through a pair of binoculars. He had missed breakfast and had taken some hardtack up the mast with him. He had just placed one of the bulky crackers in his teeth when he saw, through his glasses, a Confederate gun crew elevating a cannon until it was literally staring straight at him. The gun fired, and Evans saw nothing but smoke. Then he spotted something blurry and dark spinning toward him. A second later, the rebel projectile shot the rigging in half just below his feet. Evans tumbled into a sail, frantically pawed at some shroud lines, and managed to slow his fall enough to land on the deck shaken but unbroken. Only after he had taken a quick inventory of his arms and legs did Evans realize he had swallowed the hardtack whole.

About an hour into the bombardment, shells from the ships set fire to the fort's largest stable. A herd of panic-stricken horses burst out of the flaming structure only to emerge in the middle of a hail of bursting shells. The crazed and wounded animals ran madly back and forth on the parade ground, wild with terror and pain. Several of them, disemboweled by shell fragments, careened in circles with their intestines unwinding in the sand like purple ropes. Finally, all of the horses were killed or put out of their misery.

In the apocalyptic din and smoke of the shelling, it became harder and harder for Lamb's gunners to find their range, especially when limited to one shot every 30 minutes. One frustrated battery commander decided, on his own, that it would be better to use up ammunition and score hits than to ration it and keep missing. Using the wreckage of a blockade runner as an aiming point, he concentrated fire on the USS *Powhatan*. (Indeed, one of his shots may well have been the one that poor Evans saw coming straight at him.) On his third try, he struck her fair. Two subsequent rounds punched holes in the gunboat's hull, and two more shells exploded inside her, doing considerable structural damage but miraculously not killing anyone. The *Powhatan* shipped water and took on a starboard list, but her skipper ordered some of the cannon shifted to the port side, restoring balance well enough to resume firing.

Throughout the day, Porter's fleet actually sustained more casualties from its own artillery than from Confederate fire. The big Parrott guns, which tended to overheat and suffer metal fatigue when fired for long periods of time, had a well-deserved reputation as widow-makers. One exploded on the USS *Juanita* shortly after 2 p.m., disemboweling one gunner, decapitating another, killing two more with shrapnel, and wounding eight other men. The *Juanita* moved out of line. Admiral Porter, prowling in the *Malvern*, quickly steamed alongside and inquired brusquely why the *Juanita* had dropped out. "My 100-pounder has exploded," her captain replied.

Porter thundered: "Then why in hell don't you go back and use your other guns?" Sheepishly, the *Juanita* returned to her station and resumed firing, while the messboys sprinkled fresh ashes on her blood-puddled gun deck.

After bombarding both faces of the fort for almost three hours, in mid-afternoon several warships concentrated their fire on the symbolic targets of the bastion's two flagstaffs. The one on the Northeast Bastion went first; the other flag, planted atop the Mound Battery, proved a more difficult target. Several hundred shots were lobbed at it before it finally went down. Almost immediately, a 20-year-old private from the 36th North Carolina Regiment, Christopher Bland, from Calabash, volunteered to raise another flag. It was an almost suicidal undertaking, since the flagstaff had no halyard and Bland was forced to shinny up the pole and tie the banner on by hand. But the fire directed against the Mound Battery slacked off when he appeared, as though in tribute to his bravery. Shortly after Bland returned safely to earth, another shell clipped one corner of the flag and left it dangling like an old rag. Once more, Bland came forward and clawed his way up the splintered pole. This time, there was no gallant suspension of fire; one enemy shell whizzed by so close it ruffled the young man's hair. But he refastened the flag, and this time it remained, as though charmed by the aura of his courage, for the rest of the day.

The Mound Battery was singled out for terrific punishment. Ammo was as limited as it was for all the other guns, but the Mound's elevation gave its gunners an edge. Early in the duel, the Mound gunners shot off the foremast of one of the ships firing at them, and at about 3 p.m. they sent a Columbiad shell into the boiler of the USS *Mackinac*. The engine blew apart with a horrific explosion, and for a moment the roar of cannon was challenged by the screams of scalded seamen. Observing the effects of this one devastating hit, three more Federal ships ganged up on the Mound Battery, raining such a torrent of projectiles on it that the gunners were forced to take shelter in their bombproof for the rest of the afternoon.

By ordering his men to spend most of their time in their shelters, Lamb was keeping his casualties low. But the damage to his firepower was mounting. By late afternoon, five gun carriages had been smashed and two big cannon dismounted. The fort's gunfire had become erratic, and the gunners, deafened and choking from both smoke and the constant rain of sand, were growing less efficient. Even so, Fort Fisher continued to score hits. One shell tore through the hull of the USS *Pontoosuc* and exploded in the paymaster's office, starting a fire that caused the gunboat to veer out of line for a time.

Perhaps the most serious damage the Union fleet sustained that afternoon was caused by a hit on the USS *Osceola*. The *Osceola* was struck by a ten-inch shot three feet below the waterline. The shell passed through a layer of sandbags and exploded inside a boiler furnace, critically burning six sailors. The boiler room flooded and the *Osceola* dropped out of line, hoisting the signal flags for "Sinking!" Makeshift repairs eventually checked the flooding, but the vessel was out of the fight for good.

Porter's gun crews were getting less efficient, too. Their hands and faces were blistered and cut, their tongues were swollen from the gunpowder fumes, their noses were bleeding from concussion, and many of them were staggering as they moved. Their morale was wounded as well — Parrott guns had exploded on four more ships, killing or wounding 37 men. Nevertheless, this caused only a temporary -- and on the receiving end, unnoticeable -- slackening of fire.

Admiral Porter was, on the whole, pleased with the way things seemed to be going. At one point he remarked to some of his aides that Fort Fisher was beginning to look like a patient who had been ravaged by smallpox. He sailed constantly up and down all three bombardment lines, and woe to the captain who took his ship out of the fight for anything but drastic reasons. Observing one warship drawing out of line, Porter drew alongside and bellowed: "Where are you going?"

"To repair the damage to my side," replied the retiring skipper.

Porter surveyed the damage, thought it minor, and yelled: "Go back to your place, or I will send you and your boat to the bottom!"

By now it was 4:30 p.m. Colonel Lamb had just received the bad news that his Brooke battery, which had been served valiantly all afternoon by the crewmen from the *Chickamauga*, had taken a direct hit. Then he looked up and was startled to see General Whiting and three of his staff officers puffing their way up the ladder to the Pulpit. Whiting had departed for the fort three hours earlier, as soon as he had received Lamb's signal that the long-dreaded assault had begun, but was only now arriving. Much of the delay was caused by a lack of transportation. When Whiting had arrived at the docks near Battery Buchanan, there were no horses to be found. (Almost every horse in the fort was dead by then.) So Whiting and his aides had walked to the Pulpit, through a storm of shellfire — a distance of more than a mile.

Ever mindful of military protocol, Lamb offered to let his superior officer take command. Whiting waved aside the suggestion, and replied that he had come only to take a firsthand look and to render whatever help he could. He also brought Lamb the welcome news that two companies of reinforcements had just arrived by ferry from Fort Caswell. Even more heartening was the news that the first elements of General Robert Hoke's division had arrived and were en route from Wilmington to Sugar Loaf Hill, six miles north of the fort.

The first of Hoke's troops on the scene was the brigade of General William Kirkland, 1,300 hard-bitten veterans. Kirkland arrived at Sugar Loaf Hill at about the time the shelling started at Fort Fisher. After inspecting the earthworks at Sugar Loaf, Kirkland rode across to the coast and contacted the fort's support force — 1,200 Junior and Senior Reserves and a handful of cannon at Battery Gatlin, an isolated earthwork covering one of the most likely landing beaches north of the fort itself. After inspecting all the terrain between Sugar Loaf and Battery Gatlin, and after riding south and watching, awestruck, the naval bombardment, Kirkland deployed his men in positions from which they could either aid Lamb or repel an enemy landing.

Another general also arrived late that afternoon: Ben Butler. He was amazed at the spectacle of Porter's fleet slowly disengaging, and he was reduced to sputters of rage by the news that his "Pet" had been exploded without him, and had failed to do much of anything. Butler immediately requested a confrontation with Porter. But Porter had had enough for one day, and brushed off Butler by saying that he was too tired to meet with anyone at that moment. Porter proposed a council of war on the following morning and pointedly invited only two men: General Weitzel, Butler's subordinate who would actually be in tactical command of the landing force, and one of Weitzel's staff.

As the fleet withdrew to its anchorage, seven miles offshore, Porter counted the day's cost. Several of his ships had been damaged by the fort's guns, but only a couple were too badly hurt to fight. There were 65 sailors killed or wounded -- three times as many casualties as Lamb had sustained -- but only 20 were caused by enemy fire. (The rest were the result of bursting Parrott rifles.) In Porter's estimation, this rate of loss was acceptable, even cheap, considering the prize at stake.

Lamb, for his part, was glad for the coming of darkness, and happily surprised to learn that damage to the fort was not nearly as great as it had appeared to be at the height of the bombardment. His tactic of keeping the men under cover had paid off handsomely, for he had lost only 4 killed and 19 wounded. The parade ground was so littered with dud shells and cooling roundshot that it looked as if a shipload of bowling balls had been overturned in mid-air and dumped inside the fort. Smoking shell fragments, jagged and reeking, lay everywhere like shards of broken pottery. Every wooden structure inside the walls was battered, and about half of the barracks had burned down, but damage to the earthen walls themselves was minimal. Only two cannon had been knocked out and a handful of mounts damaged.

Exhausted, Lamb nevertheless wrote out a prompt and detailed report for Bragg, Lee, and Jefferson Davis, which concluded: "I am unable to know what damage was done [to the enemy], but I am certain the injury inflicted upon them far exceeds the injury their bombardment did to us. Our Heavenly Father has protected my garrison this day, and I feel He will sustain us in defending our homes against the invader."

Butler's Landing Goes Awry

During the night, there was some reshuffling of Confederate troops at Fort Fisher. Four additional companies landed by ferry from Fort Caswell, bringing the garrison's total strength to an unprecedented 871 men. Lamb decided to send 500 of his youngest Junior Reserves to Fort Caswell as replacements for the men he was sent, but for the moment that would have to wait. The entire garrison spent a sleepless night, repairing damage and guarding against a night attack.

Admiral Porter's men, too, spent a stoic night, repairing their ships, fusing shells for the next day's fighting, and putting down fresh ashes. Aboard General Butler's transports, the mood of the men designated for the landing force was actually rather jubilant. Most of them were less worried about getting shot at in the morning than they were delighted about the prospect of getting off the stinking ships for the first time in two weeks.

When the sun rose, many men exchanged perfunctory and rather ironic Christmas greetings; this would not be a day of peace. General Weitzel was rowed to the *Malvern* at 6:30 a.m. for his conference with Admiral Porter. Porter explained why he had deemed it expedient to set off the powder-boat before Butler's return, and admitted that the experiment had been a flop. But not so the previous day's bombardment, he insisted. The erratic nature of the return fire from Fort Fisher had led Porter to the totally erroneous conclusion that his ships had all but silenced Lamb's artillery. Weitzel was not so sure; he had worked with Porter before, at New Orleans, and he remembered how wildly Porter had overestimated the effect of the mortar bombardment on Forts Jackson and St. Phillip. Weitzel suggested that Porter send his lighter gunboats to "run the bar" into the Cape Fear River itself. If the bombardment had been as effective as Porter claimed it was, then it should be safe. And once the warships were on the western side of the fort, where there were no walls, they could pound Lamb's batteries to pieces at their leisure.

Porter declined, saying that if he sent gunboats through the inlet he would almost certainly loose at least one vessel to rebel torpedoes. Weitzel testily suggested that it might be better to lose one gunboat to enemy mines than to loose 500 men in an unsupported ground attack. Again, Porter refused, in effect contradicting his own opinion that the fort's guns had been silenced. He reported later that running the bar "might have been sport to General Butler, but it would have been death to the gunboats...I would certainly not have been influenced by General Butler's opinion in nautical matters, or risked my vessels to amuse him."[1] In their ungentlemanly squabbles that followed, Butler accused Porter of having "torpedoes on the brain," which prompted Porter to describe the general as "an ignorant liar."

So Weitzel returned from Porter's flagship without any promises of naval support on the river side, where the fort was most vulnerable. Porter did agree to detach ships for the purpose of shelling Battery Gatlin and Battery Anderson into submission, however. When those earthworks had been silenced, the Army could land and march against Fort Fisher from the north. Meanwhile, the majority of the fleet would return to the previous day's stations, where they would continue to pound the fort as before.

At 7 a.m. on Christmas morning, Porter signaled his ships to weigh anchor and form their line of battle. Butler, anxious to see what damage Porter had done the day before, ordered his own vessel, the USS *Chamberlain*, to steam close to the beach. Butler's ship came into range at about 10 a.m., and he was greeted by a salvo from the Northeast Bastion that all but hid the vessel from sight behind a grove of waterspouts. Butler decided he had seen enough and quickly retired to his original position at the head of the troopships.

Led once again by the USS *New Ironsides*, the Union fleet

assumed the same formation as the day before, and a general bombardment commenced about 10:30.

Like everyone else on his transport, young Edward King Wrightman, serving with the 3rd New York Regiment, observed the bombardment with emotions of awe and a keen sense of history in the making. Only a day later, while the events were crystalline in his mind, Wrightman wrote a vivid description to his brother:

> I can imagine nothing like the bellowing of our fifteen inch guns. The belching of a volcano with accompanying explosions may suggest a corresponding idea. The din was deafening. Above the fort the countless flash and puffs of smoke from bursting shells spoke for the accuracy of our guns while occasionally columns of sand heaved high in the air [and] suggested that possibly the [fort's] casements were not so safe and cozy after all. "I'd rather Johnny'd be where them eggs is breaking than me," was the sententious remark of a philosophic who stood with his hands in his pockets on the deck of [the] *Weybosset*. His comrades rolled the quids in their mouths and responded in chorus, with quiet earnestness, "Them's my sentiments."[2]

Within the walls of Fort Fisher, Lamb restated his strict orders to conserve ammunition: One round per gun every 30 minutes was the rule. He admitted that "the temptation to concentrate the whole of the available fire of the fort on a single frigate...and destroy her was very great," but he had already used one-sixth of the fort's ammunition, and he felt compelled to husband every round to repel the land attack he felt sure was imminent.

Conditions inside the fort were becoming chaotic. Most of the Union shells seemed to be landing within the walls and exploding on the open ground near the blackened remains of the barracks and stables. One Confederate survivor, observing the interior of the fort from the vantage point of what was left of the Brooke battery, swore there was so much shrapnel on the ground that "it would have been possible to walk from one side of the fort to the other without touching the sand."[3]

Lamb's batteries began to take hits. A ten-inch Columbiad in the Pulpit's battery was blown off its carriage when a bursting enemy shell touched off the powder charge already loaded in the piece. But Fort Fisher was still scoring hits as well. Lieutenant Daniel

Perry of the 36th North Carolina Regiment dueled a Union warship all afternoon with his battery of eight-inch Columbiads, scoring seven hits on his adversary while suffering six men wounded and one gun disabled in return.

While the main bombardment worked up its tempo, Porter ordered Captain Oliver Glisson, commanding the USS *Santiago de Cuba*, to lead 17 vessels north and take on Batteries Gatlin and Anderson. These two outlying earthworks covered the proposed landing beach north of Fort Fisher. Glisson opened fire at about 11 a.m.

The gun crews at those two Confederate positions were shaken by their first taste of shelling. Only after the greatest exertions, oaths, threats, and demonstrations of personal courage could their commander, Lieutenant Colonel John Read, get them to return fire at all. Standing in an exposed position, Read was urging his gunners on when a shell from one of Glisson's ships exploded beside him. It tore off most of his left arm, leaving it hanging from his shoulder by a few strands of muscle and cartilage. Still conscious, Read turned over command of the vital positions to the field artillery commander, Captain Thomas J. Southerland. Then he permitted himself to be led off the field for amputation. His last order to Southerland was simple: "Repel the landing at all costs!"

Unnerved by the mutilation of their commanding officer, however, the gun crews stopped firing altogether and hunkered down behind their earthworks. Southerland gave up trying to shame them into returning fire, and concentrated on readying his field guns and his handful of infantry to stop the anticipated attack.

At noon, Captain Glisson himself rowed over to Butler's ship and reported that the rebel shore batteries were silent. The landing could go ahead as planned. Butler seemed edgy and irresolute. "I shall land only 500 men," he announced, rather to Glisson's amazement.

"It would be better to land more," Glisson replied, "for I fear we may have bad weather tomorrow, which might make it difficult to land more men."

"If the weather's going to be that bad," growled Butler, "perhaps we had better not land any."

Nevertheless, Butler gave the order, and the landing com-

menced. First into the longboats were 450 men of the 142nd New
York and 112th New York Regiments. As they began pulling for
shore, a cheer rose from the sailors on Glisson's warships. In
charge of establishing the beachhead was Brigadier General
Newton M. Curtis, a 29-year-old native of De Peyster, New York.
An aggressive, some said reckless, officer, Curtis fully expected to
lead his men over the walls of Fort Fisher in a matter of hours.
Eager to begin, Curtis was the first man into the surf, at about 2
p.m. His troops splashed ashore behind him, rifles held high above
the frigid water.

Curtis and his skirmishers ran up on the beach and planted the
U.S. flag atop a sand dune. They were about five miles north of
Fort Fisher and a mere 400 yards from Battery Anderson. Soon,
Curtis had 500 men spread out in skirmish formation and a detach-
ment of engineers busily constructing entrenchments. General
Weitzel came ashore at the end of the first wave and personally
approved what he saw.

As yet, not one shot had been fired at the Federal landing force.
The single company of the 42nd North Carolina Regiment still
clinging to what was left of Battery Anderson was not in any shape
to resist. Its sole operable cannon, a 20-pounder, had been put out
of action by a shell from one of Glisson's ships, and the men were
trembling with fright from the pounding they had taken. At the first
sight of Curtis's New Yorkers advancing spiritedly on their position, they raised a white flag. The surrender token was sighted first
by some of Glisson's sailors. Several ships lowered their longboats,
and an impromptu rowing contest ensued to see which ship would
get to take the surrender first. Curtis and his infantry were also
running toward the white flag, but it was slow going in the deep
sand. A boat from the USS *Britannia* captured the flag before
anyone else got there.

The New Yorkers arrived in time to see the Confederate prisoners being led glumly into captivity. One of the Federal officers
observed that the prisoners were "very poor specimens of men,
and...still poorer specimens of soldiers. Many of them were not
over fifteen years of age."[4]

Relieved by the lack of opposition, General Butler ordered the
rest of the landing force into the boats. The remainder of Curtis's

brigade landed first, followed by the 2nd Brigade under Colonel Galusha Pennypacker. The divisional commander, General Ames, came ashore with Pennypacker's men. Ames was supervising the landing of the 3rd Brigade when he suddenly heard rifle fire beyond the beachhead perimeter.

Confederate General Kirkland had begun moving his regiment as soon as he realized that the much-feared landing had occurred. He spread his small force in a semicircle and slowly probed toward the landing area, driving into a line of Federal pickets and wounding a few of Ames's men with volleys aimed in the general direction of the beachhead. Once he got a firsthand look at the strength of the Federal landing force, and realized he was moving a single under-strength regiment with one artillery piece against three brigades backed by approximately 100 naval guns, Kirkland prudently decided not to push his luck. Instead, he fell back and assumed a defensive posture, covering the Wilmington Road and the approaches to Fort Fisher. One of his men, however, took advantage of the confusion and the proximity of the enemy to desert. From this deserter, General Ames learned that the rest of General Hoke's division of veteran Confederates was on its way to the area.

Meanwhile, Porter was having second thoughts about the plan to sail through New Inlet and rake the fort from its open side. He could make no decision on the matter until he had accurate information about the location and depth of the ever-changing channel; the charts he had were out of date, and the wreckage of several blockade runners had altered the pattern of tidal flow, deepening the channel in some places and creating new sandbars in others. Porter detached Commander John Guest and a squadron of nine gunboats to New Inlet, with orders to gather information about the depth and configuration of the channel.

Since the channel was directly under and only a few hundred yards from the guns of Battery Buchanan, and since it could also be fired on from the Mound Battery, the task of sounding and charting it was a virtual suicide mission. So Porter chose the one man in his fleet who had made a career out of taking suicide missions and coming back alive from them: Will Cushing.

Cushing and 15 volunteers got into a launch and were towed to

Commander Guest's gunboats. Guest had assembled a little flotilla of nine longboats, one from each warship, and had instructed them to follow Cushing into the channel and take soundings at his direction. As disdainful of death as always, Cushing had donned his full-dress uniform for the occasion -- a touch of theater that he probably couldn't resist because of the spectacle and the size of his audience for this exploit. Sitting primly beneath a blue and white flag, his buttons and braid glowing in the wintry sunlight, he made an irresistible target. But at first, not a shot was fired at him. The rebel gun crews just stared in amazement as he led his cockleshell fleet into what had to be, at that moment, one of the most dangerous patches of water in the world.

This gentlemanly cease-fire did not last long. It was obvious what Cushing's men were trying to do, and it was a matter of military necessity to prevent them from doing it. Despite the covering fire from Guest's gunboats, the Confederates began throwing everything they had at Cushing's little squadron. As irony would have it, the first casualties were suffered inside Fort Fisher. One of the Brooke guns, swiveled to point at the channel, exploded. The barrel split from muzzle to breach and sprayed chunks of hot iron in all directions. One gunner was decapitated, another was nailed to the sand by a huge shard of iron through his stomach, and a third man rolled in frenzied circles, crying that he was on fire. The dazed and bleeding survivors held the man down and ripped off his clothes; it wasn't fire that tormented him, they soon discovered, but thousands of grains of sand and gunpowder that had been driven into his skin by the force of the explosion.

An hour later the other Brooke gun exploded, although this time without causing serious casualties. Now defunct, the Brooke battery was abandoned. The surviving *Chickamauga* sailors were sent to Battery Buchanan.

Cushing and his men, incredibly, remained unscathed, despite so many near-hits that the boat crews had to stop and bail out the launches several times. They sounded the channel as far as Zeek's Island, but couldn't find any passage straight enough and deep enough to admit the gunboats into the Cape Fear River. By 3:30 p.m., Cushing decided there was no further reason to risk his men, and his expedition began retiring toward the covering line of gunboats. But now, after hundreds of close escapes, the little flotilla's luck ran out. A roundshot from Battery Buchanan struck the longboat from the USS *Tacony*, blowing it in half and severing both legs off a crewman. Cushing and the rest of his men made it back to their respective ships without further damage or casualties, bringing an end to the brave but futile mission.

While Cushing's men were probing for a way through the inlet, the Union bombardment of Fort Fisher continued unabated. Lamb was conferring with General Whiting in the Pulpit when word came that the Brookes were out of action. This left one whole section of the seaface silenced. To draw the enemy's attention from that fact, Lamb decided now was the proper moment to unmask his biggest weapon, the 150-pounder Armstrong.

As soon as the order came for them to open fire, the Armstrong's crew jumped to their posts with enthusiasm. For two days, they had been hunkering down in their stinking bombproof shelter, sand raining into their hair and food, unable to experience the satisfaction of fighting back. Now they had the chance to respond, and they made the most of it. Lamb directed their fire personally. The Armstrong's first shot ripped off a Union ship's smokestack. The second and third shots missed. The fourth, however, penetrated both sides of a frigate's hull, forcing the stricken vessel to duck out of line and retire. Lamb joined the gunners in a cheer.

After only a half-hour of firing, the Armstrong fell silent again, by Lamb's order. He had just received the alarming news that the enemy had landed and that Battery Anderson had surrendered after token resistance. Whiting fired off telegrams to Kirkland, to Bragg, and to Hebert in Smithville, asking for all the reinforcements and ammunition they could send. Kirkland, of course, could spare no one, as he was already stretched dangerously thin. From the other two generals, there was no reply at all. After a reasonable interval, Whiting sent another message to Bragg: "A large body of the enemy has landed near the fort, deploying as skirmishers. May be able to carry me by storm. Do the best I can. All behaving well. Order supports to attack."[5]

That was the last message that got through that day. A soldier from the 142nd New York Regiment found and cut the telegraph wire not long afterward.

The detachments of Junior Reserves that had been ordered over to Fort Holmes on Smith Island -- more to get the kids out of harm's way than to reinforce, since Fort Holmes was not under attack -- waited patiently, under scattered fire, near Battery Buchanan. But the steamboat never came for them. Finally, the teenagers were compelled to return to Fort Fisher's bombproofs, which meant a march at double-time across the heavily shelled parade ground. They were, of course, terrified, and their morale was not improved when one 16-year-old private was cut in half by a bursting Union shell. Observing the survivors scurrying for cover in the dugouts beneath the Pulpit, General Whiting called down to them: "There go North Carolina's pets!" One white-faced young-ster yelled back: "Well, she's got a damned bad way of showing it!"

Several hundred more Junior Reserves, unable to find room in the bombproofs, had been stationed at a campsite north of the fort. On Christmas afternoon, not long after Battery Anderson gave up, the commander of the 8th Junior Reserves walked to the Union beachhead and offered to surrender his entire command. He was determined that none of his boys should die that day. During the surrender negotiations, one of the young recruits asked what sort of treatment they would get as prisoners of war. "Probably better treatment than you're used to in the Confederate Army," replied the Federal officer who was handling the negotiations.

"We can't be any worse off," declared one of the Junior Reserv-ists standing nearby. "We have never received a cent of pay nor scarcely anything to eat except what we picked up." There was a general chorus of agreement. Spontaneously, the entire unit stepped forward and gave itself up to the pleased but startled officers of the 117th New York.

After watching the young Confederate prisoners being marched away, Generals Curtis and Weitzel deployed their men into skir-mish lines and advanced in a southerly direction until they were about 800 yards from Fort Fisher's landface. The generals halted their troops and went ahead to study the objective. Weitzel, in particular, was impressed. He noted with dismay the log palisade — which appeared but lightly damaged by the naval shelling — the height of the earthen walls, and the fact that there were at least 17 operable cannon facing his men, all of them presumably crammed with grape and canister. Weitzel had seen infantry assault such a position once before, at Battery Wagner near Charleston, and the memory of that gruesome failure was still fresh in his mind. From what he could see, he estimated that Fort Fisher would be four times harder to take than Battery Wagner. Shaking his head, he walked back to the landing site and prepared to report these pessimistic conclusions to General Butler.

General Curtis was not preconditioned by such bad memories. He led his New Yorkers boldly across the sandy, moderately wooded ground to a point about 150 yards from the landface. There, his troops overran a partly finished earthwork and captured a fieldpiece without losing a man. As Curtis and his men were digging in all around the captured redoubt, they spotted a Confederate courier galloping through the sally port on the river side of the fort. A Yankee sharpshooter shot him dead in the saddle, then sprinted forward and captured the dispatches which the unfortunate lad had been attempting to deliver.

Acting with remarkable initiative, some of Curtis's men had by now crawled to within 75 yards of the log palisade. They sent back reports that it was not nearly as unharmed as it looked from a distance. Numerous hits from the naval bombardment had splintered many of the logs and left gaps large enough to crawl through.

General Curtis's aide-de-camp, a lieutenant named George Ross, had also been involved in the bloody repulse at Battery Wagner, and the closer he looked at Fort Fisher the more he became convinced that this was not as tough an objective. Given the damage to the palisade, Ross decided it was possible to penetrate the fort at the bridge and sally port near the river. There were, to be sure, two field guns stationed there, but at the moment there were no gun crews visible anywhere near them.

A sharpshooter from the 142nd New York, Henry Blair, actually got within 15 yards of the entrance to the sally port. He saw no one guarding the position, but he could see a knot of Confederates crouched inside a dugout. He couldn't resist firing a blind shot into the bombproof. Not until after the war did he learn that he had, in fact, struck down one of Lamb's men. Another Yankee sharpshooter captured a mule that had fled the shelling and was wandering, wild-eyed, near the river bank.

Braving the naval bombardment, a lieutenant named Wailing sprinted forward through a hole in the log palisade and actually captured one of the fort's flags -- a regimental or company banner that had just been blown from its staff by a naval shell. When General Curtis saw Wailing make it to the base of the earthen ramparts, scoop up the flag, and return to the Union lines without a shot being fired at him, be was convinced that the fort could be stormed using only the forces already landed. He dispatched a courier to General Ames, telling him to hasten forward with every man he had. Then he waited. And waited. Finally, unable to sit still any longer, he went back to the captured earthwork, where he had left most of his troops. There he found two more regiments that had recently arrived. Incensed, Curtis demanded to know why these men had not been sent forward. Because, their commanding officers explained, Curtis's order to advance had been overridden by an order that had just arrived from General Butler: All Federal troops were to withdraw.

Thunderstruck, Curtis quickly penciled a message to Butler: "Your order to retire is held in abeyance that you may know the true condition of the fort: the garrison has offered no resistance; the flagstaff...was cut by a naval shot and one of my officer's brought from the parapet the garrison flag...my skirmishers are now at the parapet...."[6] Curtis was certain that Butler would rescind his withdrawal order as soon as this new information was received.

While Curtis was waiting for a response to his message to Butler, the naval bombardment suddenly stopped. It was 5 p.m., and if Curtis ever really had an opportunity to storm the fort, it now disappeared in the gathering winter darkness. Whether Curtis would have succeeded is an arguable point. The seemingly de-serted appearance of the landface fortifications was deceptive -- all the gun crews and supporting infantry were out of sight in their dugouts, taking shelter from the bombardment. Curtis probably could have penetrated the sally port before the two fieldpieces guarding it could have been manned, but once inside, he would have found himself in a hornet's nest. Unless he could have been massively and quickly reinforced, his chances of actually capturing the whole fort were very slim. Still, boldness counts for a great

377

deal at such moments, and it was possible, just barely, that he might have pulled it off. But the assault should have been launched between the time the courier was killed and the moment the shelling stopped. After the bombardment ceased, and silence and safety returned to the walls, any attempt to storm the landface would have been a bloody and desperate enterprise.

That conclusion is supported by what happened next. Only a few minutes after the Union shelling stopped, the landface was fully manned by fired-up, cheering Confederate troops. They were led by Major James Reilly -- the same Reilly who, as a lonely ordnance sergeant, had surrendered Fort Johnston to the Wilmington militia in January 1861. Now Reilly ordered his men to fire at will at the Yankees beyond the log palisade.

Other officers tried to get the Junior Reserves out of their shelters and onto the ramparts. Most of them refused to budge, although the majority finally got into motion after their officers waded into them with kicks, oaths, threats, and blows from the flats of their swords.

A few of the youngsters showed a fierce eagerness to fight back. One young man, finding he was too short to aim and fire over the high sandbagged parapet, climbed on a gun mount and straddled one of the cannon barrels. He clung to his perch like a spider, firing repeatedly, until he was wounded.

Now that Porter's guns were silent, Lamb could concentrate all his resources on the landface. Soon he had more than 700 men on the line, blazing furiously into the darkness. They were joined by the fieldpieces near the sally port, which lashed the underbrush with grapeshot. All of this shooting was probably beneficial to the garrison's morale, but they only managed to wing a few Yankee stragglers. Before 6 p.m., Curtis and his men, responding to a direct order from General Weitzel, began withdrawing. Soon the firing died down, as Lamb's men realized there was no one shooting back. The garrison stood guard all night, expecting an assault -- indeed, almost eager for one, after the pummeling they had endured -- but no attack came.

What had happened? When General Weitzel reported back to Butler that afternoon, he stated that Fort Fisher appeared barely touched by the naval bombardment, that it remained as formidable as ever. Weitzel recommended that no assault be launched until the Navy had disabled all of the Confederate guns on the landface. "It would be butchery," Weitzel told Butler, to attack otherwise. But General Butler had too much riding on this operation to give up quite that easily. He sent Weitzel back for another look, along with one of his staff, a trusted engineer officer, for a second opinion.

The weather was worsening by the hour. The ships' barometers were falling, and the seas off Confederate Point were becoming choppy. Butler was facing a tough decision. If he left his troops ashore and bad weather cut them off from resupply or reinforcement, he might lose the entire force. On the other hand, General Grant had specifically ordered him not to withdraw, once a landing had been made, until the fort was taken. Well, Butler could always waffle a bit; after all, he had only landed one-third of his army.

As he was debating these points with himself, Butler was brought face-to-face with the Confederate deserter from Kirkland's unit. When he learned that General Hoke's entire veteran division was close at hand, Butler grew more disturbed. He ordered his ship to steam closer to the fort so he could make a personal inspection. After taking a look, he decided Weitzel was correct: Fort Fisher had not been softened up enough by the naval bombardment. While he was wrestling with his final decision, a staff officer brought him a new report. "General," the man said, "you have got to provide for those troops on shore some way tonight, either that or get them off, because it's getting so rough that we cannot land much longer."

That settled it. Butler had visions of his 2,500-man landing force being driven into the sea by Hoke's 6,000 veterans while he watched impotently from offshore, cut off from the beach by thundering waves and adverse winds.

While Butler was coming to his decision, General Curtis was begging General Ames for an all-out assault on the fort. Ames countered that a renewed naval bombardment, at night, would probably kill as many Federals as Confederates. Besides, he gloomily informed Curtis, two entire brigades had already been sent back to the transports in compliance with Butler's order. At 7:30 p.m., Curtis gave up and ordered his men back to the beach. Sullenly, they obeyed.

Curtis reached the landing area just as the last of the 3rd Brigade was getting into its boats. By now, surf conditions had become dangerous. Curtis watched as white-fanged combers overturned a dozen boats and spilled their cursing occupants into the ice-cold foam. One man was pulled under by the weight of his equipment and drowned. A few of Curtis's men made it on the last few boats that got through, but by 10 p.m., with the surf still rising and a cold rain pouring down, the withdrawal was called off.

There were still 700 men on the beach, huddled in shallow entrenchments designed as much to protect them from "short" naval rounds as from any Confederate shelling. It was one of the most wretched nights any of the New Yorkers had to endure during their entire time in uniform. Shortly after the withdrawal ended, the cold rain turned to sleet. They had waded ashore with only one day's supply of food and water, and now had none left. There was every reason to suppose that the rebels would fall upon them during the night. Therefore no fires could be lit, although the beach was strewn with driftwood from all the splintered longboats. On top of that, Butler had not seen fit to issue any blankets to the landing force. Soaked, chilled to the marrow, hungry, thirsty, exhausted, and bitter, the New Yorkers shivered in their wet, sandy foxholes and kept themselves from freezing by thinking about what they would like to do to Ben Butler.

They might have derived some comfort had they known that Lamb's men, too, were passing a miserable night. Still believing that an entire Union army was encamped just beyond the palisade, the garrison could not afford to relax. Lamb, reeling with exhaustion himself by now, did what he could to effect makeshift repairs, aided by the eerie rain-prismed light given off by the burning barracks. A false alarm at 3 a.m. prompted every gun on the seaface to fire into the empty sea, wasting precious ammunition.

When the chilly, foggy dawn finally came, a red-eyed Lamb turned his telescope to the north and beheld a dark blue mass on the beach, where Curtis and his 700 blue-lipped men were trying to start fires from the soaked remains of wrecked boats. Lamb didn't know, of course, that the troops he saw were all of the Federal troops still on shore. Had he known, he would have launched an attack against them and requested Kirkland to attack simultaneously from his end of the peninsula. It wouldn't have been much of a contest — Curtis's men were physically and psychologically at low ebb, and most of their powder was too damp to fire.

Offshore, an increasingly irritable Ben Butler was also peering through the light of that dreary dawn. He saw right away that the surf was still too high to risk sending boats for the last fragment of his once-proud army. Butler must have known by now that there was no way he would come back from this expedition with his military career intact. Everything had conspired against him. The weather, Admiral Porter, the failure of the powder-boat scheme, the ineffectiveness of the naval bombardment, and now the damned incessant yawing of this ship! Bilious with both rage and nausea, Butler issued orders to the other ships that all of Curtis's men should be evacuated as soon as possible. Then, incredibly, he ordered his flagship to weigh anchor and he sailed away, by himself, toward Fort Monroe — in effect, simply abandoning part of his army to its fate.

Admiral Porter didn't learn of the fiasco on the beach until well after sundown on Christmas Day. After overseeing the withdrawal of the fleet to its anchorage, Porter was finished with a hard day and decided it was time to enjoy his long-delayed Christmas dinner of roast turkey and champagne. As he was digging in, feeling rather pleased with himself, one of his staff officers entered the room. The officer gaped at the admiral in frank amazement.

"Well, you are taking the world quietly. Don't you know what is going on?"

"No," replied Porter, without any sign of concern. "What's in the wind?"

"Why, that man Butler is reembarking his troops and is going away. He says the fort cannot be taken."

"Does he now?" mused Porter. Then he smiled. "Well, let him go. We will take the place without him. What part of the turkey will you have?"

'My Boy... You Are To Be Sacrificed'

General Curtis and his freezing men didn't get off the beach on December 26, either. The surf was as stormy as it had been on Christmas Day, and all attempts by the transports' quartermaster to float a raft full of food and water to the stranded men failed. As a result, their second night ashore was even more abysmal than the first. Rain continued to drench them, and several times Curtis became convinced that General Hoke's rebels were about to attack. Whenever he felt threatened, he signaled the offshore ships with a torch, and the faithful ironclads would steam in and lob shells into the yaupon groves to discourage any rebel concentrations.

By the middle of the second night, if Hoke had attacked, Curtis's detachment wouldn't have been able to offer much resistance. And if Hoke had known the situation, he might have made the effort. But he had just arrived on the scene, his men were tired, and hard intelligence was lacking (for no apparent reason, other than General Bragg's inertia). Except for the stretch between Danville and Greensboro, where they had marched on muddy roads through intermittent rain, Hoke's division had ridden all the way from Virginia in unheated boxcars. The cold weather had compelled them to light fires inside the cars, so they had also been breathing foul smoke for two days. Few of them had slept, most of them were

bent over with wracking coughs from the fumes, and none was in
any condition to mount a night attack against an unknown enemy
over unfamiliar ground. Hoke did confer with the officers on the
scene, of course, and found that Bragg's habitual caution was
echoed by Kirkland and others who had been close to the action.
All of them had an exaggerated idea of the strength of the Federal
landing force.

At first light on December 27, a disgusted Admiral Porter took
matters into his own hands and ordered naval launches sent ashore
for Curtis and his men. The surf was still high and a lot of men got
dunked, but there were no more drownings. By 1 p.m. General
Curtis and his entire bedraggled command were safe, guzzling hot
coffee, and turning the air purple with their condemnations of
General Ben Butler. Their attitude was summed up New Yorker
Edward Wrightman: "Everybody is disgusted...the fort was ours
and...no one but Butler prevented [us] from taking it."[1]

"Curses enough have been heaped on Butler's head," wrote
another survivor of the botched landing, "to sink him in the deepest
hole of the bottomless pit."[2] The brief skirmishing on the beach
and in front of the fort's landface had cost the Federals three killed
(including the drowned man) and 15 wounded.

His ships' ammunition about gone and the stranded infantry
rescued, Porter sailed for Beaufort. He had expended 20,271
rounds, approximately one million pounds of iron, and had lost 20
sailors killed and 63 wounded, many of the latter hideously burned
by exploding boilers or maimed by malfunctioning Parrott guns.
His feelings about Butler grew more vituperative, no doubt fueled
by the realization that some of the blame was going to fall on him
for approving so wholeheartedly the powder-boat scheme. His
officers suffered through numerous post-prandial tirades, with
Porter stomping around the wardroom, cigar in hand, damning
Weitzel as a yellow-belly and Butler as a "thief, a black-bearded
traitor, and an imbecile." The crew of the *Malvern* expressed its
feelings for Butler by striking a medal "In Commemoration of his
Heroic Conduct Before Fort Fisher." The medal was embossed
with a pair of running legs.

The more he thought about it, however, the more Porter was
glad that Butler had failed so wretchedly, and so publicly. It meant

the end of Butler's national political aspirations, for until the Fort Fisher debacle, there was a fair chance that the general might have won a shot at the Presidency. Ben Butler as President? That, Porter believed with all his heart, would have been "the greatest calamity that could have happened to the country."

In truth, Porter had contributed more than a little to the ruination of the attack. He was unwilling to battle Fort Fisher at close range, where his gunners could have aimed at specific batteries rather than just throwing tons of shot at the walls and the interior, hoping for a lucky hit. His chronic unwillingness to cooperate with the Army didn't help, either. But Porter rode out the domestic furor at sea, penning self-exonerating letters to influential friends and assuring his superiors that Fort Fisher was ripe for the taking, provided competent Army officers were put in charge of the next attempt. As he steamed away, Porter wrote to Navy Secretary Welles:

> I feel ashamed that men calling themselves soldiers should have left this place so ingloriously. It was, however, nothing more than I expected when General Butler got himself mixed up in this expedition...If this temporary failure succeeds in sending General Butler into private life, then it is not to be regretted, for it cost only a certain amount of shells, which I would expend in a month's target practice anyhow.

To his close personal friend, Assistant Navy Secretary Fox, Porter revealed on January 7 how eager he was to have another crack at the Gibraltar of the Confederacy:

> It is strange but true, that the desire to kill and destroy grows on a man, the oftener he hears shot whistle, and I must confess I and all hands are itching to go to work again at Fort Fisher. Every vessel that was in the last affair will go in -- damages are all repaired....[3]

Meanwhile, at Fort Fisher, Colonel Lamb was not displeased with the way both his men and his fort had withstood the assault. His casualties were incredibly light, considering the ferocity of the naval bombardment: 11 killed and 56 wounded. Seven guns had been damaged or dismounted, but his ordnance men were sure they could get three or four of them back in working condition without much delay.

On December 28, with Admiral Porter's fleet back on the high seas, two Confederate blockade runners slipped into Wilmington and one slipped out. That was Lamb's greatest satisfaction: As long as Fort Fisher remained unconquered, the South's last and most vital port remained in business.

Once it was apparent the Union attack had failed, General Braxton Bragg slipped into a kind of euphoria. It seems never to have seriously crossed his mind that the Federals would be back, more determined than ever. The only matter to which Bragg did address himself with some urgency was transportation, observing in a memo to Richmond that it had taken 60 hours for General Hoke's division to move the 48 miles between Greensboro and Danville. Bragg righteously concluded that this kind of performance "admits of no explanation of excuse. No army can be supported and no cause sustained where such imbecility obtains." The phrasing is ironic, in view of the criticism soon to be heaped on Bragg's grizzled head.

On matters closer to his actual sphere of command, Bragg's reports from this period reveal an almost unbelievable complacency about the future. Bragg wired Governor Vance that, although Porter's armada was only a few hours away at Beaufort, he was confident that "with present means they can be taken care of." Two days later, in another dispatch to the Confederate government, Bragg admitted having been informed that Porter's fleet was "reassembled." But he blithely conjectured that the fleet had sailed for home, "probably to Hampton Roads." Rarely has a commander so utterly misread the character and determination of his opponent.

General Whiting, who had seen the power of Porter's fleet with his own eyes, had no doubt that the late December/early January lull was just that — a breathing period, during which Admiral Porter would regroup and reinforce for another, more determined Union offensive. Why shouldn't he? His orders remained unchanged; the men were on hand and eager to make the attack; and his fleet was intact, its damage repaired, and fully resupplied with ammunition.

Yet Whiting's entreaties to Richmond were not received with any urgency. The Confederate government's bureaucratic apparatus treated them as low-priority paperwork. On New Year's Day 1865, Whiting wired Secretary of War Seddon that "it could scarcely be possible that after such extraordinary preparations" the whole operation against Fort Fisher had been abandoned. After presenting a professional, rational, yet very urgent situation report, Whiting closed with a plea for more troops and more mines to block the Cape Fear River. His report was not even sent to President Davis until January 8, a week after it was received in Richmond, and Davis didn't bother to initial the document until January 14. When he did, his only response was to send it back to Seddon with the woolly brained suggestion that "the propositions within might be advantageously referred to General Bragg." Of course, the whole purpose of Whiting's memo had been to go over Bragg's complacent head and signal Richmond that the Confederacy's last remaining port was in dire peril. Seddon received the document from Davis on January 15, added his own comment ("Refer to General Bragg, calling to his attention the endorsement of the President"), and rerouted it back into bureaucratic channels. The last annotation on this report, dated January 20 and initialed by an assistant adjutant-general, simply reads: "No further disposition required, Fort Fisher having fallen."

The saga of this vital memo reveals the depths of inertia, blindness, and sheer demoralization from which the Davis government was attempting to function. The defense of Fort Fisher was simply the most vital remaining strategic priority for the Confederacy as a whole; Richmond could be lost with much less serious consequences, and the resources to defend the fort were still available, had anyone in the chain of command above Whiting really been on top of the situation.

As irony would have it, the one man in high command on either side whose strategic interest in Wilmington suddenly peaked in the last days of 1864 was General U.S. Grant. Having reluctantly been persuaded, by Sherman's and Halleck's importuning memoranda, to allow Sherman to cut loose from his base at Savannah and strike inland to "punish" South Carolina and rip up the railroads in North Carolina, Grant now became very anxious to have a base on the Carolina coast to safeguard Sherman. Beaufort was neither large enough, nor well enough connected to the railroads to handle the job. Wilmington, on the other hand, was perfect.

By the end of 1864, Grant's commitment to a renewed attack on Fort Fisher was much stronger than ever. So was his determination to put someone in charge who would be the antithesis of Ben Butler. He chose well: Major General Alfred H. Terry. Generally regarded as one of the more intelligent officers in the U.S. Army, Terry was a Yale graduate who had distinguished himself in a number of similar operations, at Port Royal, Fort Pulaski, and Battery Monroe at Charleston.

Admiral Porter cooperated with General Terry much more than he did with General Butler. Together, they drew up plans for what was, in essence, the first modern amphibious assault in history. They took their cue from Grant's firm (and this time unambiguous) orders: "The siege of Fort Fisher will not be abandoned until its reduction is accomplished."

Porter's vessels would be closer to the fort this time, and they would be assigned specific gun batteries on which to concentrate their fire. Porter's authority over the operation would extend to the end of the preliminary naval bombardment. After the fort's guns were silenced, Porter agreed to use his entire fleet as a single gigantic battery, shifting its fire when and where Terry required. Once Terry had landed, he would assume responsibility for all tactical decisions. Rocket and semaphore signals were arranged and carefully rehearsed to insure control of this complex operation. Furthermore, Terry had his staff do something Butler had never bothered to do: interview dozens of Confederate prisoners who had firsthand knowledge of the terrain and defenses. He also pored intently over all the maps and charts he could find, and even sent reconnaissance parties ashore to gain fresh, last-minute intelligence.

Terry's landing force was comprised of the original 6,500 men Butler had sailed with, augmented by more than 2,000 reserve Negro troops. The Negroes were supposed to dig in across the neck of land north of the Union beachhead and hold it against counterattacks by General Hoke's rebels, thus guarding the rear of Terry's main assault force. Finally, to assure the success of the difficult mission, Terry turned his innate gifts of tact and charm on the still-scratchy Admiral Porter. Soon the two men were getting along splendidly, Porter even referring to Terry as "my beau ideal of a soldier and a general."

The Union armada arrived off Cape Fear on Thursday, January 12. The weather was moderate and clear, the sea calm. Colonel Lamb had been expecting to see this sight again, but it was still a shock.

Porter's first choice for a landing site was Masonboro Sound, but this proved too shallow to accommodate most of his ships. He then selected a beach about two miles south and commenced landing operations late in the afternoon. By 9 p.m., the leading elements of Federal troops had crossed the peninsula, reached the Cape Fear River, and begun entrenching. If the Confederates had launched a determined counterattack almost any time from sundown to sunrise, they almost certainly would have wrecked Terry's plans, for his men were in the open, nervous, and unsupported by the fleet. Bragg had arrived at Hoke's Sugar Loaf Hill position that afternoon, but except for sending out a few ineffectual cavalry patrols -- most of which were looking in the wrong direction -- he did nothing, except order Hoke to maintain a defensive posture.

Terry had chosen this part of the peninsula because his charts showed that about one-third of the distance from seashore to riverbank was occupied by a large pond. If he incorporated that water obstacle into his defensive line, Terry reasoned, he could free additional men from the rear-guard line to join the assault on the fort. But the "pond" turned out to be a flat depression of sand, and Terry found himself occupying a line about two miles longer than he had expected. To safeguard his rear, he would have to man that line fully, leaving him only Ames's brigades, about 3,000 men, for the actual assault. That was cutting it close. Terry didn't know how many men Lamb had, but he knew that a three-to-one numerical advantage was usually required for an attacker to succeed against a fortified position.

Admiral Porter had a suggestion. He proposed to outfit a naval landing force of 2,000 sailors and Marines, and send them against Fort Fisher's walls in conjunction with the Army assault -- preferably at widely separated points. This would force Lamb to stretch his manpower resources to the limit. Terry agreed, and they worked out the details. First, General Ames's men would strike at the fort's westernmost position, the bridged road beside the Cape Fear River that led to the sally port. As soon as the Army attack began, Porter's naval force would "board" the Northeast Bastion.

This face of the wall was chosen because the approaches were only partly covered by cannon fire directed from the seaface or the Mound Battery, and because it was close enough to the Army's thrust to permit good communications between the two forces. Porter estimated that 200 yards was the maximum distance his force should be asked to charge. To protect the assembled force while it waited for the order to charge, Porter detached all the Marine guards from his fleet, armed them with Spencer repeating rifles, and assigned them to defend a party of sailors whose job it was to construct a crude earthwork 200 yards from the fort. The majority of the sailors who would make the actual assault, however, would not be armed with rifles at all, but merely with revolvers and cutlasses.

Curtis's brigade, fittingly enough, was assigned the task of leading the Army's attack. Pennypacker's 2nd Brigade would follow 300 yards behind, and the 3rd Brigade, under General Bell, would move forward last. The right flank of Bell's brigade would actually extend to the river, so the Federals could methodically envelop the western end of the landface. The timing of both assaults would be signaled by a concerted blast of steam whistles from the entire fleet, triggered by a toot from Porter's flagship. The signal to let off steam would be given just as the Army attack was starting. Following the whistles, naval shellfire would be lifted from the landface to the seaface, and the Navy's landing party would launch its charge. The attack was scheduled for 2 p.m., January 15th.

On the afternoon of January 14, the Confederate Navy struck a blow when the gunboat *Chickamauga* steamed close to the river road and opened fire on Curtis's troops as they straggled forward. The Confederate vessel didn't have enough ammunition to inflict more than a few casualties, but the shelling had a strong moral effect. Many of Curtis's companies scattered into the heavily wooded sandhills east of the road, where hundreds of men became lost. Most of Curtis's brigade regrouped for the night at an old rebel earthwork about 900 yards north of Fort Fisher's sally port.

Inside Fort Fisher, the situation had deteriorated steadily. On January 13, Lamb had received some welcome reinforcements totaling about 700 men. He now had 1,500 men inside the walls, the strongest the garrison had ever been. No more ammunition had arrived, however, so Lamb was left to face an even more concentrated naval bombardment with a grand total of 2,328 rounds for all of his guns. Once more, he could reply only sporadically to Porter's shelling. And this time, Porter's ships were firing at closer range, so the Union gunners could focus their fire on the fort more methodically, working over one battery after another, paying most of their attention to the landface.

All day long on January 13 and 14, Porter's fleet kept up a bombardment which Lamb described as "ceaseless and terrific." One rebel survivor said it was "like Heven [sic] and Earth were Coming together." Porter's monitors, closest to the shore, tried with some success to "bowl" their 11- and 15-inch projectiles up the slope of the walls, figuring that a certain percentage would drop into Lamb's gun pits. The bombardment was so heavy that it became difficult, then impossible, to serve meals to the gun crews. The effect of Porter's improved fire can be seen in the casualty figures. Lamb had sustained less than 100 casualties during the entire December attack, but in the first 48 hours of the January bombardment, the garrison lost more than 200 killed and wounded. The Confederate dead lay where they fell -- Lamb began losing too many men on burial parties, so he ordered them to stop. But the sight of dismembered corpses scattered about on the parapets did nothing to raise the garrison's spirits.

On Friday, January 13, during the height of the day's shelling, Lamb was once again startled by the appearance of General Whiting — who had, once again, walked through shellfire all the way from the boat landing at Battery Buchanan to share the ordeal with his young colleague. When Whiting puffed up the stairs into the Pulpit, he saluted and said: "Lamb, my boy, I have come to share your fate. You and your garrison are to be sacrificed."

That was the last thing Lamb needed to hear at that moment. But he seems to have grasped, the moment he heard the words, that General Bragg would do nothing to save the fort. Gamely, he replied: "Don't say so, General; we shall certainly whip the enemy again."

Whiting then informed him that Bragg was already packing up his stores and making plans to fall back on Wilmington's inner defenses. Lamb offered General Whiting command of the garrison, but as he had in December, Whiting declined. Whiting had come, it would seem, purely for the sake of honor. He had come because Bragg would not. He had come to fight by Lamb's side, and if necessary, to die there, to expunge from his record the memory of his failure at Drewry's Bluff. And in his deepest heart, he had come to show Jefferson Davis — whose fathomless incompetence had imperiled Fort Fisher — the kind of man and true Confederate soldier William Whiting really was.

At first, Lamb's men tried to effect repairs at night, but Admiral Porter ordered his monitors to steadily shell the parapets in the darkness, so damage began accumulating rapidly. By the morning of January 14, only three or four guns remained in service along the entire landface. It was obvious to the Confederates that the enemy was advancing a large infantry force along the riverbank, but the Yankees were making good use of the cover provided by undulating terrain, thick patches of coastal forest, and the riverbank itself. Lamb could see enough to know they had already taken possession of the Cottage at Craig's Landing. Throughout the day, Lamb used his surviving guns to throw shells at the Federal troops, but every time his guns fired, a torrent of naval shells -- called in by the landing force's improved signal system -- rained down on the gun crew that had dared to shoot.

At about 2 p.m. on January 14, Lamb observed a Confederate steamboat, loaded with long-overdue supplies and ammunition for Fort Fisher, steaming blithely into Craig's Landing. Lamb fired warning shots, trying to warn the supply boat that Craig's Landing was in Federal hands, but the vessel kept going. The Yankees captured it easily. Observing this "stupid surrender," the CSS *Chickamauga* moved up and blew holes in the steamer until she sank. "This incident gave me the first intimation that Gen. Bragg was shamefully ignorant and indifferent to the situation of affairs," wrote Lamb in his account of the battle.

Bragg still had absolute control of the Cape Fear River. If he wanted to find out what was happening down at Fort Fisher, all he had to do was get on a steamer and sail downriver; he could have seen it all through a good pair of binoculars. Both supplies and reinforcements could have been sent to the fort, in secrecy and perfect safety, under cover of darkness. Yet 36 hours after the Union landings, Bragg was still so ignorant of the true situation, and so astonishingly complacent about its urgency, that he sent a steamer loaded with vital supplies straight into a landing that had been under Federal occupation for many hours — and he did it in broad daylight.

Desperate messages were sent from the fort during the evening hours of January 14. Whiting proposed that General Hoke attack the Union landing force from the north while the garrison sortied from the south, timing their attack to begin at night, when the Union fleet was unable to provide effective artillery support. Lamb had a good idea of the enemy positions, and he assembled ten companies of men for his half of this hammer-and-anvil operation. Then he waited for some telegraphic response from Bragg. He and his men waited all night, but the wires remained mute. Thus passed an excellent chance to demoralize the enemy landing force, if not utterly rout it. It was as though a spell had been cast over Braxton Bragg.

Throughout the morning of January 15, the Union landing forces made their final preparations. At sea, Admiral Porter's ships renewed their drumfire barrage against the landface of Fort Fisher. The Federal brigade commanders deployed their units and began their approach. Curtis's troops formed into a line oblique to the landface, his left flank about 600 yards from the sally port and his right flank about half that distance from the fort's northwest corner. Pennypacker's men were 300 yards behind Curtis's, and Bell's men were behind them.

On the beach above the Northeast Bastion, Porter's 2,000-man naval landing force crouched behind its shallow earthworks. The Marines in front gamely sniped at the rebels with their Spencers. On their way to the beach, they had been fired upon while cringing helplessly in their longboats, losing 50 men before they even touched the shore. Tension was high in their ranks -- that stretch of beach up ahead looked mighty empty.

At 2 p.m., General Terry ordered Ames's men forward. The

112th and 142nd New York Regiments advanced in short rushes, hugging the ground, seeking cover in the shallow depressions between sand dunes and behind screens of underbrush. The advance was led by 100 sharpshooters armed with Spencers. The sudden burst of movement alerted the Confederate defenders, and Curtis's troops were exposed to canister fire from the two heavy guns still in commission on the landface and by the two smooth-bore 12-pounders guarding the sally port. Within moments, a signal went out from the beach to Porter's ships, and a line of Union ironclads and gunboats began pouring fire onto the Confederate gun positions, driving their crews under cover.

By this time, the log palisade was so battered by the shelling that it probably protected the attackers more than the defenders. Lamb attempted to detonate his secret minefield of buried torpedoes, but the wires had long ago been severed by the naval bombardment. He ordered every gun still in commission on the seaface to try to bring the naval landing force under fire, but only three — including the two distant weapons of the Mound Battery — could bear on that target, due to the slope of the beach and the angle of the walls. Porter had chosen the route of attack cunningly.

Early that afternoon, Bragg finally sent substantial reinforcements: 1,000 men of General Jason Hagood's South Carolina brigade. Of course, he could have sent the force under cover of darkness the night before, but he chose instead to send them now, in full view of Porter's fleet. The Union ships promptly opened fire on the Confederate steamboat. The vessel turned tail and fled back up river, after landing only 350 men -- just about enough to replace the troops Lamb had lost in the past 48 hours. This pathetic force had to run the parade ground under sporadic shellfire, and reported for duty out of breath, disorganized, and terrified. Lamb sent them to the bombproofs to regain their wind. Of Bragg's attempt to send the reinforcements, Lamb later said: "Never was there a more stupid blunder committed by a commanding general."

By 2:30 p.m., it was clear the battle was reaching its climax. The Union sailors and Marines on the beach were obviously ready to go, and Curtis's sharpshooters were intermittently visible in the brush just beyond the palisade. Lamb's attention was riveted by a sudden cry from one of his lookouts: "Colonel, the enemy is about to charge!"

In those last tense moments before the assault, General Whiting scampered down the ladder and into the fort's telegraph office to fire off one final appeal to Braxton Bragg:

> The enemy are about to assault; they outnumber us heavily. We are just manning our parapets. Fleet have extended down the sea-front outside and are firing heavily. Enemy on the beach in front of us in very heavy force, not more than 700 yards from us. Nearly all land guns disabled. Attack! Attack! It is all I can say and all you can do![4]

In command of the naval landing force was an officer with a splendidly nautical name, Captain K.R. Breese. The pent-up tension of the column behind Breese was like a vast coiled spring. If the signal to attack were not given soon, Breese feared, the fire would go out of these men. Unfortunately for the naval party, neither Breese nor any of his subordinates had any training in land warfare. It did not occur to them that a rush by thin waves of men would suffer fewer casualties than a massive attack column. When the dreaded moment came, the Union sailors and Marines went forward in one dense, ungainly mob.

At 3:30 p.m. the naval bombardment suddenly ceased. There was a moment of electrically charged silence. Then came the demented banshee-shriek of every steam whistle in the Union fleet. The naval landing force went forward with a cheer, the men stumbling to gain purchase in the sand. The Mound Battery, along with the one remaining landface gun that could bear on the column -- a 10-inch Columbiad -- unleashed terrific blasts of grapeshot that raked the front of the column on its flanks, tearing down dozens of men.

Lamb ordered his infantry, and his now-unemployed gunners, to the parapets. Cheering wildly, they leaped from their dugouts and formed a line on the walls overlooking the beach. Companies fired by volleys — for as long as discipline held — so that the front of the naval column seemed to melt away as it advanced, like a candle being pushed against a hot iron. Instinctively, the Yankees at the head of the column made for a breach in the log palisade. That was as far as most of them got.

Now the howling Confederates lobbed sputtering hand grenades down on the Yankees. Rifle and pistol fire grew hotter by the second, and long-range grapeshot chewed at the edges of the chaotic mass. Every man or group of men that tried to get beyond the palisade was hit or driven back. Order and organization collapsed. The men who were left became a desperate mob, pinned down behind the remnants of the palisade. The handful of surviving Marine sharpshooters picked off a few rebels with their Spencers, but to expose oneself long enough to take aim was to court almost certain death. Everyone else in the naval column, at Porter's specific order, was colorfully but ineffectually armed with revolvers and cutlasses — about as useful under these conditions as slingshots.

Several times, officers rallied company-sized groups of sailors and led them forward into the teeth of the rebel fire in futile but incredibly valiant attempts to storm the seaface. The only result was that 21 officers were killed or wounded, and what little discipline the naval force still possessed soon vanished. The survivors broke and ran, leaving the beach carpeted with 300 dead and wounded men.

Nevertheless, the bloody sacrifice of the naval force created a vital diversion, focusing the defenders' attention on the Northeast Bastion rather than on the western end of the landface. This was where the main Union attack was finally getting underway — after, not before, the naval force's assault.

That diversion proved critical, because Curtis's attack had gone out of control. Pressured by cannon fire and musketry from the eastern half of the landface, Curtis's men veered to their right, away from the sally port and toward the fort's extreme left flank. Formations crumbled, units became intermingled, and the two leading New York regiments hit the wall at about the same time. They clambered over and through the splintered palisade, and scaled the slope of the first Confederate gun emplacement. One of the first men on top planted a flag. This romantic act drew the attention of many Confederates who had, until then, been looking in another direction. Behind Curtis's brigade, Pennypacker's men crowded forward, also breaking formation, until that end of the landface looked like an earthen dike holding back a flood of blue.

What happened when that flood burst into the fort was, in

Admiral Porter's words, "the hardest fighting that you ever saw." Having taken the first couple of traverses, the Yankees found themselves facing a long line of additional emplacements. Each was 20 or more feet high, and each was a miniature fortress in itself — and they were now defended ferociously by growing numbers of determined rebels.

Both Lamb and Whiting, gathering men as they went, ran toward the threatened sector. By the time they arrived, the battle had reached the fourth gun emplacement in line. Whiting led a counterattack that pushed the Union flag off the top and regained control of the gun pit, but only after a vicious hand-to-hand melee with rifle butts, swords, and pistols. In most places, the fighting was so close that there wasn't room to aim a rifle.

Lamb actually went out beyond the walls of Fort Fisher to get a better look at the situation. "I doubt," he wrote later, "if ever before the commander of a work went outside and looked upon the struggle for its possession." He saw a stream of bluecoats swarming over the left end of the landface, now bunching up to pass through the sally port. He returned within the walls and took personal command of an impromptu defense line forming behind the fourth traverse.

Having cleared the attackers from that emplacement, Whiting now found himself hard-pressed by fresh Yankee troops. A Union officer yelled a demand for Whiting and his handful of bloody, exhausted defenders to surrender. "Go to hell, you Yankee bastard!" Whiting yelled back. Seconds later, he was struck by two rifle balls. He was carried to the fort's hospital, bleeding heavily.

Lamb's men were holding, but shells from Battery Buchanan were now exploding all over that end of the fort, striking down friend and foe alike. The gunners there, observing only Union flags, had assumed that those positions were now occupied by the enemy, when in fact they were still hotly contested. There was nothing Lamb could do. While he was directing the defense, an aide reached him with the disgusting news that about 300 of the 350 men from Hagood's South Carolina detachment had refused to come into the line and fight. Instead, they remained cowering in the dugouts where Lamb had sent them to recover their spirits. Lamb dictated one final message to Braxton Bragg, saying that he could hold out until dark, and that if Bragg launched an all-out attack, the battle might yet be won.

Lamb now moved among the wounded, trying to rally them. All around him was a scene of utmost violence and desolation: great shattered cannon, splintered mounts, split sandbags, and mutilated men sprawled on every side.

At sea, observing that the Federal infantry was having difficulty making progress down the line of traverses, Admiral Porter ordered his gunboats to mass their fire just ahead of the attackers. Lamb figured the best way to get out from under this galling fire was to recapture one of the lost emplacements, where the attackers were taking shelter from Porter's barrage. He positioned himself at the head of a ragtag force of volunteers, ordered them to "Charge bayonets!", raised his sword, and led them forward. After running about six feet, he was struck in the hip by a Minie ball.

Lamb was carried to Battery Buchanan, where the Confederates were preparing to make a last stand. The bayonet charge he tried to lead never materialized. Behind him, the fight raged from traverse to traverse, the Confederates yielding only when the pressure grew intolerable, fighting every yard of the way with a cornered ferocity that won their foes' admiration. By 5 p.m., half of the fort was in Union hands. By nightfall, the unburied dead were beginning to smell.

Lamb found himself placed on a stretcher next to General Whiting, who bore his pain "uncomplainingly." Observing his young friend, Whiting said: "Lamb, when you die, I will assume command, and I will not surrender the fort." Lamb, who had no intention of dying if he could help it, gritted his teeth and made no reply.

The penultimate act of the saga was a pathetic farce. General Braxton Bragg, after ignoring every message sent to him throughout the day, finally made a response of sorts after dark, when resistance had been all but extinguished and when the defenders had almost run out of ammunition. A Confederate steamboat landed near Battery Buchanan, bearing not reinforcements, but a Georgia militia general named Colquitt. He was taken to the hospital dugout and presented to Colonel Lamb. He had been sent, he informed Lamb, to take command.

"Of what?" the embittered and agonized Lamb incredulously asked.

One nearby Confederate casualty, who had broken into the medicinal whiskey and was disgusted beyond endurance by what had been permitted to happen that day, raised himself on one elbow, unholstered a big Navy Colt, and drew a bead on one of Colquitt's dapper aides. A more sober hand gently pushed aside the pistol. Just at that tense moment, a bedraggled and powder-blackened soldier stuck his head into the dugout and announced that there were Yankees only a few yards away, demanding surrender. General Colquitt and his nattily dressed staff hastily retreated to their steamer and headed for Wilmington at full speed.

Fort Fisher surrendered at 10 p.m., just as their vessel cleared the wharf.

In contrast to the desperate messages being sent by Lamb and Whiting, Braxton Bragg's dispatches to the outside world were a model of flabbergasting equanimity. Having somehow convinced himself that Fort Fisher could be held indefinitely with its present resources, Bragg began reporting fantasy as though it were fact, assuring both Richmond and Raleigh that rumors of the fort's dire situation were totally unfounded. He even told Governor Vance that Whiting had reported the successful repulse of an enemy assault, although not one of Whiting's telegrams even remotely hinted at such a thing. He also claimed that he had landed sufficient reinforcements to hold the fort against any threat, and that he had perfect confidence in the outcome of the battle. Where he obtained that confidence remains a mystery, for there was surely nothing in the pleas from the fort to encourage it.

What Bragg had expected General Colquitt to do -- other than, by his very arrival on the scene, to offer an outrageous insult to both Lamb and Whiting -- likewise remains unfathomable. Colquitt seems to have been a competent enough officer. But he was, after all, only one man, stepping cold into a chaotic and violent situation with orders to take over the battle from the two men who knew more about what was going on than anyone else in the Confederate Army. Bragg's judgment in this instance seems more than just mistaken, and begins to look like temporary derangement.

Bragg simply refused to believe that Fort Fisher was in extremis until Colquitt wired him from the last telegraph station on Confederate Point still in rebel hands. Colquitt's message said that the fort had been overrun, that all the troops had either surrendered or were milling about in confusion at the tip of the peninsula, and that he himself had barely escaped capture. To make sure Bragg took him seriously, Colquitt ended his message with the statement: "There is no mistake in this information."

Bragg was thunderstruck. Now he flailed about, trying to salvage the unsalvageable. He ordered General Hebert at Smithville to send a reliable man across the river to inform Lamb that General Bragg had ordered "No surrender." Hebert wired back, around midnight, with a terseness bordering on contempt: "Last information is that Fort Fisher has surrendered. I await orders."

An hour later, Bragg broke the news to Richmond: "I am mortified at having to report unexpected capture of Fort Fisher...particulars not known...."

When the sun rose on January 16, the interior of Fort Fisher presented a sight that was never forgotten by any of its witnesses. "If Hell is what it is said to be," wrote one Yankee sailor, "then the interior of Fort Fisher is a fair comparison." Recalled another witness:

> The rebel dead were still lying around the fort when I was there, quite numerous, half covered with sand and many of them dreadfully mangled. Many of the guns were dismounted and some were broken to pieces...pieces of shot and shell, and whole ones as large as pumpkins, of all kinds, sizes and shapes, Arms, accoutrements, clothing, broken torn and half buried in sand...I can't attempt to describe it to you.[5]

Over 1,000 tons of scrap iron were collected from inside the walls, remnants of the 50,000 projectiles that had been fired to subdue the Gibraltar of the Confederacy.

Four hundred of Lamb's men were killed or wounded, but their Alamo-like stand had inflicted much more serious losses on their adversaries. In addition to nearly 300 casualties in the naval column, Terry's infantry had suffered another 900 killed or wounded. The dying continued even after the fighting stopped —

and not just in the field hospitals. On the morning of January 16, some drunken sailors, roaming the fort looking for loot and souvenirs, carried a torch into the fort's powder magazine. The resulting massive blast killed or injured another 300 men. Colonel Lamb survived his bullet wound, and his captivity, and was deservedly lionized as a hero. General Whiting, whose bravery at Fort Fisher more than atoned for his odd failure at Drewry's Bluff, died in a Yankee prison camp, his honor washed clean.

The night after Fort Fisher succumbed, a Confederate blockade runner, commanded by one of those dashing Englishmen who flocked to the trade, followed some phony signal lights and anchored in the Cape Fear River. The captain celebrated by holding a party for his crew and passengers, complete with imported brandy. At one point, he rapped for silence and called for a toast.

"Gentlemen, we have anchored again upon the soil of battleworn, grand old Dixie!"

"Hip, hip, huzzah!" chorused the tipsy guests.

At that exact moment, a Federal officer in full uniform threw open the door, doffed his hat, and said: "Gentlemen, you are now a prize to Admiral Porter's squadron. However, as paroled prisoners, you are at liberty to finish your repast."

When Porter heard the story, he laughed until tears were squeezed from his eyes.

RECESSIONAL —THE LAST GOOD BATTLE OF BRAXTON BRAGG

Even with Fort Fisher gone, General Braxton Bragg could have held onto Wilmington for a long time, if he had possessed the will and intelligence to make full use of the resources he still had: several very strong forts and a force of infantry almost equal to the enemy's. An active and determined defense could have kept Admiral Porter's navy out of the estuary for weeks, giving the Confederate naval command time to rush to completion the iron-clad CSS *Wilmington*. Had that powerful vessel been able to join the fight, Porter might never have taken Wilmington before the war ended.

Instead of doing any of these things, however, Bragg's first knee-jerk reaction to the fall of Fort Fisher was to order Fort Caswell blown up. Then he concentrated all his forces around Fort Anderson, in effect giving Porter control of the inlets and enabling him to take his own undisturbed time getting his ships across the bar.

The main magazine of Fort Caswell contained 100,000 pounds of precious gunpowder. When it was blown up, people in Fayetteville heard the explosion, 100 miles away. One eyewitness, much closer than that, described it this way:

> Our house was near and facing the river, and directly across the harbor from us was Fort Caswell. While I was trying to pierce the darkness over the water in search of approaching lights, I looked toward this fort and beheld the most astonishing sight I have ever seen. As I looked a vivid flash of light shot through the darkness and traveled with lightning rapidity toward the fort, and then, as if a mighty volcano had sprung its blazing contents from the sea and into the sky, a great light flashed up from Caswell, accompanied by a roar and a jar that smashed the glass in our house like [the] wave of an earthquake.[1]

Reinforcing success, General Grant now transferred an entire army corps, the 23rd under General John Schofield, from Tennessee to the coast. While this massive infusion of strength was being readied, Terry's troops dug in defensively and the Navy methodically swept the Cape Fear River for mines. These proved to be more of a threat than a danger, although Porter did lose one ship; if the technology available to Richmond had been equal to the design of the weapons, Porter would have lost a lot more. Will Cushing remained in the thick of things, leading patrols up the river, running mine-sweeping operations, and helping to design a fake wooden monitor that was later used, with great success, to draw the fire of the gunners at Fort Anderson.

Schofield's army arrived on February 9, and the Federal offensive was resumed two days later. Hoke was still entrenched across the north end of the Cape Fear peninsula, so Schofield attempted two turning movements. The first one, by way of Masonboro Sound, failed due to high water conditions. The second, on February 14, failed because Hoke guessed what Schofield was going to do and concentrated his artillery in just the right place. Schofield then took advantage of his naval resources to transfer his main thrust to the west bank of the Cape Fear River, aiming toward Fort Anderson. Porter's gunboats had been daily battering the work and had already damaged it. On February 17, Schofield was ready to attack the position. He wired Admiral Porter succinctly: "General Cox will move against Ft. Anderson in the morning. Please give it a good shelling." Porter did. His men were becoming experts at fort-reduction.

As soon as Cox's four brigades began their attack, Bragg ordered Fort Anderson abandoned, despite the fact that it was still strong enough to give Cox plenty of trouble. The Confederates fell back to a defensive line along Town Creek, about eight miles north of Fort Anderson. This line should have been a strong one, since all the bridges had been burned and there was no ford for a distance of 15 miles inland. But still the bad luck and blundering continued. An old scow was inadvertently left on the south bank, and with it, the Federals turned the defenders' flank, capturing 400 men and easily rolling up the whole position.

Some of the fiercest resistance was offered by battery of field guns under command of a Chowan County sergeant named B.F. Hunter. Hunter and his men stood their ground even after the South Carolina troops on either side had fled. Hunter's men fired like demons at the oncoming Yanks. As the enemy closed to within yards of his gun, Hunter was hailed by a Yankee officer and admonished to surrender while he had the chance. "If you fire that gun again, I will kill you!" shouted the Union officer. Hunter yelled back: "Kill, and go to hell!" Then he ordered his gunner to pull the lanyard one last time. Moments later, Hunter was wrestled to the ground and would have been spitted on a dozen bayonets, had not that same Federal officer intervened. Pushing aside his men, the officer ordered them to spare Hunter's life, saying, "He's too brave a man to be killed."

There was more sharp fighting on Hoke's end of the line as he pulled back from the peninsula, but in no place were the defenders able to do more than slow the enemy's advance for a few hours. The final resistance was offered in Wilmington itself, where a lone rebel battery, stationed at the intersection of Market and Front streets, lobbed shells into the advance guard of the 16th Kentucky Regiment on Eagle Island.

Once Wilmington was in Union hands, Schofield was under orders to take Goldsboro as soon as possible, to open rail connections with Wilmington, and to stockpile supplies in Goldsboro for General Sherman's army. But Schofield found so few railroad cars in Wilmington that he decided to shift operations to New Bern instead.

By the end of the first week of March 1865, Schofield had moved General Cox forward out of New Bern at the head of two Federal divisions, totaling about 13,000 men. Ahead of them, dug in on the far bank of Southwest Creek, just below Kinston, was Bragg. Bragg had Hoke's division and was under orders to delay the Federals as long as he could, so that General Joseph E. Johnston and the meager Army of Tennessee could concentrate for a blow against Sherman.

The two forces made contact at a place known as Wise's Forks, where the Trent and Dover roads intersect near the Neuse River. There was some artillery skirmishing on March 7, but Bragg didn't want to start a serious battle until General D.H. Hill joined him with 2,000 reinforcements — a motley group indeed, comprised partly of grizzled veterans from the Army of Tennessee and partly of fresh-faced boys of the N.C. Junior Reserves. There was no man in the Confederate Army (with the possible exception of William Lamb) who despised Braxton Bragg more than D.H. Hill, who had been rudely sacked by Bragg after the Battle of Chickamauga. But Hill had choked down his pride, mainly because Joe Johnston had begged him to. Both men would be on their best behavior during this engagement.

Hill's column arrived just before daybreak on March 8. Now strengthened to about 9,000 men, Bragg unleashed Hoke in a stinging attack on the Federal left flank. Hoke's men went forward with their usual elan, swept through all resistance, and took almost 1,000 prisoners. Hill attacked somewhat later, on the right flank, assuming from the sounds of battle that Hoke had solidly pinned the Federals. Hill's thrust was hampered, however, when three-fourths of the Junior Reserves laid down in a field and refused to advance another foot. Eventually, Hill was forced to retire to his starting point. Nevertheless, the first day had brought a smart little victory for Bragg.

Cox was reinforced by an entire division of Yankees late in the day. His men spent March 9 digging in, felling trees in front of their earthworks, and creating a strong defensive front. Bragg sent Hoke to probe this line, but Hoke reported that the entrenchments were too strong for a frontal attack.

On March 10, Bragg decided to sent Hoke on another flanking

movement to the right, while Hill made a demonstration in front.
The next-to-useless Junior Reserves were kept back in the Confederate trenches, to be used strictly in a defensive role. Some of these
boys were destined to fight stoutly at Bentonville, but they were
still too raw for much to be expected of them on this occasion.

Hoke began his approach march at 3 a.m. under cover of a
chilling rain that kept the Federal pickets huddled in their holes. By
morning, it looked to Cox's men as if the rebels had pulled back
their right flank during the night, perhaps as the prelude to a
general retreat. Colonel Henry Splaine, commanding the Union left
flank, was ordered to ride toward the rebel lines with a small escort
of cavalry and "not to return until he had seen the enemy and made
an intelligent estimate of their strength." After a time, one of the
officers riding with Splaine admonished him to ride no further --
the Confederates, he said, were right across this strip of no man's
land, at the edge of the opposite woods. Splaine searched until his
eyes ached, but the misty drizzle obscured all details. Finally he
spurred his horse on once more, muttering, "I am ordered to see
them, and I shall obey."

About 70 yards from rebel lines, the little reconnaissance party
was hailed by a "noble looking" Confederate officer leaning
nonchalantly against a cannon. This fellow took out a white
handkerchief, waved it, and called, "Come on in!" Splaine decided
to stall for time as he was now in a position to see a fairly broad
segment of the Confederate line. He brazenly inspected the area
with his field glasses, calmly counting gun emplacements and
regimental flags, while distracting the rebel officer by waving a
hanky of his own and replying: "Won't you please come here? I
want to speak with you on a most important matter."

This Alphonse-and-Gaston routine continued when the Confederate wagged his handkerchief reassuringly and said: "Oh, come on
in, it's all right." When Splaine demurred, still quite cool and
unperturbed, the Confederate grew exasperated. Patting the
fieldpiece, he barked: "If you don't come right in, I will fire."

Splaine had played this gambit about as far as it was going to go,
and the men around him were shaking with tension. Their eyes
were riveted on the Confederate cannon's mouth, and their minds
were busily computing the likely spread of a load of grapeshot at a

range of 70 yards. By now, however, Splaine had seen enough to give him a very precise idea of how many men and guns were opposite his own entrenchments. To the men around him he quietly said: "We're in a bad fix. Obey me, and we'll come out all right; otherwise, we perish...if we attempt to turn now, they will shoot us down. We must pretend we are going to surrender, and so sure will they be that we mean it, that they will become careless while glorying over their fancied prize...when we are almost within their lines, I shall order, `One, two, three, turn,' and at that command, turn quickly...and ride for dear life."

After convincing the impatient rebel battery commander that they were indeed ready to give up, the little band rode forward calmly until they were only 20 yards from the gun position. Then Splaine gave the word. When the Confederates recovered their wits, astonished at this example of "Yankee impudence," they unleashed hundreds of shots at the galloping men. Astonishingly, no one was wounded, although Splaine's boot-heel and shoulder strap were shot off, and his saddle was almost knocked from his horse by the impact of another ball. A man riding close by had his pistol blown from his hand, and every other member of the lucky patrol counted at least two bullet holes in his clothing when they finally stopped riding, deep in the trees on the Federal side.

Hoke's rebels managed to get into good position without being discovered. Just after noon they rose up and charged, howling the rebel yell. One Massachusetts soldier who witnessed the attack described it this way: "Out into the open they came, screaming...a great gray billowing, surging forward...through shell and canister...furious, determined, persistent."[2]

Hearing the outburst of gunfire, Hill attacked on his end. He succeeded in overrunning a line of Federal trenches before coming up against greatly superior forces, well dug in and amply supported by artillery. Gallant as Hoke's attack was, it too made no headway against the strong and resolutely defended Federal earthworks. Bragg wisely called off both attacks before his casualties became too severe.

That night, Bragg and his little army withdrew across the Neuse River. It took Schofield ten days to repair the railroad bridge at Kinston and throw across a pontoon bridge for his wagons and infantry; then he marched into Goldsboro without meeting further resistance. Bragg and Hoke retreated until they linked up with General Johnston, and both men left their mark on the hopeless but valiant encounter at Bentonville. Bragg's contribution, alas, was once again a negative one. (See *Volume I: Silk Flags And Cold Steel*.)

Confederate losses at the Battle of Wise's Forks amounted to approximately 1,500 killed, wounded, or captured. Federal losses were 65 killed, 319 wounded, and almost 2,000 taken prisoner. Bragg kept a firm grasp on this battle, and his men fought magnificently for him. But he simply didn't have the resources to convert a successful delaying action into a major victory — and little would have been changed, in a strategic sense, if he had.

He could take some satisfaction, perhaps, in having partly redeemed his reputation. Still, the inexplicable mystery is why he didn't show the same kind of resolution and grip during the battle for Fort Fisher, when at issue was the last lifeline port of the Confederacy. At Wise's Forks, Bragg didn't hesitate to send Hoke's division against veteran troops, dug in behind strong breastworks and an abatis of fallen timber, massively supported by artillery; nor did Hoke hesitate or his men falter in their attack. Yet at Fort Fisher, Bragg had obdurately refused to send that same division against a thin line of raw soldiers, nervously dug in behind little more than sand dunes, and totally unsupported by field artillery for at least three-fourths the length of their position. (See Appendix C.)

Contemplating the generalship of Braxton Bragg during his last two engagements -- one a handsome little victory, and the other a catastrophic and avoidable defeat -- the modern historian is forced to shake his head in wonder and repeat the words uttered by Robert E. Lee's cavalry commander, General Nathan B. Forrest, when he learned that Bragg had failed to follow up his hard-won victory at Chickamauga: "What does he fight battles for?"

There was one more skirmish -- if that is the word for it -- before the war's final actions moved away from the coastal region of North Carolina for good. The *Albemarle*'s sister ship, the CSS *Neuse*, which had been lying idle for almost a year at her anchorage near Kinston, was at last ordered to build up steam and provide cover for Bragg's withdrawal from Wise's Forks.

The *Neuse* dutifully chugged downstream until her crew spotted some Union cavalry. The Confederates fired a few desultory rounds at the Yankees, then set their ironclad on fire and abandoned her. Fortunately for posterity, before the fires could reach the ship's magazine, the intense heat ignited a loaded cannon, blowing a gaping hole in her bottom and sinking her. The *Neuse* was raised from the muddy riverbed in 1963, and proved to be a treasure trove for archaeologists. She enjoys a new career today as a tourist attraction in a museum near Kinston. It is a role she fulfills much better than that of a warship, for she reminds those who visit her of that proud morning when the CSS *Albemarle* set forth to challenge one of the most powerful navies in the world, and for one brief moment of triumph ruled supreme on the inshore waters of North Carolina.

APPENDIX A
ARTILLERY
TERMS

The size and relative power of an artillery piece is most commonly measured by the diameter of the bore -- i.e., the muzzle, or "business end" of the piece, from which the projectile emerges. Modern artillery pieces are described either in millimeters or inches.

Civil War weapons, too, were often described in terms of inches, but there were other, more specialized, terms as well. To avoid confusion, following is a brief primer of some of the terms used in this book.

Types of bores. Civil War weapons were either *smoothbore* or *rifled*. In smoothbore weapons, the inner surface of the cast-metal barrel is smooth. The projectile ("cannonball") tended to fit rather loosely in the barrel of a smoothbore, and this shortened the range and reduced the accuracy of the weapon. Nevertheless, until the mid-19th century, smoothbore weapons (both artillery and small arms) were the rule, partly because they were easier to load and much easier to manufacture.

In a rifled weapon, long grooves spiral down the length of the inner surface of the barrel. These grooves impart a spin to the projectile as it is fired from the barrel, and the spin creates a gyroscopic effect that greatly improves both range and accuracy. By the time of the Civil War, rifled artillery (and small arms) was becoming the rule, and smoothbores were increasingly considered obsolete. Nevertheless, military tactics were still largely based on the much shorter range and inaccurate fire of smoothbore weapons, which accounted for much of the slaughter suffered by both armies, particularly in the early days of the war.

Types of smoothbores. Long-barreled, low-elevation weapons using heavy powder charges were generally referred to as *guns* (although this term could also be used generically to refer to any artillery piece). The most common type of ammunition for smoothbore guns was the solid cannonball, or *roundshot*.

Shorter-barreled smoothbore weapons, lighter than guns of the same caliber, were called *howitzers*. They were frequently installed on small vessels and fired lighter powder charges. Their barrels were capable of higher elevations than comparably sized guns.

The most potent smoothbores were the *Columbiads*. These long, heavy pieces could fire large roundshot, or explosive shells packed with heavy powder charges, at high elevations.

Mortars were blunt, stubby smoothbores whose barrels were capable of firing at very high elevations. This made them useful for lobbing shells at targets behind protective walls or ridges, because the shell traveled in a high arc and dropped almost vertically on the target.

Some Civil War cannon, especially those of very distinctive shape or design, were known by the names of their designers. Examples used in this book include the Whitworth, Parrott, Dahlgren, Armstrong, and Brooke pieces. Thus, an "8-inch Brooke" or a "100-pounder Parrott" described not only the caliber of the weapon, but also its distinguishing shape.

Size of ammunition. An even more common way of categorizing artillery was by the weight of the projectile it fired. A "32-pounder," then, was not a cannon that weighed 32 pounds (this type of weapon, without mount, actually weighed anywhere from 3,000 to more than 7,000 pounds), but rather was a cannon that fired a 32-pound projectile. Perhaps the largest artillery piece employed in the North Carolina campaigns was the 150-pounder Armstrong briefly used by the Confederates in the defense of Fort Fisher. It fired a solid-shot projectile that weighed as much as a man.

Types of ammunition. There were several types of artillery ammunition in the Civil War period. The classic "cannonball" was referred to as *solid shot* or *roundshot*. Instead of exploding, it inflicted damage by sheer smashing power. If conditions were right, roundshot could be ricocheted across water like a skipping stone in order to punch holes in the hulls of wooden ships at the waterline.

Shells were hollow projectiles filled with gunpowder, timed to explode with a fuse. They inflicted damage by exploding on or over the target, spreading hot fragments of their metal casings throughout the area.

Grapeshot or *canister* consisted of bunches of small roundshot bound together or bagged so they could be loaded and fired as a single projectile. Once fired, the balls sprayed out in a cone-shaped pattern. In effect, this ammunition turned the cannon into a giant shotgun. It wasn't effective for bombarding fortifications, but it was extremely deadly at moderate ranges as an anti-personnel weapon. In a pinch, during desperate close-range encounters, cannons were sometimes loaded with handfuls of scrap metal, nails, broken bayonets, musket balls, or anything else that was handy. At one point, this tactic was used to help repel Pickett's Charge at Gettysburg. In North Carolina, it was employed by Union gunners at the Battle of Bentonville, inflicting ghastly casualties on the attacking rebels.

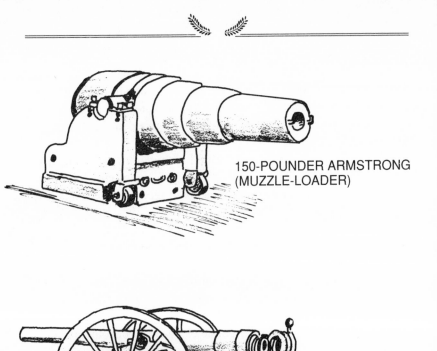

150-POUNDER ARMSTRONG
(MUZZLE-LOADER)

2.75- INCH, 12-PDR. WHITWORTH OF LAMB'S "FLYING BATTERY"

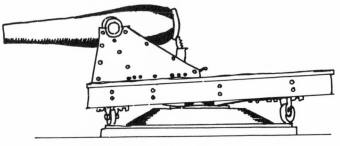

8-IN COLUMBIAD
ON BARBETTE CARRIAGE

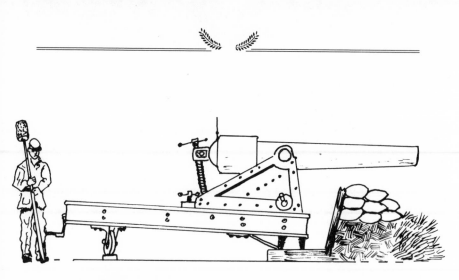

100-PDR. PARROTT ON IRON
BARBETTE CARRIAGE

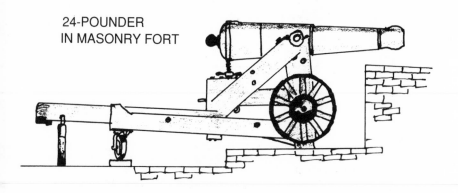

24-POUNDER
IN MASONRY FORT

APPENDIX B
A MASSACRE
AT
PLYMOUTH?

One of the best-selling nonfiction titles in recent years was James McPherson's one-volume history of the Civil War era, *Battle Cry of Freedom*. On page 793, McPherson reprints an alleged eyewitness account of a massacre of captured Negro soldiers, by Confederate General Robert Hoke's men, after the fall of Plymouth. Because McPherson's excellent book is so authoritative, and because it was so favorably reviewed, most readers will probably accept the account at face value. McPherson himself recounts the story without comment, indicating his own acceptance of it as truth. Some readers may wonder why there is no similar account of such an atrocity in Chapter 21 of this book.

The reason is simple: The preponderance of evidence indicates that this massacre never took place.

First, here is an account from the *Official Records of the War of Rebellion*, Volume VII, pp. 459-460, which was reproduced in McPherson's book:

> Samuel Johnson, being duly sworn, deposes and says:
> I am orderly sergeant in Co. D, 2d U.C. Colored Cavalry...upon the capture of Plymouth by the rebel forces all the negroes found in blue uniform, or with any outward marks of a Union soldier upon him [sic], was killed. I saw some taken into the woods and hung. Others I saw stripped of all their clothing and then stood on the banks of the

river with their faces riverward, and there they were shot. Still others were killed by having their brains beaten out by the butt-end of the muskets in the hands of the rebels. All were not killed the day of the capture. Those that were not were placed in a room with their officers, they [the officers] having previously dragged through the town with ropes around their necks, where they were kept confined until the following morning, when the remainder of the black soldiers were killed. The regiments most conspicuous in these murderous transactions were the 8th N.C. and, I think, the 6th N.C.

Samuel [his X mark] Johnson

Witnessed by John I. Davenport, lieutenant and acting aide-de-camp. Sworn and subscribed to before me this 11th day of July, 1864,

John Cassels, Captain and Provost-Marshal

Sergeant Johnson's affidavit was presented at a meeting held in 1909 by the men responsible for making the final editorial corrections to the history of the 103rd Pennsylvania Regiment — a volume which contains by far the most detailed account of the siege of Plymouth ever published. Besides the veterans from the 103rd, there were also present on that day some men from a sister regiment, the 101st Pennsylvania. Not one man in the room recalled any such incident. Many expressed amazement, since the captured Union officers, at least, had been loosely confined. It was deemed impossible for any such mass executions to have occurred without being observed, and without being protested by someone.

Everyone at the meeting, several dozen Union veterans of the battle, agreed that Robert Hoke's handling of the surrender was "courteous and considerate," and that the rebels in his command appeared reasonably disciplined at all times.

Before publishing the 103rd's history, its editor, Luther S. Dickey, investigated Johnson's claims and appended a lengthy discussion of them to the finished volume. He did this, he said, not to exonerate the Confederates, but simply to get at the truth, whatever it might be.

What is the truth? One interesting clue is a note attached to Sergeant Johnson's affidavit — a note that for some reason was not included in McPherson's book. The note appears to have been appended to the affidavit by another Union officer named Ould. It states flatly: "This is a villainous lie and badly told at that. Samuel Johnson is a bad affidavit man, whatever may be his other excellencies...." (*Official Records*, Volume VII, p. 468.)

Letters of inquiry were sent to Robert Hoke and to other prominent North Carolina veterans who were on the scene, asking for further information. Hoke was ill and close to death at the time, so there was no reply from him. The Honorable Walter Clark, chief justice of the North Carolina Supreme Court and compiler of the mammoth *History of the North Carolina Regiments*, replied that no Union prisoners "of any color" were killed at Plymouth. He was seconded by John W. Graham, formerly of the 56th North Carolina Regiment: "I have no hesitation in saying that the reputed killing of any colored troops the day after the capture of Plymouth...is entirely untrue. I heard of nothing of the kind at that time nor have I ever heard of it since until the receipt of your letter." Both of these gentlemen, it should be noted, had reputations for the highest integrity.

The worst information Dickey could unearth indicated that a number of Negro soldiers and white Unionists, fearful of what might happen to them after the surrender, fled into the surrounding woods and swamps. Individually, some of them were hunted down and killed -- in this case, "shot while trying to escape" happens to be the cliche of truth. Although these killings were brutal and unfortunate, they were not in any sense a "massacre" of unarmed and helpless prisoners. As Dickey eventually concluded on page 270 of the *History of the 103rd Pennsylvania Volunteers*:

> When the writer began this investigation it was with the expectation of, in a measure, verifying the affidavit of the negro, Sergeant Johnson. It was not with the motive of doing justice, especially to the victorious Confederates of Plymouth, but merely to tell the whole truth on the battle of Plymouth, in which his regiment had done its full duty. In his careful research for the truth he became convinced that an injustice had been done the Confederates who had captured his Regiment, and that as an impartial historian, these facts should be recorded in this volume.

APPENDIX C
THE CURIOUS
BEHAVIOR OF
BRAXTON
BRAGG

In defense of his actions -- or rather his inaction -- during the struggle for Fort Fisher, General Bragg advanced the following excuses:

> 1. His cavalry failed to supply him with accurate and timely information about the enemy's strength and location;
>
> 2. "No power on earth could have prevented the enemy from landing...";
>
> 3. The Union blocking line across the peninsula, at the rear of Terry's assault force, was too strong to be attacked;
>
> 4. Porter's fleet would have cut any Confederate attack to pieces with enfilade fire from the ocean;
>
> 5. Much of Fort Fisher's garrison was drunk and offered only spotty resistance;
>
> 6. Up until Sunday evening, January 15, the messages Bragg's headquarters received from the fort indicated that Lamb was holding his own and needed no help.

Excuse No. 6 is such a subjective distortion that it needs little comment. The texts of all but one of the telegrams sent by Whiting

and Lamb have survived, and there is nothing in them that any rational commander could possibly mistake for optimism.

The other reasons are worth some examination, however, in view of the magnitude of what was at stake and the catastrophic results of the battle's outcome.

Bragg's cavalry went were Bragg told them to go -- or should have told them to go. They were second-rate troops, but he had been on the Wilmington front long enough to know that. And he had been a professional soldier long enough to know that to get maximum performance from such men, a commander must give them very precise orders and make sure they obey them. Second-rate or not, though, Bragg's horsemen were not stupid enough to follow one of his vague directives -- to ride down the beach and make a reconnaissance on horseback. As Lamb scathingly re-marked in one of his postwar essays: "To those familiar with the Carolina seacoast at night, and how a man on horseback looms up like a dromedary in the desert, it will not be surprising that these horse-marines, not wishing to become targets for the Federal sharpshooters, followed the example of General Bragg and his army and retired for the night...Cavalry on the beach at night to watch the enemy! A reconnaissance that an officer could have made on foot within an hour...."[1]

If the horsemen weren't giving Bragg the information he needed to make decisions, he had only to get on a steamboat, make a quick run downstream, and see for himself what was going on. The peninsula was more open to observation from that direction than it was from the fort. With a good pair of binoculars, Bragg could have even identified individual men on shore. As Lamb acidly remarked:

> To know the position of the enemy, to be informed promptly of the movements which he is executing, to gather sufficient facts from which his designs may be understood, is the first care of a command-ing general, who should spare no labor or risk to arrive at such information...No commanding general ever had such an opportunity to watch the movements of the enemy, and direct the management of his forces with such slight personal danger as General Bragg....
>
> ...The women, children, and old men, who watched the battle from the farm houses across the river, knew more about what was going on in his command than did General Braxton Bragg.[2]

The terrain south of Masonboro Sound had been inspected by three experienced generals before Bragg arrived on the scene: Whiting, Pierre Beauregard, and James Longstreet. All three men concluded that it would be impractical and very dangerous for the enemy to make a landing there, if the sector were resolutely defended. The land between the sound and the fort abounded with high dunes, gullies, and underbrush at right angles to the direction a landing force would have to take. Defending troops could be moved to oppose a landing without being seen by Union ships offshore. There was, moreover, a long stretch of riverbank tall enough to hide and protect thousands of men. Even a few hundred sharpshooters, taking advantage of this landscape, could have inflicted havoc on Terry's landings with little risk to themselves from Union gunboats. Yet Terry was allowed to land his troops as if he were on a peacetime training maneuver. Not one shot was fired at him.

Bragg had at his disposal one of the best veteran divisions in the Army of Northern Virginia, led by an aggressive and highly intelligent officer, Robert F. Hoke. The troops manning Terry's defensive line were as numerous, or nearly so, but most of them had never been shot at. Their morale was reportedly high, but then most units that have never been under fire start off with "high morale." They were entrenched, to be sure, but how strong could the entrenchments have been after less than 24 hours of construction? Lastly, they were supported only by a handful of field guns, and those were massed on the riverside flank, where they could duel with the CSS *Chickamauga*. Bragg had strong superiority in field artillery in general, and a monopoly on it if he had attacked east of the riverbank.

As far as a daylight attack was concerned, it would have taken only a few minutes for Hoke's men to charge the distance from their cover to the Negro soldiers' trenches. Most of Porter's ships were firing on Fort Fisher, and they would have needed several minutes to retrain their guns on an infantry attack — leaving not enough time to inflict serious damage. Bragg avoided even discussing the option of a night attack, during which Porter's cannon would have been helpless. Although night attacks were impossible to control in those days, the utter simplicity of the tactical problem made that almost irrelevant. One didn't need a West Point education to see that a night attack was Bragg's smartest tactical choice. Such an assault, in conjunction with a sortie from the fort, would almost certainly have thrown Terry's units into chaos. It could well have turned the battle into a stunning Southern victory.

Bragg's final point -- that much of the Fort Fisher garrison was too drunk to fight -- is nothing more than an egregious slander. It was based, if rooted in anything factual at all, on the story of the angry soldier who drew his pistol on Colquitt. Lamb's first act, upon taking command of the fort in July 1862, was to cashier an officer for intoxication on duty. There was some social drinking with the blockade runners in the Cottage, but within the walls of the fort, neither Lamb nor the men in his command were permitted alcohol. No doubt there were some illegal bottles hoarded by the garrison, but surely not enough to stupefy a thousand men.

Testimony from Union sources as well as Confederate confirms that the resistance offered by Lamb's entire garrison, with the sorry exception of Hagood's South Carolinians, was fierce and unyielding. Indeed, the resistance was so fierce that for about an hour, from 4 p.m. until Porter's gunners found the range of the positions still occupied by the defenders, Terry's men were fought to a complete standstill, and were even thrown back in some places.

Braxton Bragg was charged with defending the most important piece of land remaining in Confederate hands anywhere. There was no point in husbanding Hoke's troops for a "more favorable time," because there could not be a more important time. If Fort Fisher fell, everything else Bragg did would be more or less irrelevant. If ever there were a case where risks were justified, it was during the battle for Fort Fisher. At stake was the survival of the Confederacy — nothing less. Whether Bragg really believed Hoke could repel the Union landings or break through the defensive line between Sugar Loaf Hill and the fort, it was his duty to make a supreme effort. Making it, and failing in the attempt, would have gained him honor. Not making it only consolidated his reputation as one of the most reviled and detested figures in the Confederate hierarchy.

NOTES

CHAPTER 1: SEIZING THE FORTS

1. Herring and Williams, *Fort Caswell in War and Peace*, pp. 22-23.
2. *Official Records of the War of Rebellion*, Volume 51, III, p. 6.
3. Curtis, *Reminiscences of Wilmington and Smithville*, pp. 19-20.
4. Herring and Williams, p. 34.
5. Ibid, p. 36.
6. Curtis, p. 21.

CHAPTER 2: "WE HAVE ON THESE WATERS SOME BRAVE AND SKILFUL SEAMEN"

1. Davis, *Boy Colonel of the Confederacy*, pp. 76-77.
2. Hill, *A History of North Carolina in the War Between the States*, p. 158.
3. Mahan, *The Influence of Sea Power on History*, p. 27.
4. *Official Naval Records*, Volume I/6/p. 42.

CHAPTER 4: HATTERAS LOST

1. Merrill, "The Hatteras Expedition," p. 212.
2. Ibid, p. 214.
3. Ibid, p. 205.
4. Hill, *A History of North Carolina in the War Between the States*, p. 170.
5. *Civil War Naval Chronology*, pp. 22-23.

CHAPTER 5: A DAY AT THE RACES

1. Hill, *A History of North Carolina in the War Between the States*, p. 178.

CHAPTER 6: BURNSIDE'S EXPEDITION — THE COAST CONQUERED

1. Davis, *Boy Colonel of the Confederacy*, pp. 89-90.
2. Hill, *A History of North Carolina in the War Between the States*, p. 186.
3. *Official Records of the War of Rebellion*, Volume 4, p. 573.
4. Ibid, Volume 1/iv/p. 682.
5. Davis, p. 98.
6. Merrill, *The Rebel Shore*, p. 81.
7. Hill, p. 263.

CHAPTER 7: STORMY WEATHER

1. Day, *My Diary of Rambles with Burnside's Coastal Division*, p. 28.
2. Walcott, *History of the 21st Massachusetts*, p. 26.
3. Ibid, p. 27.
4. Day, p. 23.
5. Roe, *The Twenty-Fourth Regiment, Massachusetts Volunteers*, p. 46.
6. Ibid, p. 49.
7. Day, p. 32.
8. Ibid, p. 33.

CHAPTER 8: THE BATTLE OF ROANOKE ISLAND

1. Hill, *A History of North Carolina in the War Between the States*, p. 207.
2. Barrett, *The Civil War in North Carolina*, p. 74, from a statement made by Captain Henry McCrae.
3. Parker, *Recollections of a Naval Officer*, p. 228-229.
4. Ibid, p. 230.
5. Ibid, p. 232.
6. Walcott, *History of the 21st Massachusetts*, p. 27.
7. Day, *My Diary of Rambles with Burnside's Coastal Division*, p. 35.
8. Ibid, p. 36.

9. Barrett, p. 81.

10. Loving, *Civil War Letters of George Washington Whitman*, p. 76.

11. Day, p. 37.

12. Ibid, p. 38.

13. Walcott, p. 37.

14. Merrill, *The Rebel Shore*, pp. 100-101.

15. Quoted in Walcott, p. 55.

CHAPTER 9: ZOUAVES AMOK — THE BURNING OF WINTON

1. Quoted in Parramore, "The Burning of Winton," Chapter 7, *Roanoke-Chowan News Civil War Supplement*, p. 70.

2. Ibid, p. 76.

CHAPTER 10: "YOU MAY RELY ON A HARD FIGHT" — DISASTER AT NEW BERN

1. Davis, *Boy Colonel of the Confederacy*, p. 83.

2. Ibid, p. 86.

3. Ibid, p. 99.

4. Ibid, p. 100.

5. Ibid, p. 101.

6. Ibid, p. 107.

7. Walcott, *History of the 21st Massachusetts*, p. 75.

8. Ibid, p. 76.

9. Ibid. pp. 76-77.

10. Mann, *History of the 45th Massachusetts*, appendix.

11. Hawkins, "Early Coastal Operations in North Carolina, *Battles and Leaders of the Civil War*, Volume I, p. 668.

12. Dollard, *Recollections of the Civil War*, p. 53.

13. Ibid, p. 54.

14. Roe, *The 24th Regiment, Massachusetts Volunteers*, p. 82.

15. Dollard, p. 62.

16. Ibid, p. 65.

17. Barrett, *The Civil War in North Carolina*, p. 103.

18. Underwood, *History of the 26th North Carolina*, p. 24.

19. Walcott, p. 78.
20. Barrett, p. 20.

CHAPTER 11: AFTERMATH — THE SKIRMISH AT SOUTH MILLS

1. Roe, *The 24th Regiment, Massachusetts Volunteers*, pp. 95-96.
2. Davis, *Boy Colonel of the Confederacy*, p. 130.
3. Hawkins, *Battles and Leaders of the Civil War*, Volume I, pp. 655-656.

CHAPTER 12: THE SIEGE OF FORT MACON

1. *Official Records of the War of Rebellion*, Volume 9, I, p. 277.
2. Branch, *The Siege of Fort Macon*, p. 37.

CHAPTER 13: BURNSIDE DEPARTS

1. *Official Records of the War of Rebellion*, Volume 9, I, p. 374.
2. *Official Records*, Volume 9, I, p. 302.
3. Roe, *The 24th Regiment, Massachusetts Volunteers*, p. 122.
4. Barrett, *The Civil War in North Carolina*, p. 173.
5. Ibid, p. 174.

CHAPTER 14: GENERAL FOSTER TAKES COMMAND

1. Hill, *A History of North Carolina in the War Between the States*, p. 300.
2. Day, *My Diary of Rambles with Burnside's Coastal Division*, p. 47.
3. Ibid, p. 55.
4. Roe, *The 24th Regiment, Massachusetts Volunteers*, p. 134.
5. Williams, *The Civil War Diary of J.K. Carpenter*, p. 14.
6. Kirwan, *History of the 17th Massachusetts*, p. 120.

CHAPTER 15: "CLOSE ONE, SIR!" — RAIDS ALONG THE RIVERS

1. Barrett, *The Civil War in North Carolina*, p. 139.
2. Roske and van Doren, *Lincoln's Commando*, pp. 124-125.
3. Day, *My Diary of Rambles with Burnside's Coastal Division*, p. 56.
4. Roske and van Doren, p. 128.

CHAPTER 16: FOSTER'S MARCH ON GOLDSBORO

1. Kirwan, *History of the 17th Massachusetts*, pp. 146-146.
2. Ibid, p. 149.
3. Mann, *History of the 45th Massachusetts*, p. 106.
4. Barrett, *The Civil War in North Carolina*, pp. 142-143.
5. Mann, p. 321.
6. Kirwan, pp. 149-150.
7. Gammons, *The Third Massachusetts Regiment*, p. 34.
8. *New York Herald* correspondent's book on the Goldsboro campaign, p. 31.
9. Gammons, p. 87.

CHAPTER 17: D.H. HILL COMES...AND GOES

1. *Raleigh Progress*, March 1, 1863; quoted in Barrett, *The Civil War in North Carolina*, p. 150.
2. Davis, *Boy Colonel of the Confederacy*, p. 242.
3. Barrett, p. 156.
4. Ibid, p. 160.
5. Ibid, p. 164.
6. Williams, *Civil War Diary of K.J. Carpenter*, p. 13.
7. *Roanoke-Chowan News*, Civil War Supplement, Chapter 8, p. 88.

CHAPTER 18: BUFFALOES AND OTHER SCOURGES

1. Barrett, *The Civil War in North Carolina*, p. 172.
2. Ibid, p. 173.
3. *Roanoke-Chowan News*, Civil War Supplement, p. 130; letter originally appeared in the *Montgomery Mail* and was reprinted in the *Raleigh Progress* on May 28, 1863.

4. Dillard, *The Civil War in Chowan County*, p. 13.
5. *Roanoke-Chowan News*, p. 98.
6. Ibid, p. 99.
7. Ibid, p. 125.
8. Dillard, p. 13.
9. *Roanoke-Chowan News*, p. 119.
10. *Official Naval Records*, Volume 8, p. 95.
11. *Official Records of the War of Rebellion*, Volume 29, I, p. 912.
12. Barrett, pp. 178-179.
13. Daniels, *The Diary of Captain Henry A. Chambers*, pp. 182-183.

CHAPTER 19: PICKETT DOES NOT CHARGE

1. Barrett, *The Civil War in North Carolina*, p. 202.
2. Scharf, *History of the Confederate Navy*, p. 396.

CHAPTER 20: THE VOYAGE OF THE DEADLY TURTLE

1. Scharf, *History of the Confederate Navy*, p. 405.
2. Still, *The Career of the Confederate Ironclad "Neuse,"* p. 9.
3. Still, *Iron Afloat*, p. 158 -- from a letter from James Cooke to Thomas Scharf.
4. Ibid, p. 158.

CHAPTER 21: THUNDER ON ALBEMARLE SOUND

1. Nichols, *Fighting in North Carolina Waters*, p. 79.
2. *Official Naval Records*, Volume 9, p. 655.

CHAPTER 23: THE NOOSE TIGHTENS, THE PREY ELUDES

1. Wise, "Lifeline of the Confederacy," p. 147 and p. 224.
2. Neely, "The Perils of Running the Blockade...", p. 105. Neely perhaps goes too far in debunking the swashbuckler stereotype; for a balancing and invigorating counterview, see any of James Sprunt's collections of blockade-running yarns. As a young man, Sprunt ran the blockade, and his salty tales still make vivid reading.

Clearly, he recounts only the exciting and exceptional incidents, not the routine runs, but he is a trustworthy historian within those limits.

CHAPTER 24: THE STATE GOES INTO BUSINESS

1. Wise, "Lifeline of the Confederacy," p. 335.

CHAPTER 25: WILMINGTON AT WAR

1. Thomas, *Letters From the Colonel's Lady*, p. 31.
2. James R. Randall to his fiancee, August 28, 1862, quoted in Wood, "Port Town at War," p. 157.
3. *Official Records of the War of Rebellion*, Volume 1, pp. 486-487.
4. Wood, p. 157.
5. Howell, *The Book of Wilmington*, p. 125.
6. Ibid, pp. 120-212.
7. Gragg, "Fort Fisher," pp. 3-4.
8. Wood, pp. 143-144.
9. Ibid, p. 149.
10. Ibid.
11. Ibid, pp. 96-97.

CHAPTER 26: "A PARCEL OF CATS WATCHING A BIG RATHOLE"

1. Merrill, "Men, Monotony, and Mouldy Beans..." p. 55.
2. Wood, "Port Town at War," p. 167.
3. Lass, "Sleepless Sentinels...", p. 25.
4. Merrill, p. 50.
5. Figures culled from Wise, "Lifeline of the Confederacy," p. 138, and pp. 300-301.
6. Wise, p. 488.

CHAPTER 27: THE SAND CASTLE OF COLONEL LAMB

1. Lamb, *Colonel Lamb's Story*, p. 2.

2. Stick, *Bald Head Island*, p. 45; the quote is actually in reference to the construction of a fort on Smith Island, but the methods and some of the same people were used in both projects.

3. Thomas, *Letters from the Colonel's Lady*, p. 45.

4. Ibid, p. 44.

5. Gragg, "Fort Fisher," p. 32.

6. Lamb, p. 9.

7. Ibid, p. 46.

8. *Official Records of the War of Rebellion*, Volume 42, pp. 1253 and 1295.

9. Ibid, pp. 1295-1296.

CHAPTER 28: BEN BUTLER AND HIS PET

1. Longacre, *From Antietam to Fort Fisher*, p. 220.

2. Gragg, "Fort Fisher," p. 102.

3. *The New York Times*, December 30, 1864, quoted in Price and Sturgill, "Shock and Assault at Fort Fisher," pp. 35-36.

4. Stoltz, *Braxton Bragg*, p. 480.

CHAPTER 29: THE FIRST ATTACK

1. Curtis, *Reminiscences of Wilmington and Smithville*, p. 21.

CHAPTER 30: BUTLER'S LANDING GOES AWRY

1. *Official Naval Records*, Volume 11, p. 270.

2. Longacre, *Antietam to Fort Fisher*, pp. 223-224; Wrightman was in the forefront of the charge that breached the fort's walls on January 15, 1865 and was most likely the second or third Yankee soldier to die inside those walls. Longacre's book contains a deeply moving account by Wrightman's father of his trip to Fort Fisher to recover his son's body, complete with excellent descriptions of the setting.

3. Gragg, "Fort Fisher," p. 146.

4. Ibid, p. 155.

5. *Official Records of the War of Rebellion*, Volume 42, I, p. 994.

6. Ibid, p. 983.

CHAPTER 31: "MY BOY...YOU ARE TO BE SACRIFICED"

1. Longacre, *Antietam to Fort Fisher*, p. 225.
2. Gragg, "Fort Fisher," p. 194.
3. Merrill, "Fort Fisher and the Wilmington Campaign: Letters from Rear Admiral David Porter," p. 467.
4. Lamb, *Colonel Lamb's Story*, p. 26.
5. Wood, "Port Town at War," p. 211.

CHAPTER 32: RECESSIONAL: THE LAST GOOD BATTLE OF BRAXTON BRAGG

1. Herring and Williams, *Fort Caswell in War and Peace*, p. 52.
2. Kirwan, *History of the 17th Massachusetts*, pp. 346-347.

APPENDIX C: THE CURIOUS BEHAVIOR OF BRAXTON BRAGG

1. Lamb, "Defence and Fall of Fort Fisher," p. 355.
2. Ibid, p. 352.

BIBLIOGRAPHY

Sources relevant to the trilogy as a whole:

Ashe, Samuel A'Court, *History of North Carolina*, Volume II, The Reprint Press, Spartinburg, 1971.

Barrett, John G., *The Civil War in North Carolina*, University of North Carolina Press, Chapel Hill, 1963.

Barrett, John G., and Yearns, W. Buck, *North Carolina Civil War Documentary*, University of North Carolina Press, Chapel Hill, 1980.

Butler, Lindley S., and Watson, Alan D., *The North Carolina Experience — An Interpretive and Documentary History*, University of North Carolina Press, Chapel Hill, 1984.

Clark, Walter (editor), *Histories of the Several Regiments and Battalions from North Carolina in the Great War, 1861-65*, Published by the State of North Carolina, Goldsboro, 1901 (four volumes).

Commager, Henry Steele (editor), *The Official Atlas of the Civil War*, Thomas Yoseloff Inc., New York, 1958.

Corbitt, D.L. (editor), *Pictures of the Civil War Period in North Carolina*, North Carolina Department of Archives and History, Raleigh, 1958.

Esposito, Vincent J. (editor), *The West Point Atlas of American Wars*, Frederick Praeger, New York, 1960 edition.

Gilham, William, *Manual of Instruction for the Volunteers and Militia*, West and Johnson, Richmond, Virginia, 1861.

Johnson, Robert Underwood, and Buel, Clarence Clough (editors), *Battles and Leaders of the Civil War*, Commemorative Edition in four volumes, Thomas Yoseloff, Inc., New York, 1956.

Jordan, Weymouth T. (editor), *North Carolina Troops, 1861-65*, in ten volumes, North Carolina Department of Archives and History, Raleigh, 1981.

Lefler, Hugh T., and Newsome, Albert R. (editors), *North Carolina — The History of a Southern State*, University of North Carolina Press, Chapel Hill, 1963 and 1975 editions.

McPherson, James M., *Battle Cry of Freedom*, Oxford University Press, New York, 1988.

McWhiney, Grady, and Jamieson, Perry, *Attack and Die — Civil War Tactics and the Southern Heritage*, University of Alabama Press, 1982.

Mitchell, Joseph R., *Military Leaders of the Civil War*, G. P. Putnam's Sons, New York, 1972.

Official Records, The War of the Rebellion, Volume LXVII, "Operations in the Carolinas," Thomas Settle, 1865.

Tucker, Glenn, *Front Rank*, North Carolina Confederate Centennial Commission, Raleigh, 1962.

Sources relevant to Volume 3, "The Coast":

Ammen, Daniel, *The Atlantic Coast*, reprint edition, Blue and Gray Press, circa 1961.

Anderson, Bern, *By Sea and By River — The Naval History of the Civil War*, Alfred A. Knopf, New York, 1962.

Barry, Richard S., "Fort Macon: Its History," *North Carolina Historical Review*, April 1950.

Black, Wilfred W., (editor), "Civil War Letters of E.N. Boots from New Bern and Plymouth," *North Carolina Historical Review*, April 1959.

The Blockade — Runners and Raiders, Time-Life History of the Civil War, Time-Life Books, Alexandria, Virginia, 1983.

Branch, Paul, *The Siege of Fort Macon*, Herald Printing Co., Morehead City, 1986 edition.

Bright, Leslie A., *The Blockade-Runner "Modern Greece" and her Cargo*, Archaeology Section, Division of Archives and History, North Carolina Department of Cultural Resources, Raleigh, 1977.

Burger, Nash K., *Confederate Spy — Rose O'Neale Greenhow*, Franklin Watts, Inc., New York, 1967.

Carrison, Daniel J., *The Navy from Wood to Steel, 1860-1890*, Franklin Watts, Inc., New York, 1965.

Causey, Don, "The Naked Battle," *The State Magazine*, March 1981.

Civil War Chronology, Naval History Division, Navy Department, Washington D.C., 1971.

Curtis, Walter Gilman, *Reminiscences of Wilmington and Smithville*, Herald Job Office, Southport, North Carolina, circa 1901.

Daniels, Selby, and Pearce, T.H., *The Diary of Captain Henry A. Chambers*, Broadfoot's Bookmark, Wendell, North Carolina, 1983.

Davis, Archie K., *Boy Colonel of the Confederacy — The Life and Times of Henry King Burgwyn, Jr.*, University of North Carolina Press, Chapel Hill, 1985.

Davis, William C., (editor), *The Embattled Confederacy — Volume III, The Images of War, 1861-1865*, Doubleday & Co., Garden City, 1982.

Davis, William C., (editor), *Fighting for Time — Volume IV, The Images of War, 1861-1865*, Doubleday & Co., Garden City, 1983.

Day, D. L., *My Diary of Rambles With Burnside's Coastal Division*, privately printed, Milford, Massachusetts, 1884.

Dickey, Luther S., *History of the 103rd Regiment, Pennsylvania Volunteer Infantry*, Chicago, 1910.

Dillard, Richard, *The Civil War in Chowan County*, privately printed, Edenton, 1916; reprinted, 1965, by Chowan High School, Tyner, North Carolina.

Dollard, Robert, *Recollections of the Civil War*, privately printed, South Dakota, 1906.

Dyer, Frederich H., *A Compendium of the War of Rebellion*, Thomas Yoseloff, New York, 1959.

Edmunds, Thomas F., "Operations in North Carolina, 1861-1862," Papers of the Military Historical Society of Massachusetts, Volume IX, Boston, 1912.

Evans, Clement A., (editor), *Confederate Military History, Volume IV — North Carolina*, Confederate Publishing Co., Atlanta, 1899.

Feuer, A.B., "Sailors Into the Breach," *America's Civil War Magazine*, July 1988.

Gammons, John R., *The Third Massachusetts Regiment in the War of the Rebellion*, Providence, Rhode Island, 1906.

Gragg, Rod, "Fort Fisher: The Confederate Goliath 1861-1864," master's thesis, University of South Carolina, 1979.

Hagood, Jason, *Memoirs of the War of Secession*, Columbia, South Carolina, 1910.

Hawkins, Rush C., "Early Coast Operations in North Carolina," *Battles and Leaders of the Civil War, Volume I*, Thomas Yoseloff, New York, 1956.

Herring, Ethel, and Williams, Carole, *Fort Caswell in War and Peace*, Broadfoot's Bookmark, Wendell, North Carolina, 1975.

Hill, Daniel Harvey, *A History of North Carolina in the War Between the States, Volume I — Bethel to Sharpsburg*, Edwards & Broughton, Raleigh, 1926.

Holzman, Robert S., *Stormy Ben Butler*, Macmillan and Co., New York, 1954.

Howell, Anthony J., *The Book of Wilmington*, privately published, Wilmington, circa 1930.

Johnson, Robert E., "Investment by Sea -- the Civil War Blockade," *American Neptune*, January 1972.

Kirwan, Thomas, *Memorial History of the Seventeenth Regiment, Massachusetts Volunteer Infantry*, Salem Press, Salem, Massachusetts, 1911.

Laas, Virginia J., "Sleepless Sentinels: The North Atlantic Blockading Squadron, 1862-1864," *Civil War History*, Kent State University, Ohio, March 1985.

Lamb, William, *Colonel Lamb's Story of Fort Fisher*, Blockade-Runner Museum, Carolina Beach, North Carolina, 1966.

Lamb, William, and Bragg, Braxton, "Defence and Fall of Fort Fisher," Southern Historical Society Papers, Volume X, Richmond, 1882.

Lee, Lawrence, *The History of Brunswick County, North Carolina*, Heritage Press, Charlotte, 1980.

Lewis, Emanuel R., *Seacoast Fortifications of the United States — An Introductory History*, Presidio Press, 1979.

Longacre, Edward G, (editor), *From Antietam to Fort Fisher — The Civil War Letters of Edward King Wrightman*, Farleigh Dickenson University Press, Cranbury, New Jersey, 1985.

Loving, Jerome M., (editor), "Civil War Letters of George Washington Whitman from North Carolina," *North Carolina Historical Review*, January 1973.

Loy, Ursula, and Worthy, Pauline, *Washington and the Pamlico*, Washington, North Carolina, Beaufort County Bicentennial Commission, 1976.

Mahan, Albert Thayer, *The Influence of Sea Power on History*, Hill & Wang, New York, 1957.

Mann, Albert W., (editor), *History of the Forty-Fifth Regiment, Massachusetts Volunteer Militia*, Boston, 1908.

Melton, Maurice, *The Confederate Ironclads*, Thomas Yoseloff, New York, 1968.

Merrill, James M., "The Battle for Elizabeth City", U.S. Naval Institute Proceedings, March 1957.

Merrill, James M., "The Fort Fisher and Wilmington Campaign: Letters from Rear Admiral David D. Porter," *North Carolina Historical Review*, October 1958.

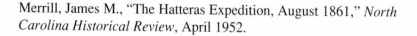

Merrill, James M., "The Hatteras Expedition, August 1861," *North Carolina Historical Review*, April 1952.

Merrill, James M., "Men, Monotony, and Mouldy Beans -- Life on Board Civil War Blockaders," *American Neptune*, January 1956.

Merrill, James M., *The Rebel Shore*, Little, Brown & Co., Boston, 1957.

Murray, Paul, and Barlett, Stephen R., (editors), "The Letters of Stephen Caulker Bartlett Aboard USS `Lanapee', January to August 1865," *North Carolina Historical Review*, January 1956.

Neely, Mark E., "The Perils of Running the Blockade: The Influence of International Law in an Era of Total War," *Civil War History*, Kent State University, Ohio, June 1986.

Nichols, Roy F., "Fighting in North Carolina Waters," *North Carolina Historical Review*, January 1963.

New York Herald, correspondents unnamed, *The Kinston, Whitehall, Goldsboro Expedition*, W.W. Howe, New York, 1890.

Oliver, William H., "Blockade-Running from Wilmington," *Confederate Veteran*, January 1895.

Parker, William H., *Recollections of a Naval Officer, 1841-1865*, Scribners & Sons, New York, 1883.

Parramore, Thomas C., et. al., "Civil War Supplement," *Roanoke-Chowan News*, 1960.

Parramore, Thomas C., "The Burning of Winton in 1862," *North Carolina Historical Review*, January 1962.

Pearce, T.H., "Where Cavalry Fought the Navy," *The State Magazine*, June 15, 1971.

Pohoresky, W.L., *Fort Macon, North Carolina During the Civil War*, The Print Shop, Havelock, North Carolina, 1970.

Pohoresky, W. L., *Newport, North Carolina During the Civil War*, The Print Shop, Havelock, North Carolina, 1978.

Price, Charles L., and Sturgill, Claude C., "Shock and Assault in the First Battle of Fort Fisher," *North Carolina Historical Review*, January 1970.

Reed, Rowena, *Combined Operations During the Civil War*, U.S. Naval Institute Press, Annapolis, 1978.

"Roberts, Captain" (C. Augustus Hobart-Hampden), *Never Caught*, reprint edition, Blockade-Runner Museum, Carolina Beach, North Carolina, 1967.

Robinson, William Morrison, Jr., *The Confederate Privateers*, Yale University Press, New Haven, Connecticut, 1928.

Roe, Alfred S., *The Twenty-Fourth Regiment, Massachusetts Volunteers*, Worchester, Massachusetts, 1907.

Roske, Ralph J., and Van Doren, Charles, *Lincoln's Commando*, Harper and Brothers, New York, 1957.

Ross, Malcolm, *The Cape Fear*, (Rivers of America Series), Holt, Rinehart and Winston, New York, 1965.

Roush, J. Fred, *The Civil War in Dare County*, U.S. Department of the Interior, National Park Service, Manteo, North Carolina, 1961.

Sauers, Richard A., "Laurels for Burnside -- The Invasion of North Carolina," *Blue and Gray Magazine*, May 1988.

Scharf, J. Thomas, *History of the Confederate States Navy*, Joseph McDonough, Albany, New York, 1894.

Seitz, Don C., *Braxton Bragg, General of the Confederacy*, reprint edition, Freeport, New York, 1971.

Sprunt, James, *Chronicles of the Cape Fear River*, reprint edition, Spartanburg, South Carolina, 1974.

Sprunt, James, "Tales of the Cape Fear Blockade," *North Carolina Booklet*, February 1902.

Sprunt, James, "Running the Blockade," Southern Historical Society Papers, Volume XXIV, 1896.

Sprunt, James, *Tales and Traditions of the Lower Cape Fear*, Wilmington, 1896.

Squires, John D., "The Confederate Navy on the North Carolina Sounds," unpublished dissertation, 1965, copy in author's possession.

Stackpole, Lewis F., "The Department of North Carolina Under General Foster," Papers of the Massachusetts Military Historical Society, Volume IX, Boston, 1912.

Stick, David, *Bald Head — A History of Smith Island and Cape Fear*, Broadfoot Publishing Co., Wendell, North Carolina, 1985.

Still, William C., "The Career of the Confederate Ironclad `Neuse'", *North Carolina Historical Review*, January 1966.

Still, William C., *Iron Afloat — The Story of the Confederate Ironclads*, Vanderbilt University Press, 1971.

Taylor, Thomas, *Running the Blockade*, London, 1896.

Thomas, Cornelius, (editor) *Letters from the Colonel's Lady: Correspondence of Mrs. William Lamb Written From Fort Fisher*, Charles Towne Preservation Trust, Winnabow, North Carolina, 1965.

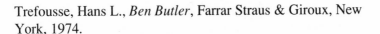

Trefousse, Hans L., *Ben Butler*, Farrar Straus & Giroux, New York, 1974.

Underwood, George C., *History of the Twenty-Sixth Regiment of North Carolina Troops in the Great War, 1861-1865*, reprint edition, Broadfoot's Bookmark, Wendell, North Carolina, 1978.

Wadell, Alfred M., *Some Memories of My Life*, Edwards and Broughton, Raleigh, 1908.

Walcott, Charles F., *History of the Twenty-First Regiment, Massachusetts Volunteers*, Boston, 1882.

West, Richard B., *Mr. Lincoln's Navy*, Longmans Green & Co., New York, 1957.

Williams, Julie C., (editor), *War Diary of Kinchen Jahu Carpenter*, privately published, Rutherfordton, North Carolina, 1955.

Wise, Stephen, "Lifeline of the Confederacy: Blockade-Running During the American Civil War," Ph.D. thesis, University of South Carolina, 1983.

Wood, Richard Everett, "Port Town at War: Wilmington, North Carolina 1860-1865," Ph.D. thesis, Florida State University, 1976.

INDEX

445

Confederate Point, 254,324,328,379, 400
Confederate ships:
    Ad-Vance, 284-293, 306
    Albemarle, 90, 233-237, 241-247,
    249-253, 259-267, 409-410
    Annie, 291-292
    Appomattox, 78, 88-89
    Banshee, 280-281, 315
    Banshee II, 317
    Beaufort, 19-20, 22, 88-89
    Black Warrior, 89
    Chickamauga, 305-306, 355, 360,
    364, 373, 390, 392, 423
    Cornubia, 315
    Curlew, 44, 79
    Don, 291-292, 300
    Ella and Annie, 315, 349
    Ellis, 19, 88-89, 167, 170, 172
    Fanny, 43-46, 88-89, 167
    Forrest, 79
    Gordon, 23
    Hansa, 291-292, 304-305
    Hebe, 331-332
    Hope, 314
    Junaluska, 44
    Kate, 298
    Little Hattie, 351
    Mariner, 23
    Modern Greece, 279
    Neuse, 184, 234-236, 409-410
    North Carolina, 304, 306
    Oregon, 19
    Raleigh, 19, 22, 44, 88, 256-257, 259,
    303-304, 306
    Rattlesnake, 319
    Robert E. Lee, 315
    Seabird, 44, 88-89
    Stonewall, 317
    Tallahassee, 305-306
    Thomas L. Wragg, 275
    Virginia (formerly USS *Merrimac*),
    108, 225, 234
    Wild Rover, 319
    Wilmington, 304, 403
    Winslow, 19, 22, 24
    York, 22-23
Confederate States Navy, 3, 22, 60, 75,
    225, 284, 293, 303-305, 390
Cooper River, 282

Cornwallis, Lord, 114
"the Cottage," 329, 345, 392, 424
Craig's Landing, 328, 392
Craven County, 199
Crimean War, 106, 326
Croatan Sound, 57
Croatan Works, 105-106, 110
Crossan, Thomas M. (Lieutenant
    Commander, CSN), 22, 284, 288-289
Culpepper Locks, 126, 130
Currituck County, 221
Currituck Sound, 126
Curtis, Newton M. (Brigadier General,
    USA), 371, 375-381, 383-384, 390,
    393-394, 396
Curtis, Walter, 12
Cushing, William Baker (Lieutenant,
    USN), 167-172, 225, 253-267, 331,
    337, 350, 372-374, 404
Cypress Swamp, 258

D

Dahlgren gun, 68, 96, 226, 412
Daniel, Junius (Brigadier General, CSA),
    193
Danville, Virginia, 343, 383, 386
Dardingkiller (Sergeant, USA), 8-10
Davis, Jefferson, 15, 20, 56-57, 61, 104,
    125, 223-225, 234, 283, 286, 305,
    327, 334-335, 337-338, 341, 366, 387,
    392
Dearing, James (Colonel, CSA), 224, 230
Decatur, Stephen (USN), 168
Delafield, Richard (General, USA), 347
Dillard, Dr. Richard, Sr., 215, 219
Dismal Swamp (see "Great Dismal
    Swamp")
Dismal Swamp Canal, 1, 20, 44, 88, 126,
    131, 220
Dover Swamp, 175
Drewry's Bluff, Battle of, 225, 336, 392,
    401
Dunn, John (USA), 130
DuPont, Samuel (Admiral, USN), 25, 53-
    54, 192, 313

E

447

Hunter, B.F. (Sergeant, CSA), 405
Hunter, "Tornado," 79
Hyde County, 62, 99

I

ironclads (under "Confederate ships," see
"*Albemarle*," "*Neuse*," "*Raleigh*," and
"*Virginia*"; also see "monitors," "USS
Merrimac," "USS *Monitor*," and
"USS *New Ironsides*")

J

Jackson, Stonewall (General, CSA), 101,
333
Jacksonville, N.C., 170
Jacobs, Ferris (Major, USA), 204
James River, 225, 342
James River Squadron, 225
Johnson, Samuel (Sergeant, USA), 417-
419
Johnston, G.W. (Colonel, CSA), 34
Johnston, Joseph E. (General, CSA), 333-
335, 406, 409
Jones, Colonel (CSA), 256
Jones, J.E. (Ensign, USN), 256
Jones, J.R. (Colonel, USA), 203-204
Jones, John Paul (USN), 168
Jones County, 209
Jordan, J.V. (Colonel, CSA), 66, 81
Junior Reserves, 352, 355, 365, 367, 375,
378, 406-407

K

Keen, Martha, 94, 97
Kelly, Captain (CSA), 255-256
Kentucky Military Institute, 239
"King Cotton," 271-272, 275
Kinnakeet, N.C., 47
Kinston, N.C., 121-122, 125, 151-152,
177-178, 181-184, 188, 193, 203, 224-
226, 228, 230, 406, 408-410
Kirkland, William (General, CSA), 365,
372, 374, 379-380, 384
Knoxville, Tennessee, 55, 202

L

Lamb, John C. (Lieutenant Colonel,
CSA), 172-173
Lamb, Sarah (nee Chafee), 296, 325, 329-
330
Lamb, William (Colonel, CSA), 279-280,
288-290, 306, 319, 324-332, 335, 343,
345, 353-355, 358-361, 363-369, 374,
376, 378, 380, 385-386, 389, 391-395,
397-401, 406, 421-422, 424
Lamb's Corner, N.C., 128
Lay, John L., 260
Lee, H.C. (Colonel, USA), 186-187
Lee, Robert E. (General, CSA), 152, 164,
191, 203, 209, 219, 223-224, 230,
236, 239, 252, 305, 334-335, 343,
366, 409
Lee, Samuel Phillips (Admiral, USN),
260-261, 310-311, 315, 332, 340
Lewis, Gaston (Major, CSA), 116
Lincoln, Abraham, 7, 10, 25-26, 28, 30,
48, 53, 137, 151-152, 210, 272, 342
Lincolnton, N.C., 239
Little Creek, 166
Liverpool, England, 271, 280, 291-292,
297, 317, 319
Longstreet, James (Major General, CSA),
191-192, 202, 423
Loyall, Benjamin P. (Lieutenant, CSN),
76, 80, 225-227, 235
Lynch, William F. (Commodore, Flag
Officer, CSN), 44-45, 78, 80-81, 88-
89, 170, 235-236, 304-305

M

Macomb, W.H. (Commander, USN), 261-
262, 267
Maffitt, John (Commander, CSN), 3
Magruder, John (Colonel, CSA), 26
Mahan, Albert Thayer, 21
Mallory, Stephen R., 39, 234-235, 293,
306
Malvern Hill, Battle of, 124
Manassas (Bull Run), Battle of, 26, 39,
53, 55, 67, 325, 333
Mansfield, J.F.K. (Brigadier General,
USA), 48
Martin County, 172

P

Paine, Charles J. (Brigadier General, USA), 345
Palmer, General (USA), 199
Pamlico River, 148, 198-199
Pamlico Sound, 1, 17, 39-40, 48, 57, 61, 63, 71, 73, 108, 125, 201, 249
Parke, John G. (Brigadier General, USA), 69, 83, 114, 117, 125-126, 136-137, 139, 141, 143, 145
Parker, William H. (Captain, CSN), 20, 78-80, 89
Parrott gun, 44, 96, 114, 136, 139-140, 142-145, 178, 197, 240-241, 244, 246, 250, 279, 317, 362, 364-365, 384, 412
"partisan rangers," 148, 161, 183, 209, 211, 218
Pasquotank County, 220
Pasquotank River, 1, 88, 126, 128
Pedrick (Captain, the *Escort*), 201-202
Pender, Josiah, 10-11
Peninsula Campaign, 147-148
Penny, Henry, 26
Pennypacker, Galusha (Colonel, USA), 372, 390, 393, 396
Perry, Daniel (Lieutenant, CSA), 369-370
Petersburg, Virginia, 39, 90, 151, 206, 252, 354
Pettigrew, James J. (Brigadier General, CSA), 186, 193, 196-197, 199-201
Pickett, George (Major General, CSA), 224, 226, 228, 230-231, 236, 239, 249, 413
Piedmont, 1, 7, 124, 323
Pinckney, Robert F. (Flag Officer, CSN), 305
Pitt County, 192
Plymouth, N.C., 62, 148, 153, 163, 167, 172-173, 198, 211, 218, 236-237, 239-241, 244-245, 247-249, 252-253, 259-260, 266-267, 417-419
Pollocksville, N.C., 149
Pool, S.D. (Colonel, CSA), 165
Port Royal, South Carolina, 53-54, 133, 388
Porter, David D. (Admiral, USN), 41, 90, 261, 304, 306, 309-310, 314, 339-342, 345, 347-351, 353, 357-360, 362-365, 367-368, 370, 372, 378, 381, 384-386, 388-394, 396-398, 401, 403-404, 421, 423-424
Porter, John, 234, 236
Portsmouth, 19, 34, 37, 43
Potecasi Creek, 97, 205-206
Potter, Edward E. (Colonel, General, USA), 149-150, 204-205
Prince, General (USA), 199
privateers, Confederate, 15-16, 20-29, 39
"Pulpit," 290, 327, 343, 358-359, 364, 369, 374-375, 391

R

Rainbow Banks, 163
Raleigh, N.C., 1, 7, 16, 33, 53, 56, 60, 70, 90, 101, 106-107, 124-125, 147-148, 152, 191, 212, 285-286, 399
Raleigh Standard, 98
Ransom, Matt (General, CSA), 206-208, 221-222, 224, 244, 247-248
Ransom, Robert (Brigadier General, CSA), 125, 149, 151
Rappahannock River, 225
Rawl's Creek, 166
Read, John (Lieutenant Colonel, CSA), 370
Reilly, James (Sergeant, USA; Major, CSA), 8-10, 378
Reno, Jesse (Brigadier General, USA), 69, 71, 83-85, 114-116, 118, 126, 128-131
Revolutionary War, 28, 114, 212, 324
Rhind, Alexander (Commander, USN), 350-352
Richmond, Virginia, 2-3, 16, 21, 29, 31, 33, 39, 41, 56-57, 60-63, 65-66, 75, 87, 91, 104-106, 122, 125, 135, 147-148, 151-152, 164, 192, 197, 211, 235-236, 252, 273, 276, 280-281, 286, 291-293, 298, 301, 305-306, 316, 319-320, 334-335, 338, 345, 350, 386-387, 399-400, 404
Richmond Examiner, 91
Roanoke Island, 31, 39-41, 43-44, 47, 57, 61-65, 70, 73, 75-77, 86, 88, 90-91, 93-94, 97-99, 104-105, 108, 114, 129, 147, 150, 215, 218, 226, 261, 283

Roanoke River, 1, 99, 148, 163-164, 168, 173, 219, 234, 240, 244-245, 260, 262, 265

"Roasted Ditch," 128-129

Robertson, B.H. (General, CSA), 193, 197

Robinson, Tom, 81

Rocky Mount, N.C., 204

Rodman, Isaac (Colonel, USA), 117

Roe, F.A. (Lieutenant Commander, USN), 250, 252

Rowan, Stephen C. (Commander, USN), 88, 90, 94-97, 108, 110, 114, 119, 121, 157-158, 163

Royal Navy, 272, 275, 277, 300-301

S

Salem, N.C., 122, 124

Salisbury, N.C., 325

Savannah, Georgia, 22, 53, 274, 333, 342-343, 387

Scharf, J. Thomas (Midshipman, CSN), 225-227

Schofield, John M. (General, USA), 304, 404-406, 408

Scotland Neck, N.C., 149

Scotland Neck Mounted Rifles, 149

Scott, Winfield (General, USA), 25, 53-54, 157

Seddon, James A., 283, 291-292, 315, 387

Seminole Wars, 84

Senior Reserves, 365

Sevastopol, Ukraine, 106-108, 326

Seven Days Battles, 239

Seward, Clarence, 48

Seward, William H., 48

Shackleford Bank, 133, 137, 143

Shaffner, Dr. J.F. (CSA), 124

Shallowbag Bay, 76

Shalotte Inlet, 311

Sharps rifle, 257

Shaw, H.M. (Colonel, CSA), 45, 47, 66, 77, 83-84, 86-87

Sherman, Thomas (General, USA), 68

Sherman, William Tecumseh (General, USA), 220, 318, 342-343, 387, 405-406

Signal Corps, 141, 143

Sinclair, James (Colonel, CSA), 104, 116

Singletary, George B. (Colonel, CSA),150

Slocum Creek, 108, 110

Small, Ned (Captain, CSA), 218

Smith, Melancton (Captain, USN), 249-250

Smith, Peter, 234-235

Smith Island, 274, 310, 324, 375

Smithville, N.C., 7-10, 12, 254, 285, 331, 354, 360, 374, 400

South Carolina, 16, 34, 53, 181, 310, 320, 387, 397, 405

South Mills, 90, 126, 128, 130

Southerland, Thomas J. (Captain, CSA), 370

Southport, N.C. (see also "Smithville"), 7

Sparta, N.C., 204-205

Spear, S.P. (Colonel, USA), 206-208

Spencer rifles, 390, 393-394, 396

Spinola, F.B. (General, USA), 199-201

Splaine, Henry (Colonel, USA), 407-408

Springfield rifle, 170, 217

Spruill, Colonel (CSA), 108

St. George's, Bermuda, 287

Stanly, Edward, 150-151

Steele, Jonothan, 280

Stringham, Silas (Commodore, USN), 27, 33-34, 36, 38-39, 54

Stuart, "Jeb" (General, CSA), 163

Suffolk, Virginia, 90, 221-222

Sugar Loaf Hill, 364-365, 389, 424

T

Tabor Island, 240

"Tar Heel," 149, 150, 237, 248

Tar River, 1, 148, 204

Tarboro, N.C., 165-167, 204, 234

Taylor, James Fauntleroy II (Petty Officer, CSN), 287

Taylor, Marble Nash, 49

Taylor, Zachary, 225

Tennessee, 124, 160, 404

Terry, Alfred H. (Major General, USA), 388-389, 393, 400, 404, 421, 423-424

The New York Times, 352

Thorburn, Lieutenant Colonel (CSA), 285-286

Trantner's Creek, 149-150